RUGBY
The Records

Chris Rhys

Jean-Pierre Rives, the French captain, en route *to the Grand Slam in 1981. Here Rives breaks clear of the Welsh back row of Burgess (No 7) and Squire (No 8), at the Parc des Princes. France won 19–15.*

GUINNESS BOOKS

Introduction

Chris Rhys started freelance journalism in 1974 and has now written some 20 books on sport as well as co-authoring *Sports Challenge* and *Rugby Facts and Feats* for Guinness Books.

He is the researcher for BBC's 'Brain of Sport', ITV's 'Sporting Triangles', 'Big Match Live', 'Midweek Sports Special' and numerous other regional Radio and TV programmes.

Rugby is his first love and he played for London Welsh and Somerset.

The year 1987 was a momentous one for Rugby Football. The inaugural World Cup was an unqualified success. One of the healthier tasks for rugby authorities in the future will be to channel the experience gained from the World Cup, to work on a structure to benefit all rugby-playing nations, but without subjecting emerging countries to worthless defeats by major powers.

This book focuses on the World Cup, with detailed information on the structure of the game in the 16 competing Nations, plus South Africa and the Soviet Union. A major innovation is the vastly improved statistical breakdown of the results of Internationals, which now include all points scorers in International rugby. The theme is taken a stage further by the inclusion of the same service for the emerging Nations. In these days of indecision as to what constitutes an International, *Rugby The Records* has unearthed the results of the matches between the International Rugby Board nations and the emerging countries.

There are also features on Great Players, Great Matches, the famous grounds plus a section devoted to the unusual and those who have achieved greatness on other sporting fronts.

An old cliché exists that records are there only to be broken, a fact that can be an author's nightmare. The introduction to Chapter 8 outlines the basis for acknowledging international record status used in this book. Records have been verified to the end of June 1987, but obviously some may be overtaken by events and time. One fact, though, is certain to remain, that the game of Rugby Union with its 120 participating countries is now unquestionably the world's foremost amateur sport.

Chris Rhys,
June 1987

Editor: Beatrice Frei
Design and Layout: Alan Hamp

© Chris Rhys and Guinness Superlatives Ltd, 1987

Published in Great Britain by Guinness Superlatives Ltd, 33 London Road, Enfield, Middlesex

Typeset in Linotron 202 Times, 9/10pt.
by Dorchester Typesetting Group Limited, Dorchester, Dorset
Printed in Great Britain by R. J. Acford, Chichester

'Guinness' is a registered trade mark of Guinness Superlatives Ltd

British Library Cataloguing in Publication Data
Rhys, Chris
　Guinness rugby: the records.
　1. Rugby football—Records
　I. Title
796.33'3'09　　GV945.4

ISBN 0-85112-450-X

Contents

Cover illustration: *Laurent Rodriguez (France) feeds the ball back for the Five Nations XV against the Overseas XV during the International Rugby Board's Centenary Game at Twickenham in April 1986. The Overseas XV won easily by 32 points to 13. (Colorsport)*

Note: Rugby records are in a transitional state. The author respects each country's decision to award caps in matches they consider to be of international status, and home career points totals and caps will in some cases differ from previously published records.

I THE 1987 WORLD CUP

New Zealand, efficiently and deservedly, won the first World Cup held in Australia between 22 May and 20 June 1987. In the final they beat France 29–9 with a controlled display. Critics described the final as boring and stereotyped, but New Zealand cannot be faulted for safety-first tactics, in a match with so much at stake.

France had beaten the co-favourites Australia in the semifinal, in a match described as the finest game of rugby ever, especially when a place in the final was the prize. France squeezed in with a late Serge Blanco try, converted by Camberabero, after the lead had constantly changed hands.

Wales, surprisingly, proved themselves the best of the British Isles sides. A dreadful 49–6 defeat in the semifinal against New Zealand, with Huw Richards sent off, found the Welsh with the unwanted nickname of the '49ers', but Paul Thorburn's marvellous touchline conversion of Adrian Hadley's last-second try brought a worthy third place. England threatened, then fell foul of Wales in the quarter-final, while Ireland and Scotland never really came to terms with Antipodean opposition in the quarter-finals.

For Australia, the Cup was a series of tragic disappointments. Co-favourites, and co-hosts, they stuttered none too convincingly through a hard game with England in the Pool match, bolstered by a David Campese try which certainly should not have been awarded; shouldered arms at the death against France; then, in a match of total anticlimax for the Wallabies, were beaten by Wales after having David Codey sent off as early as the fifth minute.

The emerging nations were often out of their depth. Romania and Argentina, the scourges of so many International Board teams, had arrived with their cupboard almost bare; Tonga and Japan struggled; Zimbabwe were outclassed, and, although the United States and Canada gave genuine hope for the future, only Italy – after a terrible start – and Fiji lived up to their reputation. Fiji, after another roasting from New Zealand, giving France an object lesson in running the ball. Italy beat Fiji, climbing back into the tournament after a 70–6 loss to the All Blacks, and showed the value of the coaching legacies of Carwyn James and Pierre Villepreux.

Many lessons will have been digested from this pioneer exercise. Injuries to key players took their toll, with many countries suffering crippling losses, making the squad system even more important. France had no wings at all: Bonneval played 20 minutes in the tournament, Berot and the first reserve Lafond took no part. For Australia, Nick Farr-Jones was a costly invalid. Wales appeared with one team and found another. Scotland were horrified to lose Rutherford and Scott Hastings. Only New Zealand made sensible use of their resources.

The World Cup committee will have noticed some points before they meet to decide the 1991 venue. In the Pool matches, the best teams all met in the very first game, thus devaluing the remainder. Indeed, it was the emerging nations who fielded weaker teams (Fiji especially so) against the better countries to save their best players for the other minnows.

As a voyage through troubled waters, the World Cup was an outstanding success. And for New Zealand, their single-mindedness, fitness and team work made it an exercise beyond compare.

POOL I

23 May 1987, Concord Oval, Sydney

AUSTRALIA 19

T: Campese (50 min), Poidevin (60 min) C: Lynagh (60 min) PG: Lynagh (21, 30, 64 min)

ENGLAND 6

T: Harrison (47 min) C: Webb (47 min)

Australia: Gould; Grigg, Slack (capt), Papworth, Campese; Lynagh, Farr-Jones; Rodriguez, Lawton, McIntyre; Cutler, Campbell, Poidevin, Coker, Tuynman

Replacement: James for Gould (78 min)

England: Rose; Harrison (capt), Simms, Salmon, Underwood; Williams, Harding; Rendall, Moore, Pearce; Dooley, Redman; Winterbottom, Rees, Richards

Replacement: Webb for Rose (2 min)

Referee: K. H. Lawrence (New Zealand) *Attendance:* 17 896

24 May 1987, Ballymore, Brisbane

UNITED STATES 21

T: Purcell (26 min), Nelson (38 min), Lambert (70 min) C: Nelson (26, 38, 70 min) PG: Nelson (20 min)

JAPAN 18

T: Taumoefolau (16, 30 min), Yoshinaga (72 min) PG: Yoshinaga (36 min), Kutsuki (54 min)

United States: Nelson; Purcell, Higgins, Helu, Lambert; Clarkson, Saunders; Bailey, Everett, Paoli; Lambert, Swords; Burlingham (capt), Warhurst, Vizard

Japan: Mukai; Taumoefolau, Yoshinaga, Onuki, Kutsuki; Hirao, Ikuta; Yasumi, Fujita, Horaguchi; Miyamoto, Hayashi (capt); Oyagi, Latu, Chida

Referee: G. Maurette (France) *Attendance:* 4500

30 May 1987, Concord Oval, Sydney

ENGLAND 60

T: Underwood (31, 56 min), Rees (39 min), Salmon (47 min), Richards (49 min), Simms (64 min), Harrison (68, 70, 80 min), Redman (79 min) C: Webb (39, 47, 49, 64, 70, 79, 80 min) PG: Webb (8, 16 min)

JAPAN 7

T: Miyamoto (42 min) PG: Matsuo (25 min)

England: Webb; Harrison (capt), Simms, Salmon, Underwood; Williams, Harding; Rendall, Moore, Chilcott; Bainbridge, Redman; Rees, Winterbottom, Richards

Replacements: Clough for Simms (68 min), Andrew for Williams (77 min)

Japan: Murai; Taumoefolau, Kutsuki, Matsuo, Onuki; Hirao, Hagimoto; Kimura, Fujita, Horaguchi; Oyagi, Kurihara; Miyamoto, Chida, Hayashi (capt)

Referee: R. Horquet (France) *Attendance:* 5500

31 May 1987, Ballymore, Brisbane
AUSTRALIA 47
  T: Penalty try (7 min), Smith (24 min), Slack (40 min),
  Leeds (43, 80 min), Papworth (56 min), Campese
  (65 min), Codey (70 min) C: Lynagh (7, 24, 40, 65, 70,
  80 min) PG: Lynagh (2 min)
UNITED STATES 12
  T: Nelson (53 min) C: Nelson (53 min) PG: Nelson
  (32 min) DG: Horton (75 min)
Australia: Leeds; Campese, Slack (capt), Papworth, Burke;
Lynagh, Smith; Lillicrap, Lawton, McIntyre; Coker, Camp-
bell; Miller, Tuynman, Codey
United States: Nelson; Higgins, Helu, Vinick, Hein; Horton,
Dickson; Horvath, Johnson, Paoli; Swords, Shiflet; Finkel,
Vizard, Ridnell
Replacements: Saunders for Dickson (35 min), Lambert for
Shiflet (24 min)
Referee: J. B. Anderson (Scotland) *Attendance:* 8300

3 Jun 1987, Concord Oval, Sydney
ENGLAND 34
  T: Winterbottom (23, 45 min), Harrison (61 min), Dooley
  (79 min) C: Webb (23, 45, 79 min) PG: Webb (10, 31, 47,
  54 min)
UNITED STATES 6
  T: Purcell (65 min) C: Nelson (65 min)
England: Webb; Harrison (capt), Clough, Salmon, Bailey;
Andrew, Hill; Chilcott, Dawe, Pearce; Bainbridge, Dooley;
Rees, Winterbottom, Richards
United States: Nelson; Purcell, Higgins, Vinick, Hein;
Clarkson, Saunders; Brendel, Everett, Bailey; Causey,
Burlingham (capt); Finkel, Vizard, Lambert
Referee: K. V. J. Fitzgerald (Australia) *Attendance:* 15 000

3 Jun 1987, Concord Oval, Sydney
AUSTRALIA 42
  T: Slack (8, 77 min), Tuynman (21 min), Burke (33,
  80 min), Grigg (46 min), Hartill (55 min), Campese
  (60 min) C: Lynagh (21, 33, 46, 77, 80 min)
JAPAN 23
  T: Kutsuki (12 min), Okidoi (23 min), Fujita (73 min)
  C: Okidoi (12 min) PG: Okidoi (2, 66 min) DG: Okidoi
  (57 min)
Australia: Campese; Grigg, Slack, Cook, Burke; Lynagh,
Smith; Rodriguez, McBain, Hartill; Cutler, Reynolds;
Poidevin (capt), Tuynman, Codey
Replacements: Papworth for Cook (17 min), Campbell for
Tuynman (69 min)
Japan: Mukai; Taumoefolau, Yoshinaga, Kutsuki, Okidoi;
Hirao, Ikuta; Kimura, Fujita, Aizawa; Sakuraba, Hayashi
(capt); Miyamoto, Latu, Kawese
Referee: J. M. Fleming (Scotland) *Attendance:* 15 000

POOL I FINAL TABLE

	P	W	D	L	F	A	Pts
Australia	3	3	0	0	108	41	6
England	3	2	0	1	100	32	4
United States	3	1	0	2	39	99	2
Japan	3	0	0	3	48	123	0

POOL 2
24 May 1987, McLean Park, Napier
CANADA 37
  T: Stuart (3 min), Frame (15, 26 min), Vaesen (43,
  76 min), Palmer (68, 72 min) C: Wyatt (3, 26 min), Rees
  (72 min) PG: Rees (70 min)
TONGA 4
  T: Valu (45 min)

Canada: Wyatt; Palmer, Vaesen, McTavish, Woods; Rees,
Stuart; Evans, Cardinal, Handson; van den Brink, de
Goede (capt); Frame, Radu, Robertson
Tonga: Etaiki; A'Si, Kuteki'Aho, Mohi, Fiela; Liava'A,
Fifita; Moto'Apauaka, Afu, Tupou; Fine, Tu'Ihalamaka;
Tuuta, Fotu, Valu (capt)
Replacements: Vaipulu for A'Si (22 min), Tahaafe for
Tu'Ihalamaka (28 min)
Referee: C. T. Norling (Wales) *Attendance:* 8000

25 May 1987, Athletic Park, Wellington
WALES 13
  T: Ring (55 min) PG: Thorburn (43 min) DG: Davies (61,
  65 min)
IRELAND 6
  PG: Kiernan (39, 40 min)
Wales: Thorburn; I. Evans, Devereux, Ring, Hadley; J.
Davies, Jones; Whitefoot, K. Phillips, S. Evans; Norster, R.
Moriarty (capt); Collins, P. Moriarty, Roberts
Ireland: McNeill; Ringland, Mullin, Kiernan, Crossan;
Dean, Bradley; Orr, Kingston, Fitzgerald; Anderson, Leni-
han (capt); McGrath, Matthews, Spillane
Replacement: Glennon for Matthews (35 min)
Referee: K. V. J. Fitzgerald (Australia) • *Attendance:* 17 500

29 May 1987, Showgrounds Oval, Palmerston North
WALES 29
  T: Webbe (4, 12, 71 min), Hadley (40 min) C: Thorburn
  (4, 71 min) PG: Thorburn (30, 56 min) DG: J. Davies
  (64 min)
TONGA 16
  T: Fiela (40 min), Etaiki (76 min) C: Liava'a (76 min)
  PG: Amone (34 min), Liava'a (80 min)
Wales: Thorburn; Webbe, Ring, Hopkins, Hadley; Dacey,
Jones; Buchanan, K. Phillips, S. Evans; Richards, R.
Moriarty (capt); P. Moriarty, P. Davies, Roberts
Replacements: Blackmore for S. Evans (40 min), J. Davies
for Dacey (58 min)
Tonga: Etaiki; Vunipola, Mohi, Kuteki'Aho, Fiela;
Amone, Fifita; Tupou, Afu, Lutua; Fine, Tu'ungafasi;
Tu'uta, Filise, Valu (capt)
Replacements: Va'eno for Tupou (44 min), Liava'a for
Amone (67 min)
Referee: D. J. Bishop (New Zealand) *Attendance:* 10 000

30 May 1987, Carisbrook, Dunedin
IRELAND 46
  T: Bradley (10 min), Crossan (28, 65 min), Spillane
  (70 min), Ringland (78 min), McNeill (79 min) C: Kiernan
  (10, 65, 70, 78, 79 min) PG: Kiernan (39, 57 min)
  DG: Kiernan (5 min), Ward (75 min)
CANADA 19
  T: Cardinal (56 min) PG: Rees (2, 18, 48 min), Wyatt
  (14 min) DG: Rees (25 min)
Ireland: McNeill; Ringland, Mullin, Kiernan, Crossan;
Ward, Bradley; Orr, McDonald, Fitzgerald; Lenihan (capt),
Anderson; McGrath, Collins, Spillane
Replacement: Kingston for McDonald (65 min)
Canada: Wyatt; Palmer, Lecky, McTavish, Woods; Rees,
Stuart; Evans, Cardinal, Handson; de Goede (capt), Hind-
son; Frame, Radu, Ennis
Referee: F. A. Howard (England) *Attendance:* 10 000

3 Jun 1987, Rugby Park, Invercargill
WALES 40
  T: I. Evans (3, 43, 65, 80 min), Bowen (49 min), Devereux
  (57 min), Hadley (67 min), A. Phillips (81 min) C:
  Thorburn (3, 43, 49, 65 min)

CANADA   9
PG: Rees (1, 26, 34 min)
Wales: Thorburn; I. Evans, Devereux, Bowen, Hadley; J. Davies (capt), Giles; Whitefoot, A. Phillips, Blackmore; Norster, Sutton; P. Moriarty, P. Davies, Roberts
Replacements: Hopkins for Bowen (72 min), R. Moriarty for P. Moriarty (77 min)
Canada: Wyatt; Palmer, Lecky, Woods, Gray; Rees, Stuart; McKellar, Svoboda, Handson; de Goede (capt), Hindson; Frame, Breen, Ennis
Replacement: Tucker for Stuart (52 min)
Referee: D. J. Bishop (New Zealand)   *Attendance:* 12 000

3 Jun 1987, Ballymore Oval, Brisbane
IRELAND   32
T: McNeill (15, 76 min), Mullin (35, 56, 76 min) C: Ward (35, 56, 72 min) PG: Ward (3, 41 min)
TONGA   9
PG: Amone (24, 48, 75 min)
Ireland: McNeill; Ringland, Mullin, Irwin, Crossan; Ward, Bradley; Langbroek, Kingston, McCoy; Lenihan (capt), Anderson; Matthews, Francis, McGrath
Tonga: Etaiki; Fiela, Mohi, Kuteki'Aho, Liava'a; Amone, Fifita; Tupou, Fungeraka, Lutua; Fine, Tu'ungafasi; Valu (capt), Felise, Kakato
Referee: G. Maurette (France)   *Attendance:* 3000

POOL 2 FINAL TABLE

	P	W	D	L	F	A	Pts
Wales	3	3	0	0	82	31	6
Ireland	3	2	0	1	84	41	4
Canada	3	1	0	2	65	90	2
Tonga	3	0	0	3	29	98	0

POOL 3
22 May 1987, Eden Park, Auckland
NEW ZEALAND   70
T: Penalty try (12 min), Jones (30 min), Kirk (38, 73 min), Taylor (45 min), Green (48, 54 min), McDowell (65 min), Kirwan (68, 72 min), Stanley (76 min), A. Whetton (80 min) C: Fox (12, 45, 54, 65, 68, 72, 73, 80 min) PG: Fox (20, 60 min)
ITALY   6
PG: Collodo (40 min) DG: Collodo (38 min)
New Zealand: Gallagher; Kirwan, Stanley, Taylor, Green; Fox, Kirk (capt.); McDowell, Fitzpatrick, Loe; Pierce, G. Whetton; A. Whetton, Jones, Shelford
Italy: Ghizzoni; Mascioletti, Collodo, Gaeteniello, Cuttita; Ambrosio, Lorigiola; Rossi, Morelli, Lupini; Berni, Gardin; Farina, Innocenti (capt.), Artuso
Referee: R. J. Fordham (Australia)   *Attendance:* 20 000

24 May 1987, Rugby Park, Hamilton
FIJI   28
T: Gale (17 min), Naiviliwasa (38 min), Nalaga (46 min), Savai (80 min)
C: Koraduadua (17, 46 min), Rokowailoa (80 min) PG: Koroduadua (21, 62 min)
ARGENTINA   9
T: Travaglini (82 min) C: Porta (82 min) PG: Porta (50 min)
Fiji: Koroduadua; Nalaga, T. Cama, Tuvula, E. Naituku; Rokowailoa, Tabulutu; Namoro, Naiviliwasa, S. Naituku; Rakoroi (capt.), Savai; Gale, Qoro, Sanday
Replacements: Nawalu for Tabalatu (25 min), Vunivalu for Gale (58 min)
Argentina: Salvat; Campo, Cuesta Silva, Turnes, J. Lanza; Porta (capt.), Gomez; Morel, Cash, Molina; Branca, Milano; Mostany, Allen, Travaglini

Replacement: Schiavio for Milano (53 min)
Referee: J. M. Fleming (Scotland)   *Attendance:* 12 000

27 May 1987, Lancaster Park, Christchurch
NEW ZEALAND   74
T: Green (2, 12, 25, 39 min), Gallagher (5, 57, 60, 76 min), Kirk (32 min), Kirwan (45 min), Penalty try (50 min), A. Whetton (70 min) C: Fox (2, 5, 12, 32, 39, 45, 50, 57, 70, 76 min) PG: Fox (20, 23 min)
FIJI   13
T: Savai (79 min) PG: Koroduadua (16, 49, 61 min)
New Zealand: Gallagher; Kirwan, Stanley, Taylor, Green; Fox, Kirk (capt.); McDowell, Fitzpatrick, Drake; Anderson, G. Whetton; A. Whetton, Jones, Shelford
Fiji: Koroduadua; Tuvulu, Lovokulu, Kubu, T. Cama; Rokowailoa, Nawalu; Taga, Rakai, Volavola; J. Cama, Savai; Kididromo, Vunivalu, Rakoroi (capt.)
Referee: W. D. Bevan (Wales)   *Attendance:* 24 000

28 May 1987, Lancaster Park, Christchurch
ARGENTINA   25
T: J. Lanza (38 min), Gomez (79 min) C: Porta (80 min) PG: Porta (16, 20, 53, 56, 74 min)
ITALY   16
T: Innocenti (50 min), Cuttita (60 min) C: Collodo (50 min) PG: Collodo (25, 55 min)
Argentina: Salvat; J. Lanza, Cuesta Silva, Madero, P. Lanza; Porta (capt.), Yanguela: Dengra, Cash, Molina; Branca, Carrosio; Schiavio, Allen, Travaglini
Replacement: Gomez for Yanguela (65 min)
Italy: Tebaldi; Mascioletti, Gaetaniello, Barba, Cuttita; Collodo, Lorigiola; Rossi, Galeazzo, Lupini; Gardin, Gollela; Pavin, Innocenti (capt.), Zanon
Referee: R. C. Quittenton (England)   *Attendance:* 5000

31 May 1987, Carisbrook, Dunedin
ITALY   18
T: Cuttita (11 min), Cucchiella (44 min), Mascioletti (58 min) PG: Collodo (36 min) DG: Collodo (4 min)
FIJI   15
T: Naiviliwasa (67 min) C: Koroduadua (67 min) PG: Koroduadua (49, 62 min) DG: Qoro (31 min)
Italy: Tebaldi; Mascioletti, Gaeteniello, Barba, Cuttita; Collodo, Ghini; Cucchiella, Romagnoli, Lupini; Gardin, Collela; Dolfato, Innocenti (capt.), Farina
Fiji: Koroduadua; T. Cama, Salusalu, Mitchell, Tuvula; Rakowailoa, Nawalu; Volavola, Naiviliwasa, Naituku; Nadolo, Sanday; Savai, Qoro, Rakoroi (capt.)
Replacements: Natluku for Tuvulu (20 min), Kubu for Natluku (62 min)
Referee: K. H. Lawrence (New Zealand)   *Attendance:* 6000

1 Jun 1987, Athletic Park, Wellington
NEW ZEALAND   46
T: Kirk (13 min), Brooke (39 min), Stanley (49 min), Earl (67 min), Crowley (71 min), A. Whetton (75 min) C: Fox (13, 39, 49, 67, 71, 75 min) PG: Fox (39, 75 min)
ARGENTINA   15
T: J. Lanza (57 min) C: Porta (57 min) PG: Porta (16, 30, 36 min)
New Zealand: Crowley; Kirwan, Stanley, McCahill, Wright; Fox, Kirk (capt.); Loe, Fitzpatrick, Drake; Pierce, G. Whetton; A. Whetton, Brooke, Earl
Argentina: Angaut; Campo, Madero, Turnes, J. Lanza; Porta (capt.), Gomez; Dengra, Cash, Molina; Branca, Carrosio; Allen, Schiavio, Travaglini
Replacements: Mostany for Travaglini (44 min), P. Lanza for Turnes (65 min)
Referee: R. C. Quittenton (England)   *Attendance:* 30 000

POOL 3 FINAL TABLE

	P	W	D	L	F	A	Pts
New Zealand	3	3	0	0	190	34	6
Fiji	3	1	0	2	56	101	2
Italy	3	1	0	2	40	110	2
Argentina	3	1	0	2	49	90	2

Fiji scored six tries, Italy five, and Argentina four.

POOL 4

23 May 1987, Eden Park, Auckland
ROMANIA 21
   T: Paraschiv (72 min), Toader (76 min), Hodorca (80 min)
   PG: Alexandru (23, 44, 48 min)
ZIMBABWE 20
   T: Tsimba (7, 63 min), Neill (17 min) C: Ferreira (63 min)
   PG: Ferreira (27, 54 min)
Romania: Toader; Marin, David, Tofan, Lungu; Alexandru, Paraschiv (capt.); Bucan, Grigore, Leonte; Dumitras, L. Constantin; S. Constantin, Raducanu, Muriaru
Replacements: Hodorca for Marin (5 min), Ion for Alexandru (60 min)
Zimbabwe: Ferreira; Kaulbach, K. Graham, Tsimba, Barrett; Brown, Jellicoe (capt.); Elcombe, Bray, Tucker; D. Buitendag, Martin; Sawyer, Gray, Neill
Replacement: A. Buitendag for Tsimba (67 min)
Referee: S. R. Hilditch (Ireland)   *Attendance:* 4000

23 May 1987, Lancaster Park, Christchurch
SCOTLAND 20
   T: White (2 min), Duncan (80 min) PG: G. Hastings (12, 22, 36, 45 min)
FRANCE 20
   T: Sella (50 min), Berbizier (58 min), Blanco (65 min)
   C: Blanco (65 min) PG: Blanco (24, 33 min)
Scotland: G. Hastings; Duncan, Robertson, Wyllie, Tukalo; Rutherford, Laidlaw; Milne, Deans (capt.), Sole; White, Tomes; F. Calder, Jeffrey, Paxton
Replacement: Tait for Rutherford (17 min)
France: Blanco; Lagisquet, Sella, Charvet, Estève; Mesnel, Berbizier; Garuet, Dubroca (capt.), Ondarts; Condom, Lorieux; Erbani, Champ, Rodriguez
Referee: F. A. Howard (England)   *Attendance:* 17000

28 May 1987, Athletic Park, Wellington
FRANCE 55
   T: Charvet (18, 78 min), Sella (26 min), Andrieu (42 min), Camberabero (45 min), Erbani (53 min), Laporte (57 min), Lagisquet (68, 75 min) C: Laporte (18, 26, 42, 53, 57, 68, 75, 78 min) PG: Laporte (50 min)
ROMANIA 12
   PG: Bezuscu (15, 23, 31, 34 min)
France: Blanco; Lagisquet, Sella, Charvet, Andrieu; Laporte, Berbizier; Garuet, Dubroca (capt.), Armary; Haget, Condom; Champ, Erbani, Carminati
Replacement: Camberabero for Blanco (14 min)
Romania: Ion; Toader, Tofan, David, Lungu; Bezuscu, Paraschiv (capt.); Opris, Ilca, Pascu; L. Constantin, Veres; Necula, Raducanu, Dumitru
Replacement: Grigore for Ilca (12 min)
Referee: D. J. Fordham (Australia)   *Attendance:* 5500

30 May 1987, Athletic Ground, Wellington
SCOTLAND 60
   T: Tait (4, 38 min), Duncan (10, 61 min), Oliver (17 min), G. Hastings (25 min), Paxton (31, 45 min), Jeffrey (74 min) C: G. Hastings (4, 10, 21, 25, 31, 38, 45, 74 min)
ZIMBABWE 21
   T: D. Buitendag (48 min) C: Grobler (48 min)

   PG: Grobler (13, 35, 56, 63, 66 min)
Scotland: G. Hastings; Duncan, Tait, Robertson, Tukalo; Wyllie, Oliver; Sole, Deans (capt.), Milne; Tomes, Campbell-Lamerton; Jeffrey, F. Calder, Paxton
Zimbabwe: Ferreira; S. Graham, A. Buitendag, K. Graham, Barrett; Grobler, Jellicoe (capt.); Elcombe, Bray, Tucker; Martin, Sawyer; Gray, D. Buitendag, Neill
Referee: D. I. H. Burnett (Ireland)   *Attendance:* 5000

2 Jun 1987, Eden Park, Auckland
FRANCE 70
   T: Modin (4, 13, 57 min), Dubroca (17 min), Rodriguez (38, 73 min), Charvet (52, 56 min), Camberabero (61, 67, 75 min), Laporte (77 min), Estève (62 min) C: Camberabero (4, 13, 17, 52, 56, 57, 61, 67, 77 min)
ZIMBABWE 12
   T: Kaulbach (66 min) C: Grobler (66 min)
   PG: Grobler (4, 69 min)
France: Camberabero; Andrieu, Bonneval, Charvet, Estève; Mesnel, Modin, Tolot, Dubroca (capt.), Ondarts; Lorieux, Condom; Carminati, Joinel, Rodriguez
Replacements: Sella for Bonneval (20 min), Laporte for Sella (43 min)
Zimbabwe: Ferreira; Kaulbach, Tsimba, K. Graham, Barrett; Grobler, Jellicoe (capt.); Elcombe, Gray, Tucker; Martin, Sawyer; Gray, D. Buitendag, Neill
Replacements: Nicholls for Elcombe (27 min), Kloppers for Martin (37 min)
Referee: W. D. Bevan (Wales)   *Attendance:* 4000

2 Jun 1987, Carisbrook, Dunedin
SCOTLAND 55
   T: Tait (5, 23 min), Jeffrey (18, 40, 42 min), Duncan (22 min), G. Hastings (68, 80 min), Tukalo (78 min) C: G. Hastings (4, 17, 20, 22, 37, 42, 65, 78 min) PG: G. Hastings (15 min)
ROMANIA 28
   T: Murariu (40, 80 min), Toader (48 min) C: Alexandru (48 min), Ion (80 min) PG: Alexandru (33, 56, 62, 68 min)
Scotland: G. Hastings; Duncan, Tait, S. Hastings, Tukalo; Wyllie, Laidlaw; Sole, Deans (capt.), Rowan; White, Tomes; Jeffrey, F. Calder, Paxton
Replacements: Cramb for S. Hastings (1 min), Campbell-Lamerton for Tomes (42 min)
Romania: Ion; Pilotschi, Lungu, Tofan, Toader; Alexandru, Paraschiv (capt.); Bucan, Grigore, Leonte; S. Constantin, L. Constantin; Murariu, Dumitras, Raducanu
Replacement: Dumitru for Raducanu (20 min)
Referee: S. Hilditch (Ireland)   *Attendance:* 10000

POOL 4 FINAL TABLE

	P	W	D	L	F	A	Pts
France	3	2	1	0	145	44	5
Scotland	3	2	1	0	135	69	5
Romania	3	1	0	2	61	130	2
Zimbabwe	3	0	0	3	53	151	0

QUARTER FINALS

6 Jun 1987, Lancaster Park, Christchurch
NEW ZEALAND 30
   T: A. Whetton (51 min), Gallagher (70 min) C: Fox (51, 70 min) PG: Fox (18, 25, 38, 58, 60, 67 min)
SCOTLAND 3
   PG: G. Hastings (18 min)
New Zealand: Gallagher; Kirwan, Stanley, Taylor, Green; Fox, Kirk (capt.); McDowell, Fitzpatrick, Drake; Pierce, G. Whetton; A. Whetton, Jones, Shelford
Replacement: McCahill for Taylor (17 min)

Scotland: G. Hastings; Duncan, Tait, Robertson, Tukalo; Wyllie, Laidlaw; Sole, Deans (capt.), Milne; White, Tomes; Turnbull, F. Calder, Paxton
Referee: D. I. H. Burnett (Ireland)   *Attendance:* 30 000

7 Jun 1987, Concord Oval, Sydney
AUSTRALIA   33
   T: McIntyre (14 min), Smith (17 min), Burke (22, 63 min)
   C: Lynagh (14, 17, 22, 63 min) PG: Lynagh (2, 8, 50 min)
IRELAND   15
   T: McNeill (69 min), Kiernan (80 min) C: Kiernan (69, 80 min) PG: Kiernan (57 min)
Australia: Campese; Grigg, Slack (capt.), Papworth, Burke; Lynagh, Farr-Jones; Lillicrap, Lawton, McIntyre; Cutler, Campbell; Poidevin, Miller, Tuynman
Replacements: Smith for Farr-Jones (5 min)
Ireland: McNeill; Ringland, Mullin, Kiernan, Crossan; Dean, Bradley; Orr, Kingston, Fitzpatrick; Lenihan (capt.), Anderson; Matthews, McGrath, Spillane
Replacements: Francis for Spillane (57 min), Irwin for Mullin (67 min)
Referee: J. B. Anderson (Scotland)   *Attendance:* 17 800

7 Jun 1987, Concord Oval, Sydney
FRANCE   31
   T: Lorieux (20 min), Rodriguez (30, 40 min), Lagisquet (76 min) C: Laporte (20, 30, 76 min) PG: Laporte (9, 17 min) DG: Laporte (80 min)
FIJI   16
   T: Qoro (15 min), Damu (78 min) C: Koroduadua (78 min) PG: Koroduadua (38, 64 min)
France: Blanco; Charvet, Sella, Mesnel, Lagisquet; Laporte, Berbizier; Ondarts, Dubroca (capt.), Garuet; Haget, Lorieux; Champ, Erbani, Rodriguez
Replacement: Camberabero for Blanco (79 min)
Fiji: Kubu; Damu, Salusalu, T. Cama, Mitchell; Koroduadua, Nawalu; Namoro, Rakai, Naituku; Rakaroi (capt.), Savai; Sanday, Qoro, Naiviliwasa
Replacements: Rokiowailoa for Savai (45 min), Lovoroku for Qoro (53 min)
Referee: C. T. Norling (Wales)   *Attendance:* 12 000

8 Jun 1987, Ballymore Oval, Brisbane
WALES   16
   T: Roberts (23 min), Jones (45 min), Devereux (80 min) C: Thorburn (23, 80 min)
ENGLAND   3
   PG: Webb (73 min)
Wales: Thorburn; I. Evans, Devereux, Bowen, Hadley; J. Davies, Jones; Buchanan, A. Phillips, Young; R. Moriarty (capt.), Norster; Collins, Roberts, P. Moriarty
Replacements: Richards for Norster (73 min)
England: Webb; Harrison (capt.), Simms, Salmon, Underwood; Williams, Harding; Rendall, Moore, Pearce; Dooley, Redman; Winterbottom, Rees, Richards
Replacement: Chilcott for Rendall (24 min)
Referee: R. Horquet (France)   *Attendance:* 15 000

SEMIFINALS
13 Jun 1987, Concord Oval, Sydney
FRANCE   30
   T: Lorieux (40 min), Sella (44 min), Lagisquet (54 min), Blanco (80 min) C: Camberabero (40, 44, 54, 80 min) PG: Camberabero (59, 79 min)
AUSTRALIA   24
   T: Campese (46 min), Codey (64 min) C: Lynagh (46, 64 min) PG: Lynagh (7, 29, 76 min) DG: Lynagh (4 min)

France: Blanco; Camberabero, Sella, Charvet, Lagisquet; Mesnel, Berbizier; Ondarts, Dubroca (capt.), Garuet; Lorieux, Condom; Champ, Erbani, Rodriguez
Australia: Campese; Grigg, Slack (capt.), Papworth, Burke; Lynagh, Farr-Jones; Lillicrap, Lawton, McIntyre; Campbell, Cutler; Miller, Poidevin, Coker
Replacements: Herbert for Papworth (8 min), Codey for Campbell (20 min)
Referee: J. B. Anderson (Scotland)   *Attendance:* 17 800

14 Jun 1987, Ballymore Oval, Brisbane
NEW ZEALAND   49
   T: Shelford (2, 73 min), Drake (8 min), Kirwan (22, 25 min), A. Whetton (59 min), Stanley (62 min), Brooke-Cowden (68 min) C: Fox (2, 8, 22, 25, 59, 62, 73 min)
   PG: Fox (35 min)
WALES   6
   T: Devereux (55 min) C: Thorburn (55 min)
New Zealand: Gallagher; Kirwan, Stanley, Taylor, Green; Fox, Kirk (capt.); Drake, Fitzpatrick, McDowell; Pierce, G. Whetton; A. Whetton, Brooke-Cowden, Shelford
Replacement: McCahill for Stanley (73 min)
Wales: Thorburn; I. Evans, Devereux, Bowen, Hadley; J. Davies, Jones; Buchanan, K. Phillips, Young; Richards, R. Moriarty (capt.); Collins, P. Davies, P. Moriarty
Replacement: Sutton for Collins (40 min)
Sending-off: Richards (71 min)
Referee: K. V. J. Fitzgerald (Australia)   *Attendance:* 25 000

THIRD-PLACE MATCH
18 Jun 1987, Rotorua International Stadium
WALES   22
   T: Roberts (29 min), P. Moriarty (40 min), Hadley (80 min) C: Thorburn (40, 80 min) PG: Thorburn (5, 43 min)
AUSTRALIA   21
   T: Burke (31 min), Grigg (39 min) C: Lynagh (31, 39 min) PG: Lynagh (12, 46 min) DG: Lynagh (54 min)
Wales: Thorburn; I. Evans, Devereux, Ring, Hadley; J. Davies, Jones; Buchanan, A. Phillips, Blackmore; R. Moriarty (capt.), Sutton; Roberts, Webster, P. Moriarty
Australia: Leeds; Grigg, Burke, Slack (capt.), Campese; Lynagh, Smith; Lillicrap, Lawton, McIntyre; Cutler, Coker; Poidevin, Codey, Tuynman
Replacements: Farr-Jones for Grigg (46 min), Rodriguez for Lillicrap (76 min)
Sending-off: Codey (5 min)
Referee: F. A. Howard (England)   *Attendance:* 20 000

WORLD CUP FINAL
20 Jun 1987, Eden Park, Auckland
NEW ZEALAND   29
   T: Jones (17 min), Kirk (63 min), Kirwan (66 min) C: Fox (17 min) PG: Fox (46, 56, 69, 77 min) DG: Fox (14 min)
FRANCE   9
   T: Berbizier (80 min) C: Camberabero (80 min)
   PG: Camberabero (44 min)
New Zealand: Gallagher; Kirwan, Stanley, Taylor, Green; Fox, Kirk (capt.); McDowell, Fitzpatrick, Drake; Pierce, G. Whetton; A. Whetton, Jones, Shelford
France: Blanco; Camberabero, Sella, Charvet, Lagisquet; Mesnel, Berbizier; Ondarts, Dubroca (capt.), Garuet; Lorieux, Condom; Champ, Erbani, Rodriguez
Referee: K. V. J. Fitzgerald (Australia)   *Attendance:* 48 035

Serge Blanco dives over for France's winning try v. Australia in the 1987 World Cup semifinal.

PROFILE OF THE WORLD CHAMPIONS

	Age	Ht	Wt	Occupation	Province
John Gallagher	23	1.90 m	85 kg	Policeman	Wellington
John Kirwan	21	1.90 m	92 kg	Representative	Auckland
Joe Stanley	29	1.78 m	83 kg	Transporter	Auckland
Warwick Taylor	27	1.78 m	79 kg	Clerk	Canterbury
Craig Green	25	1.78 m	79 kg	Farmer	Canterbury
Grant Fox	25	1.75 m	76 kg	Representative	Auckland
David Kirk	26	1.73 m	72 kg	Doctor	Auckland
Steve McDowell	25	1.81 m	101 kg	Representative	Auckland
Sean Fitzpatrick	23	1.83 m	92 kg	Carpenter	Auckland
John Drake	27	1.83 m	103 kg	Financier	Auckland
Murray Pierce	29	1.98 m	107 kg	Policeman	Wellington
Gary Whetton	26	1.98 m	106 kg	Manager	Auckland
Alan Whetton	27	1.91 m	99 kg	Transporter	Auckland
Michael Jones	22	1.85 m	92 kg	Student	Auckland
Wayne Shelford	28	1.87 m	102 kg	PE Teacher	North Harbour

HIGHEST SCORES

New Zealand	74	Fiji	13	Christchurch
New Zealand	70	Italy	6	Auckland
France	70	Zimbabwe	12	Auckland
England	60	Japan	7	Sydney
Scotland	60	Zimbabwe	21	Wellington
Scotland	55	Romania	28	Dunedin
France	55	Romania	12	Wellington

MOST TRIES IN A MATCH

4   Ieuan Evans (Wales) v Canada
4   Craig Green (New Zealand) v Fiji
4   John Gallagher (New Zealand) v
    Fiji

WORLD CUP RECORDS

Most points
Grant Fox (New Zealand)   126
Mike Lynagh (Australia)   82
Gavin Hastings (Scotland)   62
Didier Camberabero (France)   53
Jon Webb (England)   43
Guy Laporte (France)   42
Paul Thorburn (Wales)   37

Most tries
John Kirwan (New Zealand)   6
Craig Green (New Zealand)   6

Most drop goals
Jonathan Davies (Wales)   3

Most penalties
Grant Fox (New Zealand) v
   Argentina   6
Grant Fox (New Zealand) v
   Scotland   6

MOST POINTS IN A MATCH

30   Didier Camberabero (France) v
     Zimbabwe (Auckland)
27   Gavin Hastings (Scotland) v
     Romania (Dunedin)
26   Grant Fox (New Zealand) v Fiji
     (Christchurch)

2 INTERNATIONAL RUGBY BOARD COUNTRIES

The International Board consists of the eight major rugby-playing nations of the world – the four British Unions (England, Ireland, Scotland and Wales), France, and the three Southern Hemisphere countries, New Zealand, Australia and South Africa.

The first meeting took place at Manchester on 5 December 1887 with representatives from England, Scotland and Wales in attendance. Australia, New Zealand and South Africa were admitted to the International Board in 1948, France in 1978. Until the arrival of the emerging nations, international caps were only given for appearances against these eight countries.

This chapter outlines the growth and development of rugby in each Board country, the current structure and the principal domestic competitions.

England

Foundation 1871
Colours White shirts and shorts
Ground Twickenham
Capacity 54 500
No of clubs 1794
No of players 325 000

On 26 January 1871, 32 representatives from 20 clubs met at Pall Mall Restaurant in central London to form the Rugby Football Union. The founder members were Blackheath, Richmond, Wellington College, Guy's Hospital, Harlequins, King's College, St Paul's, Civil Service, Marlborough Nomads, Queen's House, West Kent, Wimbledon Hornets, Gipsies, Clapham Rovers, Flamingoes, Lausanne, Addison, Mohicans and Belsize Park. The first eight clubs still flourish.

Membership was fixed at 5s (25p) per year, with an annual subscription of the same sum. The meeting was convened by Edwin Ash of Richmond RFC. Among the items on the agenda was a desire to formulate acceptable rules and to sanction a challenge from Scotland to play the first international. A ban on 'hacking' was agreed. Laws of the game were to be drawn up.

Of course the game had been played since the famous day in 1823 when schoolboy William Webb Ellis was first reputed to have picked up the ball and run with it at Rugby School. But, as Association Football had created the Football Association in 1863, it was necessary for Rugby Football to do the same to draw up basic rules and laws.

Several of the leading Scottish and Irish clubs joined the Union, but with the foundation of their own Unions (1873 and 1879 respectively) those clubs withdrew to assume their natural allegiance. Today the Rugby Union is still open for all to join.

The crucial figure in those early days was George Rowland Hill (later knighted). Secretary of the Rugby Union from 1881–1904 and President from 1904–7, he was instrumental in the consolidation of the Rugby Union from those humble beginnings to the game's guiding light throughout the world.

Hill presented the famous amendment to the northern clubs' 'broken-time' proposal in the dispute of 1893, and his sincerity did much to ensure that rugby should remain amateur as conceived by its founders. As a tribute to his memory and his services to the game, the Rowland Hill Memorial Gates were erected at Twickenham at a cost of £6000 before a special Four Nations Memorial Match on 5 October 1929.

'Broken-time' has been a controversial issue since the turn of the century. Whether amateur rugby players should be recompensed for loss of wages as a result of participation in the game has been the longest-running saga in rugby, but the latest episode has developed on the international front. In 1987 the RFU decided that, at the discretion of each union, players on tour could be compensated for loss of earnings to the tune of up to £15 a day.

At a meeting held at the Westminster Palace Hotel, London, on 20 September 1893, two Yorkshire representatives of the Rugby Union, J. A. Millar and M. N. Newsome, proposed that, 'players be allowed compensation for bona fide loss of time'. Rowland Hill moved an amendment, 'that this meeting, believing that the above principle is contrary to the true spirit of the game and its spirit, declines to sanction the same'. The amendment was carried by 282 votes to 136, and several of the northern clubs, many of whose players worked in the mines, promptly announced their withdrawal from the Rugby Union. This led to the formation of the Northern Union, which later became the Rugby Football League.

The RFU's contribution to the game has been immense, helping to spread the game throughout the world. Most countries, especially the emerging ones, are grateful for the guidance that has come from Twickenham, the RFU's home since 1910. And if there are future problems, the game can be assured that the RFU will offer counsel.

By the 1987–8 season England should be in a position to join about 60 other countries in the world whose rugby is organized in a league system. This has developed from sponsored leagues decided on percentage totals and it is hoped that the new structure will answer critics of the way English rugby is organized. The country's top clubs are understandably loath to take part if it means losing any of the long-standing (and lucrative) friendly fixtures with major English and Welsh sides.

The knock-out John Player Cup, the County Championship (recently devalued) and the Divisional play-offs are the other major events.

ENGLAND – INTERNATIONAL RECORDS

TEAM RECORDS
Highest score
*Overall**
41 v France (41–13) 1907 Richmond
v individual countries
30 v Scotland (30–18) 1980 Murrayfield
36 v Ireland (36–14) 1938 Dublin
25 v Wales (25–0) 1896 Blackheath (London)
41 v France (41–13) 1907 Richmond
16 v N. Zealand (16–10) 1973 Auckland
18 v S. Africa (18–9) 1972 Johannesburg
23 v Australia (23–6) 1976 Twickenham
England beat Japan 60–7 in 1987 (World Cup).

Biggest winning points margin
Overall
37 v France (37–0) 1911 Twickenham
v individual countries
20 v Scotland (26–6) 1977 Twickenham
22 v Ireland (36–14) 1938 Dublin
25 v Wales (25–0) 1896 Blackheath
37 v France (37–0) 1911 Twickenham
13 v N. Zealand (13–0) 1936 Twickenham
9 v S. Africa (18–9) 1972 Johannesburg
17 v Australia (20–3) 1973 Twickenham
17 v Australia (23–6) 1976 Twickenham

Highest score by opposing team
Overall
42 N. Zealand (15–42) 1985 Wellington
by individual countries
33 Scotland (6–33) 1986 Murrayfield
26 Ireland (21–26) 1974 Twickenham
34 Wales (21–34) 1967 Cardiff
37 France (12–37) 1972 Colombes
42 N. Zealand (15–42) 1985 Wellington
35 S. Africa (9–35) 1984 Johannesburg
30 Australia (21–30) 1975 Brisbane

Biggest losing points margin
Overall
27 v N. Zealand (15–42) 1985 Wellington
27 v Scotland (6–33) 1986 Murrayfield
v individual countries
27 v Scotland (6–33) 1986 Murrayfield
22 v Ireland (0–22) 1947 Dublin
25 v Wales (0–25) 1905 Cardiff
25 v France (12–37) 1972 Colombes
27 v N. Zealand (15–42) 1985 Wellington
26 v S. Africa (9–35) 1984 Johannesburg
16 v Australia (3–19) 1984 Twickenham

Most points by England in an International Championship season
82   1913–4

Most tries by England in an International Championship season
20   1913–4

Most tries by England in an international
9 v France (35–8) 1906 Parc des Princes
9 v France (41–13) 1907 Richmond
9 v France (39–13) 1914 Colombes
England scored 13 tries v Wales at Blackheath in 1881, before uniform scoring was adopted.

Most tries against England in an international
8 by Wales (6–28) 1922 Cardiff

INDIVIDUAL RECORDS
Most capped player
Overall
A. Neary 43 1971–80
in individual positions
Full-back
W. H. Hare 25 1974–84
Wing
M. A. C. Slemen 31[2] 1976–84
Centre
P. W. Dodge 32[1] 1978–85
Fly-half
W. J. A. Davies 22 1913–23

Scrum-half
S. J. Smith 28 1973–83
Prop
G. S. Pearce 34 1979–87
Hooker
J. V. Pullin 42 1966–76
Lock
W. B. Beaumont 34 1975–82
Flanker
A. Neary 43 1971–80
No 8
J. P. Scott 31[2] 1978–84
[1]*David Duckham, England's most capped back, played 14 times at centre, and 22 times on the wing, making a total of 36 caps. M. P. Weston won 5 of his 29 caps as a fly-half, and 24 in the centre.*
[2]*Scott was capped three times as a lock.*

Longest international career
13 seasons   J. Heaton 1935–47

Most internationals as captain
21   W. B. Beaumont 1978–82

Most points in internationals
240   W. H. Hare (23 appearances)

Most points in an international
22   D. Lambert v France 1911 Twickenham

Most tries in internationals
18   C. N. Lowe (25 appearances) 1913–23

Most tries in an international
5   D. Lambert v France 1907 Richmond (on first appearance)

Most conversions in an international
6   J. E. Greenwood v France 1914 Paris
6   G. W. Parker v Ireland 1938 Dublin
L. Stokes kicked 6 v Wales at Blackheath in 1881, before uniform scoring was adopted.
J. Webb converted 7 v Japan in 1987 (World Cup).

Most points in an International Championship season
44   W. H. Hare (4 appearances) 1983–4

Most tries in an International Championship season

8 C. N. Lowe (4 appearances) 1913–4

Most conversions in an International Championship season

7 G. S. Conway (4 appearances) 1923–4

Most penalty goals in an International Championship season

14 W. H. Hare (4 appearances) 1982–3

Most points on overseas tour

48 W. N. Bennett (4 appearances) 1975 Australia

W. H. Hare scored 79 points on the North American tour of 1982, but this was not in an IB nation.

Most points in any tour match

36 W. N. Bennett v Western Australia 1975 Perth

Most tries in any tour match

4 A. J. Morley v Western Australia 1975 Perth

4 P. S. Preece v New South Wales 1975 Sydney

R. E. Webb scored 4 tries v Canada in 1967, and J. Carlton scored 4 tries against Mid-West at Cleveland in 1982.

ENGLAND'S LEADING CAP WINNERS

A. Neary   43
J. V. Pullin   42
P. J. Wheeler   41
D. J. Duckham   36
D. P. Rogers   34
W. B. Beaumont   34
J. P. Scott   34
G. S. Pearce   34
P. W. Dodge   32
W. W. Wakefield   31
F. E. Cotton   31
M. A. C. Slemen   31
E. Evans   30

ENGLAND – COUNTY CHAMPIONSHIP

1st System

1889 Yorkshire, undefeated, declared champions by the Rugby Union.
1890 Yorkshire, undefeated, declared champions.

2nd System

	Champions	Group winners
1891	Lancashire	Gloucestershire, Surrey, Yorkshire
1892	Yorkshire	Kent, Lancashire, Midlands
1893	Yorkshire	Cumberland, Devon, Middlesex
1894	Yorkshire	Gloucestershire, Lancashire, Midlands
1895	Yorkshire	Cumberland, Devon, Midlands

3rd System

	Champions	Runners Up	Venue
1896	Yorkshire	Surrey	Richmond
1897	Kent	Cumberland	Carlisle
1898	Northumberland	Midlands	Coventry
1899	Devon	Northumberland	Newcastle
1900	Durham	Devon	Exeter
1901	Devon	Durham	West Hartlepool
1902	Durham	Gloucestershire	Gloucester
1903	Durham	Kent	West Hartlepool
1904	Kent	Durham	Blackheath
1905	Durham	Middlesex	West Hartlepool
1906	Devon	Durham	Exeter
1907	Devon } Durham } Joint Champions		West Hartlepool and Exeter
1908	Cornwall	Durham	Redruth
1909	Durham	Cornwall	West Hartlepool
1910	Gloucestershire	Yorkshire	Gloucester
1911	Devon	Yorkshire	Headingley
1912	Devon	Northumberland	Devonport
1913	Gloucestershire	Cumberland	Carlisle
1914	Midlands	Durham	Leicester
1915–19	Suspended owing to First World War		
1920	Gloucestershire	Yorkshire	Bradford

4th System

	Winners	Runners Up	Venue
1921	Gloucestershire 31–4	Leicestershire	Gloucester
1922	Gloucestershire 19–0	North Midlands	Birmingham
1923	Somerset 8–6	Leicestershire	Bridgwater
1924	Cumberland 14–3	Kent	Carlisle
1925	Leicestershire 14–6	Gloucestershire	Bristol
1926	Yorkshire 15–14	Hampshire	Bradford
1927	Kent 22–12	Leicestershire	Blackheath
1928	Yorkshire 12–8	Cornwall	Bradford
1929	Middlesex drew with Lancashire		Twickenham
	Middlesex 9–8	Lancashire	Blundellsands
1930	Gloucestershire 13–7	Lancashire	Blundellsands
1931	Gloucestershire 10–9	Warwickshire	Gloucester
1932	Gloucestershire 9–3	Durham	Blaydon
1933	Hampshire 18–7	Lancashire	Boscombe
1934	East Midlands 10–0	Gloucestershire	Northampton
1935	Lancashire 14–0	Somerset	Bath
1936	Hampshire 13–6	Northumberland	Gosforth
1937	Gloucestershire 5–0	East Midlands	Bristol
1938	Lancashire 24–12	Surrey	Blundellsands
1939	Warwickshire 8–3	Somerset	Weston-super-Mare
1940–6	Suspended owing to Second World War		
1947	Lancashire 14–3	Gloucestershire	Gloucester
1948	Lancashire 5–0	Eastern Counties	Cambridge
1949	Lancashire 9–3	Gloucestershire	Blundellsands
1950	Cheshire 5–0	East Midlands	Birkenhead Park
1951	East Midlands 10–0	Middlesex	Northampton
1952	Middlesex 9–6	Lancashire	Twickenham
1953	Yorkshire 11–3	East Midlands	Bradford
1954	Middlesex 24–6	Lancashire	Blundellsands
1955	Lancashire 14–8	Middlesex	Twickenham
1956	Middlesex 13–9	Devon	Twickenham
1957	Devon 12–3	Yorkshire	Plymouth
1958	Warwickshire 16–8	Cornwall	Coventry
1959	Warwickshire 14–9	Gloucestershire	Bristol
1960	Warwickshire 9–6	Surrey	Coventry
1961	Cheshire 0–0	Devon	Plymouth
	Cheshire 5–3	Devon	Birkenhead Park

1962	Warwickshire 11–6	Hampshire	Twickenham
1963	Warwickshire 13–10	Yorkshire	Coventry
1964	Warwickshire 8–6	Lancashire	Coventry
1965	Warwickshire 15–9	Durham	Hartlepool
1966	Middlesex 6–0	Lancashire	Blundellsands
1967	Durham 14–14	Surrey	Twickenham
	Durham 0–0	Surrey	Durham
1968	Middlesex 9–6	Warwickshire	Twickenham
1969	Lancashire 11–9	Cornwall	Redruth
1970	Staffordshire 11–9	Gloucestershire	Burton-on-Trent
1971	Surrey 14–3	Gloucestershire	Gloucester
1972	Gloucestershire 11–6	Warwickshire	Coventry
1973	Lancashire 17–12	Gloucestershire	Blundellsands
1974	Gloucestershire 22–12	Lancashire	Blundellsands
1975	Gloucestershire 13–9	Eastern Counties	Gloucester
1976	Gloucestershire 24–9	Middlesex	Richmond
1977	Lancashire 17–6	Middlesex	Blundellsands
1978	North Midlands 10–7	Gloucestershire	Moseley
1979	Middlesex 19–6	Northumberland	Twickenham
1980	Lancashire 21–15	Gloucestershire	Vale of Lune
1981	Northumberland 15–6	Gloucestershire	Gloucester

1982	North Midlands 3–7	Lancashire	Moseley
1983	Gloucestershire 19–7	Yorkshire	Bristol
1984	Gloucestershire 36–18	Somerset	Twickenham
1985	Middlesex 12–9	Notts, Lincs and Derby	Twickenham
1986	Warwickshire 16–6	Kent	Twickenham
1987	Yorkshire 22–11	Middlesex	Twickenham

COUNTY CHAMPIONSHIP RECORDS
Most points in a season
253   Lancashire 1979–80

Most tries in a season
42   Lancashire 1979–80

Most county career points
462   Peter Butler (Gloucestershire)

INTER-SERVICES CHAMPIONS

1920	Navy	1947	RAF	1968	Army	1933	Army	1960	Army	1981	Navy
1921	Navy	1948	Triple tie	1969	Army	1934	Army	1961	Navy	1982	RAF
1922	Navy	1949	Army/RAF	1970	Navy	1935	Triple tie	1962	RAF	1983	Army
1923	RAF	1950	Army	1971	RAF	1936	Army	1963	Army	1984	Triple tie
1924	Triple tie	1951	Navy	1972	Army	1937	Army	1964	Army	1985	RAF
1925	Army/RAF	1952	Army	1973	Navy	1938	Navy	1965	Army	1986	RAF
1926	Army	1953	Army	1974	Navy	1939	Navy	1966	Navy	1987	Navy
1927	Navy	1954	Triple tie	1975	Triple tie	1946	Army	1967	Army		
1928	Army	1955	RAF	1976	Army						
1929	Army	1956	Triple tie	1977	Navy	**OUTRIGHT WINS**					
1930	Army	1957	Army	1978	Triple tie	25	Army				
1931	Navy	1958	RAF	1979	RAF	16	Navy				
1932	Army	1959	RAF	1980	Army	11	RAF				

NON-INTERNATIONAL TOURING DEFEATS IN ENGLAND

Cambridge University
| Beat Australia | 13–3 | Cambridge 1957–8 |

Combined Midlands & East Midlands
| Beat Australia | 16–5 | Leicester 1908 |

East Midlands
| Beat Australia | 11–8 | Leicester 1975 |

Lancashire & Cheshire
| Beat Australia | 9–8 | Blundellsands 1947–8 |

Leicester & East Midlands
| Beat South Africa | 30–21 | Leicester 1931–2 |

Midland Counties
| Beat Australia | 8–3 | Coventry 1957–8 |

Midland Counties West
| Beat New Zealand | 16–8 | Moseley 1972–3 |

Midland Division
| Beat Australia | 16–10 | Leicester 1981 |
| Beat New Zealand | 19–13 | Leicester 1983 |

North East Counties
| Beat Australia | 17–14 | Newcastle 1966–7 |

Northern Counties
| Beat Australia | 16–13 | Gosforth 1973 |

North West Counties
| Beat Australia | 6–3 | Blundellsands 1957–8 |
| Beat New Zealand | 16–14 | Workington 1972–3 |

Northern Division
| Beat New Zealand | 21–9 | Otley 1979 |

Oxford University
| Beat Australia | 12–6 | Oxford 1957–8 |
| Beat South Africa | 6–3 | Twickenham 1969–70 |

South & South West Counties
| Beat Australia | 14–5 | Bath 1973 |

South West Counties
| Beat Australia | 9–0 | Camborne 1966–7 |

Western Counties
| Beat Australia | 9–8 | Bristol 1957–8 |

West Midlands
| Beat Australia | 17–9 | Coventry 1966–7 |

FOUNDATION OF ENGLISH CLUBS

Order of foundation		Year
6	Bath	1865
40	Bedford	1886
11	Birkenhead Park	1871
49	Birmingham	1911
2	Blackheath	1858
8	Bradford	1866
43	Bristol	1888
37	Broughton Park	1882
29	Camborne	1878
13	Cambridge University	1872
21	Coventry	1874
14	Exeter	1872
50	Fylde	1919
16	Gloucester	1873
25	Gosforth	1877
17	Halifax	1873
7	Harlequins	1866
12	Harrogate	1871
31	Hartlepool Rovers	1879
30	Headingley	1878
48	Huddersfield	1909
46	Hull and East Riding	1901
35	Leicester	1880
1	Liverpool	1857
44	London Irish	1898
27	London Scottish	1878
39	London Welsh	1885
3	Manchester	1860
51	Metropolitan Police	1923
15	Middlesbrough	1872
28	Morley	1878
18	Moseley	1873
20	New Brighton	1873
34	Northampton	1880
24	Northern	1876
26	Nottingham	1877
32	Nuneaton	1879
53	Orrell	1927
10	Oxford University	1869
23	Plymouth Albion	1876
4	Richmond	1861
33	Rosslyn Park	1879
52	Roundhay	1924
19	Rugby	1873
42	St Ives	1887
5	Sale	1861
22	Saracens	1876
47	Sheffield	1902
45	Wakefield	1901
9	Wasps	1867
38	Waterloo	1883
36	West Hartlepool	1881
41	Wilmslow	1886

NB Guy's Hospital, founded 1843, were the first closed club.

MIDDLESEX SEVENS

WINNERS

1926	Harlequins
1927	Harlequins
1928	Harlequins
1929	Harlequins
1930	London Welsh
1931	London Welsh
1932	Blackheath
1933	Harlequins
1934	Barbarians
1935	Harlequins
1936	Sale
1937	London Scottish
1938	Metropolitan Police
1939	Cardiff
1940	St Mary's Hospital
1941	Cambridge University
1942	St Mary's Hospital
1943	St Mary's Hospital
1944	St Mary's Hospital
1945	Notts
1946	St Mary's Hospital
1947	Rosslyn Park
1948	Wasps
1949	Heriot's FP
1950	Rosslyn Park
1951	Richmond II
1952	Wasps
1953	Richmond
1954	Rosslyn Park
1955	Richmond
1956	London Welsh
1957	St Luke's College
1958	Blackheath
1959	Loughborough Colleges
1960	London Scottish
1961	London Scottish
1962	London Scottish
1963	London Scottish
1964	Loughborough Colleges
1965	London Scottish
1966	Loughborough Colleges
1967	Harlequins
1968	London Welsh
1969	St Luke's College
1970	Loughborough Colleges
1971	London Welsh
1972	London Welsh
1973	London Welsh
1974	Richmond
1975	Richmond
1976	Loughborough Colleges
1977	Richmond
1978	Harlequins
1979	Richmond
1980	Richmond
1981	Rosslyn Park
1982	Stewart's Melville FP
1983	Richmond
1984	London Welsh
1985	Wasps
1986	Harlequins
1987	Harlequins

WINS

10	Harlequins
9	Richmond (inc. 1 win by Richmond 2nd VII)
8	London Welsh
6	London Scottish
5	Loughborough Colleges
5	St Mary's Hospital
4	Rosslyn Park
3	Wasps
2	Blackheath, St Luke's College (now Exeter University)
1	Barbarians, Cambridge University, Cardiff, Heriot's FP, Met Police, Notts (now Nottingham), Sale, Stewart's Melville FP

Early days at the Middlesex Sevens; London Welsh (in possession) beat Blackheath 6–0 in the final of the 1930 tournament before deserted terraces.

JOHN PLAYER CUP

1971–2
Semifinals: Coventry 6, Gloucester 6*
          Moseley 18, Wilmslow 10
          Gloucester win on 'away team' rule
Final: Gloucester 17 (1PG, 2DG, 2T), Moseley 6
          (1G)
GLOUCESTER: E. J. F. Stephens; R. J. Clewes, J. A.
  Bayliss, R. Morris, J. Dix; T. Palmer, M. H. Booth;
  M. A. Burton, M. J. Nicholls (capt), R. J. Cowling, A.
  Brinn, J. S. Jarrett, J. A. Watkins, M. J. Potter, R.
  Smith.
Scorers – Tries: Dix, Morris
         Penalty goals: Stephens
         Dropped goals: Palmer, Booth
MOSELEY: S. A. Doble; K. Hatter, M. K. Swain,
  C. W. McFadyean, R. Kerr; J. F. Finlan, J. G.
  Webster (capt); C. C. Morrell, D. E. Lane, J.
  Griffiths, R. Morris, N. E. Horton, T. J. Smith, J. C.
  White, I. N. Pringle.
Scorers – Try: Swain
         Conversion: Doble
Referee: R. Lewis

1972–3
Semifinals: London Welsh 15, Bristol 8
          Sale 6, Coventry 35
Final: Coventry 27 (1G, 2PG, 1DG, 3T), Bristol 15
          (5PG)
COVENTRY: P. A. Rossborough; D. J. Duckham
  (capt), C. S. Wardlow, G. W. Evans, P. S. Preece;
  A. R. Cowman, W. J. Gittings; K. E. Fairbrother, J.
  D. Gray, J. M. Broderick, R. N. Creed, B. F. Ninnes,
  I. R. Darnell, J. Barton, B. C. Holt.
Scorers – Tries: Barton, Duckham, Evans, Gray
         Conversion: Rossborough
         Penalty goals: Rossborough (2)
         Dropped goal: Cowman
BRISTOL: P. M. Knight; M. J. W. Dandy, C. J.
  Williams, R. J. Swaffield, A. J. Morley; A. H.
  Nicholls (capt), A. F. A. Pearn; A. J. Rogers, J. V.
  Pullin, M. J. Fry, A. C. Munden, D. E. J. Watt, R. J.
  Orledge, R. C. Hannaford, D. M. Rollitt.
Scorers – Penalty goals: Pearn (5)
Referee: R. F. Johnson

1973–4
Semifinals: Coventry 23, Rosslyn Park 4
          Orrell 3, London Scottish 12
Final: Coventry 26 (2G, 2PG, 2T), London Scottish
          6 (2PG)
COVENTRY: P. A. Rossborough; R. C. Barnwell, D.
  Foulks, B. J. Corless, D. J. Duckham (capt); A. R.
  Cowman, W. J. Gittings; K. E. Fairbrother, J.
  Gallagher, J. M. Broderick, R. Walker, B. F. Ninnes,
  I. R. Darnell, L. J. Rolinson, R. Cardwell.
Scorers – Tries: Duckham (2), Barnwell, Gittings
         Conversions: Rossborough (2)
         Penalty goals: Rossborough (2)
LONDON SCOTTISH: G. B. Stevenson; D. G. Fowlie,
  A. A. Friell, A. G. Biggar, R. R. Keddie; D. E. Bell,
  R. D. Crerar; A. E. Corstorphine, D. A. Pickering,
  M. S. Lovett, R. A. McKenzie, A. F. McHarg, G.

Fraser, M. A. Biggar (capt), C. W. Thorburn.
Scorers – Penalty goals: Bell (2)
Referee: M. H. Titcomb

1974–5
Semifinals: Bedford 13, Coventry 6
          Morpeth 6, Rosslyn Park 28
Final: Bedford 28 (4G, 1T), Rosslyn Park 12 (3T)
BEDFORD: A. M. Jorden; R. Demming, J. M.
  Howard, R. Chadwick, D. Wyatt; W. N. Bennett, A.
  Lewis; C. J. Bailward, N. Barker, B. Keen, E. F.
  Edwards, R. M. Wilkinson, C. Hooker, A. J. Hollins,
  D. P. Rogers (capt).
Scorers – Tries: Demming (2), Wyatt, Bailward, Keen
         Conversions: Bennett (4)
ROSSLYN PARK: R. A. Codd; R. G. Fisher, C. D.
  Saville, M. B. Bazalgette, D. J. McKay; P. A.
  Treseder, L. E. Weston; R. L. Barlow, P. d'A.
  Keith-Roach (capt), N. P. Hinton, P. G. Anderson,
  N. D. Mantell, A. K. Rodgers, A. G. Ripley, G. Link.
Scorers – Tries: McKay (2), Fisher
Referee: R. F. Johnson

1975–6
Semifinals: Sale 3, Gosforth 12
          Rosslyn Park 12, Wakefield 6
Final: Gosforth 23 (2G, 1PG, 2T), Rosslyn Park 14
          (1PG, 1DG, 2T)
GOSFORTH: B. Patrick; S. M. Griffin, J. K. Britten,
  H. E. Patrick, J. S. Gustard; R. W. Breakey, M.
  Young (capt); A. J. Cutter, D. F. Madsen, C. White,
  A. J. Preston, T. C. Roberts, J. J. O. Short, P. J.
  Dixon, D. Robinson.
  Replacement: P. Levinson (for White after 21 mins).
Scorers – Tries: B. Patrick, Roberts, Gustard, Robinson
         Conversions: Young (2)
         Penalty goal: Young
ROSSLYN PARK: P. A. Treseder; M. P. Bulpitt, C. P.
  Kent, S. Fluskey, J. L. Moyes; C. S. Ralston, L. E.
  Weston; N. P. Hinton, P. d'A. Keith-Roach (capt), G.
  Lloyd-Roberts, R. Mordell, A. K. Rodgers, N. D.
  Mantell, A. G. Ripley, D. Starling.
  Replacement: L. Byrne (for Treseder after 33 mins).
Scorers – Tries: Ripley, Bulpitt
         Penalty goal: Weston
         Dropped goal: Ralston
Referee: N. R. Sanson

1976–7
Semifinals: London Welsh 12, Gosforth 18
          Waterloo 11, Saracens 6
Final: Gosforth 27 (2G, 1PG, 3T), Waterloo 11
          (1PG, 2T)
GOSFORTH: B. Patrick; J. S. Archer, H. E. Patrick,
  J. K. Britten, J. S. Gustard; R. W. Breakey, M.
  Young; A. J. Cutter, D. F. Madsen, C. White, D.
  Robinson, J. Hedley, T. C. Roberts, R. M. Uttley
  (capt), P. J. Dixon.
Scorers – Tries: Robinson (2), Dixon, Archer, Hedley
         Conversions: B. Patrick (2)
         Penalty goal: B. Patrick
WATERLOO: S. G. Tickle; J. N. Spaven, G. T.

Jackson, S. F. Christopherson, M. A. Flett; I. Ball, D. J. Carfoot; D. Reed, C. D. Fisher (capt), F. Blackhurst, K. Hancock, K. F. Short, M. F. Billingham, L. Connor, K. Lunt.
Scorers – Tries: Christopherson, Tickle
          Penalty goal: Ball
Referee: P. E. Hughes

1977–8
Semifinals: Leicester 25, Coventry 16
          Harlequins 6, Gloucester 12
Final: Gloucester 6 (1G), Leicester 3 (1PG)
GLOUCESTER: P. E. Butler; R. J. Clewes, B. J. Vine, R. Jardine, R. R. Mogg; C. G. Williams, P. R. Howell; M. A. Burton, S. G. F. Mills, G. A. F. Sargent, J. A. Watkins (capt), S. B. Boyle, J. H. Fidler, J. F. Simonett, V. J. Wooley.
Scorers – Try: Mogg
          Conversion: Butler
LEICESTER: W. H. Hare; M. J. Duggan, P. W. Dodge, B. P. Hall (capt), R. G. Barker; B. Jones, S. Kenney; S. P. Redfern, P. J. Wheeler, R. E. Needham, S. R. Johnson, N. J. Joyce, A. G. Hazlerigg, G. J. Adey, D. J. Forfar.
Scorer – Penalty goal: Hare
Referee: R. C. Quittenton

1978–9
Semifinals: Gosforth 3, Moseley 6
          Wasps 7, Leicester 43
Final: Leicester 15 (1G, 2PG, 1DG), Moseley 12 (1G, 1PG, 1DG)
LEICESTER: W. H. Hare; M. Newton, T. Burwell, P. W. Dodge, R. C. Barnwell; L. Cusworth, S. Kenney; S. P. Redfern, P. J. Wheeler (capt), R. J. Cowling, S. R. Johnson, N. J. Joyce, A. G. Hazlerigg, G. J. Adey, I. R. Smith.
Scorers – Try: Kenney
          Conversion: Hare
          Penalty goals: Hare (2)
          Dropped goal: Hare
MOSELEY: R. Akenhead; A. Thomas, M. K. Swain, B. J. Corless, R. Laird; M. J. Cooper (capt), C. J. Gifford; K. J. Astley, G. N. K. Cox, W. H. Greaves, N. C. Jeavons, R. Field, B. Ayre, D. R. Nutt, J. D. Beale.
Replacements: A. Watson-Jones (for Corless after 30 mins), S. King (for Nutt after 50 mins).
Scorers – Try: Laird
          Conversion: Akenhead
          Penalty goal: Akenhead
          Dropped goal: Cooper
Referee: A. Welsby

1979–80
Semifinals: Harlequins 9, Leicester 16
          Rosslyn Park 6, London Irish 6*
          London Irish won on 'away team' rule
Final: Leicester 21 (4PG, 3DG), London Irish 9 (1G, 1PG)
LEICESTER: W. H. Hare; R. C. Barnwell, C. R. Woodward, P. W. Dodge, T. R. Burwell; L. Cusworth, S. Kenney; S. P. Redfern, P. J. Wheeler (capt), R. J. Cowling, S. R. Johnson, N. J. Joyce, N. K. Gillingham, G. J. Adey, I. R. Smith.

Scorers – Penalty goals: Hare (4)
          Dropped goals: Cusworth (2), Hare
LONDON IRISH: D. A. Leopold; R. McKibbin, A. R. McKibbin, P. O'Donnell, C. A. Meanwell; H. C. Condon, B. W. Murphy; L. White, G. G. Beringer, J. A. Newberry, J. B. O'Driscoll (capt), J. M. Sheehan, M. J. Smythe, K. S. Short, W. Jones.
Replacement: D. A. McCracken (for Smythe after 43 mins).
Scorers – Try: Smythe
          Conversion: Meanwell
          Penalty goal: Meanwell
Referee: C. J. High

1980–1
Semifinals: London Scottish 12, Leicester 18 (a.e.t.)
          Gosforth 24, Moseley 3
Final: Leicester 22 (2G, 2PG, 1T), Gosforth 15 (1G, 3PG)
LEICESTER: W. H. Hare; K. Williams, P. W. Dodge, C. R. Woodward, R. C. Barnwell; L. Cusworth, S. Kenney; S. P. Redfern, P. J. Wheeler (capt), R. J. Cowling, S. R. Johnson, N. J. Joyce, N. Jackson, G. J. Adey, I. R. Smith.
Replacement: A. P. Collington (for Johnson after 82 mins).
Scorers – Tries: Kenney, Barnwell, Hare
          Conversions: Hare (2)
          Penalty goals: Hare (2)
GOSFORTH: B. Patrick; J. S. Archer, R. W. Breakey, A. J. MacMillan, N. H. McDowell; D. Johnson, M. Young; J. A. H. Bell, R. Cunningham, C. White (capt), S. M. Smith, T. C. Roberts, S. Bainbridge, J. L. Butler, T. R. Anderson.
Scorers – Try: Cunningham
          Conversion: Johnson
          Penalty goals: Johnson (2), Patrick
Referee: R. C. Quittenton

1981–2
Semifinals: Moseley 12, Leicester 4
          Coventry 9, Gloucester 18
Final: Gloucester 12 (4PG), Moseley 12 (3PG, 1DG)
          (After extra time: title shared)
GLOUCESTER: P. Ford; P. Pritchard, P. A. Taylor, S. G. Parsloe, R. R. Mogg; L. Jones, S. J. W. Baker; P. J. Blakeway, S. G. F. Mills (capt), M. Preedy, J. Gadd, S. B. Boyle, J. Orwin, M. Teague, M. Longstaff.
Replacements: G. A. F. Sargent (for Preddy after 40 mins), P. Wood (for Longstaff after 65 mins).
Scorers – Penalty goals: Ford (4)
MOSELEY: M. J. Cooper; J. M. Goodwin, J. E. Desborough, D. W. Shorrock, R. D. Lawson; M. H. Perry, I. S. Sutherland; S. D. Adcaster, G. N. J. Cox, T. F. Corless, D. G. Warren, J. S. Davidson, A. Recardo, D. R. Nutt (capt), N. C. Jeavons.
Scorers – Penalty goals: Perry (3)
          Dropped goal: Perry
Referee: R. C. Quittenton

1982–3
Semifinals: Coventry 3, Bristol 23
          London Scottish 9, Leicester 30

Final: Bristol 28 (3G, 2PG, 1T), Leicester 22 (1G, 4PG, 1T)

BRISTOL: I. H. Duggan; A. J. G. Morley, R. A. Knibbs, S. T. Hogg, J. F. Carr; S. Barnes, R. M. Harding; R. J. Doubleday, K. M. Bogira, A. Sheppard, P. Polledri, N. J. C. Pomphrey, A. H. Troughton, R. Hesford, M. Rafter (capt).

Replacement: D. J. Palmer (for Bogira after 29 mins).

Scorers – Tries: Carr (2), Hogg, Hesford
Conversions: Barnes (3)
Penalty goal: Barnes

LEICESTER: I. Dobson; B. Evans, P. W. Dodge, C. R. Woodward, R. C. Barnwell; L. Cusworth, N. C. Youngs; S. B. Redfern, P. J. Wheeler, S. P. Redfern, S. R. Johnson (capt), M. V. Foulkes-Arnold, N. K. Gillingham, I. R. Smith, D. Richards.

Replacement: I. Bates (for Barnwell after 37 mins).

Scorers – Tries: Evans, Smith
Conversion: Cusworth
Penalty goals: Cusworth (4)

Referee: R. C. Quittenton

1983–4

Semifinals: Bristol 21, Harlequins 18
Nottingham 3, Bath 12

Final: Bath 10 (1PG, 1DG, 1T), Bristol 9 (1G, 1PG)

BATH: C. R. Martin; D. M. Trick, J. A. Palmer, A. Rees, B. Trevaskis; J. P. Horton, R. J. Hill; G. J. Chilcott, R. Cunningham, M. R. Lee, N. Gaymond, N. C. Redman, R. A. Spurrell (capt), J. P. Hall, P. D. Simpson.

Scorers – Try: Simpson
Penalty goal: Palmer
Drop goal: Horton

BRISTOL: P. C. Cue; A. J. G. Morley, R. A. Knibbs, S. T. Hogg, J. F. Carr; S. Barnes, R. M. Harding; R. J. Doubleday, D. J. Palmer, A. Sheppard, P. Polledri, N. J. C. Pomphrey, P. J. Stiff, M. Rafter (capt), D. L. Chidgey.

Scorers – Try: Harding
Conversion: Barnes
Penalty goal: Barnes

Referee: R. C. Quittenton

1984–5

Semifinals: Coventry 10, London Welsh 10*
Gloucester 11, Bath 12
London Welsh won on 'more tries' rule

Final: Bath 24 (2G, 4PG), London Welsh 15 (5PG)

BATH: C. R. Martin; D. M. Trick, J. A. Palmer, S. J. Halliday, B. Trevaskis; J. P. Horton, R. J. Hill; G. J. Chilcott, G. Bess, M. R. Lee, N. Gaymond, N. C. Redman, R. A. Spurrell (capt), J. P. Hall, P. D. Simpson.

Replacement: J. Guscott (for Trevaskis after 40 mins).

Scorers – Tries: Trick, Chilcott
Conversions: Palmer (2)
Penalty goals: Palmer (4)

LONDON WELSH: M. Ebsworth; J. Hughes, R. A. Ackerman, D. Fouhy, C. F. W. Rees (capt); C. Price, M. H. J. Douglas, T. W. Jones, B. Light, B. Bradley, E. Lewis, J. Collins, S. Russell, M. Watkins, K. Bowring.

Scorers – Penalty goals: Price (5)

Referee: R. C. Quittenton

1985–6

Semifinals: Leicester 6, Bath 10
Wasps 11, London Scottish 3

Final: Bath 25 (3G, 1PG, 1T), Wasps 17 (1G, 1PG, 2T)

BATH: C. R. Martin; D. M. Trick, J. A. Palmer (capt), S. J. Halliday, A. H. Swift; S. Barnes, R. J. Hill; G. J. Chilcott, G. Dawe, M. R. Lee, J. S. C. Morrison, N. C. Redman, R. A. Spurrell, J. P. Hall, P. D. Simpson.

Scorers – Tries: Swift, Spurrell, Hill, Simpson
Conversions: Trick (3)
Penalty goal: Trick

WASPS: N. C. Stringer; S. T. Smith, R. M. Cardus (capt), R. Pellow, M. D. Bailey; G. L. Rees, S. M. Bates; G. Holmes, A. Simmons, J. A. Probyn, J. Bonner, M. C. F. Pinnegar, M. Rigby, D. Pegler, M. A. Rose.

Replacement: P. Balcombe (for Bates after 36 mins).

Scorers – Tries: Stringer, Pellow, Balcombe
Conversion: Stringer
Penalty goal: Stringer

Referee: F. A. Howard

Bath take the lead for the first time during the 1987 John Player Cup final through this try from centre Simon Halliday (in white). Bath won the final 19–12 to record their fourth successive win and set another record in remaining unbeaten in 20 successive matches in the competition.

1986–7

Semifinals: Orrell 7, Bath 31
Wasps 13, Leicester 6
Final: Bath 19 (2G, 1PG, 1T), Wasps 12 (1G, 1PG, 1DG)

BATH: C. R. Martin; A. H. Swift, J. A. Palmer, S. J. Halliday, B. Trevaskis; S. Barnes, R. J. Hill (capt); D. M. B. Sole, R. G. R. Dawe, G. J. Chilcott, J. S. C. Morrison, N. C. Redman, A. Robinson, J. P. Hall, D. W. Egerton.
Replacements: J. Guscott (for Swift after 45 mins), G. Bess (for Dawe after 25 mins)

Scorers – Tries: Redman (2), Halliday
Conversions: Barnes (2)
Penalty goal: Barnes

WASPS: G. H. Davies; S. T. Smith, K. G. Simms, R. A. P. Lozowski, M. D. Bailey; C. R. Andrew, S. M. Bates; P. A. G. Rendall, A. Simmons, J. A. Probyn, M. C. F. Pinnegar, J. Bonner, M. A. Rigby, D. J. Pegler (capt), M. A. Rose.

Scorers – Try: Davies
Conversion: Andrew
Penalty goal: Davies
Dropped goal: Andrew

Referee: F. A. Howard

Alan Morley, the Bristol and England wing who holds the world record for number of tries in first class rugby. By 1987 Morley – here in white putting pressure on New Zealanders Parkinson (right) and Batty (left) – had amassed 436 tries in club, representative and international matches.

JOHN PLAYER CUP RECORDS

Most appearances in Final
5   Leicester

Most appearances in Semifinal
8   Coventry
8   Leicester

Most Semifinal defeats
6   Coventry

Most Semifinal appearances without reaching a Final
3   Harlequins

Most points in Final
50   (Bristol 28, Leicester 22 – 1983)

Most points by winners
28   (Bedford – 1975, Bristol – 1983)

Most points by losers
22   (Leicester – 1983)

Widest margin of victory
20   (Coventry 26, London Scottish 6 – 1974)

Most points by an individual in Final
16   John Palmer (4PG, 2C) (1985)
Dusty Hare has scored a total of 43 points in four appearances in Finals (9PG, 2DG, 3C, 1T).

Most appearances by an individual in Finals
5   P. W. Dodge, S. P. Redfern, P. J. Wheeler

Most tries in Final
2   J. F. Carr 1983

2   R. Demming 1975
2   D. J. Duckham 1974
2   D. J. McKay 1975
2   D. Robinson 1977
2   N. C. Redman 1987

Most appearances in final stages
(up to start of 1987–8 season)
49   Coventry

Most points in final stages
937   Coventry

Most consecutive wins
19   Bath 1984–7

Highest score since competition began
Gloucester 87, Exeter University 3 (First Round 1985–6)

Ireland

Foundation 1879
Colours Green shirts, white shorts
Ground Lansdowne Road, Dublin
Capacity 58 000
No of clubs 225
No of players 11 000

A great deal of myth and confusion surround the formation of the Irish Rugby Union. This was probably due to the lack of surviving minutes for historians to delve into. Ireland twice formed a Union, in 1874 and 1879. Whatever the political differences today, rugby in Ireland unites people. Not surprisingly, then, Ulster were miffed that they were not invited to the first meeting in Dublin in November 1874. Ulster formed their own Northern Union in the meantime, and in 1879 the two merged to form the Irish Rugby Football Union.

The Irish benefited to the tune of two centenaries, in 1974 and 1979.

Trinity College, founded in 1854, lays claim to being one of the oldest in the world, North of Ireland FC (1859) also being high on the list. A set of rules was drawn up by Charles Barrington (related to the six times British Open squash champion Jonah Barrington) and R. M. Wall who sent a circular to the other clubs: 'We have forwarded the rules by which we play in the hope that for the future we may be able to secure players thoroughly acquainted with the science of the game, a want that has hitherto proved an obstacle to our efficiency on the field.'

Rugby in the early days did well to survive other interests in the country. Association Football, Gaelic Football and Hurling were all popular in a country with a small population. Four branch Unions – Ulster, Leinster, Munster and Connacht – with members elected onto the IRFU quickly organized their own competitions. Leinster (1882), Ulster (1885), Munster (1886) and Connacht (1896) organized Senior Cups which are today central to the success of the game in Ireland. In addition to the Senior Cup, each province runs a Senior League and Senior and Junior Schools' Cups. The inter-provincial tournament is regarded as the forerunner to the International trial.

IRELAND – INTERNATIONAL RECORDS

TEAM RECORDS

Highest score
Overall*
27 v Australia (27–12) 1979 Brisbane
v individual countries
26 v England (26–21) 1974 Twickenham
26 v Scotland (26–8) 1953 Murrayfield
21 v Wales (21–24) 1979 Cardiff
21 v Wales (21–7) 1980 Dublin
21 v Wales (21–9) 1985 Cardiff
25 v France (25–5) 1911 Cork
25 v France (25–6) 1975 Dublin
10 v N. Zealand (10–10) 1973 Dublin
15 v S. Africa (15–23) 1981 Cape Town
27 v Australia (27–12) 1979 Brisbane
*Ireland beat Romania 60–0 in 1986.

Biggest winning points margin
Overall
24 v France (24–0) 1913 Cork
v individual countries
22 v England (22–0) 1947 Dublin
21 v Scotland (21–0) 1950 Dublin
16 v Wales (19–3) 1925 Belfast
24 v France (24–0) 1913 Cork
No win v N. Zealand
3 v S. Africa (9–6) 1965 Dublin
15 v Australia (27–12) 1979 Brisbane

Highest score by opposing team
38 S. Africa (0–38) 1912 Dublin
by individual countries
36 England (14–36) 1938 Dublin
32 Scotland (9–32) 1984 Dublin
34 Wales (9–34) 1976 Dublin
29 France (9–29) 1986 Paris
17 N. Zealand (9–17) 1935 Dublin
38 S. Africa (0–38) 1912 Dublin
20 Australia (10–20) 1976 Dublin

Biggest losing points margin
Overall
38 v S. Africa (0–38) 1912 Dublin
v individual countries
22 v England (14–36) 1938 Dublin

23 v Scotland (9–32) 1984 Dublin
29 v Wales (0–29) 1907 Cardiff
23 v France (3–26) 1976 Paris
15 v N. Zealand (0–15) 1905 Dublin
38 v S. Africa (0–38) 1912 Dublin
18 v Australia (15–33) 1987 Sydney (World Cup)

Most points by Ireland in an International Championship season
71   1982–3

Most tries by Ireland in an International Championship season
12   1927–8 and 1952–3

Most tries by Ireland in an international
6 v France (24–0) 1913 Cork
6 v Scotland (26–8) 1953 Murrayfield

Most tries against Ireland in an international
10 by S. Africa (0–38) 1912 Dublin

INDIVIDUAL RECORDS

Most capped player
Overall
C. M. H. Gibson 69 1964–79
in individual positions
Full-back
T. J. Kiernan 54 1960–73
Wing
T. M. Ringland 30 1981–7
Centre
C. M. H. Gibson 40(69)[1] 1964–79
Fly-half
J. W. Kyle 46 1947–58
Scrum-half
M. Sugden 28 1925–31
Prop
P. A. Orr 58 1976–87
Hooker
K. W. Kennedy 45 1965–75
Lock
W. J. McBride 63 1962–75

Flanker
J. F. Slattery 61 1970-84
No 8
W. P. Duggan 39(41)[2] 1975–84
[1]*Gibson won 40 caps as a centre, 25 at fly-half and 4 as a wing.*
[2]*Duggan won 39 caps at No 8 and 2 as a flanker.*

Longest international career
16 seasons   A. J. F. O'Reilly 1955–70
16 seasons   C. M. H. Gibson 1964-79
Gibson's career ended during a Southern Hemisphere season.

Most internationals as captain
24   T. J. Kiernan 1963–73

Ireland's most prolific points scorer, Ollie Campbell, puts over his third penalty in Ireland's 24–9 defeat by England at Twickenham in 1980. Campbell scored 217 points for his country between 1976–84.

Most points in internationals
217   S. O. Campbell (22 appearances) 1976–84

Most points in an international
21   S. O. Campbell v Scotland 1982 Dublin
21   S. O. Campbell v England 1983 Dublin

Most tries in internationals
14   G. V. Stephenson (41 appearances) 1920–30
Stephenson also played once against NSW.

Most tries in an international
3   J. P. Quinn v France 1913 Cork
3   E. O'D. Davy v Scotland 1930 Murrayfield
3   S. Byrne v Scotland 1953 Murrayfield
R. Montgomery scored 3 tries against Wales at Birkenhead in 1887, but this was before uniform scoring was adopted. K. Crossan scored 3 tries against Romania in 1986.

Most conversions in an international
4   P. F. Murray v Scotland 1932 Murrayfield
4   R. J. Gregg v Scotland 1953 Murrayfield
M. J. Kiernan kicked 7 conversions against Romania in 1986.

Most points in an International Championship season
52   S. O. Campbell (4 appearances) 1982–3

Most tries in an International Championship season
5   J. E. Arigho (3 appearances) 1927–8

Most conversions in an International Championship season
7   R. A. Lloyd (4 appearances) 1912–3

Most penalty goals in an International Championship season
14   S. O. Campbell (4 appearances) 1982–3

Most points on overseas tour
60   S. O. Campbell (5 appearances) 1979 Australia
M. J. Kiernan scored 65 points in Japan 1985

Most points in any tour match
19   A. J. P. Ward v Australian Capital Territory 1979 Canberra
19   S. O. Campbell v Australia 1979 Brisbane
M. J. Kiernan scored 25 points in the second match against Japan 1985

Most tries in any tour match
3   A. T. A. Duggan v Victoria 1967 Melbourne
3   J. F. Slattery v SA President's XV 1981 East London
3   M. J. Kiernan v Gold Cup XV 1981 Oudtshoorn, SA
T. M. Ringland scored 3 tries v Japan at Osaka 1985

IRELAND'S LEADING CAP WINNERS

C. M. H. Gibson 69	J. D. Clinch 30
W. J. McBride 63	J. L. Farrell 29
J. F. Slattery 61	B. G. M. Wood 29
P. A. Orr 58	A. J. F. O'Reilly 29
T. J. Kiernan 54	M. Sugden 28
M. I. Keane 51	J. S. McCarthy 28
J. W. Kyle 46	M. J. Kiernan 28
K. W. Kennedy 45	A. M. Magee 27
G.V. Stephenson 42	A. R. Dawson 27
W. P. Duggan 41	M. G. Molloy 27
N. J. Henderson 40	J. J. Moloney 27
R. J. McLoughlin 40	J. C. Walsh 26
S. Millar 37	R. M. Young 26
J. R. Kavanagh 35	J. B. O'Driscoll 26
W. A. Mulcahy 35	G. R. Beamish 25
E. O'D. Davy 34	K. D. Mullen 25
H. P. MacNeill 34	F. P. K. Bresnihan 25
T. M. Ringland 31	A. T. A. Duggan 25
D. G. Lenihan 31	B. J. McGann 25
A. C. Pedlow 30	T. O. Grace 25
G. T. Hamlet 30	S. A. McKinney 25
W. E. Crawford 30	C. F. Fitzgerald 25

NON-INTERNATIONAL TOURING DEFEATS IN IRELAND

Combined Provinces
Beat South Africa Belfast 1964–5	8–3
Beat Australia Belfast 1968	9–3

Combined Universities
Beat South Africa Dublin 1964–5	12–10

Munster
Beat Australia Limerick 1966–7	11–8
Beat New Zealand Limerick 1978	12–0
Beat Australia Cork 1981	15–6

Ulster
Beat Australia Belfast 1984	15–13

IRELAND – RECENT INTER-PROVINCIAL MATCHES

1983–4	1984–5	1985–6	1986–7
Leinster 22, Munster 13	Ulster 16, Leinster 3	Ulster 23, Munster 3	Munster 6, Ulster 13
Connacht 9, Ulster 4	Connacht 9, Munster 15	Connacht 9, Leinster 6	Connacht 6, Leinster 41
Leinster 20, Ulster 16	Ulster 28, Connacht 6	Leinster 15, Munster 6	Ulster 37, Connacht 6
Munster 29, Connacht 7	Leinster 15, Munster 9	Ulster 16, Connacht 6	Leinster 15, Munster 3
Ulster 13, Munster 12	Ulster 14, Munster 6	Ulster 19, Leinster 13	Ulster 15, Leinster 12
Leinster 29, Connacht 6	Leinster 14, Connacht 3	Munster 16, Connacht 9	Connacht 11, Munster 9

FOUNDATION OF IRISH CLUBS

Order of foundation		*Year*						
31	Academy (formerly Belfast Royal)	1975	*27*	Galwegians	1922	*28*	Sunday's Well	1924
24	Ballymena	1922	*13*	Garryowen	1884	*30*	Terenure College	1941
14	Bangor	1886	*23*	Instonians	1919	*1*	Trinity College Dublin	1854
10	Bective Rangers	1881	*6*	Lansdowne	1872	*5*	University College Cork	1872
11	Blackrock College	1882	*17*	Malone	1892	*22*	University College Dublin	1910
25	Bohemians	1922	*12*	Monkstown	1883	*8*	University College Galway	1874
26	CIYMS	1922	*2*	NIFC	1859	*4*	Wanderers	1870
9	Clontarf	1876	*29*	Old Belvedere	1930			
15	Collegians	1890	*16*	Old Wesley	1891			
18	Cork Constitution	1892	*19*	Palmerston	1899			
21	Dolphin	1902	*3*	Queen's University Belfast	1869			
7	Dungannon	1873	*20*	St Mary's College	1900			

RECENT IRISH SENIOR CUP WINNERS

Province	1983–4	1984–5	1985–6	1986–7
Leinster	Wanderers	Old Wesley	Lansdowne	Lansdowne
Ulster	Malone	Ards	Bangor	Instonians
Munster	Young Munster	Cork Constitution	Shannon	Shannon
Connacht	Corinthians	Corinthians	Galwegians	Galwegians

Scotland

Foundation 1873
Colours Dark blue shirts, white shorts
Ground Murrayfield, Edinburgh
Capacity 72 500
Record Attendance 104 000 (world record) Scotland v Wales 1975
No of clubs 129
No of players 26 500

The Scottish Rugby Union was formed in 1873, two years later than the Rugby Union. Six clubs formed the Union, Edinburgh Academicals, Glasgow Academicals, West of Scotland, Royal High School Former Pupils, Merchistonians and Edinburgh University. Further clubs, originally affiliated to the Rugby Union in England, transferred their allegiance back north of the border, bringing the basic organizational structure to the Scottish scene. Of the original six, Edinburgh University, Glasgow Academicals and West of Scotland had joined the Rugby Union soon after its formation in 1871.

Two years before the formation of the Scottish RFU the first international had been played. Organized by Edinburgh Academicals (thanks to their English RFU connections), Scotland won the match by a goal and a try to a try at Raeburn Place, Edinburgh, on 27 March 1871.

Scotland rightly claim to have been innovators of several of rugby's better ideas. The first purpose-built rugby ground was established at Inverleith, Edinburgh, in 1899. Murrayfield became the permanent ground in 1924, and in 1959 the new stadium became the first to install undersoil heating, which to this day guarantees play during the depths of winter. Back in 1883, the Scots invented Seven-a-Side rugby. Melrose butcher Ned Haig devised this form of the game as a fund-raiser for the ailing border club. The game was an overnight success at Melrose and has now spread throughout the world.

In 1973, the Scottish RFU sanctioned a club championship of seven divisions of 14 clubs each, bringing the leading sides together with promotion and relegation between divisions. Each club plays 13 matches, and there is a midwinter break. The Inter District competition between the South, Edinburgh, Glasgow, the North and Midlands, and the Anglo-Scots is a yardstick for international selection, while the Border League and other local leagues continue to flourish. Significantly, the standard of Scottish international rugby has benefited from this competitive element, with the national XV winning the Grand Slam in 1984, and adopting in the 1980s a style of open play admired throughout the world.

SCOTLAND – INTERNATIONAL RECORDS

TEAM RECORDS

Highest score
*Overall**
35 v Wales (35–10) 1924 Inverleith
  (Edinburgh)
v individual countries
33 v England (33–6) 1986
  Murrayfield
32 v Ireland (32–9) 1984 Dublin
35 v Wales (35–10) 1924 Inverleith
31 v France (31–3) 1912 Inverleith
25 v N. Zealand (25–25) 1983
  Murrayfield
10 v S. Africa (10–18) 1960 Port
  Elizabeth
24 v Australia (24–15) 1981
  Murrayfield
Scotland beat Zimbabwe 60–21 in 1987 (World Cup).

Biggest winning points margin
Overall
28 v France (31–3) 1912 Inverleith
v individual countries
27 v England (33–6) 1986
  Murrayfield
23 v Ireland (32–9) 1984 Dublin
25 v Wales (35–10) 1924 Inverleith
28 v France (31–3) 1912 Inverleith
No win v N. Zealand

6 v S. Africa (6–0) 1906 Hampden
  Park (Glasgow)
9 v Australia (24–15) 1981
  Murrayfield

Highest score by opposing team
Overall
44 S. Africa (0–44) 1951 Murrayfield
by individual countries
30 England (18–30) 1980
  Murrayfield
26 Ireland (8–26) 1953 Murrayfield
35 Wales (12–35) 1972 Cardiff
28 France (22–28) 1987 Paris (Parc
  des Princes)
40 New Zealand (15–40) 1981
  Auckland
44 S. Africa (0–44) 1951 Murrayfield
37 Australia (12–37) 1984
  Murrayfield

Biggest losing points margin
Overall
44 v S. Africa (0–44) 1951
  Murrayfield
v individual countries
20 v England (6–26) 1977
  Twickenham
21 v Ireland (0–21) 1950 Dublin

23 v Wales (12–35) 1972 Cardiff
20 v France (3–23) 1977 Parc des
  Princes
27 v N. Zealand (3–30) 1987
  Auckland
44 v S. Africa (0–44) 1951
  Murrayfield
25 v Australia (12–37) 1984
  Murrayfield

Most points by Scotland in an International Championship season
86   1983–4

Most tries by Scotland in an International Championship season
17   1924–5

Most tries by Scotland in an international
8 v Wales (35–10) 1924 Inverleith
Scotland scored 12 tries v Wales at Raeburn Place in 1887, but this was before uniform scoring was adopted.

Most tries against Scotland in an international
9 by S. Africa (0–44) 1951
  Murrayfield

INDIVIDUAL RECORDS

Most capped player
Overall
C. T. Deans 53 1978–87
in individual positions
Full-back
A. R. Irvine 47[1] 1972–82
Wing
A. R. Smith 33 1955–62
Centre
J. M. Renwick 51[2] 1972–84
Fly-half
J. Y. Rutherford 42 1979–87
Scrum-half
R. J. Laidlaw 43 1980–87
Prop
A. B. Carmichael 50 1967–78
Hooker
C. T. Deans 53 1978–87
Lock
A. J. Tomes 48 1976–87
Flanker
W. I. D. Elliot 29 1947–54
No 8
J. A. Beattie 26 1980–87
[1]*Irvine was chosen 4 times as a wing.*
[2]*Renwick played once on the wing, as a replacement.*

Longest international career
14 seasons   W. C. W. Murdoch
  1935–48

Most internationals as captain
19   J. McLauchlan   1973–9

Most points in internationals
273*   A. R. Irvine (50 appearances)
  1972–82
**Includes one penalty try.*

Most points in an international
21   A. G. Hastings v England 1986
  Murrayfield
Hastings scored 27 points v Romania in 1987 (World Cup). C. Mair scored 30 points v Japan in 1977.

Most tries in internationals
24   I. S. Smith (32 appearances)
  1924–33

Most tries in an international
4   W. A. Stewart v Ireland 1913
  Inverleith
4   I. S. Smith v France 1925
  Inverleith

4   I. S. Smith v Wales 1925 Swansea
G. C. Lindsay scored 5 tries v Wales at Raeburn Place in 1887, but this was before uniform scoring was adopted. In 1925 I. S. Smith scored 6 tries in succession – the last 3 of the match v France, and the first 3 of the next match v Wales.

Most conversions in an international
5   F. H. Turner v France 1912
  Inverleith
5   J. W. Allan v England 1931
  Murrayfield
A. G. Hastings kicked 8 v Romania, 8 v Zimbabwe in 1987 (both World Cup).

Most points in an International Championship season
52   A. G. Hastings (4 appearances)
  1985–6

Most tries in an International Championship season
8   I. S. Smith (4 appearances)
  1924–5

Most conversions in an International Championship season
8   P. W. Dods (4 appearances)
  1983–4

Most penalty goals in an International Championship season
14   A. G. Hastings (4 appearances)
   1985–6

Most points on overseas tour
56   W. Lauder (5 appearances)
   Australia 1970
56   A. R. Irvine (4 appearances)
   New Zealand 1981
C. D. R. Mair scored 100 points in the Far East in 1977, but this was not in an IB nation.

Most points in any tour match
24   D. W. Morgan v Wellington
   1975 Wellington, NZ
24   A. R. Irvine v King Country
   1981 Taumarunui, NZ
24   A. R. Irvine v Wairarapa-Bush
   1981 Masterton, NZ
P. W. Dods scored 43 points v Alberta in 1985, but this was not in an IB nation.

Most tries in any tour match
3   A. R. Smith v Eastern Transvaal
   1960 Springs, SA
K. R. F. Bearne scored 5 tries v Ontario Universities in 1964, and A. J. W. Hinshelwood scored five against Quebec in 1964, but these were not in an IB nation.

FOUNDATION OF SCOTTISH CLUBS

Order of foundation		Year
15	Ayr	1897
17	Boroughmuir	1919
1	Edinburgh Acads	1857
5	Edinburgh Wands	1868
9	Gala	1875
13	Glasgow Acads	1886
21	Glasgow High/Kelvinside	1982
8	Hawick	1873
14	Heriot's F.P.	1890
18	Howe of Fife	1922
2	Jedforest	1885
19	Jordanhill	1972
11	Kelso	1876
5	Kilmarnock	1868
7	Langholm	1872
12	Melrose	1877
4	Royal High	1867
16	Selkirk	1907
20	Stewart's Melville	1973
9	Watsonians	1875
2	West of Scotland	1865

SCOTLAND'S LEADING CAP WINNERS

C. T. Deans   53
J. M. Renwick   52
A. R. Irvine   51
A. B. Carmichael   50
A. J. Tomes   48
A. F. McHarg   44
R. J. Laidlaw   44
J. McLauchlan   43
J. Y. Rutherford   42
H. F. McLeod   40
D. M. D. Rollo   40
I. G. Milne   40
K. W. Robertson   39
I. A. M. Paxton   34
A. R. Smith   33
I. S. Smith   32
F. A. L. Laidlaw   32
I. R. McGeechan   32
D. G. Leslie   32
N. S. Bruce   31
I. H. P. Laughland   31
G. L. Brown   30
W. I. D. Elliot   29
W. M. Simmers   28
P. K. Stagg   28
J. W. Y. Kemp   27
K. J. F. Scotland   27
P. C. Brown   27
J. H. Calder   27
D. I. Johnston   27
D. Drysdale   26
J. C. McCallum   26
G. P. S. Macpherson   26
G. R. T. Baird   26

J. A. Beattie   26
W. E. Maclagan   25
J. B. Nelson   25
J. P. Fisher   25
J. W. Telfer   25
G. D. Stevenson   24
M. A. Biggar   24
J. Aitken   24
M. C. Morrison   23
M. J. Campbell-Lamerton   23
J. N. M. Frame   23
W. C. C. Steele   23
B. H. Hay   23
D. R. Bedell-Sivright   22
A. Robson   22
S. Wilson   22
R. J. Arneil   22
R. G. MacMillan   21
W. P. Scott   21
W. E. Kyle   21
J. M. B. Scott   21
J. R. Paterson   21
W. B. Welsh   21
P. W. Kininmonth   21
A. J. W. Hinshelwood   21
D. W. Morgan   21
W. Cuthbertson   21
C. Reid   20
D. S. Davies   20
J. C. Dykes   20
W. R. Logan   20
J. C. Dawson   20
J. T. Greenwood   20
J. W. C. Turner   20
N. A. MacEwan   20

SCOTLAND – CLUB CHAMPIONSHIP

First played 1973–4. Until 1981–2, 11 games played; 13 games played from 1982–3. Figures in brackets – points scored.

1973–4   Hawick (19)[1]
1974–5   Hawick (20)
1975–6   Hawick (22)[2]
1976–7   Hawick (18)[3]
1977–8   Hawick (21)
1978–9   Heriot's F.P. (20)
1979–80   Gala (19)
1980–81   Gala (22)[2]
1981–2   Hawick (20)
1982–3   Gala (24)
1983–4   Hawick (26)[2]
1984–5   Hawick (24)
1985–6   Hawick (24)
1986–7   Hawick (24)

[1]*Tied with West of Scotland; Hawick won on better points difference.*
[2]*100 per cent record.*
[3]*Tied with Gala; Hawick won play-off.*

Wales

Foundation 1880
Colours Scarlet shirts,
    white shorts
Ground National Stadium,
    Cardiff
Capacity 64 500
No of clubs 187
No of players 40 000

Arguably the most fanatical of the four British Unions, it comes somewhat as a surprise to learn that Wales was the last of the home nations to form a Union. This was accomplished in March 1880 at the Tenby Hotel, Swansea. Present were Lampeter, Llandeilo and Llandovery (where the game was played ten years earlier), Cardiff, Newport, Swansea, Llanelli, Merthyr, Brecon, Pontypool and Bangor. An immediate bonus was the foundation of the 'Big Four' – Llanelli (1872), Newport (1874), Swansea (1875) and Cardiff (1876), immediately after the first senior Welsh club Neath (1871). The South Wales Union had been in operation since 1875, and the Welsh Union were able to build upon the structure of the SWU and the major clubs. Indeed, cynics suggest that the Welsh only followed the other Home Unions because they wanted international rugby, a wish that was granted at Blackheath on 19 February 1881. England won by seven goals, six tries and a dropped goal to nil, and refused to play the Welsh the following season.

Twelve years after that ignominious defeat Wales were International champions. The Big Four, geographically close, were instrumental in this transformation. Newport was the best team in the land, losing just seven games in four years from 1891–5. Cardiff, not far behind, had experimented with the four threequarter system to which the club found initially easier to adapt than the national XV. Llanelli lost just twice in 1894–5 and Swansea were unbeaten in a season.

From 1900–11 Wales were nearly invincible. They won the championship six times, and the Triple Crown six times. During those eleven years they lost just seven times. A mini Golden Era in the 1950s was followed by another in the 1970s. Apart from a barren spell in the recession of the 1920s, where rugby, strongest in the industrial heartland of Wales, seemed to slump in sympathy, the Welsh contribution both on and off the field has been immense. The parade of great players – Gareth Edwards, J. P. R. Williams, Cliff Morgan and the outside-half factory, Mervyn Davies – stretches back to the days of Reggie Gibbs, players who have graced the rugby fields of the world with their skill. Behind the scenes it was Wales, thrashed 24–3 by South Africa in Durban in 1964, who advocated the squad system. The 1971 British Lions in New Zealand and the 1974 Lions in South Africa were indebted to a vast Welsh contribution. Although the 1980s had failed to turn up a side to match this glorious heritage, the fine third place in the World Cup proves that the red jerseys will once more be triumphant on the world's rugby fields.

WALES – INTERNATIONAL RECORDS

TEAM RECORDS
Highest score
Overall
49 v France (49–14) 1910 Swansea
v individual countries
34 v England (34–21) 1967 Cardiff
35 v Scotland (35–12) 1972 Cardiff
34 v Ireland (34–9) 1976 Dublin
49 v France (49–14) 1910 Swansea
16 v N. Zealand (16–19) 1972 Cardiff
 6 v S. Africa (6–6) 1970 Cardiff
28 v Australia (28–3) 1975 Cardiff

Biggest winning points margin
Overall
42 v France (47–5) 1909 Colombes
(Paris)
v individual countries
25 v England (25–0) 1905 Cardiff
23 v Scotland (35–12) 1972 Cardiff
29 v Ireland (29–0) 1907 Cardiff
42 v France (47–5) 1909 Colombes
 5 v N. Zealand (13–8) 1953 Cardiff
No win v S. Africa
25 v Australia (28–3) 1975 Cardiff

Highest score by opposing team
Overall
49 v New Zealand (6–49) 1987
    Brisbane (World Cup)
by individual countries
25 England (0–25) 1896 Blackheath
35 Scotland (10–35) 1924 Inverleith
21 Ireland (24–21) 1979 Cardiff
21 Ireland (7–21) 1980 Dublin
21 Ireland (9–21) 1985 Cardiff
23 France (15–23) 1986 Cardiff
49 N. Zealand (6–49) 1987 Brisbane
    (World Cup)
24 S. Africa (3–24) 1964 Durban
28 Australia (9–28) 1984 Cardiff

Biggest losing points margin
Overall
43 v New Zealand (6–49) 1987
    Brisbane (World Cup)
v individual countries
25 v England (0–25) 1896 Blackheath
25 v Scotland (10–35) 1924 Inverleith
16 v Ireland (3–19) 1925 Belfast

11 v France (3–14) 1985 Paris
43 v N. Zealand (6–49) 1987
    Brisbane (World Cup)
21 v S. Africa (3–24) 1964 Durban
19 v Australia (9–28) 1984 Cardiff

**Most points by Wales in an
International Championship season**
102   1975–6

**Most tries by Wales in an
International Championship season**
21   1909–10

**Most tries by Wales in an
international**
11 v France (47–5) 1909 Colombes

**Most tries against Wales in an
international**
8 by Scotland (10–35) 1924 Inverleith
*England scored 13 tries v Wales in 1881 and
Scotland 12 tries in 1887, but this was before
uniform scoring was adopted.*

INDIVIDUAL RECORDS

Most capped player
Overall
J. P. R. Williams 55 1969–81
in individual positions
Full-back
J. P. R. Williams 54(55)[1] 1969–81
Wing
K. J. Jones 44[2] 1947–57
Centre
S. P. Fenwick 30 1975–81
Fly-half
C. I. Morgan 29[3] 1951–8
Scrum-half
G. O. Edwards 53 1967–78
Prop
G. Price 41 1975–83
Hooker
B. V. Meredith 34 1954–62
Lock
A. J. Martin 34 1973–81
Flanker
W. D. Morris 32(34)[4] 1967–74
No 8
T. M. Davies 38 1969–76

[1]*Williams won one cap as a flanker.*
[2]*T. G. R. Davies, 46 caps, won 35 as a wing, and 11 as a centre.*
[3]*P. Bennett, 29 caps, won one at full-back, as a replacement, one on the wing and two at centre, once as a replacement.*
[4]*Morris won his first two caps at No 8.*

Longest international career
14 seasons W. J. Trew 1900–13
14 seasons T. H. Vile 1908–21
14 seasons H. Tanner 1936–49

WALES'S LEADING CAP WINNERS
J. P. R. Williams 55
G. O. Edwards 53
T. G. R. Davies 46
K. J. Jones 44
G. Price 41
T. M. Davies 38
D. Williams 36
R. M. Owen 35
B. V. Meredith 34
D. I. E. Bebb 34
W. D. Morris 34
A. J. Martin 34
W. J. Bancroft 33
B. Price 32
J. R. G. Stephens 32
G. A. D. Wheel 32
J. J. Williams 30
S. P. Fenwick 30
W. J. Trew 29
C. I. Morgan 29
P. Bennett 29
J. Squire 29
R. W. Windsor 28
A. J. Gould 27
W. C. Powell 27

Most internationals as captain
18 A. J. Gould 1889–97

Most points in internationals
166 P. Bennett (29 appearances) 1969–78

Most points in an international
19 J. Bancroft v France 1910 Swansea
19 K. S. Jarrett v England 1967 Cardiff
19 P. Bennett* v Ireland 1976 Dublin
Bennett scored 34 points v Japan in 1975.

Most tries in internationals
20 G. O. Edwards (53 appearances) 1967–78
20 T. G. R. Davies (46 appearances) 1966–78

Most tries in an international
4 W. Llewellyn* v England 1899 Swansea
4 R. A. Gibbs v France 1908 Cardiff
4 M. C. R. Richards v England 1969 Cardiff
on first appearance.
I. Evans scored 4 tries v Canada in 1987 (World Cup).

Most conversions in an international
8 J. Bancroft v France 1910 Swansea

Most points in an International Championship season
52 P. H. Thorburn (4 appearances) 1985–6

Most tries in an International Championship season
6 R. A. Gibbs 1907–8
6 M. C. R. Richards 1968–9

Most conversions in an International Championship season
11 J. Bancroft (4 appearances) 1908–9

Most penalty goals in an International Championship season
16 P. H. Thorburn (4 appearances) 1985–6

Most points on overseas tour
55 S. P. Fenwick (7 appearances) Australia 1978

Most points in any tour match
15 K. S. Jarrett v Otago 1969 Dunedin, NZ

Most tries in any tour match
3 M. C. R. Richards v Otago 1969 Dunedin, NZ

Wales' leading try scorers Gareth Edwards (No 9) and Gerald Davies (releasing ball) put the Irish defence under pressure during the 16–12 win at Cardiff in 1973. Both players scored 20 tries for their country.

M. C. Thomas	27	J. Young	23
H. J. Morgan	27	D. L. Quinnell	23
R. C. C. Thomas	26	R. W. R. Gravell	23
A. E. I. Pask	26	T. R. Prosser	22
S. J. Watkins	26	B. L. Williams	22
J. Taylor	26	W. O. G. Williams	22
G. Travers	25	S. J. Dawes	22
H. Tanner	25	R. A. Ackerman	22
B. John	25	T. J. Davies	21
N. R. Gale	25	E. M. Jenkins	21
W. D. Thomas	25	B. Thomas	21
T. D. Holmes	25	W. R. Willis	21
E. Gwyn Nicholls	24	D. Watkins	21
R. T. Gabe	24	W. G. Davies	21
D. J. Lloyd	24	W. Llewellyn	20
J. J. Hodges	23	A. F. Harding	20
E. C. Davey	23	J. Webb	20
J. A. Gwilliam	23	A. Skym	20
R. H. Williams	23		

Phil Bennett takes the final pass and heads towards the line to score a marvellous try for Wales against Scotland in 1977. Bemused Scottish defenders lie in his wake.

FOUNDATION OF WELSH CLUBS

Order of foundation		Year
7	Aberavon	1876
13	Abertillery	1885
8	Bridgend	1878
6	Cardiff	1876
12	Cross Keys	1885
10	Ebbw Vale	1880
16	Glamorgan Wanderers	1893
2	Llanelli	1872
14	London Welsh	1885
11	Maesteg	1882
1	Neath	1871
15	Newbridge	1890
3	Newport	1874
9	Penarth	1880
18	Pontypool	1901
5	Pontypridd	1876
19	South Wales Police	1969
4	Swansea	1874
17	Tredegar	1899

NON-INTERNATIONAL TOURING DEFEATS IN WALES

(IB countries)

Abertillery and Ebbw Vale
Beat Australia	6–5	1957–8

Bridgend
Beat Australia	12–9	1981–2

Cardiff
Beat South Africa	17–0	1906–07
Beat Australia	24–8	1908–09
Beat Australia	11–3	1947–8
Beat New Zealand	8–3	1953–4
Beat Australia	14–11	1957–8
Beat Australia	14–8	1966–7
Beat Australia	14–9	1975–6
Beat Australia	16–12	1984

East Wales
Beat Australia	19–11	1973

Gwent
Beat South Africa	14–8	1969–70

Llanelli
Beat Australia	8–3	1908–09
Beat Australia	11–0	1966–7
Beat New Zealand	9–3	1972–3
Beat Australia	19–16	1984

Newport
Beat South Africa	9–3	1912–13
Beat Australia	11–0	1957–8
Beat New Zealand	3–0	1963–4
Beat South Africa	11–6	1969–70

Pontypool, Newbridge and Cross Keys
Beat Australia	12–3	1966–7

Swansea
Beat Australia	6–0	1908–9
Beat South Africa	3–0	1912–13
Beat New Zealand	11–3	1935–6
Beat Australia	9–8	1966–7

WALES – CLUB CHAMPIONS

(Since 1946–7)

1946–7	Neath	1956–7	Ebbw Vale	1967–8	Llanelli	1978–9	Pontypridd
1947–8	Cardiff	1957–8	Cardiff	1968–9	Newport	1979–80	Swansea
1948–9	Cardiff	1958–9	Pontypool	1969–70	Bridgend	1980–1	Bridgend
1949–50	Maesteg	1959–60	Ebbw Vale	1970–1	Bridgend	1981–2	Cardiff
1950–1	Newport	1960–1	Aberavon	1971–2	London Welsh	1982–3	Swansea
1951–2	Ebbw Vale	1961–2	Newport	1972–3	Pontypool	1983–4	Pontypool
1952–3	Cardiff	1962–3	Pontypridd	1973–4	Llanelli	1984–5	Pontypool
1953–4	Ebbw Vale	1963–4	Bridgend	1974–5	Pontypool	1985–6	Pontypool
1954–5	Cardiff	1964–5	Newbridge	1975–6	Pontypridd	1986–7	Neath
1955–6	Newport	1965–6	Bridgend	1976–7	Llanelli		
		1966–7	Neath	1977–8	Pontypridd		

SCHWEPPES WELSH CUP

1971–2
Semifinals: Neath 16, Cardiff 9
Llanelli 13, Aberavon 7
Final: Neath 15 (1G, 3PG), Llanelli 9 (1G, 1P)
NEATH: W. Davies; K. Collier, G. Ball, D. Jenkins, T. Poole; M. Davies (capt), D. Parker; W. Williams, N. Rees, G. Shaw, B. Thomas, B. Davies, W. Lauder, D. Morris, W. Thomas.
Scorers – Try: Parker
Conversion: Poole
Penalty goals: Poole (3)
LLANELLI: R. Davies; A. Hill, B. Thomas, R. W. R. Gravell, R. Mathias; P. Bennett (capt), S. Williams; A. Crocker, R. Thomas, D. Thomas, R. Fouracre, D. L. Quinnell, A. James, H. Jenkins, M. Trueman.
Scorers – Try: Penalty try
Conversion: Hill
Penalty goal: Hill
Referee: M. Joseph

1972–3
Semifinals: Llanelli 6, Neath 3 (at Swansea)
Cardiff 12, Swansea 8 (at Aberavon)
Final: Llanelli 30 (3G, 4PG), Cardiff 7 (1DG, 1T)
LLANELLI: R. Davies; A. Hill, R. T. E. Bergiers, R. W. R. Gravell, J. J. Williams; P. Bennett, S. Williams; A. Crocker, E. R. Thomas, C. Charles, D. Thomas (capt), D. L. Quinnell, T. David, H. Jenkins, G. Jenkins.
Scorers – Tries: Gravell, J. J. Williams, Jenkins
Conversions: Bennett (3)
Penalty goals: Bennett (4)
CARDIFF: L. Davies; W. Lewis, N. Williams, A. Finlayson, P. Lynn Jones; K. James, G. O. Edwards; R. Beard, G. Davies, G. Wallace (capt), I. Robinson, L. Baxter, R. Lane, C. Smith, M. John.
Scorers – Try: Finlayson
Dropped goal: Edwards
Referee: J. Kelleher

1973–4
Semifinals: Llanelli 16, Pontypool 14 (at Aberavon)
Aberavon 9, Cardiff 4 (at Bridgend)
Final: Llanelli 12 (4PG), Aberavon 10 (2PG, 1T)
LLANELLI: C. Griffiths; A. Hill, D. Nicholas, R. W. R. Gravell, J. Walters; B. Thomas, S. Williams; A. Crocker, R. Thomas (capt), C. Charles, D. B. Llewellyn, W. D. Thomas, D. L. Quinnell, H. Jenkins, G. Jenkins.
Scorers – Penalty goals: Hill (4)
ABERAVON: K. Davies; S. Roper, M. Swain, I. Hall, A. Rees; J. Bevan, R. C. Shell; C. Williams, M. Howells (capt), J. Owen, R. Davies, A. J. Martin, W. T. Mainwaring, K. Evans, O. Alexander.
Scorers – Try: Roper
Penalty goals: Martin (2)
Referee: R. Lewis

1974–5
Semifinals: Llanelli 35, Bridgend 6 (at Swansea)
Aberavon 10, Pontypridd 9 (at Cardiff)
Final: Llanelli 15 (1PG, 3T), Aberavon 6 (2PG)

LLANELLI: K. Coslett; A. Hill, R. T. E. Bergiers, R. W. R. Gravell, J. J. Williams; P. Bennett (capt), S. Williams; A. Crocker, E. R. Thomas, D. B. Llewellyn, A. James, R. Powell, P. May, H. Jenkins, T. P. David.
Scorers – Tries: Hill, Bennett, David
Penalty goal: Hill
ABERAVON: K. Davies; S. Roper, J. Thomas, G. Rees, D. Condon; A. Rees, R. C. Shell; C. Williams, M. Howells (capt), J. Owen, O. Alexander, A. J. Martin, W. T. Mainwaring, P. Clarke, R. Davies.
Scorers – Penalty goals: G. Rees (2)
Referee: S. Lewis

1975–6
Semifinals: Llanelli 10, Ebbw Vale 4 (at Swansea)
Swansea 22, Pontypool 14 (at Cardiff)
Final: Llanelli 16 (4PG, 1T), Swansea 4 (1T)
LLANELLI: C. Griffiths; J. J. Williams, R. T. E. Bergiers, R. W. R. Gravell, D. Nicholas; P. Bennett (capt), S. Williams; C. Thomas, E. R. Thomas, A. Crocker, R. J. Hyndman, D. L. Quinnell, P. May, H. Jenkins, A. James.
Scorers – Try: J. J. Williams
Penalty goals: Bennett (4)
SWANSEA: W. R. Blyth; G. Jones, J. Rees, R. Davies, R. Woodward; D. S. Richards, A. Meredith; P. D. Llewellyn, J. Herdman, N. Webb (capt), M. Keyworth, G. A. D. Wheel, B. G. Clegg, P. Davies, T. P. Evans.
Scorers – Try: Richards
Referee: D. Lloyd

1976–7
Semifinals: Cardiff 15, Aberavon 6 (at Swansea)
Newport 7, Ebbw Vale 3 (at Cardiff)
Final: Newport 16 (1G, 2PG, 1T), Cardiff 15 (2G, 1PG)
NEWPORT: L. Davies; K. Davies, N. Brown, C. Webber, J. Cranton; D. Rogers, A. Billinghurst; R. Morgan, D. Ford, C. Smart (capt), R. Barrell, I. Barnard, D. Waters, J. Squire, K. W. Pole.
Scorers – Tries: K. Davies, Cranton
Conversion: Webber
Penalty goals: L. Davies, Webber
CARDIFF: J. Davies; T. G. R. Davies (capt), A. A. J. Finlayson, M. Murphy, C. Camilleri; P. Evans, G. O. Edwards; F. M. Knill, A. J. Phillips, B. G. Nelmes, T. Worgan, I. R. Robinson, C. Smith, R. Lane, R. Dudley-Jones.
Scorers – Tries: Evans, Dudley-Jones
Conversions: J. Davies (2)
Penalty goal: J. Davies
Referee: C. G. P. Thomas

1977–8
Semifinals: Newport 10, Aberavon 6 (at Cardiff)
Swansea 18, Cardiff 13 (at Aberavon)
Final: Swansea 13 (2DG, 1PG, 1T), Newport 9 (3PG)
SWANSEA: W. R. Blyth; H. Rees, A. D. Meredith (capt), G. Jenkins, A. Donovan; D. S. Richards, H.

Davies; H. Hopkins, J. Herdman, P. D. Llewellyn, T. P. Evans, G. A. D. Wheel, B. G. Clegg, R. Moriarty, M. Keyworth.
Scorers – Try: Herdman
Dropped goals: Richards, Jenkins
Penalty goal: Blyth
NEWPORT: C. Webber; K. Davies, D. H. Burcher (capt), N. Brown, D. Bale; G. L. Evans, D. B. Williams; C. Smart, S. Jones, R. Morgan, B. Lease, J. Watkins, A. Mogridge, J. Squire, G. Evans.
Scorers – Penalty goals: Webber (3)
Referee: C. Norling

1978–9
Semifinals: Bridgend 18, Llanelli 13 (at Swansea)
Pontypridd 6, Aberavon 3 (at Bridgend)
Final: Bridgend 18 (1G, 4PG), Pontypridd 12 (1G, 2PG)
BRIDGEND: J. P. R. Williams (capt); I. Davies, S. P. Fenwick, L. Thomas, V. Jenkins; I. Lewis, G. Williams; I. Stephens, G. Davies, M. James, Gareth Williams, L. Davies, R. Evans, D. Brain, G. Jones.
Replacement: C. Williams (for Fenwick after 47 mins).
Scorers – Try: Fenwick
Conversion: Fenwick
Penalty goals: Fenwick (3), Lewis
PONTYPRIDD: I. Walsh; C. Bolderson, C. Riley, J. Poole, S. Flynn; S. Lewis, R. Morgan; R. Lott, M. Alexander, W. Evans, M. Shellard, D. Shellard, R. Penberthy, C. Seldon, T. P. David (capt).
Scorers – Try: David
Conversion: Bolderson
Penalty goals: Riley, Bolderson
Referee: K. Rowlands

1979–80
Semifinals: Bridgend 18, Llanelli 10 (at Swansea)
Swansea 23, Newport 13 (at Cardiff)
Final: Bridgend 15 (1G, 3PG), Swansea 9 (3PG)
BRIDGEND: J. P. R. Williams; C. Williams, S P. Fenwick, L. Thomas, F. Owen; G. Pearce, G. Williams; M. James (capt), G. Davies, I. Stephens, Gareth Williams, J. Morgan, W. Hower, S. Ellis, G. Jones.
Scorers – Try: Owen
Conversion: Fenwick
Penalty goals: Fenwick (3)
SWANSEA: W. R. Blyth; A. H. Swift, A. Meredith, G. Jenkins, M. Wyatt; M. Dacey, D. B. Williams; P. D. Llewellyn, J. Herdman, H. Hopkins, G. Roberts, G. A. D. Wheel (capt), B. G. Clegg, T. Cheeseman, M. Keyworth.
Scorers – Penalty goals: Blyth (3)
Referee: Corris Thomas

1980–1
Semifinals: Bridgend 22, Llanelli 15 (at Swansea)
Cardiff 18, Swansea 7 (at Bridgend)
Final: Cardiff 14 (2PG, 2T), Bridgend 6 (2PG)
CARDIFF: G. Davies; D. Preece, D. H. Burcher, N. Hutchings, S. Evans; W. G. Davies, T. D. Holmes; I. Eidman, A. J. Phillips, J. Whitefoot, R. Lakin, A. Mogridge, K. Edwards, J. P. Scott (capt), B. Lease.
Scorers – Tries: Lakin, Hutchings

Penalty goals: W. G. Davies (2)
BRIDGEND: J. P. R. Williams; F. Owen, S. P. Fenwick, R. James, C. Barber; G. P. Pearce, G. Williams; M. James (capt), K. Townley, I. Stephens, G. Jones, W. Howe, J. Morgan, L. Davies, G. P. Williams.
Scorers – Penalty goals: Fenwick (2)
Referee: A. Richards

1981–2
Semifinals: Cardiff 21, Newbridge 11 (at Newport)
Bridgend 9, Aberavon 6 (at Swansea)
Final: Cardiff 12 (1G, 2PG), Bridgend 12 (3PG, 1DG)
Cardiff won on 'most tries' rule
CARDIFF: P. Rees; S. Evans, D. Barry, P. C. T. Daniels, D. Preece; W. G. Davies, T. D. Holmes; I. Eidman, A. J. Phillips, J. Whitefoot, O. Golding, R. L. Norster, K. Edwards, J. P. Scott (capt), J. R. Lewis.
Scorers – Try: Eidman
Conversion: Barry
Penalty goals: Barry (2)
BRIDGEND: H. Davies; M. Titley, P. Daniel, C. Williams, F. Owen; G. Pearce, G. Williams (capt); M. James, G. Davies, I. Stephens, G. Jones, R. Evans, W. Howe, S. Ellis, G. P. Williams.
Scorers – Penalty goals: Pearce (3)
Dropped goal: Pearce
Referee: C. Norling

1982–3
Semifinals: Pontypool 16, Bridgend 3 (at Aberavon)
Swansea 19, Newbridge 6 (at Cardiff)
Final: Pontypool 18 (1G, 4PG), Swansea 6 (2PG)
PONTYPOOL: P. Lewis; G. Davies, L. Faulkner, L. Jones, B. Taylor; M. Goldsworthy, D. Bishop; R. W. Windsor, S. Jones, G. Price, C. Huish, M. Jones, S. J. Perkins, J. Squire (capt), M. Brown.
Replacement: M. Crowley (for Windsor after 10 mins).
Scorers – Try: Taylor
Conversion: Lewis
Penalty goals: Lewis (4)
SWANSEA: W. R. Blyth; P. Gallagher, A. H. Swift, G. Jenkins, A. Emyr; M. Dacey, H. Davies; C. Williams, S. Davies, G. John, M. Davies (capt), R. D. Moriarty, B. Clegg, G. Roberts, M. Ruddock.
Scorers – Penalty goals: Blyth (2)
Referee: W. Jones

1983–4
Semifinals: Cardiff 26, Llanelli 6 (at Swansea)
Neath 12, Aberavon 3 (at Bridgend)
Final: Cardiff 24 (2G, 4PG), Neath 19 (2G, 1PG, 1T)
CARDIFF: P. Rees; G. Cordle, A. J. Donovan, M. Ring, A. M. Hadley; W. G. Davies, T. D. Holmes; J. Whitefoot, A. J. Phillips, I. Eidman, R. L. Norster, O. Golding, R. Lakin, J. P. Scott (capt), K. Edwards.
Replacement: N. Humphreys (for Hadley after 48 mins).
Scorers – Tries: Golding, Cordle
Conversions: Davies (2)
Penalty goals: Davies (4)

NEATH: N. Harris; H. E. Rees (capt), D. Jacob, K. Jones, C. Bridgwater; J. Davies, Gareth Jones; B. Williams, M. Richards, P. Langford, G. Jones, S. Dando, H. Richards, D. Morgan, L. Jones.
Scorers – Tries: Jacob (2), Gareth Jones
Conversions: Harris (2)
Penalty goal: Harris
Referee: C. Norling

1984–5
Semifinals: Cardiff 24, Pontypool 3 (at Newport)
Llanelli 24, Bridgend 10 (at Swansea)
Final: Llanelli 15 (1G, 1DG, 2PG), Cardiff 14 (2PG, 2T)
LLANELLI: M. Gravelle; P. I. Lewis, N. Davies, P. Morgan, I. Evans; G. Pearce, J. Griffiths; A. Buchanan, D. Fox, L. Delaney, P. May (capt), R. Cornelius, A. Davies, P. T. Davies, D. F. Pickering.
Scorers – Try: Griffiths
Conversion: Pearce
Penalty goals: Pearce (2)
CARDIFF: P. Rees; G. Cordle, A. J. Donovan, D. Evans, A. M. Hadley; W. G. Davies, T. D. Holmes (capt); J. Whitefoot, A. J. Phillips, I. Eidman, K. Edwards, R. L. Norster, O. Golding, J. P. Scott, G. J. Roberts.
Scorers – Tries: Phillips, Cordle
Penalty goals: Davies (2)
Referee: W. D. Bevan

1985–6
Semifinals: Cardiff 17, Bridgend 9 (at Swansea)
Newport 15, Aberavon 6 (at Cardiff)
Final: Cardiff 28 (3G, 2PG, 1T), Newport 21 (3G, 1PG)
CARDIFF: M. Rayer; G. Cordle, A. J. Donovan, M. Ring, A. M. Hadley; W. G. Davies, N. O'Brien; J. Whitefoot, A. J. Phillips (capt), I. Eidman, K. Edwards, R. L. Norster, O. Golding, J. P. Scott,

G. J. Roberts.
Scorers – Tries: Hadley (3), O'Brien
Conversions: Davies (3)
Penalty goals: Davies (2)
NEWPORT: R. Knight; M. Batten, D. Pitt, P. Daniel, J. White; P. Turner, N. Callard; J. Rawlins, M. J. Watkins (capt), R. Morgan, J. Widdecombe, A. Perry, R. Collins, D. R. Waters, R. Powell.
Scorers – Tries: Pitt, Turner, Collins
Conversions: Turner (3)
Penalty goal: Turner
Referee: K. Rowlands

1986–7
Semifinals: Cardiff 16, Neath 6 (at Swansea)
Swansea 20, Newbridge 3 (at Cardiff)
Final: Cardiff 16 (3PG, 1DG, 1T), Swansea 15 (1G, 2PG, 1DG) (after extra time)
CARDIFF: M. Rayer; G. Cordle, A. Donovan, M. Ring, A. Hadley; G. John, C. Hutchings; J. Whitefoot, A. Phillips (capt), I. Eidman, H. Stone, R. Norster, R. Lakin, G. Roberts, J. Scott.
Replacements: T. Crothers (for Roberts after 90 mins), R. Cardus (for Ring after 97 mins)
Scorers – Try: Cordle
Penalty goals: John (3)
Dropped goal: Rayer
SWANSEA: M. Wyatt; M. Titley, R. Hopkins, M. Dacey, A. Emyr; A. Clement, R. Jones; K. Colclough, P. Hitchings, D. Young, M. Colclough, R. Moriarty (capt), P. Moriarty, R. Webster, J. Thomas.
Replacement: J. Williams (for M. Colclough after 51 mins)
Scorers – Try: Hopkins
Conversion: Wyatt
Penalty goals: Wyatt (2)
Dropped goal: Clement
Referee: W. Jones

SCHWEPPES WELSH CUP RECORDS

Most appearances in Final
8 Cardiff

Most appearances in Semifinal
11 Cardiff

Most Semifinal defeats
7 Aberavon

Most Semifinal appearances without reaching a final
3 Newbridge

Most points in Final
49 (Cardiff 28, Newport 21 – 1986)

Most points by winners
30 (Llanelli – 1973)

Most points by losers
21 (Newport – 1986)

Widest margin of victory
23 (Llanelli 30, Cardiff 7 – 1973)

Most points by an individual in Final
18 Phil Bennett (4PG, 3C) 1973
Gareth Davies has scored a total of 40 points in five appearances in Finals (10PG, 5C).

Most appearances by an individual in Finals
6 J. Whitefoot
6 A. J. Phillips
6 I. Eidman
6 J. P. Scott

Most tries in Final
3 A. M. Hadley 1986

Highest score in WRU Cup matches
Pontypool 86, Ystralyfera 6 (1st round proper 1978)
Mountain Ash 114, Builth Wells 4 (preliminary round 1976)

Most points in WRU Cup matches
34 Ross Edwards, Mountain Ash v Builth Wells, 1976

LLOYD LEWIS MEMORIAL TROPHY

Man of the match award in the Welsh Cup Final. Lloyd Lewis was the rugby correspondent of the *News of the World* who died in the Paris air crash in 1974, returning home from covering the France v England match.

1975	Phil Bennett	Llanelli
1976	Phil Bennett	Llanelli
1977	Ian Barnard	Newport
1978	David Richards	Swansea
1979	Steve Fenwick	Bridgend
1980	Gareth Williams	Bridgend
1981	Bob Lakin	Cardiff
1982	Mark Titley	Bridgend
1983	David Bishop	Pontypool
1984	Gareth Jones	Neath
1985	Gary Pearce	Llanelli
1986	Adrian Hadley	Cardiff
1987	Gareth Roberts	Cardiff

France

Foundation 1920
Colours Blue shirts,
    white shorts
Ground Parc des Princes,
    Paris
Capacity 50 000
No of clubs 1794
No of players 194 600

There is a tendency to overlook the enormous role played by France in the growth and development of rugby football. It was France who took rugby into the Olympics, and it was France who, when in dispute with the Rugby Union over professionalism in the 1930s, formed FIRA – Federation Internationale de Rugby Amateur – to promote the game in European countries and in their dependencies. Their style of play since World War II, all Gallic flair and invention, has been copied the world over. And yet their recent excellence, 1987 World Cup finalists and all, has been in sharp contrast to their own rather shambolic roots.

The game is believe to have been first played by British students on a sportsfield in Le Havre in 1870. Seven years later the British students in Paris astonished the locals by playing matches in the Bois de Boulogne. The French were quick to learn, and in 1885 a Paris Selection made the trip across the Channel to play the Civil Service at Dulwich. Proximity to Britain, and the number of university and professional people with British contacts, hastened the development of rugby in the Paris area.

In 1892, with some 25 clubs in and around Paris, the French propensity for organizing events took over. Baron Pierre de Coubertin, in the throes of organizing the 1896 Olympic Games at Athens, was at the time a sort of Physical Education boss for the French capital. He set up and refereed the first club championship final in 1892, won by Racing Club 4–3 against Stade Français.

Patrick Estève, the French wing, scores a spectacular try for France in the 1984 international with England at the Parc des Princes. Covering England players are Rory Underwood (left) and Brian Barley.

Ability was put into perspective, though, with a visit by Rosslyn Park, who scored ten tries in defeating Stade Français.

The game had now begun to take a significant hold in the south and south west. In 1893, two Bordeaux clubs, Stade and Sport Athletique, met in their version of the championship final. By 1895 reports had filtered back to Baron de Coubertin's office of organized rugby in Nantes, Rouen and Lyon. The famous grass roots clubs with the short names – Pau, Dax, Agen and Brive – had sown the seeds that were to benefit French rugby so much in the future. On New Year's Day 1906, France played their first international, losing 38–5 to the all-conquering New Zealand team who had thrashed the best that Britain could offer.

The game had developed at such a pace that organization could not cope. Part of the French social calendar, the club and international scene became ill disciplined both on and off the field. Players were at a premium, and the richer clubs had no alternative but to offer cash inducements. From over the Channel the Rugby Union, eyeing trouble on a scale not encountered since the breakaway of the Rugby League clubs, issued a series of warnings. All fell on deaf ears, and, by 1931, the Rugby Union had had enough. They sent the following letter: 'Owing to the unsatisfactory condition of the game of Rugby Football as practised and played in France, neither our Union, nor the clubs or unions under our jurisdiction, will fulfil or arrange fixtures with France, or French clubs, at home or away after the end of this season until we are satisfied that the control and conduct of the game have been placed on a satisfactory basis in all essentials.'

Stripped of international competition, the French went about organizing their own opposition, and were instrumental in creating FIRA. Losses incurred by lack of international revenue were offset by playing fixtures with the emerging Romania, Germany, Italy, Czechoslovakia and others.

By 1945 France had been forgiven by the Rugby Union. In fact they would have been admitted just before World War II, which added a further six years to their exile. Celebrating their return to the fold, France promptly beat Wales 8–0 at Swansea.

In 1951, and again the following year, France were in trouble for exactly the same reasons as 20 years earlier. They promised to abandon the club championship. Eventually the matter was dropped. Perhaps the other nations were concerned that France – now a world class force with superb backs and ball-handling forwards – would be lost to the game again. Almost as though begging forgiveness, the International Board offered France full membership in 1978. Their contribution to the cause of rugby football had been a liaison in a playing capacity with no fewer than 24 countries.

Division One of the French league has four pools of ten clubs; Second, Third and subsequent divisions are regionalized. All rugby clubs play in the national league, and it is possible for a village club to go right through the system to the top.

FRANCE – INTERNATIONAL RECORDS

TEAM RECORDS
Highest score
*Overall**
37 v England (37–12) 1972 Colombes (Paris)
v individual countries
37 v England (37–12) 1972 Colombes
23 v Scotland (23–3) 1977 Parc des Princes (Paris)
29 v Ireland (29–9) 1986 Parc des Princes
23 v Wales (23–15) 1986 Cardiff
24 v N. Zealand (24–19) 1979 Auckland
25 v S. Africa (25–38) 1975 Bloemfontein
34 v Australia (34–6) 1976 Parc des Princes
France beat Zimbabwe 70–12 in 1987 (World Cup).

Biggest winning points margin
Overall
28 v Australia (34–6) 1976 Parc des Princes
France won by 56 pts (59–3) against Romania, 1924, but this was not against an IB nation.
v individual countries
25 v England (37–12) 1972 Colombes
20 v Scotland (23–3) 1977 Parc des Princes
23 v Ireland (26–3) 1976 Parc des Princes
11 v Wales (14–3) 1985 Parc des Princes
13 v N. Zealand (16–3) 1986 Nantes
5 v S. Africa (19–14) 1967 Johannesburg
28 v Australia (34–6) 1976 Parc des Princes

Highest score by opposing team
Overall
49 Wales (14–49) 1910 Swansea
S. Africa beat 'France' 55–6 at Parc des Princes on 3 January 1907, but it is not regarded as an official international match.
by individual countries
41 England (13–41) 1907 Richmond
31 Scotland (3–31) 1912 Inverleith (Edinburgh)
25 Ireland (5–25) 1911 Cork
25 Ireland (6–25) 1975 Dublin
49 Wales (14–49) 1910 Swansea
38 N. Zealand (8–38) 1906 Parc des Princes
38 S. Africa (5–38) 1913 Bordeaux
38 S. Africa (25–38) 1975 Bloemfontein
24 Australia (14–24) 1981 Sydney
24 Australia (30–24) 1987 Sydney (World Cup)

Biggest losing points margin
Overall
42 v Wales (5–47) 1909 Colombes
The 6–55 defeat by S. Africa in Paris in 1907 is regarded as unofficial.
v individual countries
37 v England (0–37) 1911 Twickenham
28 v Scotland (3–31) 1912 Inverleith
24 v Ireland (0–24) 1913 Cork
42 v Wales (5–47) 1909 Colombes
30 v N. Zealand (8–38) 1906 Parc des Princes
33 v S. Africa (5–38) 1913 Bordeaux
10 v Australia (14–24) 1981 Sydney

Most points by France in an International Championship season
98   1985–6

Most tries by France in an International Championship season
13   1975–6, 1985–6

Most tries by France in an international
6 v Ireland (27–6) 1964 Colombes
6 v England (35–13) 1970 Colombes
6 v England (37–12) 1972 Colombes
6 v England (30–9) 1976 Parc des Princes
6 v Australia (34–6) 1976 Parc des Princes
France scored 13 v Romania, 1924 (Olympics) and Zimbabwe in 1987 (World Cup).

Most tries against France in an international
11 by Wales (5–47) 1909 Colombes
S. Africa's 13 tries in the 1907 match in Paris are regarded as unofficial.

Most points on a tour (all matches)
282 in South Africa (11 matches) 1975

INDIVIDUAL RECORDS*
Most capped player
Overall
S. Blanco 54[1] 1980–7
in individual positions
Full-back
S. Blanco 46(54) 1980-7
Wing
J. Dupuy 28 1956–64
C. Darrouy 28 1957–67
Centre
R. Bertranne 39(52)[2] 1971–81
Fly-half
P. Albaladejo 23(24)[3] 1954–64
Scrum-half
P. Berbizier 35 1981–7

Prop
R. Paparemborde 42 1975–83
Hooker
P. Dintrans 39 1979–87
Lock
J. Condom[4] 41 1982–7
Flanker
J.-P. Rives 47 1975–84
No 8
L. Rodriguez 29(32)[5] 1981–7
Records as notified by F.F.R.
[1] *Blanco played 6 times on the wing, once at centre and once at fly-half.*
[2] *Bertranne played 13 times on the wing.*
[3] *Albaladejo won his first cap at full-back.*
[4] *B. Dauga, 50 caps, won 29 as lock and 21 at No 8.*
[5] *Rodriguez played 3 times as lock.*

Longest international career
13 seasons F. Haget 1975–87
Haget was first capped in a non-IB match in 1974, v IB opposition in 1975.

Most internationals as captain
34   J.-P. Rives   1979–84

Most points in internationals
265   J.-P. Romeu (22 appearances) 1973–7

Most points in an international
17   G. Camberabero v Australia 1967 Colombes
17   J.-P. Lescarboura v Ireland 1984 Paris
17   J.-P. Lescarboura v Wales 1984 Cardiff
17   G. Laporte v England 1986 Paris
D. Camberabero scored 30 pts v Zimbabwe in 1987 (World Cup).

Most tries in internationals
14   C. Darrouy (28 appearances) 1957–67
Altogether Darrouy scored 23 tries in major internationals.

Most tries in an international
3   M. Crauste v England 1962 Colombes
3   C. Darrouy v Ireland 1963 Dublin
3   E. Bonneval v Scotland 1987 Paris
A. Jauréguy v Romania 1924, and M. Celhay v Italy 1937 scored four tries.

Most conversions in an international
5   P. Villepreux v England 1972 Paris
G. Camberabero kicked 9 v Italy 1967, but this was not against an IB nation.
D. Camberabero kicked 9 v Italy in 1987 (World Cup).

Most points in an International Championship season
54   J.-P. Lescarboura (4 appearances) 1983–4

Most tries in an International Championship season
5   P. Estève (4 appearances) 1982–3

Most conversions in an International Championship season
7   P. Villepreux (4 appearances) 1971–2

Most penalty goals in an International Championship season
10   J.-P. Lescarboura (4 appearances) 1983–4

Most points on overseas tour
71   J.-P. Romeu (7 appearances) 1975 S. Africa

Most points in any tour match
19   J. L. Dehez v SW Districts (SA) 1967 George
P. Estève scored 32 points against East Japan in 1984, but this was not in an IB country.

Most tries in any tour match
4   R. Bertranne v W. Transvaal 1971 Potchefstroom
4   M. Bruel v Australian Capital Territory 1981 Canberra
P. Estève scored 8 tries against East Japan in 1984, but this was not in an IB country.

FRANCE'S LEADING CAP WINNERS
(Matches against IB countries only)

R. Bertranne 52	L. Rodriguez 29	C. Lacaze 24
B. Dauga 50	C. Darrouy 28	R. Bénésis 24
J.-P. Rives 47	J. Dupuy 28	J. Trillo 24
M. Crauste 43	C. Dourthe 28	A. Roques 23
W. Spanghero 42	J. Iraçabal 28	G. Boniface 23
R. Paparemborde 42	J.-M. Aguirre 28	C. Carrère 23
J.-L. Joinel 41	A. Cassayet 27	G. Cholley 23
J.-P. Lux 40	J. Bouquet 27	J. Gallion 23
S. Blanco 40	J.-P. Garuet 27	M. Pomathios 22
J. Prat 38	G. Basquet 26	J.-P. Romeu 22
M. Celaya 35	D. Codorniou 26	A. Lorieux 22
A. Boniface 34	F. Haget 26	M. Communeau 21
A. Domenech 34	A. Jauréguy 25	F. Moncla 21
J.-C. Skréla 34	R. Biénès 25	J.-L. Azarète 21
D. Erbani 33	E. Ribère 25	B. Chevallier 20
G. Dufau 33	M. Prat 25	P. Lacroix 20
P. Dintrans 33	L. Mias 25	C. Spanghero 20
M. Vannier 30	J. Gachassin 25	J.-L. Averous 20
E. Cester 30	J.-P. Bastiat 25	P. Sella 20
P. Berbizier 30	A. Paco 25	J. Condom 20
P. Villepreux 29	P. Albaladejo 24	

Stade Français and Lyon battle out the 1904 French Championship semifinal.

FRANCE – CLUB CHAMPIONSHIP FINALS

1892   Racing Club de France 4, Stade Français 3
1893   Stade Français 7, Racing Club de France 3
1894   Stade Français 18, Inter-Nos 0
1895   Stade Français 16, Paris Olympique 0
1896   Paris Olympique 12, Stade Français 0
1897   Stade Français won group
1898   Stade Français won group
1899   Stade Bordelais UC 5, Stade Français 3
1900   Racing Club de France 37, Stade Bordelais UC 3
1901   Stade Français beat Stade Bordelais UC on disqualification
1902   Racing Club de France 6, Stade Bordelais UC 0

1903   Stade Français 16, Stade Toulousain 8
1904   Stade Bordelais UC 3, Stade Français 0
1905   Stade Bordelais UC 12, Stade Français 3
1906   Stade Bordelais UC 9, Stade Français 0
1907   Stade Bordelais UC 14, Stade Français 3
1908   Stade Français 16, Stade Bordelais UC 3
1909   Stade Bordelais UC 17, Stade Toulousain 0
1910   FC Lyon 13, Stade Bordelais UC 8
1911   Stade Bordelais UC 14, SCUF 0
1912   Stade Toulousain 8, Racing

Club de France 6
1913   Bayonne 31, SCUF 8
1914   Perpignan 8, Tarbes 7
1920   Tarbes 8, Racing Club de France 3
1921   Perpignan 5, Stade Toulousain 0
1922   Stade Toulousain 6, Bayonne 0
1923   Stade Toulousain 3, Bayonne 0
1924   Stade Toulousain 3, Perpignan 0
1925   Perpignan 5, Carcassonne 0
1926   Stade Toulousain 11, Perpignan 0
1927   Stade Toulousain 19, Stade Français 9
1928   Pau 6, Quillan 4

1929	Quillan 11, Lezignan 8	1952	Lourdes 20, Perpignan 11
1930	Agen 4, Quillan 0	1953	Lourdes 21, Mont de
1931	Toulon 6, Lyon OU 3		Marsan 16
1932	Lyon OU 9, Narbonne 3	1954	Grenoble 5, Cognac 3
1933	Lyon OU 10, Narbonne 3	1955	Perpignan 11, Lourdes 6
1934	Bayonne 13, Biarritz 8	1956	Lourdes 20, Dax 0
1935	Biarritz 3, Perpignan 0	1957	Lourdes 16, Racing Club de
1936	Narbonne 6, Montferrand 3		France 13
1937	Vienne 13, Montferrand 7	1958	Lourdes 25, Mazamet 8
1938	Perpignan 11, Biarritz 6	1959	Racing Club de France 8,
1939	Biarritz 6, Perpignan 0		Mont de Marsan 3
1943	Bayonne 3, Agen 0	1960	Lourdes 14, Beziers 11
1944	Perpignan 20, Bayonne 5	1961	Beziers 6, Dax 3
1945	Agen 7, Lourdes 3	1962	Agen 14, Beziers 11
1946	Pau 11, Lourdes 0	1963	Mont de Marsan 9, Dax 6
1947	Stade Toulousain 10, Agen 3	1964	Pau 14, Beziers 0
1948	Lourdes 11, Toulon 3	1965	Agen 15, Brive 8
1949	Castres 14, Mont de Marsan 3	1966	Agen 9, Dax 8
1950	Castres 11, Racing Club de	1967	Montauban 11, Begles 3
	France 8	1968	Lourdes 9, Toulon 9 (Lourdes
1951	Carmaux 14, Tarbes 12		won on tries)

1969	Begles 11, Stade Toulousain 9
1970	La Voulte 3, Montferrand 0
1971	Beziers 15, Toulon 9
1972	Beziers 9, Brive 0
1973	Tarbes 18, Dax 12
1974	Beziers 16, Narbonne 14
1975	Beziers 13, Brive 12
1976	Agen 13, Beziers 10
1977	Beziers 12, Perpignan 4
1978	Beziers 31, Montferrand 9
1979	Narbonne 10, Bagneres 0
1980	Beziers 10, Stade Toulousain 6
1981	Beziers 22, Bagneres 13
1982	Agen 18, Bayonne 9
1983	Beziers 14, Nice 6
1984	Beziers 21, Agen 21*
1985	Stade Toulousain 36, Toulon 22 (after extra time)
1986	Stade Toulousain 16, Agen 6
1987	Toulon 15, Racing Club de France 12

Beziers won 3–1 on penalties.

THREE MODERN CLUBS

AGEN
Foundation 1900
Ground Stade Armendie
Capacity 18 500
Most Capped Player P. Sella   44 (v all countries)
International Players 52
Club Championship Wins 1930, 1945, 1962, 1965, 1966, 1976, 1982

A typical French market town steeped in rugby history where the game is king, Agen has 37 000 inhabitants and lies between Toulouse and Bordeaux on the banks of the Garonne. Originally Sporting Club Agen, they changed their name to Sporting Union Agen when merging with a cycle club to use the facilities at Armendie in 1907. Champions of France in 1930 and 1945, Agen enjoyed a boom period in the 1960s when the club boasted 11 internationals; Rene Benesis and Pierre Biermouret stayed for further championship successes in 1976. Their success in 1982 was based round a mobile pack and high-class three-quarters like the incomparable Philippe Sella. French RFU president Albert Ferrasse, one of the wisest figures in the game, hails from Agen. In the mid-1980s, Agen provided seven players for the powerful national team, and three more for the 'A' FIRA XV.

BEZIERS
Foundation 1911
Ground Parc Sauclières
Capacity 22 000
Most Capped Player A. Paco   25
International Players 56
Club Championship Wins 1961, 1971, 1972, 1974, 1975, 1977, 1978, 1980, 1981, 1983, 1984

Formed in 1911 by the fusion of Midi-Athletic and Sporting clubs who bought the present stadium in 1911 for £20 000. After World War I, the club, which had fallen on hard times, reappeared as another fusion with Midi-Sportif and Jeunesse Sportif. A nearby army garrison helped recruitment. Beziers won their first championship in 1961 and were runners-up in 1960, 1962 and 1964, under the tutelage of the great Pierre Danos and Raymond Barthez. This success was just reward for refusing to bow to a breakaway group who, in the 1950s, had formed a Rugby League club. For the last few years, Beziers have dominated French rugby, with ten championships between 1971 and 1984 (prop Armand Vacquerin gaining a record nine titles). Raoul Barrière, with his squad coaching, his belief in his forwards and attacking backs, inherited a junior team in 1968 who were French champions. From 1971–5 the club produced no fewer than 17 internationals in five years, with such cornerstones of the national team as Paco, Estève, Palmie, Astre, Cantoni and Vacquerin.

STADE TOULOUSAIN
Foundation 1899
Ground Stade Ernest-Wallon
Capacity 39 000
Most Capped Player J.-P. Rives (also Racing Club)   47
International Players 76
Club Championship Wins 1912, 1922, 1923, 1924, 1925, 1926, 1927, 1947, 1985, 1986

Toulouse was the second provincial city to take up rugby. The students founded the Stade Olympien des Etudients Toulouse in 1899. Four years later the club played in the championship final. In 1906 the club merged with Veto Sports which became, more simply, Stade Toulousain in 1909. During and immediately after World War I, Stade were *the* club in France with 31 internationals between 1911 and 1929, excluding the war years. The great names – Philippe and Adolphe Jaureguy, Philippe Struxiano and François Borde – were all at the club. But Toulouse had just one championship victory since that period until the purple patch in the 1980s, in spite of Rives, Skréla, Bertranne, Villepreux and Walter Spanghero. Team-work had become the order of the day rather than individual brilliance of several internationals. At last, in the mid-1980s, the 38-year famine ended thanks to the newer contingent led by those 1987 Grand Slam stars, Charvet and Bonneval.

Australia

Foundation 1949
Colours Gold shirts,
   green shorts
Nickname Wallabies
No of clubs 296
No of players 14 500

Along with cricket and boxing, rugby is one of the oldest sports in Australia; just six years after the inspiration of William Webb Ellis, mention of the game appeared in local newspapers. The armed forces were the first to play the game, which then became an integral part of the way of life in schools and universities.

Sydney University, founded in 1864, is the oldest club outside the British Isles but the oldest open club, and the major power in the early years, was the Wallaroo Club. Founded in 1870 after a newspaper advertisement, two sons of the former headmaster of Rugby School, Thomas Arnold, were amongst the first members. Dick and Montague Arnold organized championships in those areas of Sydney and Brisbane where the game had taken root.

The Australian Rugby Union was not founded until 1949. Prior to that the control of the game had been undertaken by the Southern Rugby Union, later the New South Wales Rugby Union. Queensland was under the control of the Northern Rugby Union. It explains the name Waratahs, the 1928 tourists to Britain. Most came from NSW, and wore the traditional blue shirt.

The success of Australian rugby during the 1980s has stemmed, in no small way, to the halting of a drain of players to Australian Rules and Rugby League. Australian Rules, first played in Melbourne in 1858, went their own way in 1877, upset at the rigidity of the rules as practised by Union. Fortunately, NSW and Queensland declined to join the breakaway. In 1882 NSW toured New Zealand for the first time, which involved a five-day sea journey and a stop-off in Tasmania, as opposed to a three-hour flight today.

In 1888, Britain sent their first tourists. They were away from home for over a year, lost their captain R. L. Seddon, drowned in the Murray River, and engaged in 18 matches which turned out to be against Australian Rules opposition. On 24 June 1899, the first Australian international team was formed, beating Britain 13–3 with a side containing nine players from NSW and six from Queensland. Britain won the other three tests in front of crowds over 30 000.

Rugby League grew out of one specific incident. The international Alec Burdon had broken his arm on tour and needed money for medical aid. Other players realized the financial implications of injury, and switched their attentions to League. The major coup was the signing for £150 of the outstanding Union player of the

The ultimate success – a pushover try against Wales at Cardiff. Several Australians anxiously await referee Eamonn Doyle's decision, while most Welsh defenders peer elsewhere. Australia won 28–9, the third leg of their 1984 Grand Slam.

time, Herbert 'Dally' Messenger. After the first tour to Britain in 1908, no fewer than 13 players joined the Rugby League.

The Union game, for years the poor relation to other winter sports, is now reaching a pinnacle. Union players are remaining with the game, crowds are on the increase, difficulty of co-ordination in a large country has been overcome, sponsors are keen to be associated with the sport, and the progressive views of the Board have resulted in a leading part in rugby's first World Cup.

Alan Jones, guru, motivator and fine rugby coach, gives his threequarters some hints during the hugely successful 1984 tour to Britain.

AUSTRALIA – INTERNATIONAL RECORDS

TEAM RECORDS
Highest score
Overall
37 v Scotland (37–12) 1984 Murrayfield
Australia scored 59 against Canada at Sydney in 1985 (59–3).

v individual countries
30 v England (30–21) 1975 Brisbane
37 v Scotland (37–12) 1984 Murrayfield
20 v Ireland (20–10) 1976 Dublin
28 v Wales (28–9) 1984 Cardiff
24 v France (24–14) 1981 Sydney
30 v N. Zealand (30–16) 1978 Auckland
21 v S. Africa (21–6) 1933 Durban
 8 v B. Isles (8–11) 1966 Sydney

Biggest winning points margin
Overall
25 v Scotland (37–12) 1984 Murrayfield
Australia beat Canada by 56 points (59–3) at Sydney in 1985.

v individual countries
16 v England (19–3) 1984 Twickenham
25 v Scotland (37–12) 1984 Murrayfield
18 v Ireland (33–15) 1987 Sydney (World Cup)
19 v Wales (28–9) 1984 Cardiff
10 v France (24–14) 1981 Sydney
16 v N. Zealand (26–10) 1980 Sydney
15 v S. Africa (21–6) 1933 Durban
 1 v B. Isles (6–5) 1930 Sydney

Highest score by opposing team
Overall
38 N. Zealand (13–38) 1936 Dunedin
38 N. Zealand (3–38) 1972 Auckland
by individual countries
23 England (6–23) 1976 Twickenham
24 Scotland (15–24) 1981 Murrayfield
27 Ireland (12–27) 1979 Brisbane

28 Wales (3–28) 1975 Cardiff
34 France (6–34) 1976 Paris (Parc des Princes)
38 N. Zealand (13–38) 1936 Dunedin
38 N. Zealand (3–38) 1972 Auckland
30 S. Africa (11–30) 1969 Johannesburg
31 B. Isles (0–31) 1966 Brisbane

Biggest losing points margin
Overall
35 v N. Zealand (3–38) 1972 Auckland
v individual countries
17 v England (3–20) 1973 Twickenham
17 v England (6–23) 1976 Twickenham
9 v Scotland (15–24) 1981 Murrayfield
15 v Ireland (12–27) 1979 Brisbane
25 v Wales (3–28) 1975 Cardiff
28 v France (6–34) 1976 Parc des Princes
35 v N. Zealand (3–38) 1972 Auckland
25 v S. Africa (3–28) 1961 Johannesburg
31 v B. Isles (0–31) 1966 Brisbane

Most tries by Australia in an international
6 v Scotland (23–3) 1970 Sydney
Australia scored 9 against US at Sydney in 1983, and against Canada at Sydney in 1985, but these were not against IB countries.

Most tries against Australia in an international
8 by South Africa (3–28) 1961 Johannesburg

Most points on overseas tour (all matches)
500 in B. Isles/France (35 matches) 1947–8

Most tries on overseas tour (all matches)
115 in B. Isles/France (35 matches) 1947–8

INDIVIDUAL RECORDS
Most capped players
Overall
S. P. Poidevin 45 1980–7
in individual positions
Full-back
R. G. Gould 25 1980–7
Wing
B. J. Moon 31 1978–84
Centre
A. G. Slack 36 1978–87
Fly-half
M. G. Ella 25 1980–4
Scrum-half
J. N. B. Hipwell 34 1968–82
Prop
A. J. McIntyre 27 1982–7
Hooker
P. G. Johnson 42 1959–71
Lock
S. A. Williams 28 1980–5
Flanker
S. P. Poidevin 45 1980–7
No 8
S. N. Tuynman 27 (31) 1983–7
Tuynman played 4 times on the flank.

Longest international career
16 seasons   G. M. Cooke   1932–47/8
16 seasons   A. R. Miller   1952–67
Cooke's career ended during a Northern hemisphere season.

Most internationals as captain
A. G. Slack 23 1983–7

Most points in internationals
269   M. P. Lynagh 1984–7

Most points in an international
23*   M. P. Lynagh v Scotland 1984
      Murrayfield
*Lynagh scored 23 points against Canada at
Sydney in 1985 and 23 v Argentina in 1986.*

Most tries in internationals
25   D. I. Campese (34
     appearances)   1982–7

Most tries in an international
4*   G. Cornelsen v N. Zealand 1978
     Auckland
*D. I. Campese scored 4 against US at Sydney
in 1983, but this was not against an IB country.*

Most conversions in an international
3   R. R. Biilmann v S. Africa 1933
    Durban
3   P. F. Ryan v England 1963
    Sydney
3   P. E. McLean v Scotland 1982
    Sydney
3   R. G. Gould v Wales 1984
    Cardiff
3   M. P. Lynagh v Scotland 1984
    Murrayfield*
*M. P. Lynagh kicked 7 against Canada at
Sydney in 1985.*

Most points on overseas tour
154   P. E. McLean (18
      appearances) B. Isles 1975–6

Most tries on overseas tour
23   C. J. Russell 1908–23 B. Isles

**Most points in international series on
tour**
42   M. P. Lynagh (4 appearances)
     1984 B. Isles

**Most tries in international series on
tour**
4   G. Cornelsen (3 appearances)
    1978 N. Zealand

4   M. G. Ella (4 appearances) 1984
    B. Isles

Most points in any tour match
23   J. C. Hindmarsh v Glamorgan
     1975 Neath

AUSTRALIA'S LEADING CAP WINNERS
(Matches against IB countries)

S. P. Poidevin 45	K. W. Catchpole 27	P. C. Grigg 24
P. G. Johnson 42	T. A. Lawton 27	R. Phelps 23
A. R. Miller 41	G. A. Shaw 27	R. A. Smith 22
G. V. Davis 39	A. J. McIntyre 27	J. E. C. Meadows 22
J. E. Thornett 37	C. T. Burke 26	S. A. G. Cutler 22
J. N. B. Hipwell 36	R. B. Prosser 25	E. E. Rodriguez 22
A. A. Shaw 36	G. Cornelsen 25	E. T. Bonis 21
A. G. Slack 36	M. G. Ella 25	P. F. Hawthorne 21
D. I. Campese 34	R. G. Gould 25	R. J. Heming 21
B. J. Moon 31	J. K. Lenehan 24	A. N. McGill 21
N. M. Shehadie 30	J. P. L. White 24	A. S. Cameron 20
P. E. McLean 30	J. W. Cole 24	B. J. Ellwood 20
M. E. Loane 28	G. Fay 24	C. J. Windon 20
S. A. Williams 28	M. J. Hawker 24	*(to 30 June 1987)*

Most tries in any tour match
6   J. S. Boyce v Wairarapa (NZ)
    1962 Masterton

The calm authority of Andrew Slack, the Australian captain, was a key factor in his country's success during the 1980s. Here Slack (left) gets the ball away despite the attention of two Cardiff players during the Welsh club's 16–12 win on the 1984 tour to Britain.

AUSTRALIA – THE MAJOR STATES

AUSTRALIAN CAPITAL TERRITORY
Foundation   1974 (separated from NSW Country)
Ground   Canberra Stadium
Capacity   15 000
Record Attendance   12 500 ACT v South Africa 1971
Major Touring Teams Defeated   Fiji: 1969 17–9, 1985

34–23; Tonga: 1973 17–6; Wales: 1978 21–20; Italy:
1981 19–18; Argentina: 1983 35–9
Most Capped Player   D. I. Campese   34
Number of Wallabies   1
Club Champions on Most Occasions   Canberra Royals,
Queanbeyan

The acute embarrassment suffered by Wales, Argentina, Italy, Tonga and France in recent seasons on what, foolishly, has been believed to be no more than a quiet workout in convivial surroundings has saddled ACT with the role of giant-killers. Boosted by the recent inspirational talents of David Campese, supported by teammates of considerable ability, the ACT's history goes back further than the Canberra district itself.

In 1870 there were clubs in Bungendore, Gundaroo, Captains Flat, Sutton and Ginnindera; in 1878 the top Queanbeyan club was founded; Goulbourn – equally respected – was launched in 1873. There are now eight clubs in Canberra waiting for the next unsuspecting tourists. ACT has 14 clubs in all, and began their own championship in 1938 with just four clubs.

NEW SOUTH WALES

Foundation 1874 (as Southern RU)
Ground Sydney Cricket Ground
Capacity 49 000
Record Attendance 49 327 Australia v New Zealand 1980
Major Touring Teams Defeated New Zealand: 1893 25–3, 1897 27–8, 1907 14–0, 1922 14–8, 1924 18–16, 1926 26–20, 1938 12–9, 1980 9–3; British Isles: 1908 6–3, 1930 28–3, 1950 17–12, 1959 18–14; South Africa: 1937 17–6, 1965 12–3; Ireland: 1967 21–9; Scotland: 1970 28–14; Fiji: 1954 16–13, 1961 17–13, 1969 6–5, 1985 43–10; Argentina: 1986 30–18; Canada: 1985 27–6
Most Capped Player S. P. Poidevin 45
Number of Wallabies 127
Major Clubs Randwick, Parramatta, Manly, Eastern Suburbs, Western Suburbs, Northern Suburbs, Sydney University, Warringah, Eastwood, Gordon, Drummoyne

New South Wales was the first centre to feature rugby outside Great Britain. There is conflicting evidence as to whether a form of Australian Rules or Union was played on 25 July 1829 at the Soldiers barracks in Sydney. However, the Sydney University club dates from 1863, Sydney RFC and Australian RFC from 1865, the Military and Civil RFC from 1867, and Wallaroo was founded in 1870. In fact, most of the clubs were cricket clubs, rugby being played as part of keep-fit campaigns during the winter months. The rougher aspects of the game were such that Eldred Harmer tried to outlaw Union in the NSW parliament during the 1860s.

By the 1870s the game had mushroomed, with over 100 clubs in the Sydney area. Brutality was never far from the surface, a point exploited to the full by the Australian Rules fraternity. To combat a general state of indiscipline both on and off the field, the Southern Union was founded in 1874, the forerunner of the NSW RU. A northern section was opened in the Newcastle area in 1888.

The challenge against Queensland began in 1882. On 12 August the first match of the series ended in a win for NSW with a probable score in the region of 26–3. NSW then undertook a seven-match tour to New Zealand who, with Queensland, to this day provide the main opposition. Because these teams offer the major share of incoming tours, NSW are able consistently to produce a side of the highest quality; their record against overseas teams is the best of any state or province anywhere in the world.

SYDNEY – MAJOR TOURING TEAMS DEFEATED

British Isles: 1899 8–5; Ireland: 1967 30–8, 1979 16–12; England: 1975 14–10; Wales: 1978 18–16; France: 1981 16–14; Scotland: 1982 18–7; Japan: 1975 38–22

SYDNEY FIRST GRADE PREMIERSHIP WINNERS

Year	Winner	Year	Winner
1900	Glebe	1945	University
1901	Glebe and University	1946	Eastern Suburbs
1902	Western Suburbs	1947	Eastern Suburbs
1903	Eastern Suburbs	1948	Randwick
1904	University	1949	Gordon
1905	South Sydney	1950	Manly
1906	Glebe	1951	University
1907	Glebe	1952	Gordon
1908	Newtown	1953	University
1909	Glebe	1954	University
1910	Newtown	1955	University
1911	Newtown	1956	Gordon
1912	Glebe	1957	St George
1913	Eastern Suburbs	1958	Gordon
1914	Glebe	1959	Randwick
1915–8	No competition	1960	Northern Suburbs
1919	University	1961	University
1920	University	1962	University
1921	Eastern Suburbs	1963	Northern Suburbs
1922	Manly	1964	Northern Suburbs
1923	University	1965	Randwick
1924	University	1966	Randwick
1925	Glebe-Balmain	1967	Randwick
1926	University	1968	University
1927	University	1969	Eastern Suburbs
1928	University	1970	University
1929	Western Suburbs	1971	Randwick
1930	Randwick	1972	University
1931	Eastern Suburbs	1973	Randwick
1932	Manly	1974	Randwick
1933	Northern Suburbs	1975	Northern Suburbs
1934	Randwick	1976	Gordon
1935	Northern Suburbs	1977	Parramatta
1936	Drummoyne	1978	Randwick
1937	University	1979	Randwick
1938	Randwick	1980	Randwick
1939	University	1981	Randwick
1940	Randwick	1982	Randwick
1941	Eastern Suburbs	1983	Manly
1942	Manly	1984	Randwick
1943	Manly	1985	Parramatta
1944	Eastern Suburbs	1986	Parramatta

NEW SOUTH WALES COUNTRY

Foundation 1955
Major Touring Teams Defeated England: 1975 14–13; Fiji: 1961 17–16; Japan: 1975 97–20 (correct!); Italy: 1986 22–9; Canada: 1985 31–23
Capped Players None
Number of Wallabies 14

Rugby took off in New South Wales Country regions immediately after World War II. The NSW Country Rugby Union was formed in 1955, and now plays many touring sides, notably those just below the eight International Board nations. By 1984 there were 319 clubs scattered around the state, with the principal centres being in Newcastle, who withdrew from the Union in 1959, and on the Far South Coast. Goulbourn is the only club member of the old Northern Rugby Union still in existence. The Country regions have produced a host of international players who made the grade in Sydney, but spent their early careers playing outside the capital. Of these the best known is John Hipwell, the former international scrum-half and captain.

NORTHERN TERRITORY

The Northern Territory is not, as yet, a part of the Australian Rugby Union. However, there is growing respect for rugby in the outback, where the game is rapidly becoming properly structured and organized. The major clubs in the Northern Territory are Palmerston, Waratahs, South Darwin, Casuarina, Larrakeyah and Bayside.

By 1984 there were six clubs in Darwin and its environs. The season lasts from October to April in what is described as the rainy season, and a championship is held each year when clubs meet over a weekend. Far-flung centres such as Alice Springs regularly send a team to the Weekend Festival. Known as the Outback XV, they were one of nine clubs in the 1984 competition. The 1984 champions Palmerston claim that the foundation of their victory was a short second half, decreed because the casino who had sponsored the event were then open for business!

QUEENSLAND

Foundation 1883 (as Northern RU)
Ground Ballymore Oval, Brisbane
Capacity 25 000
Record Attendance 22 000 Australia v New Zealand 1985
Major Touring Teams Defeated British Isles: 1899 11–3, 1971 15–11; Scotland: 1970 16–13, 1982 18–7; New Zealand: 1980 9–3; Fiji: 1969 17–16, 1985 47–6; Italy: 1981 68–11; Japan: 1975 64–23; Argentina: 1986 59–9 (*N.B.* Brisbane beat Italy 37–19 1986)
Most Capped Player A. G. Slack 36
Number of Wallabies 74

Queensland – dominant power in the 1980s – dates its rugby history to 1867 with the first club, Brisbane RFC. Excelsior became the next some 11 years later, but Australian Rules was at the time the more popular pastime in both these clubs. But by 1882 there were three clubs in Brisbane, and others at Toowoomba, Rockhampton and Maryborough. Gympie was another rugby centre. A year later the Northern Rugby Union was founded – forerunner of the Queensland RU (remember that NSW was the Southern RU). At the turn of the century there had been visits from New Zealand and the Maoris, with Queensland in full swing with inter-state matches against NSW.

Queensland rugby has known hard times and, like NSW, suffered many defections in the early 1900s to both Australian Rules and Rugby League. The war years took their toll of the youth of the state and, by 1929, the Queensland RU was forced into a policy of reformation because a lack of interest in the postwar years was having serious consequences for the growth and development of the game within the state. By the 1980s, though, with more players ignoring the lure of Rugby League, and with good coaching in clubs and schools, Queensland was just about the most powerful provincial side in world rugby.

BRISBANE FIRST GRADE PREMIERSHIP WINNERS

Year	Winner	Year	Winner
1887	Ipswich Rangers		
1888	Union Harriers		
1889	Wallaroos		
1890	Wallaroos		
1891	Acoma		
1892	Past and Present Grammar		
1893	Boomerangs		
1894	Boomerangs		
1895	City		
1896	City		
1897	City		
1898	Past Grammar		
1899	Past Grammar		
1900	City		
1901	North Brisbane Electorate		
1902	North Brisbane Electorate		
1903	North Brisbane Electorate		
1904	North Brisbane Electorate and Valley (equal)		
1905–14	Unknown		
1915	Brothers		
1916–28	No competition		
1929	YMCA		
1930	University		
1931	University		
1932	University		
1933	YMCA		
1934	University		
1935	Eagle Junction		
1936	Eagle Junction		
1937	Eagle Junction		
1938	University		
1939	YMCA		
1940–5	No competition		
1946	Christian Brothers Old Boys		
1947	University		
1948	University		
1949	Christian Brothers		
1950	Christian Brothers		
1951	Christian Brothers		
1952	University		
1953	Christian Brothers		
1954	University		
1955	University		
1956	University		
1957	University		
1958	Southern Districts		
1959	Christian Brothers		
1960	University		
1961	GPS Old Boys	1974	Brothers
1962	University	1975	Brothers
1963	Teachers	1976	Teachers Norths
1964	University	1977	Wests
1965	University	1978	Brothers
1966	Brothers	1979	University
1967	University	1980	Brothers
1968	Brothers	1981	Brothers
1969	University	1982	Brothers
1970	University	1983	Brothers
1971	Brothers	1984	Brothers
1972	GPS	1985	Western Districts
1973	Brothers	1986	Western Districts

QUEENSLAND COUNTRY RUGBY UNION

Now flourishing in Rockhampton, Mount Isa, Townsville and Darling Downs. Most of the larger towns have their own Union, but all are amalgamated under the Country Union, which was founded in 1965. The Queensland Country XV is now regularly meeting international opposition from World Cup countries.

SOUTH AUSTRALIA

Foundation 1932
Ground Bailey Ground, Adelaide
Capacity 7500
Record Attendance 7000 South Australia v Fiji 1961
Heavy Defeats by Touring Teams 6–117 v NZ 1974, 0–99 v NZ 1984
Capped Players None
Number of Wallabies None
Major Clubs Old Collegians, Brighton, Glenelg

More than any other state or province in world rugby, South Australia collects records of the wrong sort. They are the butt of quiz questions surrounding record defeats against tourists. Yet today there are no more than ten clubs in the state, and there is no history of rugby tradition, so that conceding a century of points to powerful tourists does neither side much credit. The SARU dates back to 1932, and consisted of just two clubs in Adelaide, only one of which was properly constituted. Two years earlier the only rugby played was by members of the *Adelaide Observer* sports section. Adelaide RFC came into being in 1931, the Navy launched a team in 1932, and the same year Adelaide University followed suit. Today, some 1200 players are registered, with distinct emphasis on the more social aspects of the game!

TASMANIA

Foundation 1966
Ground Queenborough Oval
Capacity 6000
Record Attendance 4500 Tasmania v New Zealand 1968
Capped Players None
Number of Wallabies None
Major Clubs Harlequins, Glenorchy, Associates, Glen Dhu, University, Taroona, Eastern Suburbs

One of the smaller and newer Unions, and as yet happily unconcerned with representative fixtures with the world's leading touring sides. Two New Zealand ship crews first demonstrated the sport in 1926, but until 1951 a divide between north and south of the island hindered development. In 1932 there were just three clubs in the north, while a year later students at Tasmania University took up the game. However, by the end of World War II the winds of change had blown over the island. Hobart had six clubs in 1947, while Launceston and Devonport in the north suffered by comparison. The unification into the Tasmania Rugby Union in 1966 was a beneficial organizational step, but two years later a New Zealand victory by 74–0 put the state of the game on the island into perspective. With the points nearest geographically to the mainland hardly the most steeped in Australian rugby, Tasmania will allow social rugby to be of paramount importance.

VICTORIA

Foundation 1888 (as Melbourne RU)
Ground Olympic Park, Melbourne
Capacity 15 000
Most Capped Player O. L. Bridle 13
Number of Wallabies 13
Major Clubs Moorabbin, Kiwis, Power House, University, Melbourne

Victoria, home of Australian Rules football, has struggled to break down the barriers. In the early days rugby came a poor third to Australian Rules and Gaelic football; historians agree that the first British team to Australia in 1888 spent more time playing Rules than Union! The first recorded game was, naturally, in Melbourne, when the Northern Suburbs took on the remainder of Melbourne in 1888. From that seed grew the Melbourne Rugby Union. Indications of the pressures that Union players had to tolerate came in 1899 when the Victoria State XV travelled to Sydney to play New South Wales. Not only were they trounced, but, on arrival back in Melbourne, found themselves unemployed – sacked for not playing Australian Rules! News like that travelled fast, and the game slumped. By 1909 the braver elements had started afresh. With five clubs in the area, East and South Melbourne, Melbourne, St Kilda and the University, the first inter-club competition was under way. Yet by 1984, the number of clubs had only doubled despite frequent visits from touring sides. Victoria has never beaten an international team though several visiting sides have found spirited resistance.

WESTERN AUSTRALIA

Foundation 1893
Ground Perry Lakes Stadium, Perth
Capacity 15 000
Record Attendance 14 500 Western Australia v South Africa 1971
Major Touring Teams Defeated Canada: 1985 16–6
Most Capped Player R. J. Thompson 3
Number of Wallabies 1
Major Clubs Cottesloe, Nedlands, Western Suburbs

Rugby is now firmly established in Western Australia, at last overcoming the geographical isolation which had, on more than one occasion, threatened its existence. The first game dates back to 1868 in the Swan River Colony at Fremantle where the players were drawn from local ships in the harbour and pitted against the local Forces. By 1881 the games were more organized, though four years later a concentrated effort to introduce Australian Rules met with more success. But schoolmasters had accepted Union from 1876, and with the gold rush, miners and engineers looking for exercise were ready converts. But the enthusiasm fizzled out as war took away many players; by 1923 major surgery was needed. Two factors contributed to the recent resurgence. In 1962 Perth played host to the Commonwealth Games. Airport facilities were brought up to international standard, the city flourished, and touring sides saw the WARU as an eminently suitable stopover. Then, in 1971, the WARU acquired the Perry Lakes Stadium as their permanent home. With this increased stability the WARU has been able to plan ahead with confidence for the future. Overseas teams will find Western Australia no pushover.

New Zealand

Foundation 1892
Colours Black shirts
   and shorts
Nickname All Blacks
No of clubs 1150
No of players 174 750

There is a story in New Zealand folklore about a schoolboy who was asked by his teacher who the country's Prime Minister was in 1960. The boy looked suitably embarrassed. Silence. The teacher then asked who the All Black rugby captain was. No problem: Wilson Whineray, he replied, without a second's hesitation. True or not it gives some idea of the esteem in which the game is held in New Zealand. Respect from the rest of the world is mutual, reinforced by the World Cup triumph. By 1987, the New Zealand team had lost just over 100 games out of nearly 1000 matches.

Nelson, a small town on the northern coast of South Island, introduced the game to the country in 1870. Charles John Munro, educated at Sherborne School in Dorset, the son of the president of the New Zealand Chamber of Commerce, was the William Webb Ellis of New Zealand. His enthusiasm led to Nelson founding the country's first rugby club. Within a year, Wellington, across the Cook Strait on the southern tip of the North Island, had also formed a club, and challenged Nelson.

By 1876 the leading Unions – Auckland, Canterbury and Otago – had decided to play to the rules decreed by the newly formed International Rugby Board in London in 1871. The first meeting of the New Zealand Rugby Union was held in Wellington on 27 April 1893. All the major regions of the North Island were represented, but just four from the South. The founder members were Auckland, Hawke's Bay, Manawatu, Marlborough, Nelson, South Canterbury, Taranaki, Wairarapa, Wanganui, Wellington and West Coast. A touring team to Australia celebrated the birth of the NZRU, which a year later brought the rebel Unions from the South into the fold.

The Ranfurly Shield was first played for in 1901, and today it is still the symbol of inter-provincial supremacy, and one of the major competitions in world rugby.

Each Union has its own club championship. The backbone of New Zealand rugby is formed by the two major tournaments for the Unions: the Ranfurly Shield and the National League. The National League has a first division, and two regional second divisions. There are also various representative fixtures.

In 1905 the first All Blacks trampled all over the best of British on their first major overseas tour. New Zealand teams have been doing just that all over the world ever since, as any schoolboy will tell you.

NEW ZEALAND – INTERNATIONAL RECORDS

TEAM RECORDS
Highest score
Overall
49 v Wales (49–6) 1987 Brisbane
   (World Cup)
NZ scored 74 against Fiji (74–13) in 1987 World Cup.
v individual countries
42 v England (42–15) 1985
   Wellington
40 v Scotland (40–15) 1981 Auckland
17 v Ireland (17–9) 1935 Dublin
49 v Wales (49–6) 1987 Brisbane
   (World Cup)
38 v France (38–8) 1906 Parc des
   Princes
25 v S. Africa (25–22) 1981
   Auckland
38 v Australia (38–3) 1972 Auckland
38 v B. Isles (38–6) 1983 Auckland

Referee Clive Norling watches as Allan Hewson prepares to take the winning penalty in the final test in 1981 against South Africa at Eden Park, Auckland. New Zealand won 25–22 and the series 2–1 with that kick.

Biggest winning points margin
*Overall**
43 v Wales (49–6) 1987 (World Cup)
v individual countries
27 v England (42–15) 1985
 Wellington
25 v Scotland (40–15) 1981 Auckland
15 v Ireland (15–0) 1905 Dublin
43 v Wales (49–6) 1987 Brisbane
 (World Cup)
30 v France (38–8) 1906 Parc des
 Princes
17 v S. Africa (20–3) 1965 Auckland
35 v Australia (38–3) 1972 Auckland
32 v B. Isles (38–6) 1983 Auckland
**New Zealand beat Italy 70–6 in 1987 (World Cup).*

Highest score by opposing team
Overall
30 Australia (16–30) 1978 Auckland
by individual countries
16 England (10–16) 1973 Auckland
25 Scotland (25–25) 1983
 Murrayfield
10 Ireland (10–10) 1973 Dublin
16 Wales (19–16) 1972 Cardiff
24 France (19–24) 1979 Auckland
24 S. Africa (12–24) 1981 Wellington
30 Australia (16–30) 1978 Auckland
17 B. Isles (18–17) 1959 Dunedin

Biggest losing points margin
Overall
17 v South Africa (0–17) 1928
 Durban
v individual countries
13 v England (0–13) 1936
 Twickenham
No defeat v Scotland
No defeat v Ireland
5 v Wales (8–13) 1953 Cardiff
7 v France (6–13) 1973 Parc des
 Princes
17 v S. Africa (0–17) 1928 Durban
16 v Australia (10–26) 1980 Sydney
10 v B. Isles (3–13) 1971 Wellington

Most tries by New Zealand in an international
10 v France (38–8) 1906 Parc des
 Princes
New Zealand scored 12 v Fiji and Italy, both in 1987 World Cup.

Most tries against New Zealand in an international
5 by S. Africa (6–17) 1937 Auckland
5 by Australia (16–30) 1978
 Auckland

Most points on overseas tour (all matches)
868 in B. Isles/France (33 matches)
 1905–6

Most tries on overseas tour (all matches)
215 in B. Isles/France (33 matches)
 1905–6

INDIVIDUAL RECORDS
Most capped player
Overall
C. E. Meads 55 1957–71
in individual positions
Full-back
D. B. Clarke 31 1956–64
Wing
B. G. Williams 36(38)[1] 1970–8
Centre (includes 2nd five-eighth)
B. J. Robertson 34 1972–81
1st five-eighth
W. R. Smith 17 1980–5
Scrum-half
S. M. Going 29 1967–77
Prop
G. A. Knight 34 1977–85
Hooker
A. G. Dalton 37 1977–86
Lock
C. E. Meads 48(55)[2] 1957–71
Flanker
K. R. Tremain 36(38)[3] 1959–68
I. A. Kirkpatrick 36(39)[4] 1967–77
No 8
M. G. Mexted 36 1979–86
[1]*Williams won 2 caps as a centre.*
[2]*Meads won 5 caps as a flanker, 2 as a No 8.*
[3]*Tremain won 2 caps as a No 8.*
[4]*Kirkpatrick won 3 caps as a No 8.*

Longest international career
15 seasons E. E. Hughes 1907–21
15 seasons C. E. Meads 1957–71

Most internationals as captain
30 W. J. Whineray 1958–65

Most points in internationals
207 D. B. Clarke (31
 appearances) 1956–64

Most points in an international
26 A. R. Hewson v Australia 1982
 Auckland
G. Fox scored 26 points v Fiji in 1987 World Cup.

Most tries in internationals
19 S. S. Wilson (33*
 appearances) 1977–83
**Excludes one match against Romania.*

Most tries in an international
4 D. McGregor v England 1905
 Crystal Palace
J. Gallagher and C. Green both scored 4 tries v Fiji in 1987 World Cup.

Most conversions in an international
6 A. R. Hewson v Scotland 1981
 Auckland
G. Fox kicked 10 v Fiji in 1987 (World Cup).

Most points for New Zealand on overseas tour
230 W. J. Wallace (25
 appearances) 1905–6 B. Isles/
 France

Most tries for New Zealand on overseas tour
42 J. Hunter (23 appearances)
 1905–6 B. Isles/France

Most points in international series
46 A. R. Hewson (4 appearances)
 v B. Isles 1983

Most points for New Zealand in international series on tour
32 W. F. McCormick (4
 appearances) 1967 B. Isles/
 France
32 R.M. Deans (3 appearances)
 1984 Australia

Most tries for New Zealand in international series on tour
5 K. S. Svenson (4 appearances)
 1924–5 B. Isles/France
Svenson scored in each match of the international series.

Most points for New Zealand in any tour match
43 R. M. Deans v South Australia
 1984 Adelaide

Most tries for New Zealand in any tour match
8 T. R. Heeps v Northern NSW
 1962 Quirindi

Stuart Wilson, New Zealand's leading try scorer, prepares to wrong-foot Ray Mordt (South Africa) during the 1981 series between the countries.

RECORD OF NEW ZEALAND TEAMS 1884–1987

Year		Played	Won	Lost	Drawn	Points For	Points Against
1884	in New South Wales	9	9	—	—	176	17
1893	in New South Wales and Queensland	11	10	1	—	175	48
1894	New South Wales in New Zealand	1	—	1	—	6	8
1896	Queensland in New Zealand	1	1	—	—	9	0
1897	in New South Wales and Queensland	11	9	2	—	238	83
1901	New South Wales in New Zealand	2	2	—	—	44	8
1903	in Australia	11	10	1	—	281	27
1904	Great Britain in New Zealand	1	1	—	—	9	3
1905	in Australia and New Zealand	7	4	1	2	89	30
1905	Australia in New Zealand	1	1	—	—	14	3
1905–6	in the British Isles, France and North America	35	34	1	—	976	59
1907	in Australia	8	6	1	1	115	53
1908	Anglo-Welsh in New Zealand	3	2	—	1	64	8
1910	in Australia	8	7	1	—	138	78
1913	Australia in New Zealand	4	3	1	—	79	52
1913	in North America	16	16	—	—	610	6
1914	in Australia	11	10	1	—	260	69
1920	in Australia	10	9	—	1	352	91
1921	South Africa and New South Wales in New Zealand	4	1	2	1	18	31
1922	in Australia	8	6	2	—	198	102
1923	New South Wales in New Zealand	3	3	—	—	91	26
1924–5	in Australia, the British Isles, France and Canada	38	36	2	—	981	180
1925	in Australia	8	6	2	—	132	67
1925	New South Wales in New Zealand	1	1	—	—	36	10
1926	in Australia	8	6	2	—	187	109
1928	in South Africa	23	17	5	1	397	153
1928	New South Wales in New Zealand	4	3	1	—	79	40
1929	in Australia	10	6	3	1	186	80
1930	Great Britain in New Zealand	5	4	1	—	87	40
1931	Australia in New Zealand	1	1	—	—	20	13
1932	in Australia	11	9	2	—	331	135
1934	in Australia	9	7	1	1	201	107
1935–6	in the British Isles and Canada	30	26	3	1	490	183
1936	Australia in New Zealand	3	3	—	—	65	32
1937	South Africa in New Zealand	3	1	2	—	25	37
1938	in Australia	9	9	—	—	279	73
1946	Australia in New Zealand	2	2	—	—	45	18
1947	in Australia	10	8	2	—	263	113
1949	in South Africa	24	14	7	3	230	146
1949	Australia in New Zealand	2	—	2	—	15	27
1950	British Isles in New Zealand	4	3	—	1	34	20
1951	in Australia	13	13	—	—	375	86
1952	Australia in New Zealand	2	1	1	—	24	22
1953–4	in the British Isles, France and North America	36	30	4	2	598	152
1955	Australia in New Zealand	3	2	1	—	27	16
1956	South Africa in New Zealand	4	3	1	—	41	29
1957	in Australia	14	13	1	—	472	94
1958	Australia in New Zealand	3	2	1	—	45	17
1959	British Isles in New Zealand	4	3	1	—	57	42
1960	in Australia and South Africa	32	26	4	2	645	187
1961	France in New Zealand	3	3	—	—	50	12
1962	in Australia	10	9	1	—	426	49
1962	Australia in New Zealand	3	2	—	1	28	17
1963	England in New Zealand	2	2	—	—	30	17
1963–4	in the British Isles, France and Canada	36	34	1	1	613	159
1964	Australia in New Zealand	3	2	1	—	37	32
1965	South Africa in New Zealand	4	3	1	—	55	25
1966	British Isles in New Zealand	4	4	—	—	79	32
1967	Australia in New Zealand	1	1	—	—	29	9
1967	in the British Isles, France and Canada	17	16	—	1	370	135
1968	in Australia and Fiji	12	12	—	—	460	66
1968	France in New Zealand	3	3	—	—	40	24
1969	Wales in New Zealand	2	2	—	—	52	12
1970	in Australia and South Africa	26	23	3	—	789	234
1971	British Isles in New Zealand	4	1	2	1	42	48
1972	Internal Tour	9	9	—	—	355	88
1972	Australia in New Zealand	3	3	—	—	97	26
1972–3	in the British Isles, France and North America	32	25	5	2	640	266
1973	Internal Tour and England in New Zealand	5	2	3	—	88	83
1974	in Australia and Fiji	13	12	—	1	446	73
1974	in Ireland, Wales and England	8	7	—	1	127	50
1975	Scotland in New Zealand	1	1	—	—	24	—

Year	Opponent/Venue						
1976	Ireland in New Zealand	1	1	—	—	11	3
1976	in South Africa	24	18	6	—	610	291
1976	in Argentina and Uruguay	9	9	—	—	321	72
1977	British Isles in New Zealand	4	3	1	—	54	41
1977	in France and Italy	9	8	1	—	216	86
1978	Australia in New Zealand	3	2	1	—	51	48
1978	in the British Isles	18	17	1	—	364	147
1979	France in New Zealand	2	1	1	—	42	33
1979	in Australia	2	1	1	—	41	15
1979	Argentina in New Zealand	2	2	—	—	33	15
1979	in England and Scotland	11	10	1	—	192	95
1980	in Australia and Fiji	16	12	3	1	507	126
1980	Fiji in New Zealand	1	1	—	—	33	—
1980	in North America and Wales	7	7	—	—	197	41
1981	Scotland in New Zealand	2	2	—	—	51	19
1981	South Africa in New Zealand	3	2	1	—	51	55
1981	in Romania and France	10	8	1	1	170	108
1982	Australia in New Zealand	3	2	1	—	72	53
1983	British Isles in New Zealand	4	4	—	—	78	26
1983	in Australia	1	1	—	—	18	8
1983	in Scotland and England	8	5	2	1	162	116
1984	France in New Zealand	2	2	—	—	41	27
1984	in Australia	14	13	1	—	600	117
1984	in Fiji	4	4	—	—	174	10
1985	England in New Zealand	2	2	—	—	60	28
1985	Australia in New Zealand	1	1	—	—	10	9
1985	in Argentina	7	6	—	1	263	87
1986	France in New Zealand	1	1	—	—	18	9
1986	Australia in New Zealand	3	1	2	—	34	47
1986	in France	8	7	1	—	218	87
1987	World Cup	6	6	—	—	298	52
	TOTALS	**870**	**734**	**106**	**30**	**20176**	**6358**

NEW ZEALAND'S LEADING CAP WINNERS

C. E. Meads 55
A. M. Haden 41
I. A. Kirkpatrick 39
K. R. Tremain 38
B. G. Williams 38
A. G. Dalton 37
M. G. Mexted 36
B. J. Robertson 34
S. S. Wilson 34
G. A. Knight 34
W. J. Whineray 32
D. B. Clarke 31
S. M. Going 29
M. W. Shaw 29
R. W. Norton 27
B. J. Lochore 25
B. E. McLeod 24
K. F. Gray 24
I. J. Clarke 24
J. C. Ashworth 24
D. S. Loveridge 24
R. A. White 23
B. G. Fraser 23
D. J. Graham 22
D. Young 22
G. N. K. Mourie 21
K. L. Skinner 20
C. R. Laidlaw 20
I. N. MacEwan 20
P. J. Whiting 20

RANFURLY SHIELD

A challenge competition for affiliated unions of the New Zealand RFU, the shield bears the name of the Governor of New Zealand who presented the trophy in 1901. Auckland, with an unbeaten record, was declared the first winner of the Ranfurly Shield on 13 September 1902.

RANFURLY SHIELD STATISTICS

Longest tenure		*Challenges resisted*
Auckland	1960–3	25
Canterbury	1982–5	25
Hawke's Bay	1922–7	24
Auckland	1905–13	23
Canterbury	1953–6	23
Hawke's Bay	1966–9	21

Shortest tenure		*Days*
Wellington	1963	7
Auckland	1972	10
North Auckland	1960	11
Wairarapa	1950	14
South Canterbury	1950	14
Auckland	1952	14

North Auckland resisted one challenge, the other unions were beaten by the first challenger.

Highest winning margin
88 by Canterbury v North Otago 1983

Biggest attendance
52 000 Canterbury v Auckland, Christchurch 1985

INDIVIDUAL PERFORMANCES (to 1986)
Most matches
35 H. L. White, Auckland

Most points
332 R. M. Deans, Canterbury

Most tries
30 B. A. Grenside, Hawkes Bay

Most conversions
60 R. M. Deans, Canterbury

Most penalty goals
56 R. M. Deans, Canterbury

Most dropped goals
14 R. H. Brown, Taranaki
14 D. Trevathan, Otago

Most goals from a mark
3 J. H. Dufty, Auckland

Most points in a match
32 R. M. Deans, Canterbury v North Otago, 1983

Most tries in a match
6 R. A. Jarden, Wellington v East Coast, 1953

Most conversions in a match
10 R. M. Deans, Canterbury v North Otago, 1983

Most penalty goals in a match
7 R. M. Deans, Canterbury v Counties, 1984

Most dropped goals in a match
3 R. H. Brown, Taranaki v
  Wanganui, 1964

Unions which have never held the shield
Bay of Plenty, Buller, Counties,
East Coast, Horowhenua, King
Country, Mid Canterbury, Nelson
Bays, North Otago, Poverty Bay,
Thames Valley, Wairarapa Bush,
Wanganui, West Coast.

NEW ZEALAND – NATIONAL CHAMPIONSHIP

In 1975, a committee of the NZRFU was set up to organize representative rugby into a national championship. On the basis of performances over the early 1970s, 11 unions were selected for the first division competition: North Auckland, Auckland, Counties, Bay of Plenty, Hawke's Bay, Manawatu, Wellington, Marlborough, Canterbury, Otago and Southland. Each play five home and five away matches. The remaining unions were included in a second division in each island. There is promotion and relegation between the divisions. A third division was formed in 1985.

Year	Champions	Promoted	Relegated
1976	Bay of Plenty	Taranaki	N. Auckland
1977	Canterbury	N. Auckland	Marlborough
		S. Canterbury	Bay of Plenty
1978	Wellington	Bay of Plenty	Hawke's Bay
1979	Counties	Hawke's Bay	Taranaki
1980	Manawatu	Waikato	S. Canterbury
1981	Wellington	Wairarapa Bush	Southland
1982	Auckland	—	—
1983	Canterbury	—	—
1984	Auckland	Southland	Hawke's Bay
1985	Auckland	Taranaki	Waikato
1986	Wellington	Waikato	Southland

NEW ZEALAND – THE UNIONS

AUCKLAND
Foundation 1883
Ground Eden Park, Auckland
Capacity 57 000
Record Attendance 61 240 NZ v SA 1956
Major Touring Teams Defeated Australia: 1913 15–13, 1936 8–5, 1964 11–6; British Isles: 1888 4–0, 1904 13–0, 1930 19–6, 1983 13–12; South Africa: 1965 15–14; Fiji: 1951 29–16, 1954 39–9; Ireland: 1976 13–10
Most Capped Player A. M. Haden 42
Number of All Blacks 135
Ranfurly Shield 1902, 1903, 1906, 1907, 1908, 1909, 1910, 1911, 1912, 1913, 1934, 1935, 1952, 1959, 1960, 1961, 1962, 1963, 1965, 1966, 1971, 1974, 1975, 1976, 1979, 1980, 1981, 1985, 1986
First Division Champions 1982, 1984, 1985
Club Champions on Most Occasions Ponsonby

BAY OF PLENTY
Foundation 1911
Ground Rotorua Stadium
Capacity 50 000
Record Attendance 35 000 v British Lions 1983
Major Touring Teams Defeated Australia: 1982 40–16
Most Capped Player H. R. Reid 14
Number of All Blacks 16
Ranfurly Shield —
First Division Champions 1976

BULLER
Foundation 1894
Ground Victoria Ground, Westport
Capacity 5000
Record Attendance 5000 v S. Africa 1956
Major Touring Teams Defeated Australia: 1949 17–15, 1972 15–10 (with West Coast)
Most Capped Player K. S. Svenson 4
Number of All Blacks 7
Ranfurly Shield —
Club Champions on Most Occasions Westport

CANTERBURY
Foundation 1879
Ground Lancaster Park, Christchurch
Capacity 60 000
Record Attendance 60 000 v British Lions 1971
Major Touring Teams Defeated Australia: 1931 16–13, 1936 19–18, 1946 20–11, 1962 5–3, 1986 30–12; Ireland: 1976 18–4; British Isles: 1930 14–8, 1959 20–14, 1983 22–20; Scotland: 1975 20–9; South Africa: 1921 6–4, 1956 9–6; Fiji: 1951 24–22, 1957 22–16, 1974 9–4, 1980 10–4; Tonga: 1975 30–21; England: 1973 19–12
Most Capped Player I. A. Kirkpatrick 39
Number of All Blacks 140
Ranfurly Shield 1927, 1928, 1931, 1932, 1933, 1934, 1935, 1954, 1955, 1956, 1969, 1970, 1971, 1972, 1982, 1983, 1984, 1985
First Division Champions 1977, 1983
Club Champions on Most Occasions University

COUNTIES
Foundation As South Auckland 1926
  Counties (name change) 1955
Ground Pukekohe Stadium
Capacity 40 000
Record Attendance 26 500 Thames Valley-Counties v British Lions 1977
Major Touring Teams Defeated Argentina: 1979 18–11; Fiji: 1980 35–10; Japan: 1974 42–23; Western Samoa: 1976 24–4; Australia: 1982 15–9
Most Capped Player A. G. Dalton 35
Number of All Blacks 14
Ranfurly Shield —
First Division Champions 1979
Club Champions on Most Occasions Manurewa

EAST COAST
Foundation 1921
Ground Whakarua Park, Ruatoria

Capacity   5000
Record Attendance   1500 on several occasions
Most Capped Player   G. Nepia   9
Number of All Blacks   2 (including George Nepia)
Ranfurly Shield   —
Club Champions on Most Occasions   Uawa

HAWKE'S BAY
Foundation   1884
Ground   McLean Park, Napier
Capacity   35 000
Record Attendance   27 000 v Wellington 1967
Major Touring Teams Defeated   Australia: 1936 20–14, 1955 14–11, 1958 8–6, 1972 15–14; England: 1963 20–5; Western Samoa: 1976 38–0
Most Capped Player   K. R. Tremain   38 (also played for Canterbury)
Number of All Blacks   40
Ranfurly Shield   1922, 1923, 1924, 1925, 1926, 1927, 1934, 1966, 1967, 1968, 1969
Club Champions on Most Occasions   Napier HSOB

HOROWHENUA
Foundation   1893
Ground   Levin Park
Capacity   12 000
Record Attendance   4500 75th Jubilee Match 1967
Major Touring Teams Defeated   Tonga: 1969 22–10; Western Samoa: 1976 17–6
Most Capped Player   J. F. Karam   10
Number of All Blacks   2
Ranfurly Shield   1927 (combined with Manawatu)
Club Champions on Most Occasions   Levin Wanderers

KING COUNTRY
Foundation   1922
Ground   Taumarunui Park
Capacity   12 500
Record Attendance   12 500 v British Lions 1977
Major Touring Teams Defeated   Fiji: 1957 26–14; British Lions: 1966 12–6 (with Wanganui)
Most Capped Player   C. E. Meads   55
Number of All Blacks   7
Ranfurly Shield   —
Club Champions on Most Occasions   Waitete

MANAWATU
Foundation   1886
Ground   Showgrounds, Palmerston North
Capacity   25 000
Record Attendance   25 000 v British Lions 1959
Major Touring Teams Defeated   Australia: 1958 12–6, 1978 20–10; Romania: 1975 28–9
Most Capped Player   G. A. Knight   34
Number of All Blacks   30
Ranfurly Shield   1927 (combined with Horowhenua) Manawatu 1976, 1977, 1978
First Division Champions   1980
Club Champions on Most Occasions   Feilding

MARLBOROUGH
Foundation   1888
Ground   Lansdowne Park, Blenheim
Capacity   15 000
Record Attendance   13 200 v Nelson Bay 1973

Major Touring Teams Defeated   France: 1968 24–19; Fiji: 1974 21–13
Most Capped Player   A. R. Sutherland   10
Number of All Blacks   6
Ranfurly Shield   1973, 1974
Club Champions on Most Occasions   Moutere

MID CANTERBURY
Foundation   1952 (other Unions from 1904)
Ground   Showgrounds, Ashburton
Capacity   10 000
Record Attendance   5500 v Australia 1964
Major Touring Teams Defeated   Australia: 1964 16–10
Most Capped Player   None
Number of All Blacks   3
Ranfurly Shield   —
Club Champions on Most Occasions   Methven

NELSON BAYS
Foundation   1885
Ground   Trafalgar Park, Nelson
Capacity   15 000
Major Touring Teams Defeated   Tonga: 1969 22–21; Italy: 1980 13–9
Most Capped Player   T. J. Morris   3
Number of All Blacks   6
Ranfurly Shield   —
Club Champions on Most Occasions   Waimea Old Boys

NORTH AUCKLAND
Foundation   1920
Ground   Okara Park, Whangarei
Capacity   40 000
Record Attendance   40 000 v Auckland 1972
Major Touring Teams Defeated   Australia: 1946 32–19, 1958 9–8; Fiji: 1980 38–4; France: 1961 8–6; Romania: 1975 3–0; Tonga: 1969 47–5
Most Capped Player   S. M. Going   29
Number of All Blacks   25
Ranfurly Shield   1950, 1951, 1960, 1971, 1972, 1978, 1979
Club Champions on Most Occasions   Whangerei

NORTH HARBOUR
Foundation   1985
Ground   Onewa Park, Takapuna
Capacity   12 000
Most Capped Player   F. M. Botica   6
Number of All Blacks   2
Ranfurly Shield   —

NORTH OTAGO
Foundation   1904
Ground   Centennial Park, Oamuru
Capacity   7000
Major Touring Teams Defeated   Australia: 1962 14–13; Tonga: 1975 30–18
Most Capped Player   I. S. T. Smith   9
Number of All Blacks   2
Ranfurly Shield   —
Club Champions on Most Occasions   Union

OTAGO
Foundation   1881

Ground   Carisbrook, Dunedin
Capacity   45 000
Record Attendance   43 500 NZ v British Lions 1959
Major Touring Teams Defeated   Australia: 1972 26–0, 1978 10–8; British Isles: 1950 23–9, 1959 26–8, 1966 17–9; England: 1963 14–9; Fiji: 1951 26–5, 1980 18–10; Scotland: 1975 19–15
Most Capped Player   K. L. Skinner 20, C. R. Laidlaw 20
Number of All Blacks   121
Ranfurly Shield   1935, 1936, 1937, 1938, 1947, 1948, 1949, 1950, 1957
Club Champions on Most Occasions   Dunedin University

POVERTY BAY
Foundation   1890
Ground   Rugby Park, Gisborne
Capacity   17 000
Record Attendance   17 000 v British Lions 1971
Major Touring Teams Defeated   Western Samoa: 1976 28–3
Most Capped Player   R. A. White   23
Number of All Blacks   6
Ranfurly Shield   —
Club Champions on Most Occasions   Gisborne Old Boys

SOUTH CANTERBURY
Foundation   1888
Ground   Fraser Park, Timaru
Capacity   17 000
Record Attendance   17 000 v France 1961
Major Touring Teams Defeated   France: 1961 17–14; Romania: 1975 12–4
Most Capped Player   T. N. Lister   8
Number of All Blacks   21
Ranfurly Shield   1950, 1974
Club Champions on Most Occasions   Temuka

SOUTHLAND
Foundation   1887
Ground   Rugby Park, Invercargill
Capacity   23 500
Record Attendance   23 500 v France 1961
Major Touring Teams Defeated   Australia: 1913 13–8, 1931 14–8, 1936 14–6, 1946 8–6, 1952 24–9, 1958 26–8, 1962 16–11, 1978 10–7; British Isles: 1950 11–0, 1966 14–8; Fiji: 1957 13–8; Japan: 1974 39–20; France: 1979 12–11
Most Capped Player   S. T. Pokere   15
Number of All Blacks   49
Ranfurly Shield   1920, 1921, 1929, 1930, 1937, 1938, 1939–46, 1959
Club Champions on Most Occasions   Star RFC

TARANAKI
Foundation   1889
Ground   Rugby Park, New Plymouth
Capacity   40 000
Record Attendance   37 100 v S. Africa 1965
Major Touring Teams Defeated   Australia: 1931 11–10; England: 1973 6–3; Italy: 1980 30–9; Western Samoa: 1976 16–0; British Isles: 1888 1–0
Most Capped Player   D. S. Loveridge   24

Number of All Blacks   66
Ranfurly Shield   1957, 1958, 1959, 1963, 1964, 1965
Club Champions on Most Occasions   Stratford

THAMES VALLEY
Foundation   1922
Ground   Paeroa Park
Capacity   5000
Record Attendance   5000 v Australia 1962 (at Te Aroha)
Major Touring Teams Defeated   Australia: 1962 16–14; Tonga: 1969 12–10; Fiji: 1951 16–6
Most Capped Player   None
Number of All Blacks   2
Ranfurly Shield   —
Club Champions on Most Occasions   Paeroa West

WAIKATO
Foundation   1921 (as South Auckland 1909)
Ground   Rugby Park, Hamilton
Capacity   32 000
Record Attendance   32 000 v S. Africa 1956
Major Touring Teams Defeated   Australia: 1972 26–34; Fiji: 1974 13–7; France: 1961 22–3, 1979 18–15; South Africa: 1956 14–10
Most Capped Player   D. B. Clarke   31
Number of All Blacks   26
Ranfurly Shield   1951, 1952, 1953, 1966, 1980
Club Champions on Most Occasions   Hamilton Old Boys

WAIRARAPA BUSH
Foundation   Wairarapa 1886; Bush 1892
Ground   Memorial Park, Masterton
Capacity   20 000
Record Attendance   12 000 v British Isles 1971 and 1983
Major Touring Teams Defeated   Australia: 1936 19–13
Most Capped Player   B. J. Lochore   25
Number of All Blacks   24
Ranfurly Shield   as Wairarapa 1927, 1928, 1929, 1950
Club Champions on Most Occasions   Red Star, Masterton

WANGANUI
Foundation   1888
Ground   Spriggins Park, Wanganui
Capacity   22 000
Record Attendance   22 000 v British Isles 1971
Major Touring Teams Defeated   Fiji: 1951 14–11, 1980 16–11; British Isles: 1966 12–6 (with King Country); Australia: 1913 11–6
Most Capped Player   W. M. Osborne   18
Number of All Blacks   16
Ranfurly Shield   —
Club Champions on Most Occasions   Kaierau

WELLINGTON
Foundation   1879
Ground   Athletic Park, Wellington
Capacity   40 000
Record Attendance   57 000 NZ v British Isles 1959
Major Touring Teams Defeated   Australia: 1905 23–7, 1931 15–8; British Isles: 1930 12–8, 1966 20–6; England: 1973 25–16; Fiji: 1980 24–8; South Africa: 1965 23–6; Scotland: 1981 19–15

Most Capped Player S. S. Wilson 34
Number of All Blacks 129
Ranfurly Shield 1904, 1905, 1914–20, 1921, 1922, 1930, 1931, 1953, 1956, 1957, 1963, 1974
First Division Champions 1978, 1981, 1986
Club Champions on Most Occasions Petone

WEST COAST
Foundation 1890

Ground Rugby Park, Greymouth
Capacity 8000
Record Attendance 5000 v British Isles 1983
Major Touring Teams Defeated Australia: 1949 17–15 and 1972 15–10 (with Buller)
Most Capped Player R. R. King 13
Number of All Blacks 7
Ranfurly Shield —
Club Champions on Most Occasions Blaketown

South Africa

Foundation 1889
Colours Green and gold shirts, white shorts
Nickname Springboks

From a purely rugby-playing view, the problems of South Africa are one of the saddest aspects of the sport. Victims of their Government's policy, the players have little or no chance to show their outstanding skills on the world stage. The last tour to Britain was in 1969–70, the last tour to Australia in 1971, the last to France in 1974, while the 1981 tour to New Zealand was undertaken amid scenes of such anti-apartheid demonstrations that further contact seemed futile. Tours to South Africa have gradually fallen away, culminating in the decision of the 1986 British Lions not to visit the Republic. An unofficial tour by the New Zealand Cavaliers as a substitute served only to alienate further the International Board countries.

Newspaper reports suggest that rugby was played in South Africa in the 1860s. It had certainly taken a strong hold in the Cape by 1875, when local teams and British soldiers were often in opposition. The game became so popular with South Africans that in 1899 they formed their own Rugby Board, and two years later were sufficiently well organized to receive a tour from Britain. The tour was the brainchild of T. B. Herold, the Western Province secretary. Cecil Rhodes, then Prime Minister of the Cape, put up what must amount to the first sponsorship, by offering to underwrite any financial losses. Bill Maclagan led a party of 20 on a record 16-day trip to Cape Town.

The statistical breakdown of the first three British tours underlined the enthusiasm and development within South Africa. Maclagan's team won all 19 matches and had just one try scored against them. John Hammond's team of 1896 won 19 of 21 matches, but lost the fourth and last international 5–0. Mark Morrison's 1903 party struggled against nearly all the home sides, losing 8 out of 22 matches. In 1906 Paul Roos' first overseas tourists left for Britain. They won 25 of their 28 fixtures, drew one and were beaten 6–0 by Scotland and 17–0 by Cardiff. Wales have still to emulate Cardiff's feat of beating South Africa.

Domestically South Africa owes a debt to Sir Donald Currie, founder of the Currie Shipping Line. He donated a cup for the best performance against Maclagan's tourists – won by Griqualand West. When the Griquas handed the cup back to the Rugby Board, it was decided to offer the Currie Cup to the winners of the inter-provincial tournament which had started in 1899. The first winners were Western Province.

Stellenbosch University have made a remarkable contribution to the strength of the domestic game. Under A. F. Markotter and, more recently, Danie Craven, they have dominated club competitions, while Cape Town University, certainly under the influence of Boy de Villiers in the early days, helped spread the game, aided by the early Cape clubs such as Villagers of Cape Town and Hamilton. Importantly, they spread the game as students and professional men to the Provinces. The Afrikaaner farming and mining centres of the Orange Free State and Northern Transvaal were particularly receptive, so that by 1906, and the return of Paul Roos' team from Britain, rugby had become the national sport, as it has remained ever since. The Springboks have

Errol Tobias, South Africa's first black international. Tobias won eight caps between 1980–4.

always – excepting the trouncing by the 1974 British Lions – been right at the forefront of world rugby, and have still to lose at home to New Zealand.

Gradual isolation and a hardening of attitudes towards South Africa has failed to dampen the enthusiasm for the game within the country. The Currie Cup attendances at Loftus Versveld, Ellis Park and Newlands are often in excess of 50 000. The Rugby Board point to the integration of the black Unions into the fixture structure. Yet the white schools sometimes still refuse to play the black schools. Rebel tours cannot succeed, though top competition must be available to encourage those at school level to continue in the game.

While the players enjoy the benefits of the intensely competitive Currie Cup and the newer Lion Cup, South Africa will continue to be barred from the international stage for the foreseeable future. Sadly a whole generation of the world's best players have been unable to pit their skills against the recent 'kings' Australia, and perennial rivals New Zealand. They have been deprived of singing in the Welsh valleys, of the unique hospitality of the Celtic races, the English pubs and clubs, and the cauldron of the Parc des Princes, with town bands and cockerels adding to the hubbub. And they missed the World Cup too.

SOUTH AFRICA – INTERNATIONAL RECORDS

TEAM RECORDS
Highest score
Overall
44 v Scotland (44–0) 1951 Murrayfield
S. Africa beat France 55–6 at Parc des Princes (Paris) on 3 January 1907, but it is not regarded as an official international match. In 1982, at Pretoria, S. Africa beat S. America 50–18, but that was not against an IB country.

v individual countries
35 v England (35–9) 1984 Johannesburg
44 v Scotland (44–0) 1951 Murrayfield
38 v Ireland (38–0) 1912 Dublin
24 v Wales (24–3) 1964 Durban
38 v France (38–5) 1913 Bordeaux
38 v France (38–25) 1975 Bloemfontein
24 v N. Zealand (24–12) 1981 Wellington
30 v Australia (30–11) 1969 Johannesburg
34 v B. Isles (34–14) 1962 Bloemfontein

Biggest winning points margin
Overall
44 v Scotland (44–0) 1951 Murrayfield
v individual countries
26 v England (35–9) 1984 Johannesburg
44 v Scotland (44–0) 1951 Murrayfield
38 v Ireland (38–0) 1912 Dublin
21 v Wales (24–3) 1964 Durban
33 v France (38–5) 1913 Bordeaux
17 v N. Zealand (17–0) 1928 Durban
25 v Australia (28-3) Johannesburg
20 v B. Isles (34–14) 1962 Bloemfontein

Highest score by opposing team
Overall
28 B. Isles (9–28) 1974 Pretoria

by individual countries
18 England (9–18) 1972 Johannesburg
10 Scotland (18–10) 1960 Port Elizabeth
15 Ireland (23–15) 1981 Cape Town
6 Wales (6–6) 1970 Cardiff
25 France (38–25) 1975 Bloemfontein
25 N. Zealand (22–25) 1981 Auckland
21 Australia (6–21) 1933 Durban
28 B. Isles (9–28) 1974 Pretoria

Biggest losing points margin
Overall
19 v B. Isles (9–28) 1974 Pretoria
v individual countries
9 v England (9–18) 1972 Johannesburg
6 v Scotland (0–6) 1906 Glasgow
3 v Ireland (6–9) 1965 Dublin
No defeat v Wales
5 v France (14–19) 1967 Johannesburg
17 v N. Zealand (3–20) 1965 Auckland
15 v Australia (6–21) 1933 Durban
19 v B. Isles (9–28) 1974 Pretoria

Most tries by South Africa in an international
10 v Ireland (38–0) 1912 Dublin
S. Africa scored 13 tries in the 'unofficial' match v France in Paris, 1907.

Most tries against South Africa in an international
5 by B. Isles (22–23) 1955 Johannesburg
5 by N. Zealand (3–20) 1965 Auckland
5 by B. Isles (9–28) 1974 Pretoria

Most points on overseas tour (all matches)
753 in Australia/N. Zealand (26 matches) 1937

Most tries on overseas tour (all matches)
161 in Australia/N Zealand (26 matches) 1937

INDIVIDUAL RECORDS
Most capped player
Overall
F. C. H. du Preez 38 1960–71
J. H. Ellis 38 1965–76
in individual positions
Full-back
L. G. Wilson 27 1960–5
Wing
J. P. Engelbrecht 33 1960–9
Centre
J. L. Gainsford 33 1960–7
Fly-half
P. J. Visagie 25[3] 1967–71
Scrum-half
D. J. de Villiers 25[4] 1962–70
Prop
J. F. K. Marais 35 1963–74
Hooker
G. F. Malan 18 1958–65
Lock
F. C. H. du Preez 31(38)[1] 1960–71
Flanker
J. H. Ellis 38 1965–76
No 8
D. J. Hopwood 22[2] 1960–5
[1]*du Preez won 7 caps as a flanker.*
[2]*T. P. Bedford, 25 caps, won 19 at No 8 and 6 as a flanker.*

Longest international career
13 seasons   J. M. Powell 1891–1903
13 seasons   B. H. Heatlie 1891–1903

Most internationals as captain
22   D. J. de Villiers   1965–70

Most points in internationals
242   H. E. Botha (21 appearances) 1980–6

Most points in international series
43   P. J. Visagie (4 appearances) v Australia 1969
H. E. Botha scored 69 points v New Zealand Cavaliers in 1986.

Most points in an international
22   G. R. Bosch v France 1975 Pretoria
D. Mare scored 22 points in the 'unofficial' match v France in Paris, 1907.

Most tries in internationals
8   J. L. Gainsford (33 appearances) 1960–7
8   J. P. Engelbrecht (33 appearances) 1960–9
D. M. Gerber has scored 15 tries, but only 6 in matches against IB countries.

Most tries in an international
3   E. E. McHardy v Ireland 1912 Dublin
3   J. A. Stegmann v Ireland 1912 Dublin
3   K. T. van Vollenhoven v B. Isles 1955 Cape Town.
3   H. J. van Zyl v Australia 1961 Johannesburg
3   R. H. Mordt v N. Zealand 1981 Auckland
3   D. M. Gerber v England 1984 Johannesburg
Gerber (v S. America at Pretoria, 1982) and Mordt (v US at Glenville, 1981) have scored 3 tries in an international against non IB countries.

Most conversions in an international
7   A. Geffin v Scotland 1951 Murrayfield

Most points for South Africa on overseas tour
190   G. H. Brand (20 appearances) 1937 Australia/N. Zealand

Most tries for South Africa on overseas tour
22   J. A. Loubser (20 appearances) 1906–7 B. Isles/France

Most points for South Africa in international series on tour
35   H. E. Botha (3 appearances) 1981 N. Zealand

Most tries for South Africa in international series on tour
6   E. E. McHardy (5 appearances) 1912–3 B. Isles/France

Most points for South Africa in any tour match
31   H. E. Botha v Nelson Bays 1981 Nelson

Most tries for South Africa in any tour match
6   R. G. Dryburgh v Queensland 1956 Brisbane

SOUTH AFRICA'S LEADING CAP WINNERS
F. C. H. Du Preez   38
J. H. Ellis   38
J. F. K. Marais   35
J. P. Engelbrecht   33
J. L. Gainsford   33
J. T. Claassen   28
F. du T. Roux   27
L. G. Wilson   27
T. P. Bedford   25
D. J. de Villiers   25
P. J. F. Greyling   25

S. H. Nomis   25
P. J. Visagie   25
L. C. Moolman   24
D. J. Hopwood   22
A. C. Koch   22
M. Du Plessis   22
J. A. du Rand   21
M. T. S. Stofberg   21
H. E. Botha   21
J. S. Germishuys   20

SPRINGBOK HEAD
The Springbok head is a trophy awarded to the first team to beat South Africa on an overseas tour.

British Isles winners
1912   Newport
1931   East Midlands
1951   London Counties
1961   Barbarians
1969   Oxford University

Australian winners
1937   New South Wales
1965   New South Wales

New Zealand winners
1921   Canterbury
1937   New Zealand
1956   Waikato
1965   Wellington
1981   New Zealand

French winners
1968   SW France
1974   W France

South Africa's record points scorer Naas Botha reveals another facet of his game, creating a break during the third test against the British Isles in 1980. Jeff Squire (left) attempts to halt Botha's progress.

NON-TEST TOUR DEFEATS IN SOUTH AFRICA

Province	Date	Opposition	Score
Cape Colony	1910	British Isles	19–0
Combined Services	1960	New Zealand	8–3
	1969	Australia	19–3
Gazelles	1981	Ireland	18–15
Johannesburg Reef & Country	1933	Australia	13–6
Junior Springboks	1958	France	9–5
	1963	Australia	12–5
Northern Provinces	1933	Australia	16–8
	1938	British Isles	26–8
Northern Universities	1963	Australia	15–9
Pretoria	1924	British Isles	6–0
	1933	Australia	13–8
South African Country XV	1981	Ireland	17–16
South African Invitation XV	1975	France	18–3
Western Province Country	1903	British Isles	13–7
Western Province Town	1903	British Isles	12–3
	1928	New Zealand	7–3
Western Province Town & Country	1924	British Isles	7–6
	1933	Australia	4–0
	1938	British Isles	11–8
Western Province Universities	1953	Australia	24–5
	1963	Australia	11–9
Western Province, SW Districts & Boland XV	1958	France	38–8
Witwatersrand	1924	British Isles	10–6

CURRIE CUP

Winners 1889-1936
1889   Western Province
1892   Western Province
1894   Western Province
1895   Western Province
1897   Western Province
1898   Western Province
1899   Griqualand West
1904   Western Province
1906   Western Province
1908   Western Province
1911   Griqualand West
1914   Western Province
1920   Western Province
1922   Transvaal
1925   Western Province
1927   Western Province
1929   Western Province
1932   Western Province and Border
1936   Western Province
Finals 1939-56
1939   Transvaal 17, Western Province 6
1946   N. Transvaal 11, Western Province 9
1947   Western Province 16, Transvaal 12
1950   Transvaal 22, Western Province 11
1952   Transvaal 11, Boland 9
1954   Western Province 11, N. Transvaal 8
1956   N. Transvaal 9, Natal 8
Winners 1959-66
1959   Western Province
1964   Western Province
1966   Western Province
Finals 1968-86
1968   Northern Transvaal 16, Transvaal 3
1969   Northern Transvaal 28, Western Province 13
1970   Griqualand West 11, Northern Transvaal 9
1971   Northern Transvaal 14, Transvaal 14
1972   Transvaal 25, Eastern Transvaal 19
1973   Northern Transvaal 30, Orange Free State 22
1974   Northern Transvaal 17, Transvaal 15
1975   Northern Transvaal 12, Orange Free State 6
1976   Orange Free State 33, Western Province 16
1977   Northern Transvaal 27, Orange Free State 12
1978   Northern Transvaal 13, Orange Free State 6
1979   Northern Transvaal 15, Western Province 15
1980   Northern Transvaal 39, Western Province 9
1981   Northern Transvaal 23, Orange Free State 6
1982   Western Province 24, Northern Transvaal 7
1983   Western Province 9, Northern Transvaal 3
1984   Western Province 19, Natal 9
1985   Western Province 22, Northern Transvaal 15
1986   Western Province 22, Transvaal 9

THE LION CUP

Organized on a knockout basis, with the smaller Unions taking part at the start, later to be joined by the stronger Unions. First held in 1983.

Lion Cup Finals
1983   Transvaal 12, Orange Free State 24
1984   Western Province 30, Orange Free State 22
1985   Orange Free State 10, Northern Transvaal 12
1986   Transvaal 22, Orange Free State 12

SOUTH AFRICA'S OLDEST CLUBS

1875   Hamiltons (WP), Villagers (WP)
1877   Buffalo (Border)
1878   Albert (Border)
1879   Gardens (WP)
1880   Stellenbosch (WP)
1881   Malmesbury (Boland), Olympic (EP)
1882   UCT (WP), Worcester (Boland), Wellington (Boland), Cradock Rovers (NEC), Swifts (Border)
1883   Paarl (WP), George (SWD), Oudtshoorn (SWD)
1884   Pirates (Griquas)
1885   Robertson (Boland), Potchefstroom (WTvl), Beaufort West (SWD)
1886   Caledon (Boland), Tulbagh (Boland), Roslyns (SARU), Young Peoples (WP)
1887   Pirates (Border), Crusader (EP), Union (SARA)
1888   Wanderers (Tvl), Pirates (Tvl), Pretoria (NTvl)

1890 Riversdale (SWD)
1892 Swifts (EP)
1893 Albany (EP), De Beers (Griquas)
1894 Diggers (Tvl)
1895 Winter Rose (SARA)
1896 Hamediehs (SARU)
1898 Moorreesburg (Boland), Tigers (SARA), Lily Whites (SARA)
1899 Porterville (Boland)

Abbreviations
EP – Eastern Province
NEC – North East Cape
NTvl – Northern Transvaal
SARA – South African Rugby Association
SARU – South African Rugby Union
SWD – South West Districts
Tvl – Transvaal
WP – Western Province
WTvl – Western Transvaal

SOUTH AFRICA – CLUB CHAMPIONSHIP

First held in 1975, the club championship takes place in the early part of the season. Club champions from the major Provinces enter a knockout tournament in April, held over weekends.

Championship Finals
1975 Stellenbosch Univ. 28, Durban Collegians 20
1976 Pretoria Univ. 19, Stellenbosch Univ. 0
1977 Stellenbosch Univ. 12, Pretoria Harlequins 10
1978 Stellenbosch Univ. 15, Pretoria Univ. 9
1979 Stellenbosch Univ. 27, Pretoria Univ. 11
1980 Villagers (Cape Town) 14, Stellenbosch Univ. 3
1981 Stellenbosch Univ. 32, Pretoria Police 9
1982 Stellenbosch Univ. 25, Rand Afrikaans Univ. 6
1983 Pretoria Harlequins 29, Pretoria Univ. 12
1984 Stellenbosch Univ. 16, Pretoria Univ. 15
1985 Despatch (nr. Port Eliz) 28, Pretoria Univ. 6
1986 Shimlas (OFS Univ.) 14, Pretoria Univ. 6
1987 Western Province Defence 26, Despatch 8

SOUTH AFRICA – DOMESTIC RECORDS

CURRIE CUP
Highest score
Transvaal 99, Far North 9   1973

Highest winning margin
Transvaal 99, Far North 9   1973 (also highest match aggregate)

Most points
36   Gerald Bosch, Transvaal v Far North   1973

Most tries
6 Buks Marais, Boland v North Eastern Districts 1952

FIRST CLASS RECORDS
Highest score in a first-class match
Orange Free State 132, Eastern Free State 3 – inter-Provincial friendly, 1977
The margin of victory, match aggregate and second-half score of 76 points (half-time 56–0) are also records, as are the 23 tries and 20 conversions scored by OFS.

Most individual points in a match
48   De Wet Ras, Orange Free State v Eastern Free State   1977

Highest score in a First Division club match
Ammosal 160, Defence 6   1977

Most tries in a First Division club match
29   Ammosal v Defence   1977

Most individual points and tries in a First Division club match
80 points   Jannie Van der Westhuizen, Carnarvon v Williston   1972
14 tries   Jannie Van der Westhuizen, Carnarvon v Williston   1972

SOUTH AFRICA – THE UNIONS

BOLAND
Foundation   1939
Ground   Wellington
Capacity   23 000
Major Touring Sides Defeated   Australia: 1969 12–3
Most Capped Player   A. C. Koch   22
Number of Springboks   8

BORDER
Foundation   1891
Ground   East London
Capacity   22 000
Record Attendance   18 500 v British Isles 1974
Major Touring Sides Defeated   New Zealand: 1949 9–0; British Isles: 1955 14–12
Most Capped Player   J. White 10
Number of Springboks   14

EASTERN PROVINCE
Foundation   1888
Ground   Boet Erasmus Stadium, Port Elizabeth
Capacity   40 000
Record Attendance   40 000 South Africa v British Isles 1980
Major Touring Sides Defeated   British Isles: 1924 14–6, 1955 20–0
Most Capped Player   D. M. Gerber   19
Number of Springboks   29
National Club Champions   Despatch 1985

FAR NORTH
Foundation   1967
Ground   Pietersburg
Capacity   8000
Capped Players   None
Number of Springboks   None

GRIQUALAND WEST
Foundation   1896
Ground   De Beers Stadium, Kimberley
Capacity   27 000
Record Attendance   27 000 v Northern Transvaal 1970
Major Touring Sides Defeated   British Isles: 1903 8–6, 1903 11–0, 1910 8–0, 1910 9–3; Australia: 1933 14–9, 1953 13–3, 1969 21–13; France: 1967 20–14
Most Capped Player   P. J. Visagie 25
Number of Springboks   45

NATAL
Foundation   1890
Ground   King's Park, Durban
Capacity   48 000
Record Attendance   48 000   South Africa v New Zealand Cavaliers 1986
Major Touring Sides Defeated   Australia: 1953 15–14, 1963 14–13, 1969 19–14
Most Capped Player   T. P. Bedford 25
Number of Springboks   26

NORTHERN NATAL
Foundation   1973
Ground   Vryheid
Capacity   10 000
Major Touring Sides Defeated   South America: 1984 16–9 (with E. Transvaal)
Capped Players   None
Number of Springboks   None

NORTH EAST CAPE
Foundation   1966 (N.E. Districts founded in 1903)
Ground   Cradock
Capacity   14 000
Capped Players   None
Number of Springboks   None

NORTH WEST CAPE
Foundation   1968
Ground   Upington
Capacity   12 000
Capped Players   None
Number of Springboks   None

ORANGE FREE STATE
Foundation   1895
Ground   Free State Stadium, Bloemfontein
Capacity   47 000
Record Attendance   47 000 v several Tourists
Major Touring Sides Defeated   British Isles: 1924 6–3; Australia: 1953 23–13, 1953 28–3, 1963 14–8; New Zealand: 1960 9–8, 1976 15–10
Most Capped Players   P. J. F. Greyling 25, J. S. Germishuys 20
Number of Springboks   42
National Club Champions   Shimlas (University of Orange Free State) 1986
Lion Cup Wins   1983

EASTERN ORANGE FREE STATE
Foundation   1968
Ground   Harrismith
Capacity   5000
Capped Players   None
Number of Springboks   None

NORTHERN ORANGE FREE STATE
Foundation   1968
Ground   North West Stadium, Welkom
Capacity   20 000
Record Attendance   12 500 v Western Province   1986
Major Touring Sides Defeated   British Isles: 1924 6–0 (as OFS Country XV)
Capped Players   None
Number of Springboks   None

SOUTH AFRICAN RUGBY FEDERATION*
Foundation   1959
Most Capped Player   E. Tobias   11
Number of Springboks   3
Now Winelands and Western Province League (as from 1986).

SOUTH WEST AFRICA
Foundation   1916 (as Damaraland – SW Africa from 1952)
Ground   Windhoek Stadium
Capacity   26 000
Most Capped Player   J. H. Ellis   38   (record)
Number of Springboks   3

SOUTH WEST DISTRICTS
Foundation   1889
Ground   Outshoorn
Capacity   10 000
Record Attendance   10 000 v British Lions   1974
Most Capped Player   W. F. Bergh   17
Number of Springboks   3

STELLALAND
Foundation   1975
Ground   Litchenburg
Capacity   5000
Capped Players   None
Number of Springboks   None

TRANSVAAL
Foundation   1889
Ground   Wanderers and Ellis Park (both Johannesburg)
Capacity   Ellis Park 104 000
Record Attendance   100 000   South Africa v British Isles   1955
Major Touring Sides Defeated   British Isles: 1903 12–3, 1903 14–4, 1910 27–8, 1910 13–6, 1938 16–9, 1968 14–6; New Zealand: 1928 6–0; Australia: 1933 11–9, 1953 20–14, 1969 23–14, France 1975 28–22
Most Capped Player   S. H. Nomis   25
Number of Springboks   110
Lion Cup Wins   1986

EASTERN TRANSVAAL
Foundation   1947
Ground   Pam Brink Stadium, Springs
Capacity   25 000

Record Attendance 30 000 South Africa v France 1964
Major Touring Sides Defeated New Zealand: 1949 6–5; British Isles: 1962 19–16
Most Capped Player N. Riley 1
Number of Springboks 5

NORTHERN TRANSVAAL
Foundation 1938
Ground Loftus Versveld, Pretoria
Capacity 68 500
Record Attendance 68 500 on several occasions
Major Touring Sides Defeated Australia: 1953 27–11, 1969 13–3; British Isles: 1962 14–6; Wales: 1964 22–9; France: 1967 19–5; New Zealand: 1976 29–27
Most Capped Player F. C. H. Du Preez 38 (record)
Number of Springboks 50
Lion Cup Wins 1985
National Club Champions Pretoria University 1976; Pretoria Harlequins 1983

SOUTH EAST TRANSVAAL
Foundation 1968
Ground Middleburg
Capacity 10 000
Most Capped Player T. T. Fourie 1
Number of Springboks 1

WESTERN TRANSVAAL
Foundation 1920
Ground Olen Stadium, Potchefstroom
Capacity 20 000
Major Touring Sides Defeated British Isles: 1955 9–6;

France: 1958 19–18 (with N. Transvaal); Australia: 1969 18–6
Most Capped Player J. T. Classen 28
Number of Springboks 8

VAAL TRIANGLE
Foundation 1983 (formerly part of Transvaal RU)
Ground D P de Villiers Stadium, Sasolburg
Capacity 12 000
Capped Players None
Number of Springboks None

WESTERN PROVINCE
Foundation 1883
Ground Newlands, Cape Town
Capacity 58 000
Record Attendance 58 000 on several occasions
Major Touring Sides Defeated British Isles: 1903 8–4, 1910 8–0, 1938 21–11; New Zealand: 1928 10–3, 1976 12–11; Australia: 1933 13–9, 1963 12–6; France: 1964 29–11
Most Capped Players J. F. K. Marais 35, J. L. Gainsford 33, J. P. Engelbrecht 33, L. G. Wilson 27, F. du T. Roux 27, D. J. de Villiers 25, D. J. Hopwood 22, M du Plessis 22, D. J. Serfontein 19, R. J. Louw 18, H. P. J. Bekker 15
Number of Springboks 197
Lion Cup Wins 1984
National Club Champions Stellenbosch University 1975, 1977, 1978, 1979, 1981, 1982, 1984; Villagers 1980; Defence 1987

Other Unions: Lowveld, founded 1985, play at Nelspruit; South African Rugby Association, founded 1935, 266 clubs, 26 000 players.

3 INTERNATIONAL BOARD COUNTRIES – MATCH RECORDS

This section sets out the complete results of matches between International Board Countries. The score, date, and venue are listed, plus a new feature, the listing of every points scorer for every international. The records are up to 20 May 1987, and exclude World Cup.

Points system: *1875* 3 touchdowns = 1 try, 3 tries = 1 goal. *1886* Ireland, Scotland, Wales introduced points scoring, but points values varied until England joined the other countries and adopted the new IB's uniform system. *1887* T – 1 pt, G – 3 pts. The system changed as follows:

	T	C	PG	DG	GM
1890–1	1	2	2	3	3
1891–3	2	3	3	4	4
1893–1905	3	2	3	4	4
1905–48	3	2	3	4	3
1948–71	3	2	3	3	3
1971	4	2	3	3	3

Abbreviations: t/T – try, g – goal, C – conversion, PG – penalty goal, DG – dropped goal, gm/GM – goal from a mark

England v Ireland

5 Feb 1883, Whalley Range, Manchester
ENGLAND   1g 3t   T: Bolton, Tatham,
                       Twynam, Wade
                       C: Evanson
IRELAND   1t   T: Forrest

4 Feb 1884, Lansdowne Road, Dublin
IRELAND   0
ENGLAND   1g   T: Bolton
                       C: Sample

7 Feb 1885, Whalley Range, Manchester
ENGLAND   2t   T: Bolton, Hawcridge
IRELAND   1t   T: Greene

6 Feb 1886, Lansdowne Road, Dublin
IRELAND   0
ENGLAND   1t   T: Wilkinson

5 Feb 1887, Lansdowne Road, Dublin
IRELAND   2g   T: Montgomery, Tillie
                       C: Rambaut (2)
ENGLAND   0

15 Mar 1890, Rectory Field, Blackheath
ENGLAND   3t   T: Rogers, Morrison,
                       Stoddart
IRELAND   0

7 Feb 1891, Lansdowne Road, Dublin
IRELAND   0
ENGLAND   9   T: Lockwood (2), Wilson (2)
                       Toothill
                       C: Lockwood (2)

6 Feb 1892, Whalley Range, Manchester
ENGLAND   7   T: Evershed, Percival
                       C: Woods
IRELAND   0

4 Feb 1893, Lansdowne Road, Dublin
IRELAND   0
ENGLAND   4   T: Bradshaw, Taylor

3 Feb 1894, Rectory Field, Blackheath
ENGLAND   5   T: Lockwood
                       C: Taylor
IRELAND   7   T: John Lytle
                       DG: Forrest

2 Feb 1895, Lansdowne Road, Dublin
IRELAND   3   T: L. Magee
ENGLAND   6   T: Fegan, Thomas

1 Feb 1896, Meanwood Road, Leeds
ENGLAND   4   DG: Byrne
IRELAND   10   T: Sealy, Stevenson
                       C: Bulger

6 Feb 1897, Lansdowne Road, Dublin
IRELAND   13   T: Gardiner (2), Bulger
                       GM: Bulger
ENGLAND   9   T: Robinson
                       PG: Byrne (2)

5 Feb 1898, Athletic Ground, Richmond
ENGLAND   6   T: Robinson
                       PG: Byrne
IRELAND   9   T: Lindsay, Magee
                       PG: Bulger

4 Feb 1899, Lansdowne Road, Dublin
IRELAND   6   T: Allen
                       PG: Magee
ENGLAND   0

3 Feb 1900, Athletic Ground, Richmond
ENGLAND   15   T: Robinson (2),
                       Gordon-Smith
                       C: Alexander
                       DG: Gordon-Smith
IRELAND   4   DG: Allison

9 Feb 1901, Lansdowne Road, Dublin
IRELAND   10   T: Davidson, Gardiner
                       C: Irwin (2)
ENGLAND   6   T: Robinson
                       PG: Alexander

8 Feb 1902, Welford Road, Leicester
ENGLAND   6   T: Coopper, Williams
IRELAND   3   T: F. Gardiner

14 Feb 1903, Lansdowne Road, Dublin
IRELAND   6   T: Ryan
                       PG: Corley
ENGLAND   0

13 Feb 1904, Rectory Field, Blackheath
ENGLAND   19   T: Moore (2), Vivyan (2),
                       Simpson
                       C: Vivyan (2)
IRELAND   0

11 Feb 1905, Mardyke, Cork
IRELAND   17   T: Moffatt (2), Allen,
                       Maclear, Wallace
                       C: Maclear
ENGLAND   3   T: Coopper

10 Feb 1906, Welford Road, Leicester
ENGLAND   6   T: Jago, Mills
IRELAND   16   T: Tedford (2), Maclear,
                       Purdon
                       C: Gardiner, Maclear

9 Feb 1907, Lansdowne Road, Dublin
IRELAND   17   T: Caddell (2), Tedford,
                       Thrift
                       C: Parke
                       GM: Parke
ENGLAND   9   T: Imrie, Slocock
                       PG: Pickering

8 Feb 1908, Athletic Ground, Richmond
ENGLAND   13   T: Hudson (2), Williamson
                       C: Wood (2)
IRELAND   3   PG: Parke

13 Feb 1909, Lansdowne Road, Dublin
IRELAND   5   T: Parke
                       C: Pinion
ENGLAND   11   T: Palmer (2), Mobbs
                       C: Palmer

12 Feb 1910, Twickenham
| ENGLAND | 0 | |
| IRELAND | 0 | |

11 Feb 1911, Lansdowne Road, Dublin
| IRELAND | 3 | T: Tom Smyth |
| ENGLAND | 0 | |

10 Feb 1912, Twickenham
| ENGLAND | 15 | T: Roberts (2), Birkett, Brougham, Poulton |
| IRELAND | 0 | |

8 Feb 1913, Lansdowne Road, Dublin
IRELAND	4	DG: Lloyd
ENGLAND	15	T: Coates (2), Pillman, Ritson
		PG: Greenwood

14 Feb 1914, Twickenham
ENGLAND	17	T: Lowe (2), Davies, Pillman, Roberts
		C: Chapman
IRELAND	12	T: Jackson, Quinn
		C: Lloyd
		DG: Lloyd

14 Feb 1920, Lansdowne Road, Dublin
IRELAND	11	T: Dickson, Lloyd
		C: Lloyd
		PG: Lloyd
ENGLAND	14	T: Lowe, Mellish, Myers, Wakefield
		C: Greenwood

12 Feb 1921, Twickenham
ENGLAND	15	T: Blakiston, Brown, Lowe
		C: Cumberlege
		DG: Lowe
IRELAND	0	

11 Feb 1922, Lansdowne Road, Dublin
| IRELAND | 3 | T: Wallis |
| ENGLAND | 12 | T: Lowe, Gardner, Maxwell-Hyslop, Smallwood |

10 Feb 1923, Welford Road, Leicester
ENGLAND	23	T: Lowe, Corbett, Price, Smallwood, Voyce
		C: Conway (2)
		DG: Davies
IRELAND	5	T: McClelland
		C: Crawford

9 Feb 1924, Ravenhill, Belfast
IRELAND	3	T: Douglas
ENGLAND	14	T: Catcheside (2), Corbett, Hamilton-Wickes
		C: Conway

14 Feb 1925, Twickenham
| ENGLAND | 6 | T: Smallwood (2) |
| IRELAND | 6 | T: T. Hewitt, H. Stephenson |

13 Feb 1926, Lansdowne Road, Dublin
IRELAND	19	T: Cussen (2), F. Hewitt, G. Stephenson
		C: G. Stephenson (2)
		PG: G. Stephenson
ENGLAND	15	T: Haslett, Periton, Young
		C: Francis (3)

12 Feb 1927, Twickenham
ENGLAND	8	T: Gibbs, Laird
		C: Stanbury
IRELAND	6	T: H. McVicker
		PG: G. Stephenson

11 Feb 1928, Lansdowne Road, Dublin
IRELAND	6	T: Arigho, Sugden
ENGLAND	7	T: Richardson
		DG: Richardson

9 Feb 1929, Twickenham
ENGLAND	5	T: Smeddle
		C: Wilson
IRELAND	6	T: Davy, Sugden

8 Feb 1930, Lansdowne Road, Dublin
| IRELAND | 4 | DG: Murray |
| ENGLAND | 3 | T: Novis |

14 Feb 1931, Twickenham
ENGLAND	5	T: Black
		C: Black
IRELAND	6	T: McMahon
		PG: Murray

13 Feb 1932, Lansdowne Road, Dublin
IRELAND	8	T: Waide
		C: Murray
		PG: Murray
ENGLAND	11	T: Burland
		C: Burland
		PG: Burland (2)

11 Feb 1933, Twickenham
ENGLAND	17	T: Novis (2), Booth, Gadney, Sadler
		C: Kendrew
IRELAND	6	T: Hunt
		PG: Murray

10 Feb 1934, Lansdowne Road, Dublin
IRELAND	3	T: Morgan
ENGLAND	13	T: Fry (2), Meikle
		C: Gregory (2)

9 Feb 1935, Twickenham
ENGLAND	14	T: Giles
		C: Boughton
		PG: Boughton (3)
IRELAND	3	T: O'Connor

8 Feb 1936, Lansdowne Road, Dublin
| IRELAND | 6 | T: Bailey, Boyle |
| ENGLAND | 3 | T: Sever |

13 Feb 1937, Twickenham
ENGLAND	9	T: Butler, Sever
		PG: Cranmer
IRELAND	8	T: Moran (2)
		C: Bailey

12 Feb 1938, Lansdowne Road, Dublin
IRELAND	14	T: Bailey, Cromey, Daly, Mayne
		C: Crowe
ENGLAND	36	T: Giles, Bolton, Marshall, Nicholson, Prescott, Reynolds, Unwin
		C: Parker (6)
		PG: Parker

11 Feb 1939, Twickenham
ENGLAND 0
IRELAND 5 T: Irwin
C: McKibbin

8 Feb 1947, Lansdowne Road, Dublin
IRELAND 22 T: O'Hanlon (2), Mullan
(2), McKay
C: Mullan (2)
PG: Mullan
ENGLAND 0

14 Feb 1948, Twickenham
ENGLAND 10 T: Guest (2)
C: Uren (2)
IRELAND 11 T: Kyle, McKay, McKee
C: Mullan

12 Feb 1949, Lansdowne Road, Dublin
IRELAND 14 T: O'Hanlon, McKee
C: Norton
PG: Norton (2)
ENGLAND 5 T: van Ryneveld
C: Holmes

11 Feb 1950, Twickenham
ENGLAND 3 T: Roberts
IRELAND 0

10 Feb 1951, Lansdowne Road, Dublin
IRELAND 3 PG: McKibbin
ENGLAND 0

29 Mar 1952, Twickenham
ENGLAND 3 T: Boobyer
IRELAND 0

14 Feb 1953, Lansdowne Road, Dublin
IRELAND 9 T: Mortell
PG: Henderson (2)
ENGLAND 9 T: Evans
PG: Hall (2)

13 Feb 1954, Twickenham
ENGLAND 14 T: Butterfield, Regan,
Wilson
C: King
PG: King
IRELAND 3 PG: Murphy-O'Connor

12 Feb 1955, Lansdowne Road, Dublin
IRELAND 6 T: O'Reilly
PG: Henderson
ENGLAND 6 T: Butterfield, Hastings

11 Feb 1956, Twickenham
ENGLAND 20 T: Butterfield, Evans,
Jackson
C: Currie
PG: Currie (2), Allison
IRELAND 0

9 Feb 1957, Lansdowne Road, Dublin
IRELAND 0
ENGLAND 6 T: Jackson
PG: Challis

8 Feb 1958, Twickenham
ENGLAND 6 T: Ashcroft
PG: Hetherington
IRELAND 0

14 Feb 1959, Lansdowne Road, Dublin
IRELAND 0
ENGLAND 3 PG: Risman

13 Feb 1960, Twickenham
ENGLAND 8 T: Marques
C: Rutherford
DG: Sharp
IRELAND 5 T: Culliton
C: Kiernan

11 Feb 1961, Lansdowne Road, Dublin
IRELAND 11 T: Kavanagh
C: Moffett
PG: Moffett (2)
ENGLAND 8 T: Roberts, Rogers
C: Risman

10 Feb 1962, Twickenham
ENGLAND 16 T: Roberts, Sharp, Wade
C: Sharp (2)
PG: Sharp
IRELAND 0

9 Feb 1963, Lansdowne Road, Dublin
IRELAND 0
ENGLAND 0

8 Feb 1964, Twickenham
ENGLAND 5 T: Rogers
C: Willcox
IRELAND 18 T: Flynn (2), Casey, Murphy
C: Kiernan (3)

13 Feb 1965, Lansdowne Road, Dublin
IRELAND 5 T: Lamont
C: Kiernan
ENGLAND 0

12 Feb 1966, Twickenham
ENGLAND 6 T: Greenwood
PG: Rutherford
IRELAND 6 T: McGrath
PG: Kiernan

11 Feb 1967, Lansdowne Road, Dublin
IRELAND 3 PG: Kiernan
ENGLAND 8 T: McFadyean
C: Hosen
PG: Hosen

10 Feb 1968, Twickenham
ENGLAND 9 DG: Finlan
PG: Hiller (2)
IRELAND 9 PG: Kiernan (3)

8 Feb 1969, Lansdowne Road, Dublin
IRELAND 17 T: Bresnihan, Murphy
C: Kiernan (2)
DG: McGann
PG: Kiernan
ENGLAND 15 T: Duckham
PG: Hiller (4)

14 Feb 1970, Twickenham
ENGLAND 9 T: Shackleton
DG: Hiller (2)
IRELAND 3 PG: Kiernan

13 Feb 1971, Lansdowne Road, Dublin
IRELAND	6	T: Duggan, Grant
ENGLAND	9	PG: Hiller (3)

12 Feb 1972, Twickenham
ENGLAND	12	T: Ralston
		C: Hiller
		PG: Hiller (2)
IRELAND	16	T: Flynn, Grace
		C: Kiernan
		DG: McGann
		PG: Kiernan

10 Feb 1973, Lansdowne Road, Dublin
IRELAND	18	T: Grace, Milliken
		C: McGann (2)
		DG: McGann
		PG: McGann
ENGLAND	9	T: Neary
		C: Jorden
		PG: Jorden

16 Feb 1974, Twickenham
ENGLAND	21	T: Squires
		C: Old
		PG: Old (5)
IRELAND	26	T: Gibson (2), Moloney, Moore
		C: Gibson (2)
		DG: Quinn
		PG: Ensor

18 Jan 1975, Lansdowne Road, Dublin
IRELAND	12	T: Gibson, McCombe
		C: McCombe (2)
ENGLAND	9	T: Stevens
		C: Old
		DG: Old

6 Mar 1976, Twickenham
ENGLAND	12	PG: Old (4)
IRELAND	13	T: Grace
		DG: McGann
		PG: McGann (2)

5 Feb 1977, Lansdowne Road, Dublin
IRELAND	0	
ENGLAND	4	T: Cooper

18 Mar 1978, Twickenham
ENGLAND	15	T: Dixon, Slemen
		C: Young (2)
		PG: Young
IRELAND	9	DG: Ward
		PG: Ward (2)

17 Feb 1979, Lansdowne Road, Dublin
IRELAND	12	T: MacLennan
		C: Ward
		DG: Ward
		PG: Ward
ENGLAND	7	T: Bennett
		PG: Bennett

19 Jan 1980, Twickenham
ENGLAND	24	T: Scott, Slemen, Smith
		C: Hare (3)
		PG: Hare (2)
IRELAND	9	PG: Campbell (3)

7 Mar 1981, Lansdowne Road, Dublin
IRELAND	6	DG: Campbell, MacNeill
ENGLAND	10	T: Dodge, Rose
		C: Rose

6 Feb 1982, Twickenham
ENGLAND	15	T: Slemen
		C: Rose
		PG: Rose (3)
IRELAND	16	T: MacNeill, McLoughlin
		C: Campbell
		PG: Campbell (2)

19 Mar 1983, Lansdowne Road, Dublin
IRELAND	25	T: Slattery, Campbell
		C: Campbell
		PG: Campbell (5)
ENGLAND	15	PG: Hare (5)

18 Feb 1984, Twickenham
ENGLAND	12	PG: Hare (3)
		DG: Cusworth
IRELAND	9	PG: Ward (3)

30 Mar 1985, Lansdowne Road, Dublin
IRELAND	13	T: Mullin
		PG: Kiernan (2)
		DG: Kiernan
ENGLAND	10	T: Underwood
		PG: Andrew (2)

1 Mar 1986, Twickenham
ENGLAND	25	T: Richards (2), Penalty try, Davies
		C: Andrew (3)
		PG: Andrew
IRELAND	20	T: Ringland, Mullin, McCall
		C: Kiernan
		PG: Kiernan

7 Feb 1987, Lansdowne Road, Dublin
IRELAND	17	T: Kiernan, Matthews, Crossan
		C: Kiernan
		PG: Kiernan
ENGLAND	0	

England v Scotland

THE CALCUTTA CUP

3 Mar 1883, Raeburn Place, Edinburgh
SCOTLAND	1t	T: Reid
ENGLAND	2t	T: Rotherham, Bolton

1 Mar 1884, Rectory Field, Blackheath
ENGLAND	1g	T: Kindersley
		C: Bolton
SCOTLAND	1t	T: Jamieson

13 Mar 1886, Raeburn Place, Edinburgh
SCOTLAND	0	
ENGLAND	0	

5 Mar 1887, Whalley Range, Manchester
ENGLAND   1t   T: Jeffery
SCOTLAND   1t   T: Morton

1 Mar 1890, Raeburn Place, Edinburgh
SCOTLAND   0
ENGLAND   1g 1t   T: Evershed, Dyson
                        C: Jowett

7 Mar 1891, Athletic Ground, Richmond
ENGLAND   3   T: Lockwood
                    C: Alderson
SCOTLAND   9   T: W. Neilson, J. E. Orr
                    C: MacGregor (2)
                    DG: Clauss

5 Mar 1892, Raeburn Place, Edinburgh
SCOTLAND   0
ENGLAND   5   T: Bromet
                    C: Lockwood

4 Mar 1893, Headingley, Leeds
ENGLAND   0
SCOTLAND   8   DG: Boswell, Campbell

17 Mar 1894, Raeburn Place, Edinburgh
SCOTLAND   6   T: Boswell (2)
ENGLAND   0

9 Mar 1895, Athletic Ground, Richmond
ENGLAND   3   PG: Byrne
SCOTLAND   6   T: G. T. Neilson,
                    PG: G. T. Neilson

14 Mar 1896, Old Hampden Park, Glasgow
SCOTLAND   11   T: Fleming, Gedge, Gowans
                     C: Scott
ENGLAND   0

13 Mar 1897, Fallowfield, Manchester
ENGLAND   12   T: Fookes, Robinson
                     C: Byrne
                     DG: Byrne
SCOTLAND   3   T: Bucher

12 Mar 1898, Powderhall, Edinburgh
SCOTLAND   3   T: McEwan
ENGLAND   3   T: Royds

11 Mar 1899, Rectory Field, Blackheath
ENGLAND   0
SCOTLAND   5   T: Gillespie
                    C: Thomson

10 Mar 1900, Inverleith, Edinburgh
SCOTLAND   0
ENGLAND   0

9 Mar 1901, Rectory Field, Blackheath
ENGLAND   3   T: Robinson
SCOTLAND   18   T: Gillespie, Welsh, Timms,
                     Fell
                     C: Gillespie (3)

15 Mar 1902, Inverleith, Edinburgh
SCOTLAND   3   T: Fell
ENGLAND   6   T: Williams, Taylor

21 Mar 1903, Athletic Ground, Richmond
ENGLAND   6   T: Dobson, Forrest
SCOTLAND   10   T: Dallas, Simson
                     DG: Timms

19 Mar 1904, Inverleith, Edinburgh
SCOTLAND   6   T: Crabbie, Macdonald
ENGLAND   3   T: Vivyan

18 Mar 1905, Athletic Ground, Richmond
ENGLAND   0
SCOTLAND   8   T: Simson, Stronach
                    C: Scott

17 Mar 1906, Inverleith, Edinburgh
SCOTLAND   3   T: Purves
ENGLAND   9   T: Mills, Raphael, Simpson

16 Mar 1907, Rectory Field, Blackheath
ENGLAND   3   T: Peters
SCOTLAND   8   T: Purves, Simson
                    C: Geddes

21 Mar 1908, Inverleith, Edinburgh
SCOTLAND   16   T: MacLeod (2)
                     C: Geddes
                     DG: Purves, Schulze
ENGLAND   10   T: Birkett, Slocock
                     C: Lambert (2)

20 Mar 1909, Athletic Ground, Richmond
ENGLAND   8   T: Mobbs, Watson
                    C: Palmer
SCOTLAND   18   T: Tennent (2), Gilray,
                     Simson
                     C: Cunningham (3)

19 Mar 1910, Inverleith, Edinburgh
SCOTLAND   5   T: Macpherson
                    C: MacCallum
ENGLAND   14   T: Birkett (2), Berry, Ritson
                     C: Chapman

18 Mar 1911, Twickenham
ENGLAND   13   T: Birkett, Lawrie,
                     Wodehouse
                     C: Lagden (2)
SCOTLAND   8   T: Simson, Sutherland
                    C: Cunningham

16 Mar 1912, Inverleith, Edinburgh
SCOTLAND   8   T: Sutherland, Usher
                    C: MacCallum
ENGLAND   3   T: Holland

15 Mar 1913, Twickenham
ENGLAND   3   T: Brown
SCOTLAND   0

21 Mar 1914, Inverleith, Edinburgh
SCOTLAND   15   T: Will (2), Huggan
                     C: Turner
                     DG: Bowie
ENGLAND   16   T: Lowe (3), Poulton
                     C: Harrison (2)

20 Mar 1920, Twickenham
ENGLAND   13   T: Harris, Kershaw, Lowe
                     C: Greenwood (2)
SCOTLAND   4   DG: Bruce-Lockhart

19 Mar 1921, Inverleith, Edinburgh
SCOTLAND   0
ENGLAND   18   T: Brown, Edwards, King,
                     Woods
                     C: Hammett (3)

18 Mar 1922, Twickenham
ENGLAND	11	T: Lowe (2), Davies
		C: Conway
SCOTLAND	5	T: Dykes
		C: Bertram

2 Apr 1923, Inverleith, Edinburgh
SCOTLAND	6	T: Gracie, McLaren
ENGLAND	8	T: Smallwood, Voyce
		C: Luddington

15 Mar 1924, Twickenham
ENGLAND	19	T: Catcheside, Myers, Wakefield
		C: Conway (3)
		DG: Myers
SCOTLAND	0	

21 Mar 1925, Murrayfield, Edinburgh
SCOTLAND	14	T: Nelson, Wallace
		C: Drysdale, Gillies
		DG: Waddell
ENGLAND	11	T: Hamilton-Wickes, Wakefield
		C: Luddington
		PG: Luddington

20 Mar 1926, Twickenham
ENGLAND	9	T: Tucker, Voyce, Webb
SCOTLAND	17	T: Smith (2), Waddell
		C: Waddell (2)
		DG: Dykes

19 Mar 1927, Murrayfield
SCOTLAND	21	T: Smith (2), Dykes, Macpherson, Scott
		C: Gillies
		DG: Waddell
ENGLAND	13	T: Gibbs, Laird
		C: Stanbury, Stark
		PG: Stark

17 Mar 1928, Twickenham
ENGLAND	6	T: Hanley, Laird
SCOTLAND	0	

16 Mar 1929, Murrayfield
SCOTLAND	12	T: Ian Smith (2), Brown, Nelson
ENGLAND	6	T: Meikle, Novis

15 Mar 1930, Twickenham
ENGLAND	0	
SCOTLAND	0	

21 Mar 1931, Murrayfield
SCOTLAND	28	T: Mackintosh (2), Smith (2), Ford, Logan
		C: Allan (5)
ENGLAND	19	T: Tallent (2), Reeve (2)
		C: Black (2)
		PG: Black

19 Mar 1932, Twickenham
ENGLAND	16	T: Aavold (2), Black, Tanner
		C: Burland (2)
SCOTLAND	3	T: Smith

18 Mar 1933, Murrayfield
SCOTLAND	3	T: Fyfe
ENGLAND	0	

17 Mar 1934, Twickenham
ENGLAND	6	T: Booth, Meikle
SCOTLAND	3	T: Shaw

16 Mar 1935, Murrayfield
SCOTLAND	10	T: Fyfe, Lambie
		C: Fyfe (2)
ENGLAND	7	T: Booth
		DG: Cranmer

21 Mar 1936, Twickenham
ENGLAND	9	T: Bolton, Candler, Cranmer
SCOTLAND	8	T: Shaw
		C: Fyfe
		PG: Fyfe

20 Mar 1937, Murrayfield
SCOTLAND	3	PG: Duncan Shaw
ENGLAND	6	T: Sever, Unwin

19 Mar 1938, Twickenham
ENGLAND	16	T: Unwin
		DG: Reynolds
		PG: Parker (3)
SCOTLAND	21	T: Renwick (2), Shaw (2), Dick
		PG: Crawford (2)

18 Mar 1939, Murrayfield
SCOTLAND	6	T: Murdoch, Shaw
ENGLAND	9	PG: Heaton (3)

15 Mar 1947, Twickenham
ENGLAND	24	T: Bennett, Guest, Henderson, Holmes
		C: Heaton (4)
		DG: Hall
SCOTLAND	5	T: Jackson
		C: Geddes

20 Mar 1948, Murrayfield
SCOTLAND	6	T: Drummond, Young
ENGLAND	3	PG: Uren

19 Mar 1949, Twickenham
ENGLAND	19	T: van Ryneveld (2), Guest, Hosking, Kennedy
		C: Travers (2)
SCOTLAND	3	PG: Wilson

18 Mar 1950, Murrayfield
SCOTLAND	13	T: Sloan (2), Abercrombie
		C: Gray (2)
ENGLAND	11	T: Smith (2)
		C: Hofmeyr
		PG: Hofmeyr

17 Mar 1951, Twickenham
ENGLAND	5	T: White
		C: Hook
SCOTLAND	3	T: Cameron

15 Mar 1952, Murrayfield
SCOTLAND   3   T: Johnston
ENGLAND   19   T: Evans, Kendall-
Carpenter, Winn,
Woodward
C: Hall (2)
DG: Agar

21 Mar 1953, Twickenham
ENGLAND   26   T: Bazley (2), Adkins,
Butterfield, Stirling,
Woodward
C: Hall (4)
SCOTLAND   8   T: Henderson,
Weatherstone
C: Thomson

20 Mar 1954, Murrayfield
SCOTLAND   3   T: Elgie
ENGLAND   13   T: Wilson (2), Young
C: Gibbs (2)

19 Mar 1955, Twickenham
ENGLAND   9   T: Beer, Sykes
PG: Hazell
SCOTLAND   6   T: Cameron
PG: Cameron

17 Mar 1956, Murrayfield
SCOTLAND   6   T: Stevenson
PG: Smith
ENGLAND   11   T: Wiliams
C: Currie
PG: Currie (2)

16 Mar 1957, Twickenham
ENGLAND   16   T: Davies, Higgins,
Thompson
C: Challis (2)
PG: Challis
SCOTLAND   3   PG: Scotland

15 Mar 1958, Murrayfield
SCOTLAND   3   PG: Elliott
ENGLAND   3   PG: Hastings

21 Mar 1959, Twickenham
ENGLAND   3   PG: Risman
SCOTLAND   3   PG: Scotland

19 Mar 1960, Murrayfield
SCOTLAND   12   T: Arthur Smith
PG: Scotland (3)
ENGLAND   21   T: Roberts, Syrett, Young
C: Rutherford (3)
DG: Sharp
PG: Rutherford

18 Mar 1961, Twickenham
ENGLAND   6   T: Roberts
PG: Horrocks-Taylor
SCOTLAND   0

17 Mar, 1962, Murrayfield
SCOTLAND   3   PG: Scotland
ENGLAND   3   PG: Willcox

16 Mar 1963, Twickenham
ENGLAND   10   T: Drake-Lee, Sharp
C: Willcox (2)

SCOTLAND   8   T: Glasgow
C: Coughtrie
DG: Scotland

21 Mar 1964, Murrayfield
SCOTLAND   15   T: Glasgow, Bruce, Telfer
C: Wilson (3)
ENGLAND   6   T: Rogers
PG: Hosen

20 Mar 1965, Twickenham
ENGLAND   3   T: Hancock
SCOTLAND   3   DG: Chisholm

19 Mar 1966, Murrayfield
SCOTLAND   6   T: Whyte
PG: Blaikie
ENGLAND   3   DG: McFadyean

18 Mar 1967, Twickenham
ENGLAND   27   T: McFadyean (2), Taylor,
Webb
C: Hosen (3)
DG: Finlan
PG: Hosen (2)
SCOTLAND   14   T: Hinshelwood, Turner
C: Wilson
PG: Wilson (2)

16 Mar 1968, Murrayfield
SCOTLAND   6   DG: Connell
PG: Wilson
ENGLAND   8   T: Coulman
C: Hiller
PG: Hiller

15 Mar 1969, Twickenham
ENGLAND   8   T: Duckham (2)
C: Hiller
SCOTLAND   3   PG: Brown

21 Mar 1970, Murrayfield
SCOTLAND   14   T: Biggar, Turner
C: Peter Brown
PG: Peter Brown (2)
ENGLAND   5   T: Spencer
C: Hiller

20 Mar 1971, Twickenham
ENGLAND   15   T: Hiller, Neary
PG: Hiller (3)
SCOTLAND   16   T: Peter Brown, Paterson,
Rea
C: Peter Brown (2)
DG: Paterson

18 Mar 1972, Murrayfield
SCOTLAND   23   T: Peter Brown, MacEwan
DG: Telfer
PG: Peter Brown (3),
Arthur Brown
ENGLAND   9   PG: Old (3)

17 Mar 1973, Twickenham
ENGLAND   20   T: Dixon (2), Evans, Squires
C: Jorden (2)
SCOTLAND   13   T: Steele (2)
C: Irvine
PG: Morgan

2 Feb 1974, Murrayfield
SCOTLAND	16	T: Irvine, Lauder
		C: Irvine
		PG: Irvine (2)
ENGLAND	14	T: Cotton, Neary
		DG: Rossborough
		PG: Old

15 Mar 1975, Twickenham
ENGLAND	7	T: Morley
		PG: Bennett
SCOTLAND	6	PG: Morgan (2)

21 Feb 1976, Murrayfield
SCOTLAND	22	T: Lawson (2), Leslie
		C: Irvine (2)
		PG: Irvine (2)
ENGLAND	12	T: Maxwell
		C: Old
		PG: Old (2)

15 Jan 1977, Twickenham
ENGLAND	26	T: Kent, Slemen, Uttley,
		Young
		C: Hignell (2)
		PG: Hignell (2)
SCOTLAND	6	PG: Irvine (2)

4 Mar 1978, Murrayfield
SCOTLAND	0	
ENGLAND	15	T: Nelmes, Squires
		C: Young (2)
		PG: Dodge

3 Feb 1979, Twickenham
ENGLAND	7	T: Slemen
		PG: Bennett
SCOTLAND	7	T: Rutherford
		PG: Irvine

15 Mar 1980, Murrayfield
SCOTLAND	18	T: Tomes, Rutherford
		C: Irvine (2)
		PG: Irvine (2)
ENGLAND	30	T: Carleton (3), Slemen,
		Smith
		C: Hare (2)
		PG: Hare (2)

21 Feb 1981, Twickenham
ENGLAND	23	T: Davies, Slemen,
		Woodward
		C: Hare
		PG: Hare (3)
SCOTLAND	17	T: Munro (2), Calder
		C: Irvine
		PG: Irvine

16 Jan 1982, Murrayfield
SCOTLAND	9	DG: Rutherford
		PG: Irvine (2)
ENGLAND	9	PG: Dodge (2), Rose

5 Mar 1983, Twickenham
ENGLAND	12	DG: Horton
		PG: Hare (3)
SCOTLAND	22	T: Laidlaw, Smith
		C: Dods
		DG: Robertson
		PG: Dods (3)

4 Feb 1984, Murrayfield
SCOTLAND	18	T: Johnston, Kennedy
		C: Dods (2)
		PG: Dods (2)
ENGLAND	6	PG: Hare (2)

16 Mar 1985, Twickenham
ENGLAND	10	T: Smith
		PG: Andrew (2)
SCOTLAND	7	T: Robertson
		PG: Dods

15 Feb 1986, Murrayfield
SCOTLAND	33	T: Duncan, Rutherford,
		S. Hastings
		C: G. Hastings (3)
		PG: G. Hastings (5)
ENGLAND	6	PG: Andrew (2)

4 April 1987, Twickenham
ENGLAND	21	T: Penalty try, Rose
		C: Rose (2)
		PG: Rose (3)
SCOTLAND	12	T: Robertson
		C: G. Hastings
		PG: G. Hastings (2)

England v Wales

16 Dec 1882, St Helens, Swansea
WALES	0	
ENGLAND	2g 4t	T: Wade (3), Bolton,
		Henderson, Thomson
		C: Evanson (2)

5 Jan 1884, Cardigan Fields, Leeds
ENGLAND	1g 2t	T: Rotherham, Twynam,
		Wade
		C: Bolton
WALES	1g	T: Allen
		C: Lewis

3 Jan 1885, St Helens, Swansea
WALES	1g 1t	T: Jordan (2)
		C: Taylor
ENGLAND	1g 4t	T: Hawcridge, Kindersley,
		Ryalls, Teggin, Wade
		C: Payne

2 Jan 1886, Rectory Field, Blackheath
ENGLAND	2t 1gm	T: Wade, Wilkinson
		GM: Stoddart
WALES	1g	T: Stadden
		C: Taylor

8 Jan 1887, Stradey Park, Llanelli
| WALES | 0 | |
| ENGLAND | 0 | |

15 Feb 1890, Crown Flatt, Dewsbury
| ENGLAND | 0 | |
| WALES | 1t | T: Stadden |

3 Jan 1891, Rodney Parade, Newport
WALES	3	T: Pearson
		C: Bancroft
ENGLAND	7	T: Christopherson (2),
		Budworth
		C: Alderson

2 Jan 1892, Rectory Field, Blackheath
ENGLAND	17	T: Alderson, Evershed,
		Hubbard, Nichol
		C: Lockwood (2), Alderson
WALES	0	

7 Jan 1893, Cardiff Arms Park
WALES	12	T: Gould (2), Biggs
		C: Bancroft
		PG: Bancroft
ENGLAND	11	T: Marshall (3), Lohden
		C: Stoddart

6 Jan 1894, Birkenhead Park
ENGLAND	24	T: Bradshaw, Morfitt,
		Lockwood, Taylor
		C: Lockwood (3), Taylor
		GM: Taylor
WALES	3	T: Parfitt

5 Jan 1895, St Helens, Swansea
WALES	6	T: Elsey, Graham
ENGLAND	14	T: Carey, Leslie-Jones,
		Thomson, Woods
		C: Mitchell

4 Jan 1896, Rectory Field, Blackheath
ENGLAND	25	T: Cattell (2), Fookes (2),
		Morfitt (2) Mitchell
		C: Taylor, Valentine
WALES	0	

9 Jan 1897, Rodney Parade, Newport
WALES	11	T: Pearson, Boucher, Jones
		C: Bancroft
ENGLAND	0	

England piling on the pressure against Wales during the 1892 international at Blackheath, scoring another try under the posts on the way to a 17–0 victory.

2 Apr 1898, Rectory Field, Blackheath
ENGLAND	14	T: Fookes (2), F. Stout,
		P. Stout
		C: Byrne
WALES	7	T: Huzzey
		DG: Huzzey

7 Jan 1899, St Helens, Swansea
WALES	26	T: Llewellyn (4), Huzzey (2)
		C: Bancroft (4)
ENGLAND	3	T: Robinson

6 Jan 1900, Kingsholm, Gloucester
ENGLAND	3	T: Nicholson
WALES	13	T: Hellings, Trew
		C: Bancroft (2)
		PG: Bancroft

5 Jan 1901, Cardiff Arms Park
WALES	13	T: Hodges, Nicholls,
		Williams
		C: Bancroft (2)
ENGLAND	0	

11 Jan 1902, Rectory Field, Blackheath
ENGLAND	8	T: Dobson, Robinson
		C: Alexander
WALES	9	T: Gabe, Osborne
		PG: Strand-Jones

10 Jan 1903, St Helens, Swansea
WALES	21	T: Hodges (3), Owen,
		Pearson
		C: Strand-Jones (3)
ENGLAND	5	T: Dobson
		C: Taylor

9 Jan 1904, Welford Road, Leicester
ENGLAND	14	T: Elliot (2), Brettargh
		C: F. Stout
		PG: Gamlin
WALES	14	T: Llewellyn, Morgan
		C: Winfield (2)
		GM: Winfield

14 Jan 1905, Cardiff Arms Park
WALES	25	T: Morgan (2), Gabe,
		Harding, Dick Jones,
		Llewellyn, Watkins
		C: Davies (2)
ENGLAND	0	

13 Jan 1906, Athletic Ground, Richmond
ENGLAND	3	T: Hudson
WALES	16	T: Hodges, Maddocks,
		Morgan, C. Pritchard
		C: Winfield (2)

12 Jan 1907, St Helens, Swansea
WALES	22	T: Maddocks (2), Williams
		(2), Brown, Gibbs
		C: Gibbs (2)
ENGLAND	0	

18 Jan 1908, Ashton Gate, Bristol
ENGLAND	18	T: Birkett (2), Lapage,
		Williamson
		C: Wood (2), Roberts
WALES	28	T: Gabe (2), Bush, Gibbs,
		Trew

C: Winfield (2), Bush
PG: Winfield
DG: Bush

16 Jan 1909, Cardiff Arms Park
WALES 8 T: Hopkins, Williams
C: Bancroft

ENGLAND 0

15 Jan 1910, Twickenham
ENGLAND 11 T: Chapman, Solomon
C: Chapman
PG: Chapman
WALES 6 T: Gibbs, Webb

21 Jan 1911, St Helens, Swansea
WALES 15 T: Gibbs, Morgan, Spiller, Pugsley
PG: Birt
ENGLAND 11 T: Roberts, Kewney, Scholfield
C: Lambert

20 Jan 1912, Twickenham
ENGLAND 8 T: Brougham, Pym
C: Chapman
WALES 0

18 Jan 1913, Cardiff Arms Park
WALES 0
ENGLAND 12 T: Coates, Pillman
C: Greenwood
DG: Poulton

17 Jan 1914, Twickenham
ENGLAND 10 T: Brown, Pillman
C: Chapman (2)
WALES 9 T: W. Watts
C: Bancroft
DG: Hirst

17 Jan 1920, St Helens, Swansea
WALES 19 T: Powell, Shea
C: Shea
DG: Shea (2)
PG Shea
ENGLAND 5 T: Day
C: Day

15 Jan 1921, Twickenham
ENGLAND 18 T: Smallwood (2), Kershaw, Lowe
C: Hammett
DG: Davies
WALES 3 T: Ring

21 Jan 1922, Cardiff Arms Park
WALES 28 T: Bowen, Delahay, Islwyn Evans, Hiddlestone, Parker, Palmer, Richards, Whitfield
C: Rees (2)
ENGLAND 6 T: Day, Lowe

20 Jan 1923, Twickenham
ENGLAND 7 T: Price
DG: Smallwood
WALES 3 T: Michael

19 Jan 1924, St Helens, Swansea
WALES 9 T: Johnson, Tom Jones, Owen

ENGLAND 17 T: Catcheside (2), Jacob, Locke, Myers
C: Conway

17 Jan 1925, Twickenham
ENGLAND 12 T: Hamilton-Wickes, Kittermaster, Voyce
PG: Armstrong
WALES 6 T: Thomas, James

16 Jan 1926, Cardiff Arms Park
WALES 3 T: Andrews
ENGLAND 3 T: Wakefield

15 Jan 1927, Twickenham
ENGLAND 11 T: Corbett
C: Stanbury
GM: Corbett
PG: Stanbury
WALES 9 T: Andrews, Harding
PG: Male

21 Jan 1928, St Helens, Swansea
WALES 8 T: Bartlett, Dai John
C: Jones
ENGLAND 10 T: Taylor, Laird
C: Richardson (2)

19 Jan 1929, Twickenham
ENGLAND 8 T: Wilkinson (2)
C: Wilson
WALES 3 T: Morley

18 Jan 1930, Cardiff Arms Park
WALES 3 T: Jones-Davies
ENGLAND 11 T: Reeve (2)
C: Black
PG: Black

17 Jan 1931, Twickenham
ENGLAND 11 T: Burland
C: Burland
PG: Black (2)
WALES 11 T: Jones-Davies, Morley
C: Bassett
GM: Powell

16 Jan 1932, St Helens, Swansea
WALES 12 T: Boon
C: Bassett
DG: Boon
PG: Bassett
ENGLAND 5 T: Coley
C: Barr

21 Jan 1933, Twickenham
ENGLAND 3 T: Elliot
WALES 7 T: Boon
DG: Boon

20 Jan 1934, Cardiff Arms Park
WALES 0
ENGLAND 9 T: Meikle (2), Warr

19 Jan 1935, Twickenham
ENGLAND 3 PG: Boughton
WALES 3 T: Wooller

18 Jan 1936, St Helens, Swansea
WALES 0
ENGLAND 0

16 Jan 1937, Twickenham
| ENGLAND | 4 | DG: Sever |
| WALES | 3 | T: Wooller |

15 Jan 1938, Cardiff Arms Park
WALES	14	T: McCarley, I. Rees
		C: Jenkins
		PG: Jenkins (2)
ENGLAND	8	T: Candler, Sever
		C: Freakes

21 Jan 1939, Twickenham
| ENGLAND | 3 | T: Teden |
| WALES | 0 | |

18 Jan 1947, Cardiff Arms Park
WALES	6	T: Stephens, Evans
ENGLAND	9	T: White
		C: Gray
		DG: Hall

17 Jan 1948, Twickenham
| ENGLAND | 3 | PG: Newman |
| WALES | 3 | T: Ken Jones |

15 Jan 1949, Cardiff Arms Park
WALES	9	T: Les Williams (2),
		Meredith
ENGLAND	3	DG: Hall

21 Jan 1950, Twickenham
ENGLAND	5	T: Smith
		C: Hofmeyr
WALES	11	T: Cale, Cliff Davies
		C: Lewis Jones
		PG: Lewis Jones

20 Jan 1951, St Helens, Swansea
WALES	23	T: Matthews (2), Thomas
		(2), Ken Jones
		C: Lewis Jones (4)
ENGLAND	5	T: Rittson-Thomas
		C: Hewitt

19 Jan 1952, Twickenham
ENGLAND	6	T: Agar, Woodward
WALES	8	T: Ken Jones (2)
		C: Malcolm Thomas

17 Jan 1953, Cardiff Arms Park
WALES	3	PG: Davies
ENGLAND	8	T: Cannell
		C: Hall
		PG: Woodward

16 Jan 1954, Twickenham
ENGLAND	9	T: Woodward (2), Winn
WALES	6	T: Rowlands
		PG: Rowlands

22 Jan 1955, Cardiff Arms Park
| WALES | 3 | PG: Edwards |
| ENGLAND | 0 | |

21 Jan 1956, Twickenham
ENGLAND	3	PG: Allison
WALES	8	T: Davies, Robins
		C: Owen

19 Jan 1957, Cardiff Arms Park
| WALES | 0 | |
| ENGLAND | 3 | PG: Allison |

18 Jan 1958, Twickenham
| ENGLAND | 3 | T: Thompson |
| WALES | 3 | PG: T. J. Davies |

17 Jan 1959, Cardiff Arms Park
WALES	5	T: Bebb
		C: T. J. Davies
ENGLAND	0	

16 Jan 1960, Twickenham
ENGLAND	14	T: Roberts (2)
		C: Rutherford
		PG: Rutherford (2)
WALES	6	PG: T. J. Davies (2)

21 Jan 1961, Cardiff Arms Park
| WALES | 6 | T: Bebb (2) |
| ENGLAND | 3 | T: Young |

20 Jan 1962, Twickenham
| ENGLAND | 0 | |
| WALES | 0 | |

19 Jan 1963, Cardiff Arms Park
WALES	6	T: Hayward
		PG: Hodgson
ENGLAND	13	T: Owen, Phillips
		C: Sharp (2)
		DG: Sharp

18 Jan 1964, Twickenham
| ENGLAND | 6 | T: Perry, Ranson |
| WALES | 6 | T: Bebb (2) |

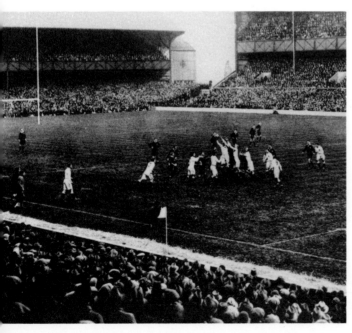

Action from the 1933 England and Wales match at Twickenham. Wales won 7–3 to record their first victory at rugby's Headquarters.

16 Jan 1965, Cardiff Arms Park
WALES 14 T: S. Watkins (2),
H. Morgan
C: T. Price
DG: D. Watkins
ENGLAND 3 PG: Rutherford

15 Jan 1966, Twickenham
ENGLAND 6 T: Perry
PG: Rutherford
WALES 11 T: Pask
C: T. Price
PG: T. Price (2)

15 Apr 1967, Cardiff Arms Park
WALES 34 T: T. G. R. Davies (2),
Jarrett, Morris, Bebb
C: Jarrett (5)
DG: Raybould
PG: Jarrett (2)
ENGLAND 21 T: Barton (2), Savage
PG: Hosen (4)

20 Jan 1968, Twickenham
ENGLAND 11 T: McFadyean, Redwood
C: Hiller
PG: Hiller
WALES 11 T: Edwards, Wanbon
C: Jarrett
DG: John

12 Apr 1969, Cardiff Arms Park
WALES 30 T: M. C. R. Richards (4),
John
C: Jarrett (3)
DG: John
PG: Jarrett (2)
ENGLAND 9 PG: Hiller (3)

28 Feb 1970, Twickenham
ENGLAND 13 T: Duckham, Novak
C: Hiller (2)
PG: Hiller
WALES 17 T: T. M. Davies, John,
J. P. R. Williams, Hopkins
C: J. P. R. Williams
DG: John

16 Jan 1971, Cardiff Arms Park
WALES 22 T: T. G. R. Davies (2),
Bevan
C: Taylor (2)
DG: John (2)
PG: J. P. R. Williams
ENGLAND 6 T: Hannaford
PG: Rossborough

15 Jan 1972, Twickenham
ENGLAND 3 PG: Hiller
WALES 12 T: J. P. R. Williams
C: John
PG: John (2)

20 Jan 1973, Cardiff Arms Park
WALES 25 T: J. C. Bevan (2),
T. G. R. Davies, Edwards,
A. J. L. Lewis
C: Bennett
PG: Taylor

ENGLAND 9 DG: Cowman
PG: Doble

16 Mar 1974, Twickenham
ENGLAND 16 T: Duckham, Ripley
C: Old
PG: Old (2)
WALES 12 T: T. M. Davies
C: Bennett
PG: Bennett (2)

15 Feb 1975, Cardiff Arms Park
WALES 20 T: T. G. R. Davies,
Fenwick, J. J. Williams
C: Martin
PG: Martin (2)
ENGLAND 4 T: Horton

17 Jan 1976, Twickenham
ENGLAND 9 PG: Hignell (3)
WALES 21 T: J. P. R. Williams (2),
Edwards
C: Fenwick (3)
PG: Martin

5 Mar 1977, Cardiff Arms Park
WALES 14 T: Edwards,
J. P. R. Williams
PG: Fenwick (2)
ENGLAND 9 PG: Hignell (3)

4 Feb 1978, Twickenham
ENGLAND 6 PG: Hignell (2)
WALES 9 PG: Bennett (3)

17 Mar 1979, Cardiff Arms Park
WALES 27 T: E. Rees, D. S. Richards,
Ringer, M. G. Roberts,
J. J. Williams
C: Martin, Fenwick
DG: W. G. Davies
ENGLAND 3 PG: Bennett

16 Feb 1980, Twickenham
ENGLAND 9 PG: Hare (3)
WALES 8 T: E. Rees, Squire

17 Jan 1981, Cardiff Arms Park
WALES 21 T: W. G. Davies
C: Fenwick
DG: W. G. Davies
PG: Fenwick (4)
ENGLAND 19 T: Hare
PG: Hare (5)

6 Mar 1982, Twickenham
ENGLAND 17 T: Carleton, Slemen
PG: Hare (3)
WALES 7 T: J. R. Lewis
DG: W. G. Davies

5 Feb 1983, Cardiff Arms Park
WALES 13 T: Squire
DG: Dacey
PG: Wyatt (2)
ENGLAND 13 T: Carleton
DG: Cusworth
PG: Hare (2)

17 Mar 1984, Twickenham
ENGLAND	15	PG: Hare (5)
WALES	24	T: Hadley
		C: H. Davies
		PG: H. Davies (4)
		DG: Dacey

20 Apr 1985, Cardiff Arms Park
WALES	24	T: J. Davies, Roberts
		C: Thorburn (2)
		PG: Thorburn (3)
		DG: J. Davies
ENGLAND	15	T: Smith
		C: Andrew
		PG: Andrew (2)
		DG: Andrew

17 Jan 1986, Twickenham
ENGLAND	21	PG: Andrew (6)
		DG: Andrew
WALES	18	T: Bowen
		C: Thorburn
		PG: Thorburn (3)
		DG: J. Davies

7 Mar 1987, Cardiff Arms Park
WALES	19	T: S. Evans
		PG: Wyatt (4)
ENGLAND	12	PG: Rose (4)

Ireland v Scotland

17 Feb 1883, Ormeau, Belfast
IRELAND	0	
SCOTLAND	1g 1t	T: Reid, Somerville
		C: Maclagan

16 Feb 1884, Raeburn Place, Edinburgh
SCOTLAND	2g 2t	T: Peterkin, Tod, Don Wauchope, Asher
		C: Berry (2)
IRELAND	1t	T: McIntosh

7 Mar 1885, Raeburn Place, Edinburgh
SCOTLAND	1g 2t	T: Reid, Peterkin, Don Wauchope
		C: Veitch
IRELAND	0	

20 Feb 1886, Raeburn Place, Edinburgh
SCOTLAND	3g 2t 1dg	T: Don Wauchope (2), Morrison (2), Macfarlan
		C: Macfarlan (3)
		DG: Asher
IRELAND	0	

19 Feb 1887, Ormeau, Belfast
IRELAND	0	
SCOTLAND	1g 2t 1gm	T: Maclagan, McEwan, Morton
		C: Berry
		GM: Berry

10 Mar 1888, Raeburn Place, Edinburgh
SCOTLAND	1g	T: Macfarlan
		C: Berry
IRELAND	0	

16 Feb 1889, Ormeau, Belfast
IRELAND	1dg	DG: Stevenson
SCOTLAND	0	

22 Feb 1890, Raeburn Place, Edinburgh
SCOTLAND	1t 1dg	T: J. E. Orr
		DG: Boswell
IRELAND	0	

21 Feb 1891, Ballynafeigh, Belfast
IRELAND	0	
SCOTLAND	14	T: Wotherspoon (3), Clauss, MacGregor
		C: Boswell (3)
		DG: McEwan

20 Feb 1892, Raeburn Place, Edinburgh
SCOTLAND	2	T: Millar
IRELAND	0	

20 Feb 1893, Ballynafeigh, Belfast
IRELAND	0	
SCOTLAND	0	

24 Feb 1894, Lansdowne Road, Dublin
IRELAND	5	T: Wells
		C: J. Lytle
SCOTLAND	0	

2 Mar 1895, Raeburn Place, Edinburgh
SCOTLAND	6	T: Welsh, Campbell
IRELAND	0	

15 Feb 1896, Lansdowne Road, Dublin
IRELAND	0	
SCOTLAND	0	

20 Feb 1897, Powderhall, Edinburgh
SCOTLAND	8	T: Turnbull
		C: T. M. Scott
		PG: T. M. Scott
IRELAND	3	T: Bulger

19 Feb 1898, Balmoral Showgrounds, Belfast
IRELAND	0	
SCOTLAND	8	T: T. M. Scott (2)
		C: T. M. Scott

18 Feb 1899, Inverleith, Edinburgh
SCOTLAND	3	PG: Donaldson
IRELAND	9	T: Campbell, Reid, Sealy

24 Feb 1900, Lansdowne Road, Dublin
IRELAND	0	
SCOTLAND	0	

23 Feb 1901, Inverleith, Edinburgh
SCOTLAND	9	T: Gillespie, Welsh (2)
IRELAND	5	T: Doran
		C: Irvine

22 Feb 1902, Balmoral Showgrounds, Belfast
IRELAND	5	T: G. Doran
		C: Corley
SCOTLAND	0	

28 Feb 1903, Inverleith, Edinburgh
SCOTLAND   3   T: Crabbie
IRELAND   0

27 Feb 1904, Lansdowne Road, Dublin
IRELAND   3   T: Moffatt
SCOTLAND   19 T: Bedell-Sivright (2),
               Timms, Macdonald, Simson
               C: Macdonald (2)

25 Feb 1905, Inverleith, Edinburgh
SCOTLAND   5   T: Timms
               C: Forrest
IRELAND   11 T: Tedford, Wallace,
               Moffatt
               C: Maclear

24 Feb 1906, Lansdowne Road, Dublin
IRELAND   6   T: Parke, Robb
SCOTLAND   13 T: Bedell-Sivright, Munro
               C: MacCallum (2)
               GM: MacLeod

23 Feb 1907, Inverleith, Edinburgh
SCOTLAND   15 T: Sanderson, Purves, Frew
               C: MacLeod, Geddes (2)
IRELAND   3   PG: Parke

29 Feb 1908, Lansdowne Road, Dublin
IRELAND   16 T: Thrift (2), Thompson,
               Beckett
               C: Parke, Hinton
SCOTLAND   11 T: MacLeod, Martin
               C: MacLeod
               PG: MacLeod

27 Feb 1909, Inverleith, Edinburgh
SCOTLAND   9   T: Lindsay-Watson,
               McGregor, Kyle
IRELAND   3   PG: Parke

26 Feb 1910, Balmoral Showgrounds, Belfast
IRELAND   0
SCOTLAND   14 T: Dobson, Walter (2),
               Stuart
               C: MacCallum

25 Feb 1911, Inverleith, Edinburgh
SCOTLAND   10 T: Simson, Angus
               DG: Munro
IRELAND   16 T: O'Callaghan, Foster,
               Adams, Quinn
               C: Hinton, Lloyd

24 Feb 1912, Lansdowne Road, Dublin
IRELAND   10 T: Foster
               DG: Lloyd
               PG: Lloyd
SCOTLAND   8   T: Turner, Will
               C: MacCallum

22 Feb 1913, Inverleith, Edinburgh
SCOTLAND   29 T: Stewart (4), Usher,
               Bowie, Purves
               C: Turner (4)
IRELAND   14 T: Schute, Stokes
               C: Lloyd (2)
               DG: Lloyd

28 Feb 1914, Lansdowne Road, Dublin
IRELAND   6   T: Quinn, McNamara
SCOTLAND   0

28 Feb 1920, Inverleith, Edinburgh
SCOTLAND   19 T: Crole (2), Angus,
               Browning
               C: Kennedy (2)
               PG: Kennedy
IRELAND   0

26 Feb 1921, Lansdowne Road, Dublin
IRELAND   9   T: Cussen, Stephenson,
               Cunningham
SCOTLAND   9   T: Hume, Sloan
               C: Maxwell

25 Feb 1922, Inverleith, Edinburgh
SCOTLAND   6   T: Bryce, Liddell
IRELAND   3   T: Clarke

24 Feb 1923, Lansdowne Road, Dublin
IRELAND   3   T: Cussen
SCOTLAND   13 T: Liddell, McQueen,
               Browning
               C: Browning (2)

23 Feb 1924, Inverleith, Edinburgh
SCOTLAND   13 T: Waddell (2), Bertram
               C: Drysdale (2)
IRELAND   8   T: G. Stephenson (2)
               C: G. Stephenson

28 Feb 1925, Lansdowne Road, Dublin
IRELAND   8   T: H. Stephenson
               C: Crawford
               PG: Crawford
SCOTLAND   14 T: Wallace, McMyn
               C: Drysdale, Dykes
               DG: Waddell

27 Feb 1926, Murrayfield, Edinburgh
SCOTLAND   0
IRELAND   3   T: Gage

26 Feb 1927, Lansdowne Road, Dublin
IRELAND   6   T: Pike, Ganly
SCOTLAND   0

25 Feb 1928, Murrayfield
SCOTLAND   5   T: Kerr
               C: Drysdale
IRELAND   13 T: Ganly, Davy, Stephenson
               C: Stephenson (2)

23 Feb 1929, Lansdowne Road, Dublin
IRELAND   7   T: Arigho
               DG: Davy
SCOTLAND   16 T: Macpherson,
               Bannerman, I. Smith,
               Simmers
               C: Dykes, Allan

22 Feb 1930, Murrayfield
SCOTLAND   11 T: Ford, Macpherson,
               Waters
               C: Waters
IRELAND   14 T: Davy (3), Crowe
               C: Murray

28 Feb 1931, Lansdowne Road, Dublin
IRELAND   8   T: Sugden, Pike
                          C: Murray
SCOTLAND   5   T: Mackintosh
                          C: Allan

27 Feb 1932, Murrayfield
SCOTLAND   8   T: Wood, Simmers
                          C: Allan
IRELAND   20   T: Lightfoot (2), Hunt,
                          Waide
                          C: Murray (4)

1 Apr 1933, Lansdowne Road, Dublin
IRELAND   6   T: Crowe, Murray
SCOTLAND   8   DG: Jackson, Lind

24 Feb 1934, Murrayfield
SCOTLAND   16   T: Dick (2), Crawford
                          C: Shaw (2)
                          PG: Allan
IRELAND   9   T: Russell (2), O'Connor

23 Feb 1935, Lansdowne Road, Dublin
IRELAND   12   T: O'Connor, Lawlor,
                          Bailey, Ridgeway
SCOTLAND   5   T: Shaw
                          C: Fyfe

22 Feb 1936, Murrayfield
SCOTLAND   4   DG: Murdoch
IRELAND   10   T: Walker, McMahon
                          DG: Hewitt

27 Feb 1937, Lansdowne Road, Dublin
IRELAND   11   T: Alexander, McMahon,
                          Moran
                          C: Bailey
SCOTLAND   4   DG: Wilson Shaw

26 Feb 1938, Murrayfield
SCOTLAND   23   T: Forrest (2), Macrae,
                          Drummond
                          C: Crawford (2),
                          DG: Dorward
                          PG: Drummond
IRELAND   14   T: Cromey, O'Loughlin,
                          Moran, Morgan
                          C: Walker

25 Feb 1939, Lansdowne Road, Dublin
IRELAND   12   T: Moran, Torrens
                          PG: McKibbin
                          GM: Sayers
SCOTLAND   3   T: Innes

22 Feb 1947, Murrayfield
SCOTLAND   0
IRELAND   3   T: Mullan

28 Feb 1948, Lansdowne Road, Dublin
IRELAND   6   T: Mullan, Kyle
SCOTLAND   0

26 Feb 1949, Murrayfield
SCOTLAND   3   PG: Allardice
IRELAND   13   T: McCarthy (2)
                          C: Norton (2)
                          PG: Norton

25 Feb 1950, Lansdowne Road, Dublin
IRELAND   21   T: Blayney, Curtis, Crowe
                          C: Norton (3)
                          PG: Norton (2)
SCOTLAND   0

24 Feb 1951, Murrayfield
SCOTLAND   5   T: Sloan
                          C: Thomson
IRELAND   6   T: O'Brien
                          DG: Henderson

23 Feb 1952, Lansdowne Road, Dublin
IRELAND   12   T: Lane, Kyle, Henderson
                          PG: Henderson
SCOTLAND   8   T: Davidson
                          C: Thomson
                          PG: Thomson

28 Feb 1953, Murrayfield
SCOTLAND   8   T: Henderson
                          C: I. Thomson
                          PG: I. Thomson
IRELAND   26   T: McCarthy, Byrne (3),
                          Mortell, Kavanagh
                          C: Gregg (4)

27 Feb 1954, Ravenhill, Belfast
IRELAND   6   T: Mortell (2)
SCOTLAND   0

26 Feb 1955, Murrayfield
SCOTLAND   12   T: Swann
                          DG: Cameron
                          PG: Elgie (2)
IRELAND   3   PG: Kelly

25 Feb 1956, Lansdowne Road, Dublin
IRELAND   14   T: Henderson, O'Reilly,
                          Kyle, O'Meara
                          C: Pedlow
SCOTLAND   10   T: Michie, Smith
                          C: McClung (2)

23 Feb 1957, Murrayfield
SCOTLAND   3   PG: Scotland
IRELAND   5   T: O'Sullivan
                          C: Berkery

1 Mar 1958, Lansdowne Road, Dublin
IRELAND   12   T: Pedlow (2)
                          PG: Henderson, Berkery
SCOTLAND   6   T: Smith, Weatherstone

28 Feb 1959, Murrayfield
SCOTLAND   3   PG: Scotland
IRELAND   8   T: Dooley
                          C: Hewitt
                          PG: Hewitt

27 Feb 1960, Lansdowne Road, Dublin
IRELAND   5   T: Wood
                          C: Hewitt
SCOTLAND   6   T: Thomson
                          DG: Scotland

25 Feb 1961, Murrayfield
SCOTLAND   16   T: Douglas, Ross (2)
                          C: Scotland (2)
                          PG: Scotland

IRELAND 8 T: Kavanagh, Hewitt
C: Moffett

24 Feb 1962, Lansdowne Road, Dublin
IRELAND 6 T: Hunter
PG: Hunter
SCOTLAND 20 T: Smith (2), Cowan
C: Scotland
DG: Coughtrie
PG: Scotlanld (2)

23 Feb 1963, Murrayfield
SCOTLAND 3 PG: Coughtrie
IRELAND 0

22 Feb 1964, Lansdowne Road, Dublin
IRELAND 3 PG: Kiernan
SCOTLAND 6 PG: Wilson (2)

27 Feb 1965, Murrayfield
SCOTLAND 6 DG: Laughland
PG: Wilson
IRELAND 16 T: McGrath, Young,
Murphy
C: Kiernan (2)
DG: Gibson

26 Feb 1966, Lansdowne Road, Dublin
IRELAND 3 PG: Kiernan
SCOTLAND 11 T: Hinshelwood (2), Grant
C: Wilson

25 Feb 1967, Murrayfield
SCOTLAND 3 PG: Wilson
IRELAND 5 T: Murphy
C: Kiernan

24 Feb 1968, Lansdowne Road, Dublin
IRELAND 14 T: Duggan (2), Bresnihan
C: Kiernan
PG: Kiernan
SCOTLAND 6 PG: Wilson (2)

22 Feb 1969, Murrayfield
SCOTLAND 0
IRELAND 16 T: Duggan, McGann,
Gibson, Bresnihan
C: Moroney (2)

28 Feb 1970, Lansdowne Road, Dublin
IRELAND 16 T: Molloy, Goodall, Gibson,
Brown
C: Kiernan (2)
SCOTLAND 11 T: Lauder, M. A. Smith,
C. I. Smith
DG: Robertson

27 Feb 1971, Murrayfield
SCOTLAND 5 T: Frame
C: P. Brown
IRELAND 17 T: Duggan (2), Grant
C: Gibson
PG: Gibson (2)

24 Feb 1973, Murrayfield
SCOTLAND 19 T: Forsyth
DG: Morgan (2),
McGeechan
PG: Morgan (2)
IRELAND 14 T: McMaster, Kiernan
PG: McGann (2)

2 Mar 1974, Lansdowne Road, Dublin
IRELAND 9 T: Milliken
C: Gibson
PG: McKinney
SCOTLAND 6 PG: Irvine (2)

1 Feb 1975, Murrayfield
SCOTLAND 20 T: Renwick, Steele
DG: Morgan, McGeechan
PG: Irvine (2)
IRELAND 13 T: Dennison, Grace
C: McCombe
PG: McCombe

20 Mar 1976, Lansdowne Road, Dublin
IRELAND 6 PG: McGann (2)
SCOTLAND 15 DG: Wilson
PG: Irvine (4)

19 Feb 1977, Murrayfield
SCOTLAND 21 T: Gammell (2), Madsen
DG: Morgan
PG: Irvine (2)
IRELAND 18 T: Gibson
C: Gibson
DG: Quinn
PG: Gibson (2), Quinn

21 Jan 1978, Lansdowne Road, Dublin
IRELAND 12 T: McKinney
C: Ward
PG: Ward (2)
SCOTLAND 9 PG: Morgan (3)

3 Mar 1979, Murrayfield
SCOTLAND 11 T: Rutherford, Irvine
PG: Irvine
IRELAND 11 T: Patterson (2)
PG: Ward

2 Feb 1980, Lansdowne Road, Dublin
IRELAND 22 T: Keane, Kennedy
C: Campbell
DG: Campbell
PG: Campbell (3)
SCOTLAND 15 T: Johnston (2)
C: Irvine (2)
PG: Irvine

21 Mar 1981, Murrayfield
SCOTLAND 10 T: Hay
DG: Rutherford
PG: Irvine
IRELAND 9 T: Irwin
C: Campbell
PG: Campbell

20 Feb 1982, Lansdowne Road, Dublin
IRELAND 21 DG: Campbell
PG: Campbell (6)
SCOTLAND 12 T: Rutherford
C: Irvine
PG: Renwick (2)

15 Jan 1983, Murrayfield
SCOTLAND 13 T: Laidlaw
DG: Renwick
PG: Dods (2)

IRELAND   15   T: Kiernan
                     C: Campbell
                     PG: Campbell (3)

3 Mar 1984, Lansdowne Road, Dublin
IRELAND   9   T: Kiernan
                     C: Murphy
                     PG: Murphy
SCOTLAND   32   T: Laidlaw (2), Penalty try,
                     Robertson, Dods
                     C: Dods (3)
                     PG: Dods (2)

2 Feb 1985, Murrayfield
SCOTLAND   15   PG: Dods (4)
                     DG: Robertson
IRELAND   18   T: Ringland (2)
                     C: Kiernan (2)
                     PG: Kiernan
                     DG: Kiernan

15 Mar 1986, Lansdowne Road, Dublin
IRELAND   9   T: Ringland
                     C: Kiernan
                     PG: Kiernan
SCOTLAND   10   T: Laidlaw
                     PG: G. Hastings (2)

21 Feb 1987, Murrayfield
SCOTLAND   16   T: Laidlaw, Tukalo
                     C: G. Hastings
                     DG: Rutherford
IRELAND   12   T: Lenehan
                     C: Kiernan
                     PG: Kiernan
                     DG: Kiernan

Ireland v Wales

12 Apr 1884, Cardiff Arms Park
WALES   2t 1dg   T: Norton, Clapp
                     DG: Stadden
IRELAND   0

12 Mar 1887, Birkenhead Park
WALES   1t 1dg   T: Morgan
                     DG: Gould
IRELAND   3t   T: Montgomery (3)

3 Mar 1888, Lansdowne Road, Dublin
IRELAND   1g 1t   T: Warren, Shanahan
            1dg   C: Rambaut
                     DG: Carpendale
WALES   0

2 Mar 1889, St Helens, Swansea
WALES   0
IRELAND   2t   T: McDonnell, Cotton

1 Mar 1890, Lansdowne Road, Dublin
IRELAND   1g   T: Dunlop
                     C: Roche
WALES   1g   T: C. Thomas
                     C: Bancroft

7 Mar 1891, Stradey Park, Llanelli
WALES   6   T: D. Samuel
                     C: Bancroft
                     DG: Bancroft
IRELAND   4   T: Lee
                     DG: Walkington

5 Mar 1892, Lansdowne Road, Dublin
IRELAND   9   T: Walsh (2), Davies
                     C: Roche
WALES   0

11 Mar 1893, Stradey Park, Llanelli
WALES   2   T: Bert Gould
IRELAND   0

19 Mar 1894, Ballynafeigh, Belfast
IRELAND   3   PG: John Lytle
WALES   0

16 Mar 1895, Cardiff Arms Park
WALES   5   T: Pearson
                     C: Bancroft
IRELAND   3   T: Crean

14 Mar 1896, Lansdowne Road, Dublin
IRELAND   8   T: Crean, Lytle
                     C: Bulger
WALES   4   DG: Gould

18 Mar 1898, Limerick
IRELAND   3   PG: Bulger
WALES   11   T: Dobson, Huzzey
                     C: Bancroft
                     PG: Bancroft

18 Mar 1899, Cardiff Arms Park
WALES   0
IRELAND   3   T: Doran

17 Mar 1900, Balmoral Showgrounds, Belfast
IRELAND   0
WALES   3   T: Davies

16 Mar 1901, St Helens, Swansea
WALES   10   T: Alexander (2)
                     C: Bancroft (2)
IRELAND   9   T: J. Ryan, Freear,
                     Davidson

8 Mar 1902, Lansdowne Road, Dublin
IRELAND   0
WALES   15   T: Nicholls, Llewellyn,
                     Llewellyn Lloyd
                     C: Brice
                     DG: Nicholls

14 Mar 1903, Cardiff Arms Park
WALES   18   T: Llewellyn (2), Gabe,
                     Morgan (2), Brice
IRELAND   0

2 Mar 1904, Balmoral Showgrounds, Belfast
IRELAND   14   T: Tedford (2), J. Wallace,
                     Thrift
                     C: Parke
WALES   12   T: Morgan (2), Gabe, Cliff
                     Pritchard

11 Mar 1905, St Helens, Swansea
WALES	10	T: Wyndham Jones, Morgan
		C: Davies (2)
IRELAND	3	T: Robinson

10 Mar 1906, Balmoral Showgrounds, Belfast
IRELAND	11	T: Thrift, Wallace, Maclear
		C: Gardiner
WALES	6	T: Morgan, Gabe

9 Mar 1907, Cardiff Arms Park
WALES	29	T: Williams (3), Jones,
		Gabe, Bush
		C: Winfield (2)
		DG: Bush
		PG: Winfield
IRELAND	0	

14 Mar 1908, Balmoral Showgrounds, Belfast
IRELAND	5	T: Aston
		C: Parke
WALES	11	T: Williams (2), Gibbs
		C: Winfield

13 Mar 1909, St Helens, Swansea
WALES	18	T: J. Jones, Hopkins, Watts,
		Trew
		C: Bancroft (3)
IRELAND	5	T: Thompson
		C: Parke

12 Mar 1910, Lansdowne Road, Dublin
IRELAND	3	T: McIldowie
WALES	19	T: Williams (3), Gibbs,
		Dyke
		DG: Bush

11 Mar 1911, Cardiff Arms Park
WALES	16	T: T. Evans, Webb, Gibbs
		C: Bancroft (2)
		PG: Bancroft
IRELAND	0	

9 Mar 1912, Balmoral Showgrounds, Belfast
IRELAND	12	T: McIvor, Brown
		C: Lloyd
		DG: Lloyd
WALES	5	T: Davies
		C: Bancroft

8 Mar 1913, St Helens, Swansea
WALES	16	T: B. Lewis (2), Jones
		C: Bancroft (2)
		PG: Bancroft
IRELAND	13	T: Quinn, Stewart
		C: Lloyd (2)
		PG: Lloyd

14 Mar 1914, Balmoral Showgrounds, Belfast
IRELAND	3	T: Foster
WALES	11	T: Bedwelty Jones, Evans,
		Wetter
		C: Lewis

13 Mar 1920, Cardiff Arms Park
WALES	28	T: B. Williams (3), Jenkins,
		Whitfield, Parker
		C: Jenkins (2), Wetter
		DG: Jenkins
IRELAND	4	DG: McFarland

12 Mar 1921, Balmoral Showgrounds, Belfast
IRELAND	0	
WALES	6	T: M. Thomas
		PG: Johnson

11 Mar 1922, St Helens, Swansea
WALES	11	T: Whitfield (2), I. Evans
		C: Samuel
IRELAND	5	T: Stokes
		C: Wallis

10 Mar 1923, Lansdowne Road, Dublin
IRELAND	5	T: Cussen
		C: Crawford
WALES	4	DG: Powell

8 Mar 1924, Cardiff Arms Park
WALES	10	T: Richards, Pugh
		DG: Watkins
IRELAND	13	T: T. Hewitt, F. Hewitt,
		G. Stephenson
		C: Crawford (2)

14 Mar 1925, Ravenhill, Belfast
IRELAND	19	T: Millin, G. Stephenson,
		Browne, H. Stephenson
		C: G. Stephenson (2)
		PG: G. Stephenson
WALES	3	T: Turnbull

13 Mar 1926, St Helens, Swansea
WALES	11	T: Harding, Hopkins,
		Herrera
		C: Rees
IRELAND	8	T: Hanrahan
		C: Stephenson
		PG: Stephenson

12 Mar 1927, Lansdowne Road, Dublin
IRELAND	19	T: Stephenson (2), Ganly (2)
		C: Stephenson (2)
		PG: Stephenson
WALES	9	T: Morgan
		C: Powell
		DG: Lewis

10 Mar 1928, Cardiff Arms Park
WALES	10	T: D. John, A. Jenkins
		C: I. Jones (2)
IRELAND	13	T: Arigho (2), Ganly
		C: Stephenson (2)

9 Mar 1929, Ravenhill, Belfast
IRELAND	5	T: Davy
		C: Stephenson
WALES	5	T: Williams
		C: Parker

8 Mar 1930, St Helens, Swansea
WALES	12	T: Skym, Arthur Jones/
		Peacock (joint)
		PG: Bassett
IRELAND	7	DG: Davy
		PG: Murray

14 Mar 1931, Ravenhill, Belfast
IRELAND	3	T: Siggins
WALES	15	T: Morley (2), Davey
		C: Bassett
		DG: Ralph

12 Mar 1932, Cardiff Arms Park
WALES	10	T: Davey, Ralph
		DG: Ralph
IRELAND	12	T: Ross (2), Lightfoot, Waide

11 Mar 1933, Ravenhill, Belfast
IRELAND	10	T: Barnes
		DG: Davy
		PG: Siggins
WALES	5	T: Bowcott
		C: Jenkins

10 Mar 1934, St Helens, Swansea
WALES	13	T: Fear, Cowey, Jenkins
		C: Jenkins (2)
IRELAND	0	

9 Mar 1935, Ravenhill, Belfast
IRELAND	9	T: Doyle
		PG: Siggins, Bailey
WALES	3	PG: James

14 Mar 1936, Cardiff Arms Park
WALES	3	PG: Jenkins
IRELAND	0	

3 Apr 1937, Ravenhill, Belfast
IRELAND	5	T: Bailey
		C: Walker
WALES	3	PG: Legge

12 Mar 1938, St Helens, Swansea
WALES	11	T: Taylor, Clement
		C: Legge
		PG: Wooller
IRELAND	5	T: Moran
		C: McKibbin

11 Mar 1939, Ravenhill, Belfast
IRELAND	0	
WALES	7	T: Willie Davies
		DG: Willie Davies

20 Mar 1947, St Helens, Swansea
WALES	6	T: B. Evans
		PG: Tamplin
IRELAND	0	

13 Mar 1948, Ravenhill, Belfast
IRELAND	6	T: Mullan, Daly
WALES	3	T: Bleddyn Williams

12 Mar 1949, St Helens, Swansea
WALES	0	
IRELAND	5	T: McCarthy
		C: Norton

11 Mar 1950, Ravenhill, Belfast
IRELAND	3	PG: Norton
WALES	6	T: K. Jones, Thomas

10 Mar 1951, Cardiff Arms Park
WALES	3	PG: Edwards
IRELAND	3	T: Kyle

8 Mar 1952, Lansdowne Road, Dublin
IRELAND	3	PG: Murphy
WALES	14	T: C. Thomas, K. Jones, Stephens
		C: Lewis Jones
		PG: Lewis Jones

14 Mar 1953, St Helens, Swansea
WALES	5	T: Griffiths
		C: T. Davies
IRELAND	3	T: Pedlow

13 Mar 1954, Lansdowne Road, Dublin
IRELAND	9	T: Gaston
		PG: Henderson, Kelly
WALES	12	DG: D. Thomas
		PG: Evans (3)

12 Mar 1955, Cardiff Arms Park
WALES	21	T: Meredith, Griffiths, Morgan, Morris
		C: Owen (3)
		PG: Owen
IRELAND	3	PG: Henderson

10 Mar 1956, Lansdowne Road, Dublin
IRELAND	11	T: Cunningham
		C: Pedlow
		DG: Kyle
		PG: Pedlow
WALES	3	PG: Owen

9 Mar 1957, Cardiff Arms Park
WALES	6	PG: T. J. Davies (2)
IRELAND	5	T: Kavanagh
		C: Pedlow

15 Mar 1958, Lansdowne Road, Dublin
IRELAND	6	T: O'Meara
		PG: Henderson
WALES	9	T: H. Morgan, B. V. Meredith, Roberts

14 Mar 1959, Cardiff Arms Park
WALES	8	T: Ashton, M. Price
		C: T. J. Davies
IRELAND	6	T: O'Reilly
		PG: D. Hewitt

12 Mar 1960, Lansdowne Road, Dublin
IRELAND	9	T: Murphy
		PG: Kelly (2)
WALES	10	T: Cresswell, Brace
		C: Morgan (2)

11 Mar 1961, Cardiff Arms Park
WALES	9	T: Richards
		PG: Richards (2)
IRELAND	0	

17 Nov 1962, Lansdowne Road, Dublin
IRELAND	3	DG: English
WALES	3	PG: Hodgson

9 Mar 1963, Cardiff Arms Park
WALES	6	T: G. Jones
		DG: Watkins
IRELAND	14	T: Casey
		C: Kiernan
		DG: English
		PG: Kiernan (2)

7 March 1964, Lansdowne Road, Dublin
IRELAND	6	PG: Keogh (2)
WALES	15	T: S. Watkins, Dawes, D. Watkins
		C: Bradshaw (3)

13 Mar 1965, Cardiff Arms Park
WALES	14	T: D. Watkins, Bebb
		C: T. Price
		DG: T. Price
		PG: T. Price
IRELAND	8	T: Flynn
		C: Kiernan
		PG: Kiernan

12 Mar 1966, Lansdowne Road, Dublin
IRELAND	9	T: Bresnihan
		DG: Gibson
		PG: Gibson
WALES	6	T: Prothero
		PG: Bradshaw

11 Mar 1967, Cardiff Arms Park
WALES	0	
IRELAND	3	T: Duggan

9 Mar 1968, Lansdowne Road, Dublin
IRELAND	9	T: M. Doyle
		DG: Gibson
		PG: Kiernan
WALES	6	DG: Edwards
		PG: D. Rees

8 Mar 1969, Cardiff Arms Park
WALES	24	T: S. Watkins, D. Williams, Morris, Taylor
		C: Jarrett (3)
		DG: John
		PG: Jarrett
IRELAND	11	T: Gibson
		C: Kiernan
		PG: Kiernan (2)

14 Mar 1970, Lansdowne Road, Dublin
IRELAND	14	T: Duggan, Goodall
		C: Kiernan
		DG: McGann
		PG: Kiernan
WALES	0	

13 Mar 1971, Cardiff Arms Park
WALES	23	T: T. G. R. Davies (2), Edwards (2)
		C: John
		DG: John
		PG: John (2)
IRELAND	9	PG: Gibson (3)

10 Mar 1973, Cardiff Arms Park
WALES	16	T: Shanklin, Edwards
		C: Bennett
		PG: Bennett (2)
IRELAND	12	T: Gibson
		C: McGann
		PG: McGann (2)

2 Feb 1974, Lansdowne Road, Dublin
IRELAND	9	PG: Ensor (3)
WALES	9	T: J. J. Williams
		C: Bennett
		PG: Bennett

15 Mar 1975, Cardiff Arms Park
WALES	32	T: Edwards, T. G. R. Davies, Faulkner, J. J. Williams, Bergiers

C: Bennett (3)
PG: Bennett (2)
IRELAND	4	T: Duggan

21 Feb 1976, Lansdowne Road, Dublin
IRELAND	9	PG: McGann (3)
WALES	34	T: T. G. R. Davies (2), Edwards, Bennett
		C: Bennett (3)
		PG: Bennett (3), Martin

15 Jan 1977, Cardiff Arms Park
WALES	25	T: Davies, J. P. R. Williams, Burgess
		C: Bennett (2)
		DG: Fenwick
		PG: Bennett (2)
IRELAND	9	PG: Gibson (3)

4 Mar 1978, Lansdowne Road, Dublin
IRELAND	16	T: Moloney
		DG: Ward
		PG: Ward (3)
WALES	20	T: Fenwick, J. J. Williams
		PG: Fenwick (4)

3 Feb 1979, Cardiff Arms Park
WALES	24	T: Martin, Ringer
		C: Fenwick (2)
		PG: Fenwick (4)
IRELAND	21	T: McLennan, Patterson
		C: Ward (2)
		PG: Ward (3)

15 Mar 1980, Lansdowne Road, Dublin
IRELAND	21	T: Irwin, O'Driscoll, Fitzgerald
		C: Campbell (3)
		PG: Campbell
WALES	7	T: Blyth
		PG: Fenwick

21 Feb 1981, Cardiff Arms Park
WALES	9	DG: Pearce
		PG: Evans (2)
IRELAND	8	T: Slattery, MacNeill

23 Jan 1982, Lansdowne Road, Dublin
IRELAND	20	T: Ringland, Finn (2)
		C: Campbell
		PG: Campbell (2)
WALES	12	T: Holmes
		C: G. Evans
		DG: Pearce
		PG: G. Evans

5 Mar 1983, Cardiff Arms Park
WALES	23	T: Wyatt, Holmes, E. Rees
		C: Wyatt
		PG: Wyatt (3)
IRELAND	9	PG: Campbell (2), MacNeill

4 Feb 1984, Lansdowne Road, Dublin
IRELAND	9	PG: Campbell (3)
WALES	18	T: Ackerman
		C: H. Davies
		PG: H. Davies (2), Bowen (2)

16 Mar 1985, Cardiff Arms Park
WALES	9	T: P. I. Lewis
		C: W. G. Davies
		PG: W. G. Davies
IRELAND	21	T: Crossan, Ringland
		C: Kiernan (2)
		PG: Kiernan (3)

15 Feb 1986, Lansdowne Road, Dublin
IRELAND	12	T: Ringland
		C: Kiernan
		PG: Kiernan (2)
WALES	19	T: P. I. Lewis, P. T. Davies
		C: Thorburn
		PG: Thorburn (3)

4 April 1987, Cardiff Arms Park
WALES	11	T: I. Evans, Norster
		PG: Wyatt
IRELAND	15	T: Dean, Mullin
		C: Kiernan (2)
		PG: Kiernan

Scotland v Wales

8 Jan 1883, Raeburn Place, Edinburgh
SCOTLAND	3g	T: Macfarlan (2) Don Wauchope
		C: Maclagan (3)
WALES	1g	T: Judson
		C: Lewis

12 Jan 1884, Rodney Parade, Newport
WALES	0	
SCOTLAND	1t 1dg	T: Ainslie
		DG: Asher

10 Jan 1885, Hamilton Crescent, Glasgow
SCOTLAND	0	
WALES	0	

9 Jan 1886, Cardiff Arms Park
WALES	0	
SCOTLAND	2g 1t	T: Clay, Todd, A. R. Don Wauchope
		C: Macleod (2)

26 Feb 1887, Raeburn Place, Edinburgh
SCOTLAND	4g 8t	T: Lindsay (5), Don Wauchope, Orr, Reid, Macmillan, McEwan, Maclagan, Morton
		C: Berry (2) Woodrow (2)
WALES	0	

4 Feb 1888, Rodney Parade, Newport
WALES	1t	T: Pryce-Jenkins
SCOTLAND	0	

2 Feb 1889, Raeburn Place, Edinburgh
SCOTLAND	2t	T: Orr, Ker
WALES	0	

1 Feb 1890, Cardiff Arms Park
WALES	1t	T: Gould
SCOTLAND	1g 2t	T: Anderson, Boswell, Maclagan
		C: McEwan

7 Feb 1891, Raeburn Place, Edinburgh
SCOTLAND	15	T: C. E. Orr, J. E. Orr, Goodhue, Clauss (2), Leggatt, Boswell
		C: McEwan
		DG: W. Neilson, Stevenson
WALES	0	

6 Feb 1892, St Helens, Swansea
WALES	2	T: Hannan
SCOTLAND	7	T: Boswell, Campbell
		C: Boswell

4 Feb 1893, Raeburn Place, Edinburgh
SCOTLAND	0	
WALES	0	T: Bert Gould, Biggs, McCutcheon
		C: Bancroft

3 Feb 1894, Rodney Parade, Newport
WALES	7	T: Fitzgerald
		DG: Fitzgerald
SCOTLAND	0	

26 Jan 1895, Raeburn Place, Edinburgh
SCOTLAND	5	T: Gowans
		C: H. O. Smith
WALES	4	GM: Bancroft

25 Jan 1896, Cardiff Arms Park
WALES	6	T: Bowen, Gould
SCOTLAND	0	

4 Mar 1899, Inverleith, Edinburgh
SCOTLAND	21	T: Gedge, Smith, Monypenny
		DG: Lamond, Gedge
		GM: Thomson
WALES	10	T: Llewellyn Lloyd, Llewellyn
		C: Bancroft (2)

27 Jan 1900, St Helens, Swansea
WALES	12	T: Llewellyn (2), Nicholls, Williams
SCOTLAND	3	T: Dykes

9 Feb 1901, Inverleith, Edinburgh
SCOTLAND	18	T: Gillespie (2), Turnbull, Flett
		C: Gillespie (2), Flett
WALES	8	T: Llewellyn Lloyd, Boots
		C: Bancroft

1 Feb 1902, Cardiff Arms Park
WALES	14	T: Llewellyn (2), Gabe (2)
		C: Strand-Jones
SCOTLAND	5	T: Welsh
		C: Gillespie

7 Feb 1903, Inverleith, Edinburgh
SCOTLAND	6	T: Kyle
		PG: Timms
WALES	0	

6 Feb 1904, St Helens, Swansea
WALES	21	T: Gabe, Jones, Morgan, Brice
		C: Winfield (3)
		PG: Winfield
SCOTLAND	3	T: Orr

4 Feb 1905, Inverleith, Edinburgh
SCOTLAND	3	T: Little
WALES	6	T: Llewellyn (2)

3 Feb 1906, Cardiff Arms Park
WALES	9	T: Hodges, Cliff Pritchard, Maddocks
SCOTLAND	3	PG: MacLeod

2 Feb 1907, Inverleith, Edinburgh
SCOTLAND	6	T: Purves, Monteith
WALES	3	PG: Winfield

1 Feb 1908, St Helens, Swansea
WALES	6	T: Trew, Williams
SCOTLAND	5	T: Purves
		C: Geddes

6 Feb 1909, Inverleith, Edinburgh
SCOTLAND	3	PG: Cunningham
WALES	5	T: Trew
		C: Bancroft

5 Feb 1910, Cardiff Arms Park
WALES	14	T: Pugsley, Spiller, Baker, Ivor Morgan
		C: Bancroft
SCOTLAND	0	

4 Feb 1911, Inverleith, Edinburgh
SCOTLAND	10	T: Turner, Scott
		DG: Munro
WALES	32	T: Gibbs (3), Spiller (2), Williams (2), Rhys Thomas
		C: Dyke (2)
		DG: Spiller

3 Feb 1912, St Helens, Swansea
WALES	21	T: Hirst, Morgan, Plummer
		C: Bancroft (2)
		DG: Trew, Birt
SCOTLAND	6	T: Will, Milroy

1 Feb 1913, Inverleith, Edinburgh
SCOTLAND	0	
WALES	8	T: C. Lewis, T. Jones
		C: C. Lewis

7 Feb 1914, Cardiff Arms Park
WALES	24	T: Ivor Davies, Wetter, Hirst
		C: Bancroft (2)
		DG: Hirst, Lewis
		PG: Bancroft
SCOTLAND	5	T: Stewart
		C: Laing

7 Feb 1920, Inverleith, Edinburgh
SCOTLAND	9	T: Sloan
		PG: Kennedy (2)
WALES	5	T: Jenkins
		C: Jenkins

5 Feb 1921, St Helens, Swansea
WALES	8	DG: Jenkins (2)
SCOTLAND	14	T: Thomson, Buchanan, Sloan
		C: Maxwell
		PG: Maxwell

4 Feb 1922, Inverleith, Edinburgh
SCOTLAND	9	T: Browning (2)
		PG: Browning
WALES	9	T: Bowen
		C: Samuel
		DG: I. Evans

3 Feb 1923, Cardiff Arms Park
WALES	8	T: Lewis
		C: A. Jenkins
		PG: A. Jenkins
SCOTLAND	11	T: Liddell, Stuart, Gracie
		C: Drysdale

2 Feb 1924, Inverleith, Edinburgh
SCOTLAND	35	T: Smith (3), Bryce, Bertram, Wallace, Waddell, Macpherson
		C: Drysdale (4)
		PG: Drysdale
WALES	10	T: Griffiths, Ivor Jones
		C: Male (2)

7 Feb 1925, St Helens, Swansea
WALES	14	T: Hopkins, Jones, Cornish
		C: Parker
		PG: Parker
SCOTLAND	24	T: Smith (4), Wallace (2)
		C: Drysdale
		PG: Drysdale

6 Feb 1926, Murrayfield, Edinburgh
SCOTLAND	8	T: Waddell
		C: Drysdale
		PG: Gillies
WALES	5	T: Herrera
		C: Everson

The much feared and respected Scotland threequarter line of 1924–5 who were all at Oxford University at the same time. L to R: A. C. Wallace, G. G. Aitken, G. P. S. Macpherson, I. S. Smith.

5 Feb 1927, Cardiff Arms Park
WALES   0
SCOTLAND   5   T: Kerr
                          C: Gillies

4 Feb 1928, Murrayfield
SCOTLAND   0
WALES   13   T: A. Jenkins, Dai John,
                          Roberts
                          C: Male (2)

2 Feb 1929, St Helens, Swansea
WALES   14   T: Roberts (2), Morgan,
                          Peacock
                          C: Ivor Jones
SCOTLAND   7   DG: Dykes
                          PG: Brown

1 Feb 1930, Murrayfield
SCOTLAND   12   T: Simmers (2)
                          C: Waters
                          DG: Waddell
WALES   9   T: G. Jones
                          C: Ivor Jones
                          DG: G. Jones

7 Feb 1931, Cardiff Arms Park
WALES   13   T: Morley, Thomas, Boon
                          C: Bassett (2)
SCOTLAND   8   T: Crichton-Miller (2)
                          C: Allan

6 Feb 1932, Murrayfield
SCOTLAND   0
WALES   6   T: Boon
                          PG: Bassett

4 Feb 1933, St Helens, Swansea
WALES   3   T: Arthur
SCOTLAND   11   T: Smith, Jackson
                          C: Fyfe
                          PG: Fyfe

3 Feb 1934, Murrayfield
SCOTLAND   6   T: Logan
                          PG: Ritchie
WALES   13   T: Cowey (2), Rees
                          C: Jenkins (2)

2 Feb 1935, Cardiff Arms Park
WALES   10   T: Jones, Wooller
                          DG: Jenkins
SCOTLAND   6   T: Thom, Shaw

1 Feb 1936, Murrayfield
SCOTLAND   3   T: Murray
WALES   13   T: Wooller, Davey, Jones
                          C: Jenkins (2)

6 Feb 1937, St Helens, Swansea
WALES   6   T: Wooller (2)
SCOTLAND   13   T: Wilson Shaw, Dick (2)
                          C: Duncan Shaw (2)

5 Feb 1938, Murrayfield
SCOTLAND   8   T: Crawford
                          C: Crawford
                          PG: Crawford
WALES   6   T: McCarley (2)

4 Feb 1939, Cardiff Arms Park
WALES   11   T: M. Davies, Travers
                          C: Wooller
                          PG: Wooller
SCOTLAND   3   PG: Crawford

1 Feb 1947, Murrayfield
SCOTLAND   8   T: Elliot
                          C: Geddes
                          PG: Geddes
WALES   22   T: K. Jones (2), B. Williams,
                          Cleaver, L. Williams
                          C: Tamplin (2)
                          PG: Tamplin

7 Feb 1948, Cardiff Arms Park
WALES   14   T: B. Williams, Matthews,
                          K. Jones
                          C: Tamplin,
                          PG: Tamplin
SCOTLAND   0

5 Feb 1949, Murrayfield
SCOTLAND   6   T: Gloag, Smith
WALES   5   T: Williams
                          C: Trott

4 Feb 1950, St Helens, Swansea
WALES   12   T: Thomas, K. Jones
                          DG: Cleaver
                          PG: Lewis Jones
SCOTLAND   0

3 Feb 1951, Murrayfield
SCOTLAND   19   T: Gordon (2), Dawson
                          C: Inglis, Thomson
                          DG: Kinninmonth
                          PG: Thomson
WALES   0

2 Feb 1952, Cardiff Arms Park
WALES   11   T: K. Jones
                          C: M. Thomas
                          PG: M. Thomas (2)
SCOTLAND   0

7 Feb 1953, Murrayfield
SCOTLAND   0
WALES   12   T: B. Williams (2), Jones
                          PG: Davies

10 Apr 1954, St Helens, Swansea
WALES   15   T: Rhys Williams, Meredith,
                          Ray Williams, Morgan
                          PG: Evans
SCOTLAND   3   T: Henderson

5 Feb 1955, Murrayfield
SCOTLAND   14   T: Smith, Nichol
                          C: Elgie
                          DG: Docherty
                          PG: Elgie
WALES   8   T: Brewer (2)
                          C: Stephens

4 Feb 1956, Cardiff Arms Park
WALES   9   T: H. Morgan, C. Morgan,
                          Davies
SCOTLAND   3   PG: Cameron

2 Feb 1957, Murrayfield
SCOTLAND	9	T: Smith
		DG: Dorward
		PG: Scotland
WALES	6	T: R. Davies
		PG: T. Davies

1 Feb 1958, Cardiff Arms Park
WALES	8	T: Wells, Collins
		C: T. Davies
SCOTLAND	3	PG: A. Smith

7 Feb 1959, Murrayfield
SCOTLAND	6	T: Bruce
		PG: Scotland
WALES	5	T: Price
		C: T. Davies

6 Feb 1960, Cardiff Arms Park
WALES	8	T: Bebb
		C: Morgan
		PG: Morgan
SCOTLAND	0	

11 Feb 1961, Murrayfield
SCOTLAND	3	T: A Smith
WALES	0	

3 Feb 1962, Cardiff Arms Park
WALES	3	PG: Rees
SCOTLAND	8	T: Glasgow, ten Bos
		C: Scotland

2 Feb 1963, Murrayfield
SCOTLAND	0	
WALES	6	DG: Rowlands
		PG: Hodgson

1 Feb 1964, Cardiff Arms Park
WALES	11	T: Bradshaw, Thomas
		C: Bradshaw
		PG: Bradshaw
SCOTLAND	3	T: Laughland

6 Feb 1965, Murrayfield
SCOTLAND	12	DG: Simmers (2)
		PG: Wilson (2)
WALES	14	T: S. Watkins, Gale
		C: T. Price
		PG: T. Price (2)

5 Feb 1966, Cardiff Arms Park
WALES	8	T: K. Jones (2)
		C: Bradshaw
SCOTLAND	3	PG: Wilson

4 Feb 1967, Murrayfield
SCOTLAND	11	T: Hinshelwood, Telfer
		C: Wilson
		DG: Chisholm
WALES	5	T: Watkins
		C: T. Price

3 Feb 1968, Cardiff Arms Park
WALES	5	T: K. Jones
		C: Jarrett
SCOTLAND	0	

1 Feb 1969, Murrayfield
SCOTLAND	3	PG: Blaikie
WALES	17	T: John, Edwards,
		M. C. R. Richards
		C: Jarrett
		PG: Jarrett (2)

7 Feb 1970, Cardiff Arms Park
WALES	18	T: Daniel, Llewelyn, Dawes, Morris
		C: Edwards (2), Daniel
SCOTLAND	9	T: Robertson
		DG: Robertson
		PG: Lauder

6 Feb 1971, Murrayfield
SCOTLAND	18	T: Carmichael, Rea
		PG: P. Brown (4)
WALES	19	T: Taylor, Edwards, John, T. G. R. Davies
		C: John, Taylor
		PG: John

5 Feb 1972, Cardiff Arms Park
WALES	35	T: Edwards (2), Bergiers, T. G. R. Davies, Taylor
		C: John (3)
		PG: John (3)
SCOTLAND	12	T: Clark
		C: P. Brown
		PG: Renwick, P. Brown

3 Feb 1973, Murrayfield
SCOTLAND	10	T: Telfer, Steele
		C: Morgan
WALES	9	PG: Bennett (2), Taylor

19 Jan 1974, Cardiff Arms Park
WALES	6	T: Cobner
		C: Bennett
SCOTLAND	0	

1 Mar 1975, Murrayfield
SCOTLAND	12	DG: McGeechan
		PG: Morgan (3)
WALES	10	T: T. P. Evans
		PG: Fenwick (2)

7 Feb 1976, Cardiff Arms Park
WALES	28	T: J. J. Williams, Edwards, T.P. Evans
		C. Bennett (2)
		DG: Fenwick
		PG: Bennett (3)
SCOTLAND	6	T: Irvine
		C: Morgan

19 Mar 1977, Murrayfield
SCOTLAND	9	T: Irvine
		C: Irvine
		DG: McGeechan
WALES	18	T: J. J. Williams, Bennett
		C: Bennett (2)
		PG: Bennett (2)

18 Feb 1978, Cardiff Arms Park
WALES	22	T: Edwards, Gravell, Fenwick, Quinnell
		DG: Bennett
		PG: Bennett
SCOTLAND	14	T: Renwick, Tomes
		PG: Morgan (2)

20 Jan 1979, Murrayfield
SCOTLAND	13	T: Irvine
		PG: Irvine (3)
WALES	19	T: E. Rees, Holmes
		C: Fenwick
		PG: Fenwick (3)

1 Mar 1980, Cardiff Arms Park
WALES	17	T: Holmes, Keen,
		D. S. Richards
		C: Blyth
		PG: Fenwick
SCOTLAND	6	T: Renwick
		C: Irvine

7 Feb 1981, Murrayfield
SCOTLAND	15	T: Tomes, Irvine (pen. try)
		C: Renwick (2)
		PG: Renwick
WALES	6	DG: Fenwick (2)

20 Mar 1982, Cardiff Arms Park
WALES	18	T: Butler
		C: G. Evans
		PG: G. Evans (4)
SCOTLAND	34	T: Calder, Renwick,
		Pollock, White, Johnston
		C: Irvine (4)
		DG: Renwick, Rutherford

19 Feb 1983, Murrayfield
SCOTLAND	15	T: Renwick
		C: Dods
		PG: Dods (3)
WALES	19	T: S. T. Jones, E. Rees
		C: Wyatt
		PG: Wyatt (3)

21 Jan 1984, Cardiff Arms Park
WALES	9	T: Titley
		C: H. Davies
		PG: H. Davies
SCOTLAND	15	T: Paxton, Aitken
		C: Dods (2)
		PG: Dods

2 Mar 1985, Murrayfield
SCOTLAND	21	T: Paxton (2)
		C: Dods (2)
		PG: Dods
		DG: Rutherford (2)
WALES	25	T: Pickering (2)
		C: Wyatt
		PG: Wyatt (4)
		DG: W. G. Davies

1 Feb 1986, Cardiff Arms Park
WALES	22	T: Hadley
		PG: Thorburn (5)
		DG: J. Davies
SCOTLAND	15	T: Duncan, Jeffrey,
		G. Hastings
		PG: G. Hastings

21 March 1987, Murrayfield
SCOTLAND	21	T: Beattie, Jeffrey
		C: G. Hastings (2)
		PG: G. Hastings (2)
		DG: Rutherford

WALES	14	T: M. Jones
		C: Wyatt
		PG: Wyatt (2)
		DG: J. Davies

France v England

3 Mar 1910, Parc des Princes, Paris
FRANCE	3	T: Communeau
ENGLAND	11	T: Hudson (2), Berry
		C: Chapman

28 Jan 1911, Twickenham
ENGLAND	37	T: Lambert (2), Pillman (2),
		Mann, A. Stoop,
		Wodehouse
		C: Lambert (5)
		PG: Lambert (2)
FRANCE	0	

8 Apr 1912, Parc des Princes, Paris
FRANCE	8	T: Dufau, Falliot
		C: Boyau
ENGLAND	18	T: Birkett, Brougham,
		Eddison, Roberts
		C: Pillman
		DG: Coverdale

25 Jan 1913, Twickenham
ENGLAND	20	T: Coates (3), Pillman (2),
		Poulton
		C: Greenwood
FRANCE	0	

13 Apr 1914, Stade Colombes, Paris
FRANCE	13	T: Andre, Capmau, Lubin-
		Lebrere
		C: Besset (2)
ENGLAND	39	T: Poulton (4), Lowe (3),
		Davies, Watson
		C: Greenwood (6)

31 Jan 1920, Twickenham
ENGLAND	8	T: Davies
		C: Greenwood
		PG: Greenwood
FRANCE	3	T: Crabos

28 Mar 1921, Stade Colombes, Paris
FRANCE	6	PG: Crabos (2)
ENGLAND	10	T: Blakiston, Lowe
		C: Hammett (2)

25 Feb 1922, Twickenham
ENGLAND	11	T: Voyce
		C: Day
		PG: Day (2)
FRANCE	11	T: Cassayet, Got, Lasserre
		C: Crabos

2 Apr 1923, Stade Colombes, Paris
FRANCE	3	PG: Beguet
ENGLAND	12	T: Conway, Wakefield
		C: Luddington
		DG: Davies

23 Feb 1924, Twickenham
| ENGLAND | 19 | T: Jacob (3), Catcheside, Young
C: Conway (2) |
| FRANCE | 7 | T: Ballarin
DG: Behoteguy |

13 Apr 1925, Stade Colombes, Paris
| FRANCE | 11 | T: Barthe, Besson, Cluchague
C: Ducousso |
| ENGLAND | 13 | T: Hamilton-Wickes, Wakefield
C: Luddington (2)
GM: Luddington |

27 Feb 1926, Twickenham
| ENGLAND | 11 | T: Aslett (2), Kittermaster
C: Francis |
| FRANCE | 0 | |

2 Apr 1927, Stade Colombes, Paris
| FRANCE | 3 | T: Vellat |
| ENGLAND | 0 | |

25 Feb 1928, Twickenham
| ENGLAND | 18 | T: Periton (2), Palmer (2)
C: Richardson (3) |
| FRANCE | 8 | T: Galia, Jaureguy
C: Verger |

1 Apr 1929, Stade Colombes, Paris
| FRANCE | 6 | T: Houdet, Ribere |
| ENGLAND | 16 | T: Aarvold (2), Gummer, Periton
C: Stanbury (2) |

22 Feb 1930, Twickenham
| ENGLAND | 11 | T: Periton, Reeve, Robson
C: Black |
| FRANCE | 5 | T: Serin
C: Ambert |

6 Apr 1931, Stade Colombes, Paris
| FRANCE | 14 | T: Clady, Galia
DG: Baillette, Gerald |
| ENGLAND | 13 | T: Burland, Smeddle, Tallent
C: Black (2) |

19 Apr 1947, Twickenham
| ENGLAND | 6 | T: Guest, Roberts |
| FRANCE | 3 | PG: Prat |

29 Mar 1948, Stade Colombes, Paris
| FRANCE | 15 | T: Pomathios, Prat, Soro
C: Alvarez
DG: Bergougnan |
| ENGLAND | 0 | |

26 Feb 1949, Twickenham
| ENGLAND | 8 | T: Cannell
C: Holmes
DG: Preece |
| FRANCE | 3 | DG: Alvarez |

25 Feb 1950, Stade Colombes, Paris
| FRANCE | 6 | T: Cazenave, Pilon |
| ENGLAND | 3 | T: Smith |

24 Feb 1951, Twickenham
| ENGLAND | 3 | T: Boobyer |
| FRANCE | 11 | T: Basquet, Prat
C: Prat
DG: Prat |

5 Apr 1952, Stade Colombes, Paris
| FRANCE | 3 | T: Pomathios |
| ENGLAND | 6 | PG: Hall (2) |

28 Feb 1953, Twickenham
| ENGLAND | 11 | T: Butterfield, Evans, Woodward
C: Hall |
| ENGLAND | 0 | |

10 Apr 1954, Stade Colombes, Paris
| FRANCE | 11 | T: Boniface, M. Prat
C: J. Prat
DG: J. Prat |
| ENGLAND | 3 | T: Wilson |

26 Feb 1955, Twickenham
| ENGLAND | 9 | T: Higgins
PG: Hazell (2) |
| FRANCE | 16 | T: Baulon, Celaya
C: Vannier (2)
DG: J. Prat (2) |

14 Apr 1956, Stade Colombes, Paris
| FRANCE | 14 | T: Dupuy, Pauthe
C: Labazuy
PG: Labazuy (2) |
| ENGLAND | 9 | T: Thompson
PG: Allison (2) |

23 Feb 1957, Twickenham
| ENGLAND | 9 | T: Jackson (2), Evans |
| FRANCE | 5 | T: Darrouy
C: Vannier |

1 Mar 1958, Stade Colombes, Paris
| FRANCE | 0 | |
| ENGLAND | 14 | T: Thompson (2), Jackson
C: Hastings
PG: Hastings |

28 Feb 1959, Twickenham
| ENGLAND | 3 | PG: Hetherington |
| FRANCE | 3 | PG: Labazuy |

27 Feb 1960, Stade Colombes, Paris
| FRANCE | 3 | PG: Vannier |
| ENGLAND | 3 | T: Weston |

25 Feb 1961, Twickenham
| ENGLAND | 5 | T: Harding
C: Willcox |
| FRANCE | 5 | T: Crauste
C: Vannier |

24 Feb 1962, Stade Colombes, Paris
| FRANCE | 13 | T: Crauste (3)
C: Albaladejo (2) |
| ENGLAND | 0 | |

23 Feb 1963, Twickenham
| ENGLAND | 6 | PG: Willcox (2) |
| FRANCE | 5 | T: G. Boniface
C: Albaladejo |

22 Feb 1964, Stade Colombes, Paris
FRANCE	3	T: Darrouy
ENGLAND	6	T: Phillips
		PG: Hosen

27 Feb 1965, Twickenham
ENGLAND	9	T: Payne
		PG: Rutherford (2)
FRANCE	6	T: Darrouy
		PG: Dedieu

26 Feb 1966, Stade Colombes, Paris
FRANCE	13	T: A. Boniface, Gachassin, Graurin
		C: Lacaze (2)
ENGLAND	0	

25 Feb 1967, Twickenham
ENGLAND	12	DG: Finlan
		PG: Hosen (3)
FRANCE	16	T: Dourthe, Duprat
		C: G. Camberabero (2)
		DG: G. Camberabero
		PG: G. Camberabero

24 Feb 1968, Stade Colombes, Paris
FRANCE	14	T: Gachassin
		C: G. Camberabero
		DG: G. Camberabero, Lacaze
		PG: G. Camberabero
ENGLAND	9	DG: Weston
		PG: Hiller (2)

22 Feb 1969, Twickenham
ENGLAND	22	T: Fielding, Rollitt, Webb
		C: Hiller (2)
		PG: Hiller (3)
FRANCE	8	T: Bonal
		C: Lacaze
		DG: Lacaze

18 Apr 1970, Stade Colombes, Paris
FRANCE	35	T: Berot, Bonal, Bourgarel, Dauga, Lux, Trillo
		C: Villepreux (4)
		DG: Berot, Villepreux
		PG: Villepreux
ENGLAND	13	T: Spencer, Taylor
		C: Jorden (2)
		PG: Jorden

27 Feb 1971, Twickenham
ENGLAND	14	T: Hiller
		C: Hiller
		PG: Hiller (3)
FRANCE	14	T: Bertranne, Cantoni
		C: Villepreux
		DG: Berot
		PG: Villepreux

26 Feb 1972, Stade Colombes, Paris
FRANCE	37	T: Duprat (2), Biemouret, Lux, Sillieres, W. Spanghero
		C: Villepreux (5)
		PG: Villepreux
ENGLAND	12	T: Beese
		C: Old
		PG: Old (2)

24 Feb 1973, Twickenham
ENGLAND	14	T: Duckham (2)
		PG: Jorden (2)
FRANCE	6	T: Bertranne
		C: Romeu

2 Mar 1974, Parc des Princes, Paris
FRANCE	12	T: Romeu
		C: Romeu
		DG: Romeu
		PG: Romeu
ENGLAND	12	T: Duckham
		C: Old
		DG: Evans
		PG: Old

1 Feb 1975, Twickenham
ENGLAND	20	T: Duckham, Rossborough
		DG: Rossborough
		PG: Rossborough (4)
FRANCE	27	T: Etchenique, Gourdon, Guilbert, Spanghero
		C: Paries (4)
		PG: Paries

20 Mar 1976, Parc des Princes, Paris
FRANCE	30	T: Paparemborde (2), Bastiat, Fouroux, Gourdon, Romeu
		C: Romeu (3)
ENGLAND	9	T: Dixon
		C: Butler
		PG: Butler

19 Feb 1977, Twickenham
ENGLAND	3	PG: Hignell
FRANCE	4	T: Sangali

21 Jan 1978, Parc des Princes, Paris
FRANCE	15	T: Averous, Gallion
		C: Aguirre (2)
		PG: Aguirre
ENGLAND	6	DG: Old (2)

3 Mar 1979, Twickenham
ENGLAND	7	T: Bennett
		PG: Bennett
FRANCE	6	T: Costes
		C: Aguirre

2 Feb 1980, Parc des Princes, Paris
FRANCE	13	T: Averous, Rives
		C: Caussade
		PG: Caussade
ENGLAND	17	T: Carleton, Preston
		DG: Horton (2)
		PG: Hare

21 Mar 1981, Twickenham
ENGLAND	12	PG: Rose (4)
FRANCE	16	T: Lacans, Pardo
		C: Laporte
		DG: Laporte (2)

20 Feb 1982, Parc des Princes, Paris
FRANCE	15	T: Pardo
		C: Sallefranque
		DG: Lescarboura
		PG: Sallefranque (2)
ENGLAND	27	T: Woodward, Carleton

C: Hare (2)
PG: Hare (5)

15 Jan 1983, Twickenham
ENGLAND	15	DG: Cusworth
		PG: Hare (4)
FRANCE	19	T: Estève, Sella,
		Paparemborde
		C: Blanco (2)
		PG: Camberabero

3 Mar 1984, Parc des Princes, Paris
FRANCE	32	T: Codorniou, Sella, Estève,
		Begu, Gallion
		C: Lescarboura
		PG: Lescarboura
		DG: Lescarboura
ENGLAND	18	T: Underwood, Hare
		C: Hare (2)
		PG: Hare (2)

2 Feb 1985, Twickenham
ENGLAND	9	PG: Andrew (2)
		DG: Andrew
FRANCE	9	DG: Lescarboura (3)

15 Mar 1986, Parc des Princes, Paris
FRANCE	29	T: Sella, Laporte, Penalty
		try, Blanco
		C: Laporte (2)
		PG: Laporte (3)
ENGLAND	10	T: Dooley
		PG: Barnes (2)

21 Feb 1987, Twickenham
ENGLAND	15	PG: Rose (4)
		DG: Andrew
FRANCE	19	T: Bonneval, Sella
		C: Berot
		PG: Berot (2)
		DG: Mesnel

France v Ireland

28 Mar 1910, Parc des Princes, Paris
FRANCE	3	T: Guillemin
IRELAND	8	T: Thompson, Smyth
		C: McClinton

25 Mar 1911, Mardyke, Cork
IRELAND	25	T: Quinn, O'Callaghan,
		Jackson (2), Heffernan
		C: Lloyd (3)
		DG: Lloyd
FRANCE	5	T: Failliot
		C: Dutour

1 Jan 1912, Parc des Princes, Paris
FRANCE	6	T: Paoli, Dufau
IRELAND	11	T: Taylor, Foster, Lloyd
		C: Taylor

24 Mar 1913, Mardyke, Cork
IRELAND	24	T: Quinn (3), Tyrrell (2),
		Patterson
		C: Lloyd (3)
FRANCE	0	

1 Jan 1914, Parc des Princes, Paris
FRANCE	6	T: Lacoste, Andre
IRELAND	8	T: Quinn, Wood
		C: Lloyd

3 Apr 1920, Lansdowne Road, Dublin
IRELAND	7	T: Price
		DG: Lloyd
FRANCE	15	T: Gayraud, Got (2),
		Jaureguy (2)

9 Apr 1921, Stade Colombes, Paris
FRANCE	20	T: Piteu (2), Cassayet,
		Boubee
		C: Crabos (4)
IRELAND	10	T: Stokes (2)
		C: Wallis (2)

8 Apr 1922, Lansdowne Road, Dublin
IRELAND	8	T: G. Stephenson
		C: Wallis
		PG: Wallis
FRANCE	3	T: Pascot

14 Apr 1923, Stade Colombes, Paris
FRANCE	14	T: Jaureguy (2), Beguet,
		Moreau
		C: Beguet
IRELAND	8	T: Douglas, McClelland
		C: Crawford

26 Jan 1924, Lansdowne Road, Dublin
| IRELAND | 6 | T: G. Stephenson, Atkins |
| FRANCE | 0 | |

1 Jan 1925, Stade Colombes, Paris
FRANCE	3	T: Ribere
IRELAND	9	T: Sugden, G. Stephenson
		PG: Crawford

23 Jan 1926, Ravenhill, Belfast
IRELAND	11	T: Stephenson (2)
		C: Hewitt
		PG: Stephenson
FRANCE	0	

1 Jan 1927, Stade Colombes, Paris
FRANCE	3	T: Ribere
IRELAND	8	T: Davy
		C: Stephenson
		PG: Stephenson

28 Jan 1928, Ravenhill, Belfast
IRELAND	12	T: Ganly (2), Arigho (2)
FRANCE	8	T: Ribere, H. Behoteguy
		C: A. Behoteguy

30 Dec 1928, Yves du Manor Stadium, Paris
| FRANCE | 0 | |
| IRELAND | 6 | T: Davy, Stephenson |

25 Jan 1930, Ravenhill, Belfast
IRELAND	0	
FRANCE	5	T: Samatan
		C: Ambert

1 Jan 1931, Stade Colombes, Paris
FRANCE 3 T: Ribere
IRELAND 0

25 Jan 1947, Lansdowne Road, Dublin
IRELAND 8 T: McKay
C: Mullan
PG: Mullan
FRANCE 12 T: Lassegue (2), Prat, Sorondo

1 Jan 1948, Stade Colombes, Paris
FRANCE 6 T: Basquet, Soro
IRELAND 13 T: Reid, McCarthy, Mullan
C: Mullan (2)

29 Jan 1949, Lansdowne Road, Dublin
IRELAND 9 PG: Norton (3)
FRANCE 16 T: Basquet, Lassegue
C: Prat (2)
PG: Prat (2)

28 Jan 1950, Stade Colombes, Paris
FRANCE 3 DG: Lauga
IRELAND 3 PG: Burges

27 Jan 1951, Lansdowne Road, Dublin
IRELAND 9 T: Nelson, Clifford
PG: Henderson
FRANCE 8 T: Olive, Matheu
C: Bertrand

26 Jan 1952, Stade Colombes, Paris
FRANCE 8 T: J. Prat
C: J. Prat
PG: J. Prat
IRELAND 11 T: McCarthy (2)
C: Notley
PG: Henderson

24 Jan 1953, Ravenhill, Belfast
IRELAND 16 T: Lawler, McCarthy, Kyle, Mortell
C: Gregg (2)
FRANCE 3 DG: Carabignac

23 Jan 1954, Stade Colombes, Paris
FRANCE 8 T: M. Prat (2)
C: J. Prat
IRELAND 0

22 Jan 1955, Lansdowne Road, Dublin
IRELAND 3 PG: Henderson
FRANCE 5 T: Domenech
C: Vannier

28 Jan 2956, Stade Colombes, Paris
FRANCE 14 T: Boniface, Baulon
C: Vannier
DG: Vannier, Bouquet
IRELAND 8 T: O'Reilly
C: Pedlow
PG: Pedlow

26 Jan 1957, Lansdowne Road, Dublin
IRELAND 11 T: Brophy, Kyle
C: Pedlow
PG: Pedlow
FRANCE 6 PG: Vannier (2)

19 Apr 1958, Stade Colombes, Paris
FRANCE 11 T: Danos
C: Labuzuy
DG: Vannier
PG: Labazuy
IRELAND 6 PG: Henderson (2)

18 Apr 1959, Lansdowne Road, Dublin
IRELAND 9 T: Brophy
DG: English
PG: Hewitt
FRANCE 5 T: Dupuy
C: Lacaze

9 Apr 1960, Stade Colombes, Paris
FRANCE 23 T: Celaya, Domenech, Moncla, Rancoule
C: Bouquet
DG: Albaladejo (3)
IRELAND 6 T: Brophy (2)

15 Apr 1961, Lansdowne Road, Dublin
IRELAND 3 PG: Kiernan
FRANCE 15 T: Gachassin
DG: Bouquet, Albaladejo
PG: Vannier, Albaladejo

14 Apr 1962, Stade Colombes, Paris
FRANCE 11 T: Mommejat, Lacaze, Crauste
C: Albaladejo
IRELAND 0

26 Jan 1963, Lansdowne Road, Dublin
IRELAND 5 T: O'Reilly
C: Kiernan
FRANCE 24 T: G. Boniface, Darrouy (3)
C: Albaladejo (3)
DG: Albaladejo, A. Boniface

11 Apr 1964, Stade Colombes, Paris
FRANCE 27 T: Crauste, Lira, Darrouy (2), Arnaudet, Herrero
C: Albaladejo (3)
DG: Dedieu
IRELAND 6 T: Casey
DG: Gibson

23 Jan 1965, Lansdowne Road, Dublin
IRELAND 3 T: Doyle
FRANCE 3 T: Darrouy

29 Jan 1966, Stade Colombes, Paris
FRANCE 11 T: Darrouy (2)
C: Lacaze
PG: Lacaze
IRELAND 6 DG: Kiernan
PG: Gibson

15 Apr 1967, Lansdowne Road, Dublin
IRELAND 6 T: Molloy
PG: Kiernan
FRANCE 11 T: Cabanier
C: G. Camberabero
DG: G. Camberabero (2)

27 Jan 1968, Stade Colombes, Paris
FRANCE 16 T: Campaes, Dauga
C: Villepreux (2)

DG: Gachassin
PG: Villepreux

| IRELAND | 6 | PG: McCombe (2) |

25 Jan 1969, Lansdowne Road, Dublin

IRELAND	17	T: Moroney
		C: Moroney
		DG: McGann
		PG: Moroney (3)
FRANCE	9	T: Trillo
		PG: Villepreux (2)

24 Jan 1970, Stade Colombes, Paris

FRANCE	8	T: Sillieres
		C: Paries
		DG: Paries
IRELAND	0	

30 Jan 1971, Lansdowne Road, Dublin

IRELAND	9	T: Grant
		PG: O'Driscoll (2)
FRANCE	9	DG: Berot
		PG: Villepreux (2)

29 Jan 1972, Stade Colombes, Paris

FRANCE	9	T: Lux
		C: Villepreux
		PG: Villepreux
IRELAND	14	T: Moloney, McLoughlin
		PG: Kiernan (2)

14 Apr 1973, Lansdowne Road, Dublin

| IRELAND | 6 | PG: Gibson (2) |
| FRANCE | 4 | T: Phliponneau |

19 Jan 1974, Parc des Princes, Paris

FRANCE	9	T: Boffelli
		C: Aguirre
		PG: Berot
IRELAND	6	PG: Ensor (2)

1 Mar 1975, Lansdowne Road, Dublin

IRELAND	25	T: Ensor, Grace, McBride
		C: McCombe (2)
		DG: McCombe (2)
		PG: McCombe
FRANCE	6	DG: Paries
		PG: Paries

7 Feb 1976, Parc des Princes, Paris

FRANCE	26	T: Pecune, Cholley, Fouroux, Rives
		C: Rives, Bastiat
		PG: Romeu (2)
IRELAND	3	PG: Robbie

19 Mar 1977, Lansdowne Road, Dublin

IRELAND	6	PG: Gibson, Quinn
FRANCE	15	T: Bastiat
		C: Aguirre
		PG: Aguirre (2), Romeu

18 Feb 1978, Parc des Princes, Paris

FRANCE	10	T: Gallion
		PG: Aguirre (2)
IRELAND	9	PG: Ward (3)

20 Jan 1979, Lansdowne Road, Dublin

| IRELAND | 9 | PG: Ward (3) |
| FRANCE | 9 | T: Caussade |

C: Aguirre
PG: Aguirre

1 Mar 1980, Parc des Princes, Paris

FRANCE	19	T: Gourdon (2)
		C: Aguirre
		DG: Pedeutour
		PG: Aguirre (2)
IRELAND	18	T: McLennan
		C: Campbell
		DG: Campbell
		PG: Campbell

7 Feb 1981, Lansdowne Road, Dublin

IRELAND	13	T: MacNeill
		PG: Campbell (3)
FRANCE	19	T: Pardo
		DG: Laporte (2)
		PG: Laporte (2), Gabernet

20 Mar 1982, Parc des Princes, Paris

FRANCE	22	T: Blanco, Mesny
		C: Gabernet
		PG: Blanco (2), Gabernet (2)
IRELAND	9	PG: Campbell (3)

19 Feb 1983, Lansdowne Road, Dublin

IRELAND	22	T: Finn (2)
		C: Campbell
		PG: Campbell (4)
FRANCE	16	T: Blanco, Estève
		C: Blanco
		PG: Blanco (2)

21 Jan 1984, Parc des Princes, Paris

FRANCE	25	T: Gallion, Sella
		C: Lescarboura
		PG: Lescarboura (4)
		DG: Lescarboura
IRELAND	12	PG: Campbell (4)

2 Mar 1985, Lansdowne Road, Dublin

IRELAND	15	PG: Kiernan (5)
FRANCE	15	T: Estève, Codorniou
		C: Lescarboura (2)
		PG: Lescarboura

1 Feb 1986, Parc des Princes, Paris

FRANCE	29	T: Berbizier, Marocco, Sella
		C: Laporte
		PG: Laporte (3), Blanco
		DG: Lafond
IRELAND	9	PG: Kiernan (3)

21 March 1987, Lansdowne Road, Dublin

IRELAND	13	T: Ringland, Bradley
		C: Kiernan
		PG: Kiernan
FRANCE	19	T: Champ (2)
		C: Berot
		PG: Berot (3)

France v Scotland

22 Jan 1910, Inverleith, Edinburgh
SCOTLAND　　27　　T: Tennent (3), Robertson (2), Angus, Gowlland
C: MacCallum (3)
FRANCE　　0

2 Jan 1911, Stade Colombes, Paris
FRANCE　　16　　T: Laterrade, Failliot (2), Peyroutou
C: Descamps (2)
SCOTLAND　　15　　T: MacCallum, Munro, Abercrombie
C: Turner
DG: Pearson

20 Jan 1912, Inverleith, Edinburgh
SCOTLAND　　31　　T: Gunn, Sutherland (2), Pearson, Will, Turner
C: Turner (5)
PG: Pearson
FRANCE　　3　　T: Communeau

1 Jan 1913, Parc des Princes, Paris
FRANCE　　3　　T: Sebedio
SCOTLAND　　21　　T: Stewart (3), Gordon (2)
C: Turner (3)

1 Jan 1920, Parc des Princes, Paris
FRANCE　　0
SCOTLAND　　5　　T: Crole
C: Kennedy

22 Jan 1921, Inverleith, Edinburgh
SCOTLAND　　0
FRANCE　　3　　T: Billac

2 Jan 1922, Stade Colombes, Paris
FRANCE　　3　　T: Jaureguy
SCOTLAND　　3　　T: Browning

20 Jan 1923, Inverleith, Edinburgh
SCOTLAND　　16　　T: McClaren (2), Bryce, Liddell
C: Drysdale (2)
FRANCE　　3　　GM: Beguet

1 Jan 1924, Stade Pershing, Paris
FRANCE　　12　　T: Jaureguy, Piquirial, Galau, Moureu
SCOTLAND　　10　　T: Wallace
DG: Waddell
PG: Davies

24 Jan 1925, Inverleith, Edinburgh
SCOTLAND　　25　　T: Smith (4), Wallace (2), Gillies
C: Gillies, Drysdale
FRANCE　　4　　DG: du Manoir

2 Jan 1926, Stade Colombes, Paris
FRANCE　　6　　T: Piquiral
PG: Gonnet

SCOTLAND　　20　　T: Wallace (3), MacMyn, Bannerman
C: Drysdale
PG: Gillies

22 Jan 1927, Murrayfield, Edinburgh
SCOTLAND　　23　　T: Waddell (2), Smith (2)
C: Gillies (3), Drysdale
PG: Gillies
FRANCE　　6　　T: Piquiral, Hutin

2 Jan 1928, Stade Colombes, Paris
FRANCE　　6　　T: Haget, Camel
SCOTLAND　　15　　T: Simmers, Paterson, Dykes, Douty, Scott

19 Jan 1929, Murrayfield
SCOTLAND　　6　　T: Paterson
PG: Brown
FRANCE　　3　　T: Behoteguy

1 Jan 1930, Stade Colombes, Paris
FRANCE　　7　　T: Bioussa
DG: Magnanou
SCOTLAND　　3　　T: Simmers

24 Jan 1931, Murrayfield
SCOTLAND　　6　　PG: Allan (2)
FRANCE　　4　　DG: Servole

1 Jan 1947, Stade Colombes, Paris
FRANCE　　8　　T: Lassegue, Terreau
C: Prat
SCOTLAND　　3　　PG: Geddes

24 Jan 1948, Murrayfield
SCOTLAND　　9　　T: Jackson
PG: Murdoch (2)
FRANCE　　8　　T: Lacaussade
C: Alvarez
PG: Prat

15 Jan 1949, Stade Colombes, Paris
FRANCE　　0
SCOTLAND　　8　　T: Elliot, Kininmonth
C: Allardice

14 Jan 1950, Murrayfield
SCOTLAND　　8　　T: Macdonald, Budge
C: Bruce-Lockhart
FRANCE　　5　　T: Merquey
C: Prat

13 Jan 1951, Stade Colombes, Paris
FRANCE　　14　　T: Mias, Porthault
C: Prat
PG: Prat (2)
SCOTLAND　　12　　T: Rose (2)
PG: Gray

12 Jan 1952, Murrayfield
SCOTLAND　　11　　T: Cordial
C: Thomson
PG: Thomson (2)
FRANCE　　13　　T: J. Prat, Basquet
C: J. Prat (2)
PG: J. Prat

10 Jan 1953, Stade Colombes, Paris
FRANCE	11	T: Bordeau
		C: Bertrand
		DG: Carabignac
		PG: Bertrand
SCOTLAND	5	T: Rose
		C: Cameron

9 Jan 1954, Murrayfield
SCOTLAND	0	
FRANCE	3	T: Brejassou

8 Jan 1955, Stade Colombes, Paris
FRANCE	15	T: Boniface, J. Prat,
		Domenech, Dufau
		PG: Vannier
SCOTLAND	0	

14 Jan 1956, Murrayfield
SCOTLAND	12	T: Kemp (2)
		PG: Smith, Cameron
FRANCE	0	

12 Jan 1957, Stade Colombes, Paris
FRANCE	0	
SCOTLAND	6	DG: Scotland
		PG: Scotland

11 Jan 1958, Murrayfield
SCOTLAND	11	T: Stevenson, Hastie
		C: Chisholm
		PG: Chisholm
FRANCE	9	T: Dupuy
		PG: Vannier

10 Jan 1959, Stade Colombes, Paris
FRANCE	9	T: Moncla
		DG: Lacaze (2)
SCOTLAND	0	

9 Jan 1960, Murrayfield
SCOTLAND	11	T: A. Smith (2)
		C: Elliot
		PG: Elliot
FRANCE	13	T: Meyer, Mericq, Moncla
		C: Vannier (2)

7 Jan 1961, Stade Colombes, Paris
FRANCE	11	T: Boniface
		C: Albaladejo
		DG: Albaladejo
		PG: Albaladejo
SCOTLAND	0	

13 Jan 1962, Murrayfield
SCOTLAND	3	PG: Smith
FRANCE	11	T: Rancoule
		C: Albaladejo
		PG: Albaladejo (2)

12 Jan 1963, Stade Colombes, Paris
FRANCE	6	DG: A. Boniface
		PG: Albaladejo
SCOTLAND	11	T: Thomson
		C: Scotland
		DG: Scotland
		PG: Scotland

4 Jan 1964, Murrayfield
SCOTLAND	10	T: Laughland, Thomson
		C: Wilson (2)

FRANCE	0	

9 Jan 1965, Stade Colombes, Paris
FRANCE	16	T: Gachassin, Pique,
		Darrouy (2)
		C: Dedieu (2)
SCOTLAND	8	T: Henderson (2)
		C: Scotland

15 Jan 1966, Murrayfield
SCOTLAND	3	T: Whyte
FRANCE	3	PG: Lacaze

14 Jan 1967, Stade Colombes, Paris
FRANCE	8	T: Duprat, Carrere
		C: Gachassin
SCOTLAND	9	DG: Simmers
		PG: Wilson (2)

13 Jan 1968, Murrayfield
SCOTLAND	6	T: Keith
		PG: Wilson
FRANCE	8	T: Duprat, Campaes
		C: G. Camberabero

11 Jan 1969, Stade Colombes, Paris
FRANCE	3	PG: Villepreux
SCOTLAND	6	T: J. Telfer
		PG: Blaikie

10 Jan 1970, Murrayfield
SCOTLAND	9	T: Smith
		PG: Lauder (2)
FRANCE	11	T: Dauga, Lux
		C: Paries
		DG: Paries

16 Jan 1971, Stade Colombes, Paris
FRANCE	13	T: Sillieres, Villepreux
		C: Villepreux (2)
		PG: Villepreux
SCOTLAND	8	T: Steele
		C: P. Brown
		PG: Smith

15 Jan 1972, Murrayfield
SCOTLAND	20	T: Telfer, Renwick, Frame
		C: A. Brown
		DG: Telfer
		PG: P. Brown
FRANCE	9	T: Dauga
		C: Villepreux
		PG: Villepreux

13 Jan 1973, Parc des Princes, Paris
FRANCE	16	T: Dourthe
		DG: Romeu
		PG: Romeu (3)
SCOTLAND	13	T: Lawson
		DG: McGeechan
		PG: Brown (2)

16 Mar 1974, Murrayfield
SCOTLAND	19	T: McHarg, Dick
		C: Irvine
		PG: Morgan, Irvine (2)
FRANCE	6	DG: Romeu
		PG: Romeu

15 Feb 1975, Parc des Princes, Paris

FRANCE	10	T: Dourthe
		DG: Astre
		PG: Paries
SCOTLAND	9	PG: Irvine (3)

10 Jan 1976, Murrayfield

SCOTLAND	6	DG: Morgan
		PG: Renwick
FRANCE	13	T: Dubertrand
		PG: Romeu (3)

5 Mar 1977, Parc des Princes, Paris

FRANCE	23	T: Paco, Harize, Bertranne, Paparemborde
		C: Romeu (2)
		PG: Romeu
SCOTLAND	3	PG: Irvine

4 Feb 1978, Murrayfield

SCOTLAND	16	T: Shedden, Irvine
		C: Morgan
		DG: Morgan
		PG: Morgan
FRANCE	19	T: Gallion, Haget
		C: Aguirre
		PG: Aguirre (3)

17 Mar 1979, Parc des Princes, Paris

FRANCE	21	T: Belascain, Malquier (2)
		DG: Aguerre
		PG: Aguerre, Aguirre
SCOTLAND	17	T: Robertson, Dickson, Irvine
		C: Irvine
		PG: Irvine

16 Feb 1980, Murrayfield

SCOTLAND	22	T: Rutherford, Irvine (2)
		C: Irvine, Renwick
		PG: Irvine (2)
FRANCE	14	T: Gallion, Gabernet
		DG: Caussade
		PG: Gabernet

17 Jan 1981, Parc des Princes, Paris

FRANCE	16	T: Blanco, Bertranne
		C: Caussade
		PG: Vivies, Gabernet

SCOTLAND	9	T: Rutherford
		C: Renwick
		PG: Irvine

6 Mar 1982, Murrayfield

SCOTLAND	16	T: Rutherford
		DG: Renwick
		PG: Irvine (3)
FRANCE	7	T: Rives
		PG: Sallefranque

5 Feb 1983, Parc des Princes, Paris

FRANCE	19	T: Estève (2)
		C: Blanco
		PG: Blanco (3)
SCOTLAND	15	T: Robertson
		C: Dods
		DG: Gossman (2)
		PG: Dods

17 Feb 1984, Murrayfield

SCOTLAND	21	T: Calder
		C: Dods
		PG: Dods (5)
FRANCE	12	T: Gallion
		C: Lescarboura
		PG: Lescarboura
		DG: Lescarboura

16 Feb 1985, Parc des Princes, Paris

FRANCE	11	T: Blanco (2)
		PG: Lescarboura
SCOTLAND	3	PG: Dods

17 Jan 1986, Murrayfield

SCOTLAND	18	PG: G. Hastings (6)
FRANCE	17	T: Berbizier, Sella
		PG: Laporte (2)
		DG: Laporte

7 Mar 1987, Parc des Princes, Paris

FRANCE	28	T: Bonneval (3), Berot
		PG: Berot (3)
		DG: Mesnel
SCOTLAND	22	T: Beattie, S. Hastings
		C: G. Hastings
		PG: G. Hastings (4)

Gareth Edwards

Cardiff and Wales

Gareth Owen Edwards played 53 times for Wales in succession. During that time Wales won seven International Championships, five Triple Crowns and two Grand Slams. He toured with the British Lions three times. In 1968 hamstring trouble limited his appearances to a meagre eight, but in 1971 he was one of the key players in the Lions first (and only) test series victory in New Zealand. Three years later he was a principal member of Willie John McBride's unbeaten Lions in South Africa.

Like his fellow Welshmen of those heady days, Barry John and Gerald Davies, he avoided that nasty tendency for fine careers to turn sour before the hero retired. When he retired in 1978 only Clive Shell and Ray Hopkins had received caps during Gareth's reign at scrum-half, and both of those were as a replacement. That, by any standards, is endurance of the highest order.

Born on 12 July 1947 at Gwaen-cae-Gurwen, Gareth Edwards was educated at Pontardawe Grammar School and Millfield. Both schools did much to instill good rugby basics. At Millfield he won the All England schools 200 yards low hurdles in record time, leaving future Commonwealth and European 400 metres Hurdles gold medallist Alan Pascoe trailing 20 yards adrift.

From Millfield, Edwards went to Cardiff College of Education and joined the Cardiff club. He was a student when first called to national honours in 1967. His second appearance was highlighted by Keith Jarrett's 19 points salvo. He engaged in two memorable half-back partnerships – first with Barry John with whom he played for Wales on 23 occasions, and later with Phil Bennett.

At the age of 20 years 7 months he became the youngest captain of Wales. One can say with hindsight that this role was not quite suitable; the responsibility of worrying about others shackled his own individual brilliance. Indeed, it was a brief reign.

Gareth Edwards has scored more tries by far than any other scrum-half in world rugby. His tally of 20 places him just behind wingers David Campese, Ian Smith and Gerald Davies on the all-time list. The types of try varied: in 1972 an 85-yard (78m) kick and chase revealing the schoolboy sprinting qualities, but often a tigerish burst to the line through a phalanx of covering defenders landed the spoils.

He retired in 1978, declining to go on tour to Australia after a strenuous winter season at home. Edwards quit while right at the top, and in this, as in his entire career, he never let down the demanding Welsh rugby fans.

Gareth Edwards blasts through flimsy English cover during the 1971 match at Cardiff.

John P. R. Williams

London Welsh, Bridgend and Wales

J. P. R. Williams was a central figure in all that was best in British rugby in the early 1970s. And at that time, it was the best in the world. Whether it be with those two triumphant British Lions teams, successful in New Zealand in 1971, and in South Africa three years later, or with the superb Welsh team that won the Grand Slam in 1971, or even the attractive, fluid play of London Welsh that drew so many to Old Deer Park, J. P. R.'s style was the same – long hair flying in the wind on a counter attack, rock-like in defence and absolutely fearless.

Yet many people overlooked another aspect of J. P. R.'s play. His physical presence and bravery were well known. He was 6ft 2in (1.85m), weighed 14 stones (88.9kg) and as a full-back was often larger than many of his forwards. Indeed, he once played against Australia in 1978 as a flanker. But he was also a tennis player of repute. In 1966,

as a Millfield schoolboy, he won Junior Wimbledon, beating future Davis Cup stalwart David Lloyd in the final. You need touch and timing in tennis, something that J. P. R.'s rugby opponents often forgot he possessed.

Born on 2 March 1949, he was educated at Bridgend GS and Millfield. Williams first played for Bridgend, and after a Welsh tour to Argentina in 1968 he joined London Welsh while studying to become a doctor at St Mary's Hospital. At the time, two factors elevated him above other contenders for the number 15 jersey in the Welsh national team – a general paucity of class full-backs and, more importantly, the new law forbidding players to kick for touch on the full outside the 25 (or 22 as it is now) had given the full-back a new role. J. P. R. was to revolutionize the game.

He took particular delight in scoring tries against the Old

Enemy. His first international try was against England in 1970, he added another in 1972, became the first full-back to score two in a match in 1976, and signed off with another match-winning effort the following year. His six international tries were a record until surpassed by Andy Irvine.

After the 1974 Lions tour to South Africa, J. P. R.'s rugby career marked time while he took his exams, and opened his own practice dealing in sports injuries. But he was part of the Grand Slam teams again in 1976 and 1978, and on his return to Bridgend was honoured with captaincy of club and country. He became the record Welsh cap winner with his 54th appearance, and collected one more before retirement. If in the last couple of years his play tailed off (as work demanded more of his time) it was only in comparison with the unique standards that he himself had set.

THE RECORDS
Most capped Welsh international 55 caps
Double international Rugby and Tennis
Record number of Grand Slam titles 3 – in 1971, 1976 and 1978 (with G. O. Edwards and T. G. R. Davies)
World's most capped full-back 54 caps

J. P. R. Williams demonstrates his defensive capabilities as he shoulder-charges the powerful French wing Jean-François Gourdon into touch barely a yard from the line. Wales won 19–13 to complete the 1976 Grand Slam.

France v Wales

1 Jan 1910, St Helens, Swansea
WALES	49	T: Gibbs (3), Morgan (2), Maddocks (2), Trew, J. Jones, Gronow C: Bancroft (8) PG: Bancroft
FRANCE	14	T: Lafitte, Mauriat C: Menrath PG: Menrath (2)

28 Feb 1911, Parc des Princes, Paris
FRANCE	0	
WALES	15	T: Morgan, Williams, Owen C: Bancroft (3)

25 Mar 1912, Rodney Parade, Newport
WALES	14	T: Davies (2), Plummer, Jones C: Thomas
FRANCE	8	T: Lesieur, Larribeau C: Boyau

27 Feb 1913, Parc des Princes, Paris
FRANCE	8	T: Failliot, Andre C: Struxiano
WALES	11	T: C. Lewis, Davies, Williams C: C. Lewis

2 Mar 1914, St Helens, Swansea
WALES	31	T: Wetter (2), Uzzell (2), Hirst, Rev. Davies, Evans C: Bancroft
FRANCE	0	

17 Feb 1920, Stade Colombes, Paris
FRANCE	5	T: Jaureguy C: Struxiano
WALES	6	T: B. Williams, Powell

26 Feb 1921, Cardiff Arms Park
WALES	12	T: J. Williams, Hodder PG: Jenkins (2)
FRANCE	4	DG: Lasserre

23 Mar 1922, Stade Colombes, Paris
FRANCE	3	T: Jaureguy
WALES	11	T: Whitfield, Cummins, I. Evans C: Jenkins

24 Feb 1923, St Helens, Swansea
WALES	16	T: Harding, M. Thomas, Baker C: A. Jenkins (2) PG: Rees
FRANCE	8	T: Lalande, Lasserre C: Larrieu

27 Mar 1924, Stade Colombes, Paris
FRANCE	6	T: Behoteguy, Lubin-Lebrere
WALES	10	T: Finch, Rickards DG: Griffiths

28 Feb 1925, Cardiff Arms Park
WALES	11	T: Finch (2), Delahay C: Parker
FRANCE	5	T: de Laborderie C: Ducousso

5 Apr 1926, Stade Colombes, Paris
FRANCE	5	T: Gerintes C: Gonnet
WALES	7	T: Watkins DG: Cornish

26 Feb 1927, St Helens, Swansea
WALES	25	T: Roberts (2), Harding (2), Thomas, Andrews, Morgan C: Male (2)
FRANCE	7	T: Prevost DG: Verger

9 Apr 1928, Stade Colombes, Paris
FRANCE	8	T: Houdet (2) C: A. Behoteguy
WALES	3	T: Powell

25 Feb 1929, Cardiff Arms Park
WALES	8	T: Arthur, Barrell C: Parker
FRANCE	3	T: A. Camel

21 Apr 1930, Stade Colombes, Paris
FRANCE	0	
WALES	11	T: Skym DG: Morgan, Powell

28 Feb 1931, St Helens, Swansea
WALES	35	T: Ralph (2), Davey, Fender, Lang, Williams, Arthur C: Bassett (5) DG: Powell
FRANCE	3	T: Petit

22 Mar 1947, Stade Colombes, Paris
FRANCE	0	
WALES	3	PG: Tamplin

21 Feb 1948, St Helens, Swansea
WALES	3	PG: O. Williams
FRANCE	11	T: Basquet, Terreau, Pomathios C: Alvarez

26 Mar 1949, Stade Colombes, Paris
FRANCE	5	T: Lassegue C: Alvarez
WALES	3	T: K. Jones

25 Mar 1950, Cardiff Arms Park
WALES	21	T: K. Jones (2), John, Matthews C: Lewis Jones (3) PG: Lewis Jones
FRANCE	0	

7 Apr 1951, Stade Colombes, Paris
FRANCE	8	T: Alvarez C: Prat PG: Alvarez
WALES	3	PG: K. Jones

22 Mar 1952, St Helens, Swansea
WALES	9	DG: A. Thomas
		PG: Lewis Jones (2)
FRANCE	5	T: Pomathios
		C: J. Prat

28 Mar 1953, Stade Colombes, Paris
FRANCE	3	PG: Bertrand
WALES	6	T: Griffiths (2)

27 Mar 1954, Cardiff Arms Park
WALES	19	T: Griffiths, B. Williams
		C: Evans (2)
		PG: Evans (3)
FRANCE	13	T: Martine, Baulon
		C: J. Prat (2)
		PG: J. Prat

26 Mar 1955, Stade Colombes, Paris
FRANCE	11	T: Baulon
		C: Vannier
		DG: M. Prat
		PG: Vannier
WALES	16	T: Thomas, Morris
		C: Owen (2)
		PG: Owen (2)

24 Mar 1956, Cardiff Arms Park
WALES	5	T: Williams
		C: Owen
FRANCE	3	T: Bouquet

23 Mar 1957, Stade Colombes, Paris
FRANCE	13	T: Dupuy, Prat, Sanac
		C: Bouquet (2)
WALES	19	T: Prosser, Howells, Faull, B. V. Meredith
		C: T. J. Davies (2)
		PG: T. J. Davies

29 Mar 1958, Cardiff Arms Park
WALES	6	T: Collins
		PG: T. J. Davies
FRANCE	16	T: Danos, Tarricq
		C: Labazuy (2)
		DG: Vannier (2)

4 Apr 1959, Stade Colombes, Paris
FRANCE	11	T: Moncla (2)
		C: Labazuy
		PG: Labazuy
WALES	3	PG: T. J. Davies

26 Mar 1960, Cardiff Arms Park
WALES	8	T: Cresswell
		C: N. Morgan
		PG: N. Morgan
FRANCE	16	T: Celaya, Lacroix, Meficq, Dupuy
		C: Vannier, Albaladejo

25 Mar 1961, Stade Colombes, Paris
FRANCE	8	T: Boniface, Saux
		C: Vannier
WALES	6	T: Pask, Bebb

24 Mar 1962, Cardiff Arms Park
WALES	3	PG: Coslett
FRANCE	0	

23 Mar 1963, Stade Colombes, Paris
FRANCE	5	T: G. Boniface
		C: Albaladejo
WALES	3	PG: Hodgson

21 Mar 1964, Cardiff Arms Park
WALES	11	T: S. Watkins
		C: Bradshaw
		PG: Bradshaw (2)
FRANCE	11	T: Crauste
		C: Albaladejo
		PG: Albaladejo (2)

27 Mar 1965, Stade Colombes, Paris
FRANCE	22	T: G. Boniface (2), Herrero (2)
		C: Dedieu (2)
		DG: Lasserre
		PG: Dedieu
WALES	13	T: Dawes, S. Watkins, Bebb
		C: T. Price (2)

26 Mar 1966, Cardiff Arms Park
WALES	9	T: S. Watkins
		PG: Bradshaw (2)
FRANCE	8	T: Duprat, Rupert
		C: Lacaze

1 Apr 1967, Stade Colombes, Paris
FRANCE	20	T: G. Camberabero, Dauga, Dourthe
		C: G. Camberabero
		DG: G. Camberabero (2)
		PG: G. Camberabero
WALES	14	T: Bebb
		C: T. Price
		DG: D. Watkins
		PG: T. Price (2)

23 Mar 1968, Cardiff Arms Park
WALES	9	T: W. K. Jones
		PG: D. Rees (2)
FRANCE	14	T: L. Camberabero, Carrere
		C: G. Camberabero
		DG: G. Camberabero
		PG: G. Camberabero

22 Mar 1969, Stade Colombes, Paris
FRANCE	8	T: Campaes
		C: Villepreux
		PG: Villepreux
WALES	8	T: Edwards, M. C. R. Richards
		C: Jarrett

4 Apr 1970, Cardiff Arms Park
WALES	11	T: Morris
		C: J. P. R. Williams
		PG: J. P. R. Williams (2)
FRANCE	6	T: Cantoni, Bonal

27 Mar 1971, Stade Colombes, Paris
FRANCE	5	T: Dauga
		C: Villepreux
WALES	9	T: Edwards, John
		PG: John

25 Mar 1972, Cardiff Arms Park

| WALES | 20 | T: T. G. R. Davies, J. C. Bevan
PG: John (4) |
| FRANCE | 6 | PG: Villepreux (2) |

24 Mar 1973, Parc des Princes, Paris

| FRANCE | 12 | DG: Romeu
PG: Romeu (3) |
| WALES | 3 | DG: Bennett |

16 Feb 1974, Cardiff Arms Park

| WALES | 16 | T: J. J. Williams
DG: Edwards
PG: Bennett (3) |
| FRANCE | 16 | T: Lux
DG: Romeu
PG: Romeu (3) |

18 Jan 1975, Parc des Princes, Paris

| FRANCE | 10 | T: Gourdon
PG: Taffary (2) |
| WALES | 25 | T: Fenwick, Cobner, T. G. R. Davies, Edwards, G. Price
C: Fenwick
PG: Fenwick |

6 Mar 1976, Cardiff Arms Park

| WALES | 19 | T: J. J. Williams
PG: Bennett (2), Fenwick (2), Martin |
| FRANCE | 13 | T: Gourdon, Averous
C: Romeu
PG: Romeu |

5 Feb 1977, Parc des Princes, Paris

| FRANCE | 16 | T: Skréla, Harize
C: Romeu
PG: Romeu (2) |
| WALES | 9 | PG: Fenwick (3) |

18 Mar 1978, Cardiff Arms Park

| WALES | 16 | T: Bennett (2)
C: Bennett
DG: Edwards, Fenwick |
| FRANCE | 7 | T: Skréla
DG: Vivies |

17 Feb 1979, Parc des Princes, Paris

| FRANCE | 14 | T: Gourdon (2)
PG: Aguirre (2) |
| WALES | 13 | T: Holmes
PG: Fenwick (3) |

19 Jan 1980, Cardiff Arms Park

| WALES | 18 | T: E. Rees, Holmes, D. S. Richards, G. Price
C: W. G. Davies |
| FRANCE | 9 | T: Marchal
C: Caussade
DG: Caussade |

7 Mar 1981, Parc des Princes, Paris

| FRANCE | 19 | T: Gabernet
PG: Laporte (3), Gabernet (2) |
| WALES | 15 | T: D. S. Richards
C: G. Evans
PG: G. Evans (3) |

6 Feb 1982, Cardiff Arms Park

| WALES | 22 | T: Holmes
PG: G. Evans (6) |
| FRANCE | 12 | T: Blanco
C: Sallefranque
PG: Sallefranque, Martinez |

19 Mar 1983, Parc des Princes, Paris

| FRANCE | 16 | T: Estève
DG: Camberabero
PG: Blanco (3) |
| WALES | 9 | T: Squire
C: Wyatt
PG: G. Evans |

18 Feb 1984, Cardiff Arms Park

| WALES | 16 | T: H. Davies, Butler
C: H. Davies
PG: H. Davies (2) |
| FRANCE | 21 | T: Sella
C: Lescarboura
PG: Lescarboura (4)
DG: Lescarboura |

30 Mar 1985, Parc des Princes, Paris

| FRANCE | 14 | T: Estève, Gallion
PG: Lescarboura (2) |
| WALES | 3 | PG: Thorburn |

1 Mar 1986, Cardiff Arms Park

| WALES | 15 | PG: Thorburn (5) |
| FRANCE | 23 | T: Sella, Lafond (2), Blanco
C: Laporte (2)
DG: Laporte |

7 Feb 1987, Parc des Princes, Paris

| FRANCE | 16 | T: Mesnel, Bonneval
C: Berot
PG: Berot (2) |
| WALES | 9 | PG: Thorburn (3) |

France v Australia

1948, Paris

| FRANCE | 13 | T: Basquet (2), Pomathios
C: Alvarez (2) |
| AUSTRALIA | 6 | PG: Tonkin (2) |

9 Mar 1958, Stade Colombes, Paris

| FRANCE | 19 | T: Crauste, Quaglio, Rancoule
C: A. Labazuy (2)
DG: M. Prat, A Labazuy |
| AUSTRALIA | 0 | |

22 Aug 1961, Sydney

| AUSTRALIA | 8 | T: Heinrich
C: Elwood
PG: Elwood |
| FRANCE | 15 | T: Lacroix, Pique, Bouguyon
DG: P. Albaladejo (2) |

11 Feb 1967, Stade Colombes, Paris
FRANCE	20	T: L. Camberabero
		C: G. Camberabero
		PG: G. Camberabero (4)
		DG: G. Camberabero
AUSTRALIA	14	T: G. Davis, Johnson
		C: Hawthorne
		PG: Hawthorne
		DG: Hawthorne

17 Aug 1968, Sydney
AUSTRALIA	11	T: Smith
		C: McGill
		PG: McGill
		DG: Ballesty
FRANCE	10	T: W. Spanghero, Boujet
		C: Villepreux, Boujet

20 Nov 1971, Toulouse
FRANCE	11	T: Skréla, Bertranne
		PG: Villepreux
AUSTRALIA	13	T: L'Estrange (2)
		C: McGill
		PG: J. McLean

27 Nov 1971, Stade Colombes, Paris
FRANCE	18	T: Boffeli
		C: Villepreux
		PG: Villepreux (4)
AUSTRALIA	9	PG: McGill, J. McLean (2)

17 Jun 1972, Sydney
AUSTRALIA	14	T: Taafe, Taylor
		PG: Fairfax (2)
FRANCE	14	T: Lux (2), Saisset
		C: Villepreux

23 Jun 1972, Brisbane
AUSTRALIA	15	PG: Fairfax (5)
FRANCE	16	T: Maso (2), W. Spanghero
		C: Villepreux, Cabrol

24 Oct 1976, Bordeaux
FRANCE	18	T: Bertranne, Paparemborde, Cholley
		C: Droitecourt (3)
AUSTRALIA	15	PG: P. McLean (4)
		DG: P. McLean

31 Oct 1976, Parc des Princes, Paris
FRANCE	34	T: Harize, Averous, Bertranne, Aguirre, Rives, Cholley
		C: Aguirre (2)
		PG: Aguirre
		DG: Astre
AUSTRALIA	6	PG: P. McLean (2)

5 Jul 1981, Ballymore, Brisbane
AUSTRALIA	17	T: Poidevin, O'Connor, Moon
		C: McLean
		PG: Richards
FRANCE	15	T: Mesny
		C: Gabernet
		PG: Blanco, Gabernet
		DG: Vivies

11 Jul 1981, Sydney Cricket Ground
AUSTRALIA	24	T: Hall, O'Connor
		C: P. E. McLean (2)
		PG: P. E. McLean (4)
FRANCE	14	T: Lacaⁱs, Elissalde
		DG: Elissalde, Sallefranque

13 Nov 1983, Clermont-Ferrand
FRANCE	15	PG: Lescarboura (3)
		DG: Lescarboura, Lafond
AUSTRALIA	15	T: Roche
		C: Campese
		PG: Campese
		DG: M. Ella, Hawker

20 Nov 1983, Parc des Princes, Paris
FRANCE	15	T: Estève
		C: Lescarboura
		PG: Gabernet, Lescarboura (2)
AUSTRALIA	6	PG: Campese
		DG: M. Ella

21 Jun 1986, Sydney Cricket Ground
AUSTRALIA	27	T: Campese
		C: Lynagh
		PG: Lynagh (6)
		DG: Lynagh
FRANCE	14	T: Blanco (2), Sella
		C: Lescarboura

France v New Zealand

1 Jan 1906, Parc des Princes, Paris
FRANCE	8	T: Cessieux, Jerome
		C: Pujol
NEW ZEALAND	38	T: Wallace (3), Abbott (2), Hunter (2), Harper (2), Glasgow
		C: Wallace (2), Tyler, Abbott

18 Jan 1925, Stade des Ponts Jumeaux, Toulouse
FRANCE	6	T: Cassayet, Ribere
NEW ZEALAND	30	T: Cooke (2), White, Porter, Steel, Svenson, Irvine, Richardson
		C: Nicholls (3)

27 Feb 1954, Stade Colombes, Paris
FRANCE	3	T: J. Prat
NEW ZEALAND	0	

22 Jul 1961, Eden Park, Auckland
NEW ZEALAND   13   T: McKay, O'Sullivan
                         C: D. B. Clarke (2)
                         DG: D. B. Clarke
FRANCE   6   DG: Albaladejo (2)

5 Aug 1961, Athletic Park, Wellington
NEW ZEALAND   5   T: Tremain
                         C: D. B. Clarke (4)
FRANCE   3   T: Dupuy

19 Aug 1961, Lancaster Park, Christchurch
NEW ZEALAND   32   T: Graham, Little, Tremain,
                          Meads, Yates
                          C: D. B. Clarke
                          PG: D. B. Clarke (3)
FRANCE   3   T: Crauste

8 Feb 1964, Stade Colombes, Paris
FRANCE   3   PG: Albaladejo
NEW ZEALAND   12   T: Caulton, Gray
                          PG: Herewini
                          DG: Laidlaw

25 Nov 1967, Stade Colombes, Paris
FRANCE   15   T: Campaes
                          PG: Villepreux (3)
                          DG: Gachassin
NEW ZEALAND   21   T: Going, Kirkpatrick, Dick,
                          Steel
                          C: McCormick (3)
                          PG: McCormick

13 Jul 1968, Lancaster Park, Christchurch
NEW ZEALAND   12   T: Kirton
                          PG: McCormick (3)
FRANCE   9   PG: Villepreux (2)
                          DG: Lacaze

27 Jul 1968, Athletic Park, Wellington
NEW ZEALAND   9   PG: McCormick (3)
FRANCE   3   PG: Villepreux

10 Aug 1968, Eden Park, Auckland
NEW ZEALAND   19   T: Going (2)
                          C: McCormick (2)
                          PG: McCormick (2)
                          DG: Cottrell
FRANCE   12   T: Trillo, Carrere, Lux
                          DG: Dourthe

10 Feb 1973, Parc des Princes, Paris
FRANCE   13   T: Dourthe, Bertranne
                          C: Romeu
                          PG: Romeu
NEW ZEALAND   6   PG: Karam (2)

11 Nov 1977, Stadium de Toulouse
FRANCE   18   T: Paparemborde
                          C: Romeu
                          PG: Romeu (3)
                          DG: Romeu
NEW ZEALAND   13   T: Williams
                          PG: McKechnie, Williams
                          DG: Robertson

19 Nov 1977, Parc des Princes, Paris
FRANCE   3   PG: Romeu
NEW ZEALAND   15   T: Wilson
                          C: McKechnie
                          PG: McKechnie, Seear
                          DG: McKechnie

7 Jul 1979, Lancaster Park, Christchurch
NEW ZEALAND   23   T: S. S. Wilson, Donaldson,
                          Watts
                          C: B. W. Wilson
                          PG: B. W. Wilson (3)
FRANCE   9   T: Mesny
                          C: Aguirre
                          DG: Caussade

14 Jul 1979, Eden Park, Auckland
NEW ZEALAND   19   T: S. Wilson, Mourie
                          C: B. Wilson
                          PG: B. Wilson (3)
FRANCE   24   T: Averous, Codorniou,
                          Caussade, Gallion
                          C: Caussade
                          PG: Aguirre
                          DG: Caussade

14 Nov 1981, Stadium de Toulouse
FRANCE   9   PG: Laporte (2)
                          DG: Gabernet
NEW ZEALAND   13   T: Wilson
                          PG: Hewson (2)
                          DG: Hewson

21 Nov 1981, Parc des Princes, Paris
FRANCE   6   PG: Laporte, Blanco
NEW ZEALAND   18   T: Shaw (pen. try), Wilson
                          C: Hewson (2)
                          PG: Hewson (2)

16 Jun 1984, Lancaster Park, Christchurch
NEW ZEALAND   10   T: Taylor
                          PG: Hewson (2)
FRANCE   9   T: Blanco
                          C: Lescarboura
                          PG: Lescarboura

23 Jun 1984, Eden Park, Auckland
NEW ZEALAND   31   T: B. Smith, Taylor, Dalton
                          C: Hewson (2)
                          PG: Hewson (5)
FRANCE   18   T: Lescarboura (2),
                          Bonneval
                          PG: Lescarboura (2)

28 Jun 1986, Lancaster Park, Christchurch
NEW ZEALAND   18   T: Brewer
                          C: Cooper
                          PG: Cooper (2)
                          DG: Botica (2)
FRANCE   9   DG: Lescarboura (3)

8 Nov 1986, Stadium de Toulouse
FRANCE   7   T: Sella
                          PG: Berot
NEW ZEALAND   19   T: W. Shelford
                          PG: Crowley (3)
                          DG: Stone, Crowley

15 Nov 1986, Beajoire Stadium, Nantes
FRANCE   16   T: Charvet, Lorieux
                          C: Berot
                          PG: Berot (2)
NEW ZEALAND   3   PG: Crowley

France v South Africa

1913, Bordeaux
FRANCE	5	T: Bruneau
		C: Andre
SOUTH AFRICA	38	T: W. Morkel, D. Morkel (2), Francis, R. Luyt, McHardy (2), Ledger, J. Morkel
		C: D. Morkel (2), G. Morkel (2)
		PG: D. Morkel

16 Feb 1952, Stade Colombes, Paris
FRANCE	3	DG: Carbignac
SOUTH AFRICA	25	T: Johnstone (2), Dinkelman, Muller, Delport, van Wyk
		C: Muller, Johnstone
		PG: Johnstone

26 Jul 1958, Newlands, Cape Town
SOUTH AFRICA	3	T: Lochner
FRANCE	3	DG: Danos

16 Aug 1958, Ellis Park, Johannesburg
SOUTH AFRICA	5	T: Fourie
		C: Gerber
FRANCE	9	PG: Lacaze
		DG: Lacaze, Martine

18 Feb 1961, Stade Colombes, Paris
FRANCE	0	
SOUTH AFRICA	0	

25 Jul 1964, Springs, South Africa
SOUTH AFRICA	6	T: Stewart
		PG: Stewart
FRANCE	8	T: Darrouy
		C: Albaladejo
		PG: Albaladejo

15 Jul 1967, Kingsmead, Durban
SOUTH AFRICA	26	T: Dirksen (2), Greyling (2), Ellis
		C: H. de Villiers (4)
		PG: H. de Villiers
FRANCE	3	T: Dourthe

22 Jul 1967, Free State Stadium, Bloemfontein
SOUTH AFRICA	16	T: Olivier, Dirksen, Engelbrecht
		C: H. de Villiers (2)
		PG: Naude
FRANCE	3	PG: Villepreux

29 Jul 1967, Ellis Park, Johannesburg
SOUTH AFRICA	14	T: Olivier, Ellis
		C: Visagie
		PG: Naude (2)
FRANCE	19	T: Cabanier, Trillo
		C: G. Camberabero (2)
		DG: G. Camberabero (2)
		PG: Lacaze

12 Aug 1967, Newlands, Cape Town
SOUTH AFRICA	6	DG: Visagie
		PG: H. de Villiers
FRANCE	6	T: Spanghero
		PG: G. Camberabero

9 Nov 1968, Bordeaux
FRANCE	9	T: Douga (2), Bonal
SOUTH AFRICA	12	PG: Visagie (4)

16 Nov 1968, Stade Colombes, Paris
FRANCE	11	T: Cester
		C: Paries
		DG: Puget, Paries
SOUTH AFRICA	16	T: Engelbrecht, D. de Villiers, Nomis
		C: Visagie (2)
		PG: Visagie

12 Jun 1971, Free State Stadium, Bloemfontein
SOUTH AFRICA	22	T: Muller, Viljoen
		C: McCallum (2)
		PG: McCallum (3)
		DG: Visagie
FRANCE	9	T: Trillo
		PG: Berot (2)

19 Jun 1971, Kings Park, Durban
SOUTH AFRICA	8	T: Cronje
		C: McCallum
		DG: Visagie
FRANCE	8	T: Bertranne
		C: Berot
		DG: Cantoni

23 Nov 1974, Stadium de Toulouse
FRANCE	4	T: Bertranne
SOUTH AFRICA	13	T: Stapelberg
		PG: Bosch (2), C. Fourie

30 Oct 1974, Parc des Princes, Paris
FRANCE	8	T: Gourdon, Dourthe
SOUTH AFRICA	10	T: Stapelberg
		PG: Bosch (2)

21 Jun 1975, Free State Stadium, Bloemfontein
SOUTH AFRICA	38	T: Whipp, Grobler, Cockrell, Oosthuizen, Pope
		C: Bosch (2), Dawie Snyman
		PG: Bosch (3), Dawie Snyman
FRANCE	25	T: Skrela, Paparemborde, Averous, Harize
		C: Pesteil (3)
		PG: Pesteil

28 Jun 1975, Loftus Versveld, Pretoria
SOUTH AFRICA	33	T: C. Fourie, du Plessis
		C: Bosch (2)
		PG: Bosch (6), C. Fourie
FRANCE	18	T: E. Paparemborde
		C: Romeu
		DG: Romeu
		PG: Romeu (3)

8 Nov 1980, Loftus Versveld, Pretoria
SOUTH AFRICA	37	T: Pienaar, Germishuys, Serfontein, Stofberg, Kahts
		C: Botha (4)
		PG: Botha (3)

FRANCE	15	T: Dintrans
		C: Vivies
		PG: Vivies (3)

England v New Zealand

2 Dec 1905, Crystal Palace, London
ENGLAND	0	
NEW ZEALAND	15	T: McGregor (4), Newton

3 Jan 1925, Twickenham
ENGLAND	11	T: Cove-Smith, Kittermaster
		C: Conway
		PG: Corbett
NEW ZEALAND	17	T: Svenson, Steel, Parker,
		M. J. Brownlie
		C: Nicholls
		PG: Nicholls

4 Jan 1936, Twickenham
ENGLAND	13	T: Obolensky (2), Sever
		DG: Cranmer
NEW ZEALAND	0	

30 Jan 1954, Twickenham
ENGLAND	0	
NEW ZEALAND	5	T: Dalzell
		C: Scott

25 May 1963, Eden Park, Auckland
NEW ZEALAND	21	T: Caulton (2), D. B. Clarke
		C: D. B. Clarke (3)
		PG: D. B. Clarke
		DG: D. B. Clarke
ENGLAND	11	T: Ranson
		C: Hosen
		PG: Hosen (2)

1 Jun 1963, Lancaster Park, Christchurch
NEW ZEALAND	9	T: McKay, Walsh
		GM: D. B. Clarke
ENGLAND	6	T: Phillips
		PG: Hosen

4 Jan 1964, Twickenham
ENGLAND	0	
NEW ZEALAND	14	T: Caulton, Meads
		C: D. B. Clarke
		PG: D. B. Clarke (2)

4 Nov 1967, Twickenham
ENGLAND	11	T: Lloyd (2)
		C: Rutherford
		PG: Larter
NEW ZEALAND	23	T: Kirton (2), Birtwistle,
		Laidlaw, Dick
		C: McCormick (4)

6 Jan 1973, Twickenham
ENGLAND	0	
NEW ZEALAND	9	T: Kirkpatrick
		C: Karam
		DG: Williams

15 Sep 1973, Eden Park, Auckland
NEW ZEALAND	10	T: Batty, Hurst
		C: Lendrum
ENGLAND	16	T: Squires, Stevens, Neary
		C: Rossborough (2)

25 Nov 1978, Twickenham
ENGLAND	6	PG: Hare
		DG: Hare
NEW ZEALAND	16	T: Oliver, Johnstone
		C: McKechnie
		PG: McKechnie (2)

24 Nov 1979, Twickenham
ENGLAND	9	PG: Hare (3)
NEW ZEALAND	10	T: Fleming
		PG: R. G. Wilson (2)

19 Nov 1983, Twickenham
ENGLAND	15	T: Colclough
		C: Hare
		PG: Hare (3)
NEW ZEALAND	9	T: Davie
		C: Deans
		PG: Deans

1 Jun 1985, Lancaster Park, Christchurch
NEW ZEALAND	18	PG: Crowley (6)
ENGLAND	13	T: Harrison, Teague
		C: Barnes
		PG: Barnes

8 Jun 1985, Athletic Park, Wellington
NEW ZEALAND	42	T: Green (2), Kirwan,
		Mexted, Shaw, Hobbs
		C: Crowley (3)
		PG: Crowley (3)
		DG: Smith
ENGLAND	15	T: Hall, Harrison
		C: Barnes (2)
		DG: Barnes

Ireland v New Zealand

25 Nov 1905, Lansdowne Road, Dublin
IRELAND	0	
NEW ZEALAND	15	T: Deans (2), McDonald
		C: Wallace (3)

1 Nov 1924, Lansdowne Road, Dublin
IRELAND	0	
NEW ZEALAND	6	T: Svenson
		PG: Nicholls

7 Dec 1935, Lansdowne Road, Dublin
IRELAND	9	T: Beamish
		PG: Bailey, Siggins
NEW ZEALAND	17	T: Mitchell, Oliver, Hart
		C: Gilbert
		PG: Gilbert (2)

9 Jan 1954, Lansdowne Road, Dublin
IRELAND	3	PG: Henderson

NEW ZEALAND   14   T: Clark, Stuart
C: Scott
PG: Scott
DG: Scott

7 Dec 1963, Lansdowne Road, Dublin
IRELAND   5   T: Fortune
C: Kiernan
NEW ZEALAND   6   T: Tremain
PG: Clarke

20 Jan 1973, Lansdowne Road, Dublin
IRELAND   10   T: Grace
PG: McGann (2)
NEW ZEALAND   10   T: Going, Wyllie
C: Karam

23 Nov 1974, Lansdowne Road, Dublin
IRELAND   6   PG: Ensor (2)
NEW ZEALAND   15   T: Karam
C: Karam
PG: Karam (3)

5 Jun 1976, Athletic Park, Wellington
NEW ZEALAND   11   T: B. J. Robertson,
Kirkpatrick
PG: Mains
IRELAND   3   PG: McGann

4 Nov 1978, Lansdowne Road, Dublin
IRELAND   6   PG: Ward (2)
NEW ZEALAND   10   T: Dalton
DG: Bruce (2)

Scotland v New Zealand

18 Nov 1905, Inverleith, Edinburgh
SCOTLAND   7   T: MacCallum
DG: E. D. Simson
NEW ZEALAND   12   T: Smith (2), Glasgow,
Cunningham

23 Nov 1935, Murrayfield, Edinburgh
SCOTLAND   8   T: Fyfe, Dick
C: Murdoch
NEW ZEALAND   18   T: Caughey (3), Hadley
C: Gilbert (3)

13 Feb 1954, Murrayfield
SCOTLAND   0
NEW ZEALAND   3   PG: Scott

18 Jan 1964, Murrayfield
SCOTLAND   0
NEW ZEALAND   0

2 Dec 1967, Murrayfield
SCOTLAND   3   DG: Chisholm
NEW ZEALAND   14   T: MacRae, Davis
C: McCormick
PG: McCormick (2)

16 Dec 1972, Murrayfield
SCOTLAND   9   PG: P. C. Brown, Irvine
DG: McGeechan

NEW ZEALAND   14   T: Wyllie, Batty, Going
C: Karam

14 Jun 1975, Eden Park, Auckland
NEW ZEALAND   24   T: Williams (2), Macdonald,
Robertson
C: Karam (4)
SCOTLAND   0

9 Dec 1978, Murrayfield
SCOTLAND   9   T: Hay
C: Irvine
DG: Irvine
NEW ZEALAND   18   T: Seear, Robertson
C: McKechnie (2)
PG: McKechnie (2)

10 Nov 1979, Murrayfield
SCOTLAND   6   PG: Irvine (2)
NEW ZEALAND   20   T: S. S. Wilson, Dunn,
Loveridge, Mexted
C: R. G. Wilson

13 Jun 1981, Carisbrook, Dunedin
NEW ZEALAND   11   T: Wilson, Loveridge
PG: Hewson
SCOTLAND   4   T: Deans

20 Jun 1981, Eden Park, Auckland
NEW ZEALAND   40   T: Wilson (3), Hewson (2),
Robertson, Mourie
C: Hewson (6)
SCOTLAND   15   T: Hay
C: Irvine
PG: Irvine (2)
DG: Renwick

12 Nov 1983, Murrayfield
SCOTLAND   25   T: Pollock
PG: Dods (5)
DG: Rutherford (2)
NEW ZEALAND   25   T: Hobbs, Fraser (2)
C: Deans (2)
PG: Deans (3)

Wales v New Zealand

16 Dec 1905, Cardiff Arms Park
WALES   3   T: Morgan
NEW ZEALAND   0

29 Nov 1925, St Helens, Swansea
WALES   0
NEW ZEALAND   19   T: Irvine (2),
M. J. Brownlie, Svenson
C: Nicholls (2)
PG: Nicholls

21 Dec 1935, Cardiff Arms Park
WALES   13   T: Rees-Jones (2), Davey
C: Jenkins (2)
NEW ZEALAND   12   T: Ball (2)
C: Gilbert
DG: Gilbert

The All Blacks (top) led by Wayne Shelford performing their 'Haka' with considerably more cohesion than the equivalent offerings of Fiji (above) and Tonga (below). The cohesion was more marked on the field as well.

David Kirk, the New Zealand captain, with the World Cup. Andy Dalton, who did not play in the tournament was the squad captain for the Cup.

The leading try scorers, John Kirwan (right) scoring his second try against Wales in the semi final, and Craig Green (right below) brought down by Serge Blanco (France) in the Final. Both New Zealanders scored six tries in the tournament.

Michael Jones, the Auckland flanker (below), voted by most critics as the outstanding player in the World Cup, charges past the French defence in the Final.

Adrian Hadley scores a last second try for Wales against Australia to bring the score to 20-21 . . . then Paul

Thorburn (arms raised) celebrates his outstanding pressure kick to bring Wales victory.

Three of the personalities of the
World Cup.
Right, Grant Fox, the New Zealand
outside half, who scored 126 points
during the tournament.
Below, Michael Lynagh, the
Australian outside half, broke the
Australian points scoring record
previously held by Paul McLean.
Below right, John Devereux, the
outstanding Wales centre who lived
up to all his early promise.

John Kirwan (left) and Alan Whetton (right) add to Fijian misery in a match that produced a new world record score; New Zealand's 74 points beating their total of 70 against Italy earlier in the tournament.

The new breed of Rugby supporter? – French and Australian fans mingle before the spectacular semi final won by France 30-24.

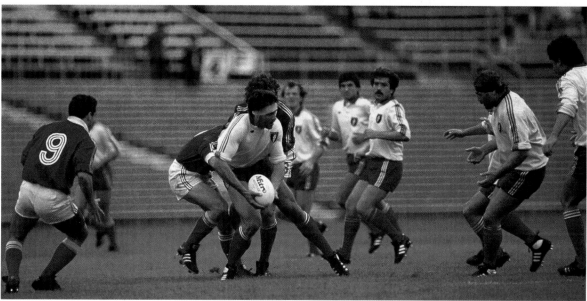

Some of the emerging Nations in action.

Top, Japan gain possession in their best performance in defeat, a free running exhibition against Australia.

Above, Romania snatch rare possession against Scotland.

Below, Tonga move forward menacingly against the green shirted Welsh defence in a positive performance before losing 29-16.

The United States move purposely forward against England.

Left, Zimbabwe celebrate their one moment of glory, a try by David Buitendag in the drubbing against Scotland.

. . . and finally the faithful dog gives his opinion of Argentina's performance against New Zealand!

19 Dec 1953, Cardiff Arms Park
WALES   13   T: Judd, K. Jones
                    C: Rowlands (2)
                    PG: Rowlands
NEW ZEALAND 8   T: Clark
                    C: Jarden
                    PG: Jarden

21 Dec 1963, Cardiff Arms Park
WALES   0
NEW ZEALAND 6   PG: Clarke
                    DG: Watt

11 Nov 1967, Cardiff Arms Park
WALES   6   PG: Gale
                    DG: John
NEW ZEALAND 13 T: Birtwistle, Davis
                    C: McCormick (2)
                    PG: McCormick

31 May 1969, Lancaster Park, Christchurch
NEW ZEALAND 19 T: Dick, McLeod, Lochore,
                    Gray
                    C: McCormick (2)
                    PG: McCormick
WALES   0

14 Jun 1969, Eden Park, Auckland
NEW ZEALAND 33 T: Skudder, MacRae,
                    Kirkpatrick
                    C: McCormick (3)
                    PG: McCormick (5)
                    DG: McCormick

Clashes between Wales and New Zealand are always competitive and currently marked by a certain lack of success by the Welsh. Here J. P. R. Williams shows the scars of battle during an encounter between Bridgend and the All Blacks in 1978.

WALES   12   T: M. C. R. Richards,
                    Jarrett
                    PG: Jarrett (2)

2 Dec 1972, Cardiff Arms Park
WALES   16   T: J. C. Bevan
                    PG: Bennett (4)
NEW ZEALAND 19 T: Murdoch
                    PG: Karam (5)

11 Nov 1978, Cardiff Arms Park
WALES   12   PG: W. G. Davies (3),
                    Fenwick
NEW ZEALAND 13 T: S. S. Wilson
                    PG: McKechnie (3)

1 Nov 1980, Cardiff Arms Park
WALES   3   PG: Fenwick
NEW ZEALAND 23 T: Mourie, Fraser, Allen,
                    Reid
                    C: Rollerson (2)
                    PG: Rollerson

Great Britain/British Isles v New Zealand

13 Aug 1904, Athletic Park, Wellington
NEW ZEALAND 9   T: D. McGregor (2)
                    PG: Wallace
GREAT BRITAIN 3   PG: Harding

21 Jun 1930, Carisbrook, Dunedin
NEW ZEALAND 3   T: Hart
GREAT BRITAIN 6   T: Reeve, Morley

5 Jul 1930, Lancaster Park, Christchurch
NEW ZEALAND 13 T: Hart, Oliver
                    C: Nicholls (2)
                    GM: Nicholls
GREAT BRITAIN 10 T: Aarvold (2)
                    C: Prentice (2)

26 Jul 1930, Eden Park, Auckland
NEW ZEALAND 15 T: McLean (2), Lucas
                    C: Strang
                    DG: Nicholls
GREAT BRITAIN 10 T: Bowcott, Aarvold
                    C: Jones, Black

9 Aug 1930, Athletic Park, Wellington
NEW ZEALAND 22 T: Porter (2), Cooke (2)
                    Strang, Batty
                    C: Strang (2)
GREAT BRITAIN 8   T: Novis
                    C: Black
                    PG: Parker

27 May 1950, Carisbrook, Dunedin
NEW ZEALAND 9   T: Roper, Elvidge
                    PG: Scott
BRITISH ISLES 9   T: Kyle, Jones
                    PG: Robins

10 Jun 1950, Lancaster Park, Christchurch
NEW ZEALAND   8   T: Crowley, Roper
                                C: Haigh
BRITISH ISLES   0

1 Jul 1950, Athletic Park, Wellington
NEW ZEALAND   6   T: Elvidge
                                PG: Scott
BRITISH ISLES   3   PG: Robins

29 Jul 1950, Eden Park, Auckland
NEW ZEALAND   11   T: Wilson, Henderson
                                C: Scott
                                DG: Scott
BRITISH ISLES   8   T: K. J. Jones
                                C: B. L. Jones
                                PG: B. L. Jones

18 Jul 1959, Carisbrook, Dunedin
NEW ZEALAND   18   PG: D. B. Clarke (6)
BRITISH ISLES   17   T: Price (2), O'Reilly,
                                Jackson
                                C: Risman
                                PG: Hewitt

15 Aug 1959, Athletic Park, Wellington
NEW ZEALAND   11   T: Caulton (2), D. B. Clarke
                                C: D. B. Clarke
BRITISH ISLES   8   T: Young
                                C: Davies
                                PG: Davies

29 Aug 1959, Lancaster Park, Christchurch
NEW ZEALAND   22   T: Caulton (2), Meads,
                                Urbahan
                                C: D. B. Clarke (2)
                                PG: D. B. Clarke
                                DG: D. B. Clarke
BRITISH ISLES   8   T: Hewitt
                                C: Faull
                                PG: Faull

19 Sep 1959, Eden Park, Auckland
NEW ZEALAND   6   PG: D. B. Clarke (2)
BRITISH ISLES   9   T: O'Reilly, Jackson,
                                Risman

16 Jul 1966, Carisbrook, Dunedin
NEW ZEALAND   20   T: McLeod, Williment,
                                Lochore
                                C: Williment
                                PG: Williment (2)
                                DG: Herewini
BRITISH ISLES   3   PG: Wilson

6 Aug 1966, Athletic Park, Wellington
NEW ZEALAND   16   T: Tremain, C. E. Meads,
                                Steel
                                C: Williment (2)
                                PG: Williment
BRITISH ISLES   12   PG: Wilson (3)
                                DG: Watkins

27 Aug 1966, Lancaster Park, Christchurch
NEW ZEALAND   19   T: Nathan (2), Steel
                                C: Williment (2)
                                PG: Williment (2)
BRITISH ISLES   6   T: Lamont, D. Watkins

10 Sep 1966, Eden Park, Auckland
NEW ZEALAND   24   T: Nathan, Dick, MacRae,
                                Steel
                                C: Williment (3)
                                PG: Williment
                                DG: Herewini
BRITISH ISLES   11   T: Hinshelwood,
                                McFadyean
                                C: Wilson
                                PG: Wilson

26 Jun 1971, Carisbrook, Dunedin
NEW ZEALAND   3   PG: McCormick
BRITISH ISLES   9   T: McLauchlan
                                PG: John (2)

10 Jul 1971, Lancaster Park, Christchurch
NEW ZEALAND   22   T: Burgess (2), Going,
                                Kirkpatrick, Williams (pen.
                                try)
                                C: Mains (2)
                                PG: Mains
BRITISH ISLES   12   T: T. G. R. Davies (2)
                                PG: John
                                DG: John

31 Jul 1971, Athletic Park, Wellington
NEW ZEALAND   3   T: Mains
BRITISH ISLES   13   T: T. G. R. Davies, John
                                C: John (2)
                                DG: John

14 Aug 1971, Eden Park, Auckland
NEW ZEALAND   14   T: Cottrell, Lister
                                C: Mains
                                PG: Mains (2)
BRITISH ISLES   14   T: Dixon
                                C: John
                                PG: John (2)
                                DG: J. P. R. Williams

18 Jun 1977, Athletic Park, Wellington
NEW ZEALAND   16   T: Going, Johnstone, Batty
                                C: Williams (2)
BRITISH ISLES   12   PG: Bennett (3), Irvine

9 Jul 1977, Lancaster Park, Christchurch
NEW ZEALAND   9   PG: Williams (3)
BRITISH ISLES   13   T: J. J. Williams
                                PG: Bennett (3)

30 Jul 1977, Carisbrook Park, Dunedin
NEW ZEALAND   19   T: Kirkpatrick, Haden
                                C: Wilson
                                PG: Wilson (2)
                                DG: Robertson
BRITISH ISLES   7   T: Duggan
                                PG: Irvine

13 Aug 1977, Eden Park, Auckland
NEW ZEALAND   10   T: Knight
                                PG: Wilson (2)
BRITISH ISLES   9   T: Morgan
                                C: Morgan
                                PG: Morgan

4 Jun 1983, Lancaster Park, Christchurch
NEW ZEALAND   16   T: M. Shaw
                                PG: Hewson (3)
                                DG: Hewson

| BRITISH ISLES | 12 | PG: Campbell (3) |
| | | DG: Campbell |

18 Jun 1983, Athletic Park, Wellington
NEW ZEALAND	9	T: Loveridge
		C: Hewson
		PG: Hewson
BRITISH ISLES	0	

2 Jul 1983, Carisbrook Park, Dunedin
NEW ZEALAND	15	T: S. Wilson
		C: Hewson
		PG: Hewson (3)
BRITISH ISLES	8	T: Baird, Rutherford

16 Jul 1983, Eden Park, Auckland
NEW ZEALAND	38	T: S. Wilson (3), Hewson,
		Hobbs, Haden
		C: Hewson (4)
BRITISH ISLES	6	PG: G. Evans (2)

England v Australia

1909, Blackheath
| ENGLAND | 3 | T: Mobbs |
| AUSTRALIA | 9 | T: Russell (2), N. Rowe |

3 Jan 1948, Twickenham
ENGLAND	0	
AUSTRALIA	11	T: Windon (2), Walker
		C: Tonkin

1 Feb 1958, Twickenham
ENGLAND	9	T: Phillips, Jackson
		PG: Hetherington
AUSTRALIA	6	PG: Lenehan
		DG: Curley

4 Jun 1963, Sydney Sports Ground
AUSTRALIA	18	T: Jones, Walsham,
		Heinrich, Davis
		C: Ryan (3)
ENGLAND	9	T: Phillips, Clarke, Godwin

8 Jan 1967, Twickenham
ENGLAND	11	T: Ashby
		C: Hosen
		PG: Hosen (2)
AUSTRALIA	23	T: Brass, Catchpole
		C: Lenehan
		PG: Lenehan, Hawthorne
		DG: Hawthorne (3)

18 Nov 1973, Twickenham
ENGLAND	20	T: Old, Neary, Ripley
		C: Rossborough
		PG: Rossborough (2)
AUSTRALIA	3	PG: Fairfax

24 May 1975, Sydney Cricket Ground
AUSTRALIA	16	T: Loane
		PG: Brown (2)
		DG: Brown, Wright
ENGLAND	9	T: Squires
		PG: Butler
		DG: Butler

31 May 1975, Ballymore, Brisbane
AUSTRALIA	30	T: Price, Smith,
		Weatherstone, Fay,
		Monaghan
		C: Brown, Wright
		PG: Brown, Wright
ENGLAND	21	T: Squires, Uttley
		C: Old (2)
		PG: Old (3)

3 Jan 1976, Twickenham
ENGLAND	23	T: Corless, Duckham,
		Lampowski
		C: Hignell
		PG: Hignell (3)
AUSTRALIA	6	PG: P. E. McLean (2)

2 Jan 1982, Twickenham
ENGLAND	15	T: Jeavons
		C: Dodge
		PG: Rose (3)
AUSTRALIA	11	T: Moon (2)
		PG: McLean

3 Nov 1984, Twickenham
ENGLAND	3	PG: Barnes
AUSTRALIA	19	T: M. Ella, Poidevin,
		Lynagh
		C: Lynagh (2)
		PG: Lynagh

Ireland v Australia

6 Dec 1947, Lansdowne Road, Dublin
IRELAND	3	PG: Quinn
AUSTRALIA	16	T: Allan, Windon, Burke,
		Tonkin
		C: McMaster (2)

18 Jan 1958, Lansdowne Road, Dublin
IRELAND	9	T: Henderson, Dawson
		PG: Pedlow
AUSTRALIA	6	T: Phelps, Summons

21 Jan 1967, Lansdowne Road, Dublin
IRELAND	15	T: Duggan, Gibson
		PG: Kiernan
		DG: Gibson (2)
AUSTRALIA	8	T: Boyce
		C: Lenehan
		DG: Hawthorne

13 May 1967, Sydney Cricket Ground
AUSTRALIA	5	T: Catchpole
		C: Lenehan
IRELAND	11	T: McGrath, Walsh
		C: Kiernan
		DG: Kiernan

26 Oct 1968, Lansdowne Road, Dublin
IRELAND	10	T: Bresnihan, Goodall
		C: Kiernan, Moroney
AUSTRALIA	3	T: Ballesty

17 Jan 1976, Lansdowne Road, Dublin
IRELAND   10   T: McMaster
                    PG: Robbie (2)
AUSTRALIA   20   T: Ryan, G. Shaw,
                    Weatherstone
                    C: P. E. McLean
                    PG: P. E. McLean (2)

3 Jun 1979, Ballymore, Brisbane
AUSTRALIA   12   T: Moon
                    C: P. E. McLean
                    PG: P. E. McLean (2)
IRELAND   27   T: Patterson (2)
                    C: Campbell (2)
                    PG: Campbell (4)
                    DG: Campbell

16 Jun 1979, Sydney Cricket Ground
AUSTRALIA   3   PG: P. McLean
IRELAND   9   PG: Campbell (3)

21 Nov 1981, Lansdowne Road, Dublin
IRELAND   12   PG: Ward (4)
AUSTRALIA   16   T: O'Connor
                    PG: P. McLean (3)
                    DG: Gould

10 Nov 1984, Lansdowne Road, Dublin
IRELAND   9   PG: Kiernan (3)
AUSTRALIA   16   T: M. Ella
                    C: Lynagh
                    DG: M. Ella (2), Lynagh

Scotland v Australia

24 Nov 1947, Murrayfield, Edinburgh
SCOTLAND   7   PG: McDonald
                    DG: Hepburn
AUSTRALIA   16   T: Kearney, Tonkin,
                    Howell, Cooke
                    C: Piper (2)

15 Feb 1958, Murrayfield
SCOTLAND   12   T: Weatherstone, Stevenson
                    PG: A. R. Smith (2)
AUSTRALIA   8   T: Thornett, Donald
                    C: Lenehan

17 Dec 1966, Murrayfield
SCOTLAND   11   T: Chisholm, Boyle
                    C: Wilson
                    PG: Wilson
AUSTRALIA   5   T: Brass
                    C: Lenehan

2 Nov 1968, Murrayfield
SCOTLAND   9   T: Hinshelwood
                    PG: Blaikie (2)
AUSTRALIA   3   PG: Smith

6 Jun 1970, Sydney Cricket Ground
AUSTRALIA   23   T: Batterham (2), Cole (2),
                    Hipwell, Rosenblum

                    C: McGill
                    PG: McGill
SCOTLAND   3   PG: Lauder

6 Dec 1975, Murrayfield
SCOTLAND   10   T: Renwick, Dick
                    C: Morgan
AUSTRALIA   3   PG: McLean

19 Dec 1981, Murrayfield
SCOTLAND   24   T: Renwick
                    C: Irvine
                    PG: Irvine (5)
                    DG: Rutherford
AUSTRALIA   15   T: Poidevin, Moon, Slack
                    PG: P. E. McLean

3 Jul 1982, Ballymore, Brisbane
AUSTRALIA   7   T: Hawker
                    PG: Hawker
SCOTLAND   12   T: Robertson
                    C: Irvine
                    PG: Irvine
                    DG: Rutherford

10 Jul 1982, Sydney Cricket Ground
AUSTRALIA   33   T: Gould (2), O'Connor
                    C: P. E. McLean (3)
                    PG: P. E. McLean (5)
SCOTLAND   9   PG: Irvine (3)

8 Dec 1984, Murrayfield
SCOTLAND   12   PG: Dods (4)
AUSTRALIA   37   T: Campese (2), Farr-Jones,
                    M. Ella
                    C: Lynagh (3)
                    PG: Lynagh (5)

Wales v Australia

12 Dec 1908, Cardiff Arms Park
WALES   9   T: Travers, Hopkins
                    PG: Winfield
AUSTRALIA   6   T: Richards, Russell

20 Dec 1947, Cardiff Arms Park
WALES   6   PG: Tamplin (2)
AUSTRALIA   0

4 Jan 1958, Cardiff Arms Park
WALES   9   T: Collins
                    PG: T. J. Davies
                    DG: C. R. James
AUSTRALIA   3   T: Miller

3 Dec 1966, Cardiff Arms Park
WALES   11   T: Dawes, Morgan
                    C: Price
                    PG: Price
AUSTRALIA   14   T: Lenehan, Cardy
                    C: Lenehan
                    PG: Lenehan
                    DG: Hawthorne

21 Jun 1969, Sydney Cricket Ground
AUSTRALIA   16   T: McGill, Smith
                       C: McGill (2)
                       PG: McGill (2)
WALES   19   T: Davies, Taylor, Morris
                       C: Jarrett (2)
                       PG: Jarrett (2)

10 Nov 1973, Cardiff Arms Park
WALES   24   T: T. G. R. Davies, Morris,
                       Windsor
                       PG: Bennett (4)
AUSTRALIA   0

21 Dec 1975, Cardiff Arms Park
WALES   28   T: J. J. Williams (3),
                       Edwards
                       C: Fenwick (2), Martin
                       PG: Fenwick
AUSTRALIA   3   PG: P. McLean

11 Jun 1978, Ballymore, Brisbane
AUSTRALIA   19   T: Crowe
                       C: P. McLean
                       PG: P. McLean (4)
WALES   17   T: T. G. R. Davies,
                       B. Williams

17 Jun 1978, Sydney Cricket Ground
AUSTRALIA   18   T: Loane
                       PG: P. McLean (3)
                       DG: P. McLean, Monaghan
WALES   8   T: T. G. R. Davies, Holmes
                       PG: W. G. Davies
                       DG: W. G. Davies

5 Dec 1981, Cardiff Arms Park
WALES   18   T: R. D. Moriarty
                       C: G. Evans
                       PG: G. Evans
                       DG: W. G. Davies
AUSTRALIA   13   T: Slack, M. Cox
                       C: P. McLean
                       PG: P. McLean

24 Nov 1984, Cardiff Arms Park
WALES   9   T: Bishop
                       C: Wyatt
                       PG: Wyatt
AUSTRALIA   28   T: Lawton, Tuynman,
                       M. Ella, Lynagh
                       C: Gould (3)
                       PG: Gould (2)

Australia v British Isles

30 Aug 1930, Sydney Cricket Ground
AUSTRALIA   6   T: Malcolm, McGhie
BRITISH ISLES   5   T: Novis
                       C: Prentice

19 Aug 1950, Brisbane Cricket Ground
AUSTRALIA   6   T: Cross
                       PG: Gardner
BRITISH ISLES   19   T: Jones, Williams
                       C: Jones (2)
                       PG: Jones (2)
                       DG: Jones

26 Aug 1950, Sydney Cricket Ground
AUSTRALIA   3   T: Burke
BRITISH ISLES   24   T: Nelson (2), Kyle,
                       Macdonald, John
                       C: Robins (2), Jones
                       PG: Jones

6 Jun 1959, Brisbane Exhibition Ground
AUSTRALIA   6   PG: Donald (2)
BRITISH ISLES   17   T: O'Reilly, Smith
                       C: Risman
                       PG: Hewitt (2)
                       DG: Scotland

13 Jun 1959, Sydney Sports Ground
AUSTRALIA   3   PG: Donald
BRITISH ISLES   24   T: Price (2), Risman,
                       O'Reilly, Dawson
                       C: Hewitt (2)
                       PG: Scotland

28 May 1966, Sydney Cricket Ground
AUSTRALIA   8   T: Miller
                       C: Ruebner
                       PG: Ruebner
BRITISH ISLES   11   T: Kennedy, McLoughlin
                       C: Rutherford
                       PG: Rutherford

4 Jun 1966, Lang Park, Brisbane
AUSTRALIA   0
BRITISH ISLES   31   T: Jones (2), Bebb, Watkins,
                       Murphy
                       C: Wilson (5)
                       PG: Wilson
                       DG: Watkins

England v South Africa

8 Dec 1906, Crystal Palace
ENGLAND   3   T: Brooks
SOUTH AFRICA   3   T: Millar

4 Jan 1913, Twickenham
ENGLAND   3   T: Poulton
SOUTH AFRICA   9   T: J. W. H. Morkel
                       PG: D. F. T. Morkel (2)

2 Jan 1932, Twickenham
ENGLAND   0
SOUTH AFRICA   7   T: Bergh
                       DG: Brand

5 Jan 1952, Twickenham
ENGLAND	3	T: Winn
SOUTH AFRICA	8	T: Du Toit
		C: Muller
		PG: Muller

7 Jan 1961, Twickenham
ENGLAND	0	
SOUTH AFRICA	5	T: Hopwood
		C: Du Preez

20 Dec 1969, Twickenham
ENGLAND	11	T: Larter, Pullin
		C: Hiller
		PG: Hiller
SOUTH AFRICA	8	T: Greyling
		C: Visagie
		PG: Visagie

3 Jun 1972, Ellis Park, Johannesburg
SOUTH AFRICA	9	PG: Snyman (3)
ENGLAND	18	T: Morley
		C: Doble
		PG: Doble (4)

2 Jun 1984, Boet Erasmus Stadium, Port Elizabeth
SOUTH AFRICA	33	T: Gerber, C. Du Plessis, Louw
		C: Heunis (3)
		PG: Heunis (5)
ENGLAND	15	PG: Hare (4)
		DG: Horton

9 Jun 1984, Ellis Park, Johannesburg
SOUTH AFRICA	35	T: Gerber (3), Stofberg, Sonnekus, Tobias
		C: Heunis (3), Tobias
		PG: Heunis
ENGLAND	9	PG: Hare (3)

Ireland v South Africa

24 Nov 1906, Belfast
IRELAND	12	T: Maclear (2), Sugar
		PG: Parke
SOUTH AFRICA	15	T: Loubser (2), Krige, A. C. Stegmann
		PG: Joubert

30 Nov 1912, Lansdowne Road, Dublin
IRELAND	0	
SOUTH AFRICA	38	T: J. A. Stegmann (3), McHardy (3), J. Morkel (2), Francis, Millar
		C: G. Morkel (3), Luyt

19 Dec 1931, Lansdowne Road, Dublin
IRELAND	3	PG: Beamish
SOUTH AFRICA	8	T: Zimmerman (2)
		C: Osler

8 Dec 1951, Lansdowne Road, Dublin
IRELAND	5	T: Browne
		C: Murphy

SOUTH AFRICA	17	T: Van Wyk (2), Ochse, Van Schoor
		C: Geffin
		DG: Brewis

17 Dec 1960, Lansdowne Road, Dublin
IRELAND	3	PG: Kiernan
SOUTH AFRICA	8	T: Gainsford, H. Van Zyl
		C: Lockyear

13 May 1961, Newlands, Cape Town
SOUTH AFRICA	24	T: Greenwood (2), Hopwood, B. P. Van Zyl (2)
		C: Nimb (3)
		PG: Nimb
IRELAND	8	T: Kiernan
		C: Kiernan
		PG: Kiernan

6 Apr 1965, Lansdowne Road, Dublin
IRELAND	9	T: McGrath
		PG: Kiernan (2)
SOUTH AFRICA	6	T: Mans
		PG: Stewart

10 Jan 1970, Lansdowne Road, Dublin
IRELAND	8	T: Duggan
		C: Kiernan
		PG: Kiernan
SOUTH AFRICA	8	T: Greyling
		C: H. O. de Villiers
		PG: H. O. de Villiers

30 May 1981, Newlands, Cape Town
SOUTH AFRICA	23	T: Gerber (2), Louw
		C: Botha
		PG: Botha
IRELAND	15	T: McGrath, McLennan
		C: Campbell (2)
		PG: Campbell

6 Jun 1981, Lansdowne Road, Dublin
IRELAND	10	T: O'Brien
		PG: Quinn (2)
SOUTH AFRICA	12	PG: Botha
		DG: Botha (3)

Scotland v South Africa

17 Nov 1906, Hampden Park, Glasgow
SCOTLAND	6	T: MacLeod, Purves
SOUTH AFRICA	0	

23 Nov 1912, Inverleith, Edinburgh
SCOTLAND	0	
SOUTH AFRICA	16	T: McHardy, J. A. Stegmann (2), W. H. Morkel
		C: P. G. Morkel, D. T. F. Morkel

16 Jan 1932, Murrayfield, Edinburgh
SCOTLAND	3	T: Lind
SOUTH AFRICA	6	T: Osler, Craven

24 Nov 1951, Murrayfield
SCOTLAND   0
SOUTH AFRICA   44   T: Durand, Van Schoor,
C. Koch (2), Delport, Van
Wyk, Muller, Dinkelmann,
Lategan
C: Geffin (7)
DG: Brewis

30 Apr 1960, Boet Erasmus, Port Elizabeth
SOUTH AFRICA   18   T: Van Zyl (2), Gerike, Van
Jaarsveldt
C: Gerber (3)
SCOTLAND   10   T: Bruce, Smith
C: Smith (2)

21 Jan 1961, Murrayfield
SCOTLAND   5   T: Smith
C: Scotland
SOUTH AFRICA   12   T: Hopwood, Claassen
PG: Du Preez (2)

17 Apr 1965, Murrayfield
SCOTLAND   8   T: Shackleton
C: Wilson
DG: Chisholm
SOUTH AFRICA   5   T: Engelbrecht
C: Mans

6 Dec 1969, Murrayfield
SCOTLAND   6   T: I. S. G. Smith
PG: I. S. G. Smith
SOUTH AFRICA   3   PG: Visagie

Wales v South Africa

1 Dec 1906, St Helens, Swansea
WALES   0
SOUTH AFRICA   11   T: Joubert, Loubser, Raaff
C: Joubert

14 Dec 1912, Cardiff Arms Park
WALES   0
SOUTH AFRICA   3   PG: D. F. T. Morkel

5 Dec 1931, St Helens, Swansea
WALES   3   T: Will Davies
SOUTH AFRICA   8   T: Daneel, Bergh
C: Osler

22 Dec 1951, Cardiff Arms Park
WALES   3   T: B. L. Williams
SOUTH AFRICA   6   T: Ochse
PG: Brewis

3 Dec 1960, Cardiff Arms Park
WALES   0
SOUTH AFRICA   3   PG: Oxlee

23 May 1964, Kings Park, Durban
SOUTH AFRICA   24   T: Marais, Hopwood, Smith
C: Oxlee (3)
PG: Oxlee (2)
DG: Wilson
WALES   3   PG: Bradshaw

24 Jan 1970, Cardiff Arms Park
WALES   6   T: Edwards
PG: Edwards
SOUTH AFRICA   6   T: Nomis
PG: H. O. de Villiers

British Isles v South Africa

30 Jul 1891, Crusader Ground, Port Elizabeth
SOUTH AFRICA   0
BRITISH ISLES   4   T: Aston, Whittaker
C: Rotherham

28 Aug 1891, Kimberley
SOUTH AFRICA   0
BRITISH ISLES   3   DG: Mitchell

5 Sep 1891, Newlands, Cape Town
SOUTH AFRICA   0
BRITISH ISLES   4   T: Aston, Maclagan
C: Rotherham

30 Jul 1896, Crusader Ground, Port Elizabeth
SOUTH AFRICA   0
BRITISH ISLES   8   T: Carey, Bulger
C: Byrne

22 Aug 1896, Johannesburg
SOUTH AFRICA   8   T: Samuels (2)
C: Cope
BRITISH ISLES   17   T: Todd, Crean, Hancock
C: Byrne (2)
DG: Mackie

29 Aug 1896, Kimberley
SOUTH AFRICA   3   T: Jones
BRITISH ISLES   9   T: Mackie
C: Byrne
DG: Byrne

5 Sep 1896, Newlands, Cape Town
SOUTH AFRICA   5   T: Larard
C: Hepburn
BRITISH ISLES   0

26 Aug 1903, Johannesburg
SOUTH AFRICA   10   T: Dobbin, Sinclair
C: Heatlie (2)
BRITISH ISLES   10   T: Skrimshire, Cave
C: Gillespie (2)

5 Sep 1903, Kimberley
SOUTH AFRICA   0
BRITISH ISLES   0

12 Sep 1903, Newlands, Cape Town
SOUTH AFRICA   8   T: Barry, Reid
C: Heatlie
BRITISH ISLES   0

6 Aug 1910, Johannesburg
SOUTH AFRICA   14   T: De Villiers, D. F. T.
Morkel, F. Luyt, Hahn
C: D. F. T. Morkel
BRITISH ISLES   10   T: Foster, Spoors
DG: Jones

27 Aug 1910, Crusader Ground, Port Elizabeth
SOUTH AFRICA   3   T: Mills
BRITISH ISLES   8   T: Spoors, Neale
C: Pillman

3 Sep 1910, Newlands, Cape Town
SOUTH AFRICA   21   T: Roos, F. Luyt, Allport,
Reyneke
C: D. F. T. Morkel (3)
PG: D. F. T Morkel
BRITISH ISLES   5   T: Spoors
C: Pillman

16 Aug 1924, Kingsmead, Durban
SOUTH AFRICA   7   T: Aucamp
DG: Osler
BRITISH ISLES   3   T: Whitley

23 Aug 1924, Johannesburg
SOUTH AFRICA   17   T: Starke, Mostert,
Van Druten, Albertyn
C: Osler
PG: Osler
BRITISH ISLES   0

17 Sep 1924, Crusader Ground, Port Elizabeth
SOUTH AFRICA   3   T: Van Druten
BRITISH ISLES   3   T: Cunningham

20 Sep 1924, Newlands, Cape Town
SOUTH AFRICA   16   T: Starke (2), Bester, Slater
DG: Starke
BRITISH ISLES   9   T: Boyce, Harris
PG: Boyce

6 Aug 1938, Johannesburg
SOUTH AFRICA   26   T: Williams (2), S. C. Louw,
Harris
C: Brand (4)
PG: Brand (2)
BRITISH ISLES   12   PG: Jenkins (3), Taylor

3 Sep 1938, Crusader Ground, Port Elizabeth
SOUTH AFRICA   19   T: Du Toit, Lochner, Bester
C: Turner (2)
PG: Turner (2)
BRITISH ISLES   3   T: Duff

10 Sep 1938, Newlands, Cape Town
SOUTH AFRICA   16   T: Turner, Bester, Lotz
C: Turner (2)
PG: Turner
BRITISH ISLES   21   T: Jones, Dancer,
Alexander, Duff
C: McKibbin
PG: McKibbin
DG: Grieve

6 Aug 1955, Ellis Park, Johannesburg
SOUTH AFRICA   22   T: Briers (2), Swart, Koch
C: Van der Schyff (2)
PG: Van der Schyff (2)

BRITISH ISLES   23   T: Pedlow, Butterfield,
Morgan, Greenwood,
O'Reilly
C: Cameron (4)

20 Aug 1955, Newlands, Cape Town
SOUTH AFRICA   25   T: Van Vollenhoven (3),
Rosenberg, Dryburgh,
Briers, Ackermann
C: Dryburgh (2)
BRITISH ISLES   9   T: Butterfield, B. Meredith
PG: Cameron

3 Sep 1955, Loftus Versveld, Pretoria
SOUTH AFRICA   6   PG: Dryburgh (2)
BRITISH ISLES   9   T: Butterfield
PG: Baker
DG: Butterfield

24 Sep 1955, Crusader Ground, Port Elizabeth
SOUTH AFRICA   22   T: Briers (2), Ulyate,
Van Vollenhoven, Reteif
C: Dryburgh (2)
DG: Ulyate
BRITISH ISLES   8   T: Greenwood, O'Reilly
C: Pedlow

23 Jun 1962, Ellis Park, Johannesburg
SOUTH AFRICA   3   T: Gainsford
BRITISH ISLES   3   T: D. K. Jones

21 Jul 1962, Durban
SOUTH AFRICA   3   PG: Oxlee
BRITISH ISLES   0

4 Aug 1962, Newlands, Cape Town
SOUTH AFRICA   8   T: Oxlee
C: Oxlee
PG: Oxlee
BRITISH ISLES   3   DG: Sharp

25 Aug 1962, Free State Stadium, Bloemfontein
SOUTH AFRICA   34   T: Roux (2), Wyness,
Gainsford, H. Van Zyl,
Claassen
C: Oxlee (5)
PG: Oxlee (2)
BRITISH ISLES   14   T: Cowan, Rowlands,
Campbell-Lamerton
C: Willcox
PG: Willcox

8 Jun 1968, Loftus Versveld, Pretoria
SOUTH AFRICA   25   T: Naude, De Villiers,
Du Preez
C: Visagie (2)
PG: Visagie (2), Naude (2)
BRITISH ISLES   20   T: McBride
C: Kiernan
PG: Kiernan (5)

22 Jun 1968, Boet Erasmus, Port Elizabeth
SOUTH AFRICA   6   PG: Naude, Visagie
BRITISH ISLES   6   PG: Kiernan (2)

13 Jul 1968, Newlands, Cape Town
SOUTH AFRICA   11   T: Lourens
C: Visagie
PG: Visagie, Naude
BRITISH ISLES   6   PG: Kiernan (2)

27 Jul 1968, Ellis Park, Johannesburg
SOUTH AFRICA 19 T: Roux, Ellis, Olivier, Nomis
C: Visagie (2)
DG: Gould
BRITISH ISLES 6 PG: Kiernan (2)

8 Jun 1974, Newlands, Cape Town
SOUTH AFRICA 3 DG: Snyman
BRITISH ISLES 12 PG: Bennett (3)
DG: Edwards

22 Jun 1974, Loftus Versveld, Pretoria
SOUTH AFRICA 9 PG: Bosch (2)
DG: Bosch
BRITISH ISLES 28 T: J. J. Williams (2), Bennett, Brown, Milliken
C: Bennett
PG: Bennett
DG: McGeechan

13 Jul 1974, Boet Erasmus, Port Elizabeth
SOUTH AFRICA 9 PG: Snyman (3)
BRITISH ISLES 26 T: Brown, J. J. Williams (2)
C: Irvine
PG: Irvine (2)
DG: Bennett (2)

27 Jul 1974, Ellis Park, Johannesburg
SOUTH AFRICA 13 T: Cronje
PG: Snyman (3)
BRITISH ISLES 13 T: Uttley, Irvine
C: Bennett
PG: Irvine

31 May 1980, Newlands, Cape Town
SOUTH AFRICA 26 T: Louw, W. Du Plessis, Van Heerden, Germishuys, Serfontein
C: Botha (3)
BRITISH ISLES 22 T: Price
PG: Ward (5)
DG: Ward

14 Jun 1980, Free State Stadium, Bloemfontein
SOUTH AFRICA 26 T: Louw, Stofberg, Germishuys, Pienaar
C: Botha (2)
PG: Botha (2)
BRITISH ISLES 19 T: O'Driscoll, Gravell
C: G. Davies
PG: G. Davies (2), Irvine

28 Jun 1980, Boet Erasmus, Port Elizabeth
SOUTH AFRICA 12 T: Germishuys
C: Botha
PG: Botha (2)
BRITISH ISLES 10 T: Hay
PG: Campbell (2)

12 Jul 1980, Loftus Versveld, Pretoria
SOUTH AFRICA 13 T: W. du Plessis
PG: Pienaar (2), Botha
BRITISH ISLES 17 T: C. Williams, Irvine, O'Driscoll

Australia v South Africa

8 Jul 1933, Newlands, Cape Town
SOUTH AFRICA 17 T: Bergh (2), Craven, Osler
C: Brand
PG: Brand
AUSTRALIA 3 PG: Billman

22 Jul 1933, Durban
SOUTH AFRICA 6 T: Waring
PG: Brand
AUSTRALIA 21 T: Loudon, Cerutti, Bennett, Sturtridge
C: Billman (3)
PG: Billman

12 Jul 1933, Johannesburg
SOUTH AFRICA 12 T: M. Louw, Turner
C: Brand
DG: Osler
AUSTRALIA 3 T: Cowper

26 Aug 1933, Boet Erasmus, Port Elizabeth
SOUTH AFRICA 11 T: White, S. Louw
C: Osler
PG: Brand
AUSTRALIA 0

2 Sep 1933, Free State Stadium, Bloemfontein
SOUTH AFRICA 4 DG: Brand
AUSTRALIA 15 T: Kelleher, Steggle, Bridle
C: Ross
DG: Cowper

26 Jun 1937, Sydney Cricket Ground
AUSTRALIA 5 T: Towers
C: Towers
SOUTH AFRICA 9 T: Bastard, Bergh
PG: Brand

17 Jul 1937, Sydney Cricket Ground
AUSTRALIA 17 T: Hodgson, Kelaher, O'Brien
C: Rankin
PG: Rankin (2)
SOUTH AFRICA 26 T: Van Reenen (2), Bergh, Babrow, Williams, Turner
C: Brand (4)

22 Aug 1953, Ellis Park, Johannesburg
SOUTH AFRICA 25 T: Lategan, Marais, Oelofse, Durand
C: Marais, Buchler
PG: Marais, Buchler
AUSTRALIA 3 PG: Sweeney

5 Sep 1953, Newlands, Cape Town
SOUTH AFRICA 14 T: Ochse, Van Wyk, Durand
C: Marais
AUSTRALIA 18 T: Jones, Stapleton, Cross, Johnson
C: Colbert (2), Stapleton

19 Sep 1953, Durban
SOUTH AFRICA 18 T: R. Bekker, Roussow, Van Wyk, H. Bekker
C: Rens (3)

AUSTRALIA 8 T: Cross
C: Colbert
PG: Solomon

26 Sep 1953, Crusader Ground, Port Elizabeth
SOUTH AFRICA 22 T: Koch, Oelofse
C: Rens
PG: Rens (2)
DG: Marais, Buchler
AUSTRALIA 9 T: Stapleton
PG: Barker (2)

26 May 1956, Sydney Cricket Ground
AUSTRALIA 0
SOUTH AFRICA 9 T: Nel, Reteif
PG: Viviers

2 Jun 1956, Brisbane
AUSTRALIA 0
SOUTH AFRICA 9 T: Dryburgh, Reteif
PG: Von Vollenhoven

5 Aug 1961, Ellis Park, Johannesburg
SOUTH AFRICA 28 T: Van Zyl (3), Gainsford,
Engelbrecht, Oxlee, Pelser,
Hopwood
C: Claassen (2)
AUSTRALIA 3 PG: Dowse

12 Aug 1961, Boet Erasmus, Port Elizabeth
SOUTH AFRICA 23 T: Van Zyl, Roux, Oxlee
C: Oxlee
PG: Oxlee (3), Wilson
AUSTRALIA 11 T: Cleary
C: Dowse
PG: Dowse (2)

13 Jul 1963, Loftus Versveld, Pretoria
SOUTH AFRICA 14 T: Bedford, Cilliers
C: Oxlee
PG: Oxlee (2)
AUSTRALIA 3 T: McMullen

10 Aug 1963, Newlands, Cape Town
SOUTH AFRICA 5 T: Penalty try
C: Oxlee
AUSTRALIA 9 T: Boyce
PG: Casey, Hawthorne

24 Aug 1963, Ellis Park, Johannesburg
SOUTH AFRICA 9 PG: Smith (3)
AUSTRALIA 11 T: Williams
C: Casey
PG Casey (2)

7 Sep 1963, Boet Erasmus, Port Elizabeth
SOUTH AFRICA 22 T: Gainsford, Naude, Malan
C: Oxlee (2)
PG: Oxlee (2), Naude
AUSTRALIA 6 PG: Casey
DG: Casey

19 Jun 1965, Sydney Cricket Ground
AUSTRALIA 18 T: Lenehan, S. Boyce
PG: Ellwood (4)
SOUTH AFRICA 11 T: Engelbrecht (2)
PG: Naude

26 Jun 1965, Lang Park, Brisbane
AUSTRALIA 12 PG: Ellwood (2), Lenehan
(2)

SOUTH AFRICA 8 T: Gainsford, Truter
C: Naude

2 Aug 1969, Ellis Park, Johannesburg
SOUTH AFRICA 30 T: Nomis (2), Roux, Ellis,
Greyling
C: Visagie (3)
PG: Visagie (3)
AUSTRALIA 11 T: Forman
C: Rosenblum
PG: Rosenblum (2)

16 Aug 1969, Kings Park, Durban
SOUTH AFRICA 16 T: Engelbrecht, Visagie
C: Visagie
PG: Visagie (2)
AUSTRALIA 9 PG: Ballesty (3)

6 Sep 1969, Newlands, Cape Town
SOUTH AFRICA 11 T: Ellis, Visagie
C: Visagie
PG: Visagie
AUSTRALIA 3 PG: Ballesty

21 Sep 1969, Free State Stadium, Bloemfontein
SOUTH AFRICA 19 T: Olivier, Roux
C: Visagie (2)
PG: Visagie (2)
AUSTRALIA 8 T: Knight
C: Ballesty
PG: Ballesty

17 Jul 1971, Sydney Cricket Ground
AUSTRALIA 11 T: R. McLean
C: McGill
PG: McGill (2)
SOUTH AFRICA 19 T: H. Viljeon, J. Viljeon,
Ellis
C: McCullum (2)
PG: McCullum
DG: Visagie

31 Jul 1971, Brisbane Exhibition Ground
AUSTRALIA 6 PG: McGill (2)
SOUTH AFRICA 14 T: Visagie (2), H. Viljeon
C: McCullum
PG: McCullum

7 Aug 1971, Sydney Cricket Ground
AUSTRALIA 6 T: Cole
PG: J. McLean
SOUTII AFRICA 18 T: Cronje, Visagie, Ellis
C: Visagie (3)
PG: Visagie

Australia v New Zealand

15 Aug 1903, Sydney Cricket Ground
AUSTRALIA 3 PG: Wickham
NEW ZEALAND 22 T: Asher, Tyler,
R. W. McGregor
C: Wallace

PG: Wallace
GM: Wallace (2)

2 Sep 1905, Tahuna Park, Dunedin
NEW ZEALAND   14   T: McMinn (2), Wrigley,
                    Cross
                    C: Francis
AUSTRALIA   3   T: McLean

20 Jul 1907, Sydney Cricket Ground
AUSTRALIA   6   PG: Carmichael
                 GM: Carmichael
NEW ZEALAND   26   T: Mitchinson (3), Seeling,
                    Hughes, Francis
                    C: Wallace (4)

3 Aug 1907, Woolloongabba Ground, Brisbane
AUSTRALIA   5   T: Messenger
                 C: Messenger
NEW ZEALAND   14   T: Wallace (2), Seeling,
                    Francis
                    C: Wallace

10 Aug 1907, Sydney Cricket Ground
AUSTRALIA   5   T: Wood
                 C: Messenger
NEW ZEALAND   5   T: Mitchinson
                 C: Wallace

25 Jun 1910, Sydney Cricket Ground
AUSTRALIA   0
NEW ZEALAND   6   T: Wilson, Fuller

27 Jun 1910, Sydney Cricket Ground
AUSTRALIA   11   T: Gilbert (2), Hodgens
                  C: Row
NEW ZEALAND   0

2 Jul 1910, Sydney Cricket Ground
AUSTRALIA   13   T: Gilbert, Row
                  C: Row (2)
                  PG: Row
NEW ZEALAND   28   T: Burns (2), Stohr (2),
                    Paterson, Mitchinson,
                    Mitchell, Paton
                    C: O'Leary (2)

6 Sep 1913, Athletic Park, Wellington
NEW ZEALAND   30   T: Lynch (3), McKenzie (2),
                    Murray, Gray, Roberts
                    C: Roberts (3)
AUSTRALIA   5   T: Carr
                 C: McMahon

13 Sep 1913, Carisbrook, Dunedin
NEW ZEALAND   25   T: Brown, Cummings,
                    Hasell, Taylor, Wilson
                    C: O'Leary (3)
                    DG: O'Leary
AUSTRALIA   13   T: Jones (2), Suttor
                  C: Simpson (2)

20 Sep 1913, Lancaster Park, Christchurch
NEW ZEALAND   5   T: Fanning
                 C: O'Leary
AUSTRALIA   16   T: Suttor (2), Jones,
                  Thompson
                  C: Hughes (2)

18 Jul 1914, Sydney Sports Ground
AUSTRALIA   0
NEW ZEALAND   5   T: McNeece
                 C: Graham

1 Aug 1914, Brisbane Cricket Ground
AUSTRALIA   0
NEW ZEALAND   17   T: Taylor (3),
                    R. W. Roberts, Lynch
                    C: E. J. Roberts

15 Aug 1914, Sydney Sports Ground
AUSTRALIA   7   T: Wogan
                 DG: Dwyer
NEW ZEALAND   22   T: R. W. Roberts (2),
                    Francis (2), McKenzie,
                    Taylor
                    C: R. W. Roberts,
                    E. J. Roberts

6 Jul 1929, Sydney Cricket Ground
AUSTRALIA   9   T: Gordon
                 PG: Lawton (2)
NEW ZEALAND   8   T: Oliver
                 C: Nepia
                 PG: Nepia

20 Jul 1929, Exhibition Ground, Brisbane
AUSTRALIA   17   T: McGhie, Crossman, Ford
                  C: Lawton
                  PG: Lawton (2)
NEW ZEALAND   9   T: Grenside, Porter
                 PG: Cundy

27 Jul 1929, Sydney Cricket Ground
AUSTRALIA   15   T: J. A. Ford, King
                  PG: Lawton (2), Towers
NEW ZEALAND   13   T: McWilliams,
                    Stringfellow, Grenside
                    C: Lilburne (2)

12 Sep 1931, Eden Park, Auckland
NEW ZEALAND   20   T: Hart, Ball
                    C: Bush
                    PG: Bush (4)
AUSTRALIA   13   T: Towers (2), Cowper
                  C: Ross (2)

2 Jul 1932, Sydney Cricket Ground
AUSTRALIA   22   T: Cerutti (2), Bridle,
                  Cowper
                  C: Lawton (2)
                  PG: Lawton (2)
NEW ZEALAND   17   T: Bullock-Douglas, Hore,
                    Purdue
                    C: Pollock (2)
                    DG: Pollock

16 Jul 1932, Exhibition Ground, Brisbane
AUSTRALIA   3   T: Steggall
NEW ZEALAND   21   T: Bullock-Douglas (2),
                    Ball, Page
                    C: Pollock
                    PG: Collins
                    DG: Pollock

23 Jul 1932, Sydney Cricket Ground
AUSTRALIA   13   T: Hemingway, Bridle,
                  Cowper
                  C: Ross, Cowper

NEW ZEALAND   21   T: Kilby, McLean, Solomon,
Manchester, Palmer
C: Collins (2), Pollock

11 Aug 1934, Sydney Cricket Ground
AUSTRALIA   25   T: Towers (2), Bridle,
McLean
C: Ross (2)
PG: Ross (3)
NEW ZEALAND   11   T: Hore, Knight, Max
C: Collins

25 Aug 1934, Sydney Cricket Ground
AUSTRALIA   3   T: Loudon
NEW ZEALAND   3   T: Hore

5 Sep 1936, Athletic Park, Wellington
NEW ZEALAND   11   T: Hart, Hadley, Watt
C: Pollock
AUSTRALIA   6   T: McLaughlin
PG: Rankin

12 Sep 1936, Carisbrook, Dunedin
NEW ZEALAND   38   T: Mitchell (2), Hart (2),
Reid (2), Rankin (2), Watt
C: Pollock (4)
PG: Pollock
AUSTRALIA   13   T: McLaughlin, Bridle
C: Rankin
PG: Rankin

23 Jul 1938, Sydney Cricket Ground
AUSTRALIA   9   PG: Carpenter (3)
NEW ZEALAND   24   T: Saxton (2), Sullivan,
Parkhill
C: Taylor (3)
PG: Taylor

6 Aug 1938, Exhibition Ground, Brisbane
AUSTRALIA   14   T: Carpenter (2), Collins
C: Carpenter
PG: Carpenter
NEW ZEALAND   20   T: Phillips, Milliken,
Bowman, Mitchell
C: Taylor (2)
DG: Morrison

13 Aug 1938, Sydney Cricket Ground
AUSTRALIA   6   T: Ramsay
PG: Hayes
NEW ZEALAND   14   T: Saxton, Bowman
C: Taylor
PG: Taylor (2)

14 Sep 1946, Carisbrook, Dunedin
NEW ZEALAND   31   T: Argus (2), Haig, Elliott,
Finlay, Smith, White
C: Scott (5)
AUSTRALIA   8   T: Eastes, Allan
C: Livermore

28 Sep 1946, Eden Park, Auckland
NEW ZEALAND   14   T: Elvidge
C: Scott
PG: Scott (3)
AUSTRALIA   10   T: Eastes, MacBride
C: Piper (2)

14 Jun 1947, Exhibition Ground, Brisbane
AUSTRALIA   5   T: Cornforth
C: Piper
NEW ZEALAND   13   T: Frazer (pen. try), Argus,
Arnold
C: Scott (2)

28 Jun 1947, Sydney Cricket Ground
AUSTRALIA   14   T: McLean
C: Allan
PG: Allan (3)
NEW ZEALAND   27   T: Argus, Kearney, Mason
C: Scott (3)
PG: (3), Thornton

3 Sep 1949, Athletic Park, Wellington
NEW ZEALAND   6   T: Moore
PG: Kelly
AUSTRALIA   11   T: Garner (2), Windon
C: Cawsey

24 Sep 1949, Eden Park, Auckland
NEW ZEALAND   9   T: Roper
DG: Smith
PG: O'Callaghan
AUSTRALIA   16   T: Solomon, Windon,
Emery
C: Allan, Cawsey
PG: Allan

23 Jun 1951, Sydney Cricket Ground
AUSTRALIA   0
NEW ZEALAND   8   T: Skinner
C: Cockerill
PG: Cockerill

7 Jul 1951, Sydney Cricket Ground
AUSTRALIA   11   T: Tooth, Shehadie
C: Rothwell
PG: Rothwell
NEW ZEALAND   17   T: Jarden (2), N. L. Wilson,
Lynch
C: Cockerill
DG: Lynch

21 Jul 1951, Brisbane Cricket Ground
AUSTRALIA   6   PG: Rothwell, Cottrell
NEW ZEALAND   16   T: Tanner, Lynch, Bell,
Haig
C: Cockerill (2)

6 Sep 1952, Lancaster Park, Christchurch
NEW ZEALAND   9   T: Fitzgerald, White
PG: Bell
AUSTRALIA   14   T: Stapleton, Barker,
Windon
C: Cottrell
DG: Solomon

13 Sep 1952, Athletic Park, Wellington
NEW ZEALAND   15   T: Hotop, Robinson
PG: Jarden, Bowden
DG: Hotop
AUSTRALIA   8   T: Windon
C: Cottrell
PG: Cottrell

29 Aug 1955, Athletic Park, Wellington
NEW ZEALAND   16   T: Clark, Vodanovich,
Jarden

C: Jarden (2)
PG: Jarden
AUSTRALIA   8   T: Jones
C: Tooth
PG: Stapleton

3 Sep 1955, Carisbrook, Dunedin
NEW ZEALAND   8   T: Jarden
C: Jarden
DG: Elsom
AUSTRALIA   0

17 Sep 1955, Eden Park, Auckland
NEW ZEALAND   3   T: Jarden
AUSTRALIA   8   T: Stapleton, Hughes
C: Stapleton

25 May 1957, Sydney Cricket Ground
AUSTRALIA   11   T: Cross
C: Tooth
PG: Tooth (2)
NEW ZEALAND   25   T: MacEwan, Hemi,
McMullen, Walsh
C: D. B. Clarke (2)
PG: D. B. Clarke (3)

1 Jun 1957, Exhibition Ground, Brisbane
AUSTRALIA   9   T: Morton
PG: Tooth (2)
NEW ZEALAND   22   T: Dixon, McMullen,
Brown, Meads
C: D. B. Clarke (2)
DG: Brown
GM: D. B. Clarke

23 Aug 1958, Athletic Park, Wellington
NEW ZEALAND   25   T: Whineray (2), Walsh (2),
Graham, McMullen, Jones
C: D. B. Clarke (2)
AUSTRALIA   3   T: Ellwood

6 Sep 1958, Lancaster Park, Christchurch
NEW ZEALAND   3   T: Brown
AUSTRALIA   6   T: Morton
PG: Curley

20 Sep 1958, Epsom Showgrounds, Auckland
NEW ZEALAND   17   T: Meads
C: D. B. Clarke
PG: D. B. Clarke (4)
AUSTRALIA   8   T: Carroll
C: Curley
PG: Curley

26 May 1962, Exhibition Ground, Brisbane
AUSTRALIA   6   PG: Scott (2)
NEW ZEALAND   20   T: B. A. Watt (2),
MacEwan, Tremain
C: D. B. Clarke
PG: D. B. Clarke
DG: D. B. Clarke

4 Jun 1962, Sydney Cricket Ground
AUSTRALIA   5   T: R. N. Thornett
C: Scott
NEW ZEALAND   14   T: Nathan, Watt
C: D. B. Clarke
PG: D. B. Clarke (2)

25 Aug 1962, Athletic Park, Wellington
NEW ZEALAND   9   T: Morrisey
PG: D. B. Clarke (2)
AUSTRALIA   9   PG: Chapman (3)

8 Sep 1962, Carisbrook, Dunedin
NEW ZEALAND   3   PG: Clarke
AUSTRALIA   0

22 Sep 1962, Eden Park, Auckland
NEW ZEALAND   16   T: Morrissey, Heeps,
Herewini
C: Clarke (2)
DG: Herewini
AUSTRALIA   8   T: Lenehan
C: Chapman
PG: Chapman

15 Aug 1964, Carisbrook, Dunedin
NEW ZEALAND   14   T: McLeod
C: Williment
PG: Williment (2)
DG: Moreton
AUSTRALIA   9   T: Marks
PG: Casey (2)

22 Aug 1964, Lancaster Park, Christchurch
NEW ZEALAND   18   T: Murdoch, Moreton,
Rangi, Gray
C: Clarke (3)
AUSTRALIA   3   T: Marks

29 Aug 1964, Athletic Park, Wellington
NEW ZEALAND   5   T: Murdoch
C: Clarke
AUSTRALIA   20   T: E. S. Boyce (2)
C: Casey
PG: Casey (3)
DG: Hawthorne

19 Aug 1967, Athletic Park, Wellington
NEW ZEALAND   29   T: Steel (2), Davis, Tremain
C: Williment (4)
PG: Williment (2)
DG: Herewini
AUSTRALIA   9   T: Batterham (2)
PG: Batterham

15 Jun 1968, Sydney Cricket Ground
AUSTRALIA   11   T: Cardy
C: McGill
PG: McGill (2)
NEW ZEALAND   27   T: Kirkpatrick (3), Kirton,
Steel, Laidlaw
C: McCormick (3)
PG: McCormick

22 Jun 1968, Ballymore Oval, Brisbane
AUSTRALIA   18   T: Hipwell
PG: McGill (5)
NEW ZEALAND   19   T: Lister, Thorne, Davis
(pen. try)
C: McCormick (2)
PG: McCormick (2)

19 Aug 1972, Athletic Park, Wellington
NEW ZEALAND   29   T: Dougan, Going,
Sutherland, Williams,
P. J. Whiting
C: Morris (3)

AUSTRALIA   6   DG: Morris
                    PG: J. J. McLean (2)

2 Sep 1972, Lancaster Park, Christchurch
NEW ZEALAND   30   T: Kirkpatrick (2),
                    Sutherland, P. J. Whiting,
                    Williams
                    C: Morris (2)
                    PG: Morris (2)
AUSTRALIA   17   T: J. J. McLean (2), Cole
                    C: J. J. McLean
                    DG: Richardson

16 Sep 1972, Eden Park, Auckland
NEW ZEALAND   38   T: Kirkpatrick, Sutherland,
                    Scown, Going, Whiting,
                    Williams
                    C: Morris (4)
                    PG: Morris (2)
AUSTRALIA   3   PG: J. J. McLean

25 May 1974, Sydney Cricket Ground
AUSTRALIA   6   T: Price
                    C: P. E. McLean
NEW ZEALAND   11   T: D. J. Robertson,
                    Kirkpatrick
                    PG: Karam

1 Jun 1974, Ballymore Oval, Brisbane
AUSTRALIA   16   T: Hipwell, Monaghan
                    C: P. E. McLean
                    PG: P. E. McLean (2)
NEW ZEALAND   16   T: Hurst, Leslie
                    C: Karam
                    PG: Karam (2)

8 Jun 1974, Sydney Cricket Ground
AUSTRALIA   6   PG: P. E. McLean (2)
NEW ZEALAND   16   T: Kirkpatrick, Batty,
                    Stevens
                    C: Karam (2)

19 Aug 1978, Athletic Park, Wellington
NEW ZEALAND   13   T: Williams
                    PG: B. W. Wilson (3)
AUSTRALIA   12   T: Batch
                    PG: Wright (2)

26 Aug 1978, Lancaster Park, Christchurch
NEW ZEALAND   22   T: Taylor, Seear,
                    S. S. Wilson
                    C: B. W. Wilson (2)
                    PG: B. W. Wilson
                    DG: Bruce
AUSTRALIA   6   PG: Wright
                    DG: Wright

9 Sep 1978, Eden Park, Auckland
NEW ZEALAND   16   T: Ashworth, S. S. Wilson
                    C: McKechnie
                    PG: McKechnie (2)
AUSTRALIA   30   T: Cornelsen (4), Pearse
                    C: Wright, Melrose
                    PG: Wright
                    DG: Melrose

28 Jul 1979, Sydney Cricket Ground
AUSTRALIA   12   PG: P. E. McLean (3)
                    DG: Melrose

NEW ZEALAND   6   PG: Wilson
                    DG: Taylor

21 Jun 1980, Sydney Cricket Ground
AUSTRALIA   13   T: Hawker, Martin
                    C: Gould
                    DG: Ella
NEW ZEALAND   9   PG: Codlin (3)

28 Jun 1980, Ballymore Oval, Brisbane
AUSTRALIA   9   T: Moon
                    C: Gould
                    PG: Gould
NEW ZEALAND   12   T: Reid
                    C: Codlin
                    PG: Codlin (2)

12 Jul 1980, Sydney Cricket Ground
AUSTRALIA   26   T: Grigg (2), O'Connor,
                    Carson
                    C: Gould (2)
                    PG: Gould
                    DG: Ella
NEW ZEALAND   10   T: Fraser
                    PG: Codlin (2)

14 Aug 1982, Lancaster Park, Christchurch
NEW ZEALAND   23   T: Mexted, Mourie, Pokere,
                    Fraser
                    C: Hewson (2)
                    PG: Hewson
AUSTRALIA   16   T: Hawker, Campese
                    C: Gould
                    PG: Gould (2)

28 Aug 1982, Athletic Park, Wellington
NEW ZEALAND   16   T: Shaw, Fraser
                    C: Hewson
                    PG: Hewson (2)
AUSTRALIA   19   T: G. A. Ella, Campese
                    C: Gould
                    PG: Gould (3)

11 Sep 1982, Eden Park, Auckland
NEW ZEALAND   33   T: Hewson, Shaw
                    C: Hewson (2)
                    PG: Hewson (5)
                    DG: Hewson, Smith
AUSTRALIA   18   T: Gould
                    C: Gould
                    PG: Gould (3)
                    DG: Hawker

20 Aug 1983, Sydney Cricket Ground
AUSTRALIA   8   T: Slack, Poidevin
NEW ZEALAND   18   T: Taylor
                    C: Hewson
                    PG: Hewson (4)

21 Jun 1984, Sydney Cricket Ground
AUSTRALIA   16   T: Reynolds, Moon
                    C: M. Ella
                    PG: M. Ella
                    DG: Gould
NEW ZEALAND   9   PG: Hewson (2)
                    DG: Hewson

4 Aug 1984, Ballymore Oval, Brisbane
AUSTRALIA   15   T: M. Ella
                    C: M. Ella
                    PG: M. Ella (2), Campese

NEW ZEALAND 19 T: Pokere
PG: Deans (5)

18 Aug 1984, Sydney Cricket Ground
AUSTRALIA 24 T: Campese
C: M. Ella
PG: M. Ella (5), Campese
NEW ZEALAND 25 T: Stone, Clamp
C: Deans
PG: Deans (5)

29 Jun 1985, Eden Park, Auckland
NEW ZEALAND 10 T: Green
PG: Crowley (2)
AUSTRALIA 9 T: Black
C: Lynagh
PG: Lynagh

9 Aug 1986, Athletic Park, Wellington
NEW ZEALAND 12 T: Brooke-Cowden
C: Cooper
PG: Cooper (2)
AUSTRALIA 13 T: Campese, Burke
C: Lynagh
PG: Lynagh

23 Aug 1986, Carisbrook, Dunedin
NEW ZEALAND 13 T: Kirk
PG: Cooper (2)
DG: Cooper
AUSTRALIA 12 PG: Lynagh (3)
DG: Lynagh

6 Sep 1986, Eden Park, Auckland
NEW ZEALAND 9 PG: Crowley (3)
AUSTRALIA 22 T: Leeds, Campese
C: Lynagh
PG: Lynagh (4)

South Africa v New Zealand

13 Aug 1921, Carisbrook, Dunedin
NEW ZEALAND 13 T: Belliss, Steel, Storey
C: M. F. Nicholls
SOUTH AFRICA 5 T: van Heerden
C: P. G. Morkel

27 Aug 1921, Eden Park, Auckland
NEW ZEALAND 5 T: McLean
C: Nicholls
SOUTH AFRICA 9 T: Sendin
C: P. G. Morkel

17 Sep 1921, Athletic Park, Wellington
NEW ZEALAND 0
SOUTH AFRICA 0

30 Jun 1928, Kingsmead, Durban
SOUTH AFRICA 17 T: Slater
PG: B. L. Osler (2)
DG: B. L. Osler (2)
NEW ZEALAND 0

21 Jul 1928, Ellis Park, Johannesburg
SOUTH AFRICA 6 PG: Osler
GM: Mostert
NEW ZEALAND 7 PG: Lindsay
DG: Strang

18 Aug 1928, Crusader Ground, Port Elizabeth
SOUTH AFRICA 11 T: Nel, de Jongh, Daneel
C: Osler
NEW ZEALAND 6 T: Stewart, Grenside

1 Sep 1928, Newlands, Cape Town
SOUTH AFRICA 5 T: van der Westhuizen
C: Osler
NEW ZEALAND 13 T: Swain
PG: Nicholls (2)
DG: Nicholls

14 Aug 1937, Athletic Park, Wellington
NEW ZEALAND 13 T: Dick
PG: Trevathan (2)
DG: Trevathan
SOUTH AFRICA 7 T: Williams
DG: White

4 Sep 1937, Lancaster Park, Christchurch
NEW ZEALAND 6 T: Sullivan (2)
SOUTH AFRICA 13 T: Turner, Bastard
C: Brand (2)
PG: Brand

25 Sep 1937, Eden Park, Auckland
NEW ZEALAND 6 PG: Trevathan (2)
SOUTH AFRICA 17 T: Babrow (2), Bergh,
Williams, Turner
C: Brand

16 Jul 1949, Newlands, Cape Town
SOUTH AFRICA 15 PG: Geffin (5)
NEW ZEALAND 11 T: Henderson
C: Scott
DG: Kearney
PG: Scott

13 Aug 1949, Ellis Park, Johannesburg
SOUTH AFRICA 12 T: Brewis, Lategan
DG: Brewis
PG: Geffin
NEW ZEALAND 6 DG: Kearney
PG: Scott

3 Sep 1949, Athletic, Kingsmead Ground, Durban
SOUTH AFRICA 9 PG: Geffin (3)
NEW ZEALAND 3 T: Goddard

17 Sep 1949, Crusader Ground, Port Elizabeth
SOUTH AFRICA 11 T: du Toit
C: Geffin
PG: Geffin
DG: Brewis
NEW ZEALAND 8 T: Johnstone, Elvidge
C: Scott

14 Jul 1956, Carisbrook, Dunedin
NEW ZEALAND 10 T: White, Jarden
C: Jarden (2)
SOUTH AFRICA 6 T: Howe
PG: Dryburgh

4 Aug 1956, Athletic Park, Wellington
NEW ZEALAND   3   T: Brown
SOUTH AFRICA   8   T: Reteif, du Rand
C: Viviers

18 Aug 1956, Lancaster Park, Christchurch
NEW ZEALAND   17   T: Dixon, Jarden, White
C: D. B. Clarke
PG: D. B. Clarke (2)
SOUTH AFRICA   10   T: Lochner, Rosenberg
C: Viviers (2)

1 Sep 1956, Eden Park, Auckland
NEW ZEALAND   11   T: Jones
C: D. B. Clarke
PG: D. B. Clarke (2)
SOUTH AFRICA   5   T: Dryburgh
C: Viviers

25 Jun 1960, Ellis Park, Johannesburg
SOUTH AFRICA   13   T: H. J. van Zyl (2)
C: Dryburgh, Lockyear
PG: Lockyear
NEW ZEALAND   0

23 Jul 1960, Newlands, Cape Town
SOUTH AFRICA   3   T: Oxlee
NEW ZEALAND   11   T: Meads
C: D. B. Clarke
PG: D. B. Clarke
DG: D. B. Clarke

13 Aug 1960, Free State Stadium, Bloemfontein
SOUTH AFRICA   11   T: Oxlee
C: Lockyear
PG: Lockyear (2)
NEW ZEALAND   11   T: McMullen
C: Clarke
PG: Clarke (2)

27 Aug 1960, Boet Erasmus Stadium, Port Elizabeth
SOUTH AFRICA   8   T: Pelser
C: Lockyear
PG: Lockyear
NEW ZEALAND   3   PG: D. B. Clarke

31 Jul 1965, Athletic Park, Wellington
NEW ZEALAND   6   T: Birtwistle, Tremain
SOUTH AFRICA   3   DG: Oxlee

21 Aug 1965, Carisbrook, Dunedin
NEW ZEALAND   13   T: Tremain, McLeod, Rangi
C: Williment (2)
SOUTH AFRICA   0

4 Sep 1965, Lancaster Park, Christchurch
NEW ZEALAND   16   T: Tremain, Rangi, Moreton
C: Williment (2)
PG: Williment
SOUTH AFRICA   19   T: Gainsford (2), Brynard (2)
C: Naude (2)
PG: Naude

18 Sep 1965, Eden Park, Auckland
NEW ZEALAND   20   T: Smith (2), Conway, Birtwistle, Gray
C: McCormick
DG: Herewini
SOUTH AFRICA   3   PG: Naude

25 Jul 1970, Loftus Versveld Stadium, Pretoria
SOUTH AFRICA   17   T: de Villiers, Nomis
C: McCallum
PG: McCallum (2)
DG: Visagie
NEW ZEALAND   6   T: Williams
PG: McCormick

8 Aug 1970, Newlands, Cape Town
SOUTH AFRICA   8   T: Jansen
C: McCallum
PG: McCallum
NEW ZEALAND   9   T: Laidlaw, Kirkpatrick
PG: McCormick

29 Aug 1970, Boet Erasmus Stadium, Port Elizabeth
SOUTH AFRICA   14   T: Muller (2)
C: McCallum
PG: McCallum (2)
NEW ZEALAND   3   PG: Williams

12 Sep 1970, Ellis Park, Johannesburg
SOUTH AFRICA   20   T: Visagie, Muller
C: McCallum
PG: McCallum (4)
NEW ZEALAND   17   T: Williams
C: Kember
PG: Kember (4)

24 Jul 1976, Kings Park, Durban
SOUTH AFRICA   16   T: Germishuys, Krantz
C: Bosch
PG: Bosch
DG: Robertson
NEW ZEALAND   7   T: Jaffray
PG: Williams

14 Aug 1976, Free State Stadium, Bloemfontein
SOUTH AFRICA   9   PG: Bosch (3)
NEW ZEALAND   15   T: Morgan
C: Going
PG: Going (2)
DG: Bruce

4 Sep 1976, Newlands, Cape Town
SOUTH AFRICA   15   T: Oosthuizen
C: Bosch
PG: Bosch (2)
DG: Snyman
NEW ZEALAND   10   T: B. J. Robertson
PG: Williams (2)

18 Sep 1976, Ellis Park, Johannesburg
SOUTH AFRICA   15   T: Kritzinger
C: Bosch
PG: Bosch (2)
DG: Bosch
NEW ZEALAND   14   T: Kirkpatrick, Going
PG: Williams
DG: Bruce

15 Aug 1981, Lancaster Park, Christchurch
NEW ZEALAND   14   T: Rollerson, Wilson, Shaw
C: Rollerson
SOUTH AFRICA   9   T: Bekker
C: H. E. Botha
DG: H. E. Botha

29 Aug 1981, Athletic Park, Wellington
NEW ZEALAND 12   PG: Hewson (4)
SOUTH AFRICA 24   T: Germishuys
                     C: Botha
                     PG: Botha (5)
                     DG: Botha

12 Sep 1981, Eden Park, Auckland
NEW ZEALAND 25   T: Wilson, Knight
                     C: Rollerson
                     PG: Hewson (3), Rollerson
                     DG: Rollerson
SOUTH AFRICA 22   T: Mordt (3)
                     C: Botha (2)
                     PG: Botha (2)

A sadly familiar sight on South Africa's 1981 tour to New Zealand. A policeman guards two protesters during the first test at Lancaster Park, Christchurch, won 14–9 by New Zealand.

4 GREAT MATCHES FROM AROUND THE WORLD

Obolensky's Match

4 January 1936, Twickenham
ENGLAND 13   NEW ZEALAND 0

England's pre-war zenith – their biggest win over New Zealand, who failed to score, and three superbly created tries to nil. It was the fourth international of the 1935–6 All Blacks tour, after wins against Scotland 18–8, Ireland 17–9 and a 13–12 defeat at Cardiff against Wales.

The three England tries are worth recalling. All three came from the wingers. The first arrived after New Zealand pressure for the first 20 minutes. England broke away. Obolensky, on his international debut, scooted around Ball and Gilbert from an orthodox threequarter movement from a scrum, using his pace to slip his cover. Two minutes from halftime Obolensky scored again. This time the try went into the annals. Cranmer broke right towards Obolensky's wing, passed on to Candler who found Obolensky on the right wing. Obolensky hesitated, cut back inside and spurted diagonally across the field beating the cover defence, before rounding the

Alexander Obolensky's second try coming up. He has just received the ball from Candler (No 10) and ducks back towards the England No 8 before outsprinting a wrong-footed All Blacks' defence.

New Zealand right wing Mitchell and the despairing Gilbert to score on his opposite wing.

England scored twice more in the second half. First Cranmer dropped a goal to increase the margin to ten points. Finally Candler and Cranmer, who had set up Obolensky's epic tries, provided the other wing Sever with a chance to show his paces in a 35-yard (32 m) sprint to the line. England's winning margin in no way flattered them.

The two Obolensky tries were the only two he scored for England in a four-match international career. Born in Leningrad on 17 February 1916, he was the son of Prince Alexis Obolensky, an officer in the Imperial Horse Guards. Fleeing from the Russian Revolution, the family came to Britain. Obolensky was educated at Kent College and Brasenose College, Oxford, gaining his rugby blue. He was still a Russian citizen when England – searching desperately for speedy wings – called upon his services. Obolensky was also playing club rugby for Rosslyn Park, and running in a few tries. After his incredible England debut that day he became a national hero overnight. Yet he played only three more games (all in 1936) for England and hardly received a pass.

On leaving Oxford, Obolensky joined the RAF. The onset of war, in which he became a Hurricane pilot, left little time for training, but he was looking forward to re-establishing himself in the 1939 season after his exams.

Tragically, that was never to be. On 29 March 1940, Obolensky's plane crashed on landing in Norfolk. He was just 24, the first rugby international to lose his life during the war. His fame rests solely on that one glorious match against New Zealand, a memory that will surely outlive us all.

ENGLAND: H. G. Owen-Smith (St Mary's Hospital); A. Obolensky (Oxford University), P. Cranmer (Richmond), R. A. Gerrard (Bath), H. S. Sever (Sale); P. L. Candler (St Bartholomew's Hospital), B. C. Gadney (Leicester, capt.); D. A. Kendrew (Leicester), E. S. Nicholson (Leicester), R. J. Longland (Northampton); C. S. H. Webb (Devonport Services), A. J. Clarke (Coventry); W. H. Weston (Northampton), E. A. Hamilton-Hill (Harlequins), P. E. Dunkley (Harlequins)

NEW ZEALAND: G. D. M. Gilbert (West Coast); N. A. Mitchell (Southland), T. H. C. Caughey (Auckland), C. J. Oliver (Canterbury), N. Ball (Wellington); E. W. T. Tindill (Wellington), M. M. N. Corner (Auckland); A. Lambourn (Wellington), W. E. Hadley (Auckland), J. Hore (Otago); S. T. Reid (Hawke's Bay), R. R. King (West Coast); J. E. Manchester (Canterbury, capt.), H. F. McLean (Auckland), A. Mahoney (Bush)

Referee: J. W. Faull (Wales)

High Summer for British Rugby

22 June 1974, Loftus Versveld, Pretoria
SOUTH AFRICA   9   BRITISH ISLES   28

The heaviest ever defeat suffered by South Africa, and final proof, if any were needed, that the British – for a short time – were the best in the world. John Dawes' 1971 team had won the series in New Zealand, the 1973 Barbarians had confirmed supremacy, but there was still the nagging doubt that South Africa, at test level, would spoil the party.

There were doubts about the team before the Lions left Britain. Gerald Davies, David Duckham and initially Mike Gibson, three of the finest threequarters ever produced in Britain and who relished the firm ground, were unavailable for business reasons. Yet as the tour progressed the Lions found that the Springboks had gone soft through isolation.

Loftus Versveld is an open bowl, over 5000 feet (1524 m) above sea level, making it ideal for attacking rugby if the lungs hold out. A unique climate and totally suited to the home side who had gone one down after losing the first test 12–3 in soggy Cape Town.

South Africa made eight changes for the match, one positional. The British Isles were happy with the team which had won in a quagmire at Newlands, and hoped to repeat the success of using England's lock Roger Uttley on the flank.

More than 63 000 witnessed the five-try rout, with only a Gerald Bosch drop goal and two penalties in reply. Leading 10–3 at half time, and then pegged back to 10–6,

the Lions ran riot with 18 points in the last quarter.

The five tries were scored by four players who really made their mark on the tour. The bedrock basis of the 1971 Lions was left intact: J. P. R. Williams, Gareth Edwards, Mervyn Davies, Willie John McBride, Fergus Slattery and Ian McLauchlan. But in this match the newer contingent stepped into the limelight. John J. Williams – known as JJ – scored two tries. He was to score four in the series, a Lions' record. The 'Welsh Whippet' was a sprinter for Wales in the Commonwealth Games, and excelled in the rarefied atmosphere. Scottish lock Gordon Brown scored a try, one of a record eight that he was to touch down on tour, confirming his immense promise in New Zealand. Dick Milliken, the Irish centre – unheralded and unranked, but a perfect foil for the more flamboyant threequarters – was also on the try list. Phil Bennett had come to the fore as replacement for Barry John for both Wales and the Lions. Now his 50-yard (45 m) solo effort, finishing with an outrageous dummy past McCullum, broke all Springbok resistance. He converted just one of the tries and kicked just one penalty (Ian McGeechan completing the scoring with a drop goal). After the match Bennett had to have six stitches in a cut foot which seriously impaired his kicking. Without that injury the score would have reached 40 points.

SOUTH AFRICA: I. D. McCullum (Natal); C. F. Pope (Western Province), J. C. P. Snyman (Orange Free State), P. J. M. Whipp (Western Province), J. S.

Germishuys (Orange Free State); G. R. Bosch (Transvaal), P. C. R. Bayvel (Transvaal); J. K. Marais (Eastern Province, capt.), D. Frederickson (Transvaal), N. S. E. Bezuidenhout (Northern Transvaal); J. G. Williams (Northern Transvaal), K. B. H. de Klerk (Transvaal); J. H. Ellis (South West Africa), M. du Plessis (Western Province), D. A. McDonald (Western Province). Replacements: D. S. L. Snyman (Western Province) for McCullum 67 mins; M. L. Vogel (Orange Free State) for D. S. L. Snyman 75 mins.

BRITISH ISLES: J. P. R. Williams (Wales); W. C. C. Steele (Scotland), R. A. Milliken (Ireland), I. R. McGeechan (Scotland), J. J. Williams (Wales); P. Bennett (Wales), G. O. Edwards (Wales); J. McLauchlan (Scotland), R. W. Windsor (Wales), F. E. Cotton (England); W. J. McBride (Ireland, capt.), G. L. Brown (Scotland); J. F. Slattery (Ireland), R. M. Uttley (England), T. M. Davies (Wales)
Referee: C. de Bruyn (South Africa)

Cornelsen – Four-Try Forward

9 September 1978, Eden Park, Auckland
NEW ZEALAND 16   AUSTRALIA 30

Greg Cornelsen, the Queensland number 8, came out of this match straight into the record books as the first (and so far only) forward to score four tries in a test match. It was also the first time that New Zealand had conceded 30 points in a test match. Moreover, it proved that Australia were a side to be reckoned with. The groundwork for the later integration of the Ellas, Campese, Slack and a new set of forwards had been laid.

New Zealand had won the first two tests of the series 13–12 at Wellington and 22–6 at Christchurch, so this was a 'dead' rubber match. Paul McLean had been invalided out of the tour, and the Australians made three changes. New Zealand, as expected, were unchanged.

Cornelsen was on the score sheet within seven minutes with his first try, scrambling the ball over the line from a lineout after a fine back movement. Tony Melrose, just 19, converted. Five minutes later, Geoff Richards, the full-back, made a penetrating run which was halted just a few metres from the line. Cornelsen gobbled up the loose ball and plunged over. New Zealand's only points of the first half came through a simple 20-metre kick from Brian McKechnie, the test cricketer.

That fine old warrior John Hipwell created the third Australian try – a bolt round the blind side, linking with Wright who passed inside for Gary Pearse to power in from 20 metres. Seven minutes after the restart, the Wallabies had scored again. Cornelsen, backing up like a good back row forward, was again first to the loose ball after another surging threequarter movement initiated by Hipwell. But with another failed conversion the lead, though handy, could have been more than 18–3.

This failure to kick goals became highlighted when the All Black Stu Wilson was involved in two tries inside three minutes. First, his fine break was carried on by Knight for Ashworth to burst over; then a kick and chase brought Wilson four points. McKechnie converted Ashworth's effort, and Wright and McKechnie swapped penalties in quick succession.

Greg Cornelsen (centre), scorer of four tries against New Zealand in 1978, charges through the Welsh defence at Cardiff in 1975.

The crucial scores then came from the visitors. With 15 minutes left, Hipwell created his third try, and Cornelsen's fourth. The scrum-half made the break, the ubiquitous Cornelsen collected the loose ball when the movement broke down, and pounced as it rolled tantalizingly into the goal area. Wright converted. With five minutes to go, Melrose capped a fine day by dropping a goal.

Greg Cornelsen, a 26-year-old superannuation consultant, had barely to move 15 metres in sum total for his four tries. His effort proved conclusively the value of support play, a feature of later teams from the Southern Hemisphere. Born in northern New South Wales on 29 August 1952, he was an automatic choice for Australia during a career in which he won 25 caps between 1973 and 1981. He played club rugby for Teachers, and state rugby for NSW Country, NSW, and Queensland. A splendid lineout jumper, and effective in the close-quarter work, Cornelsen is equally famous for his 'up the jumper' try in 1975 against Sydney, when he ran 40 yards with the ball stuffed up his jersey.

NEW ZEALAND: B. W. Wilson (Otago); S. S. Wilson (Wellington), N. M. Taylor (Bay of Plenty), B. J. Robertson (Counties), B. G. Williams (Auckland); B. J. McKechnie (Southland), M. W. Donaldson

(Manawatu); G. A. Knight (Manawatu), A. G. Dalton (Counties), J. C. Ashworth (Canterbury); F. J. Oliver (Otago, capt.), A. M. Haden (Auckland); R. G. Myers (Waikato), L. M. Rutledge (Southland), G. A. Seear (Otago)

AUSTRALIA: G. Richards (NSW); P. G. Batch (Queensland), K. J. Wright (NSW), W. A. McKid (NSW), B. J. Moon (Queensland); T. C. Melrose (NSW), J. N. B. Hipwell (NSW); C. B. Handy (Queensland), P. A. Horton (Queensland), J. E. C. Meadows (Victoria); P. W. McLean (Queensland), G. Fay (NSW); A. A. Shaw (Queensland, capt.), G. K. Pearse (NSW), G. Cornelsen (Queensland)
Referee: D. H. Millar (Otago)

Clarke's Boot Slays Rampant Lions

18 July 1959, Carisbrook, Dunedin
NEW ZEALAND   18   BRITISH ISLES   17

New Zealand won the first test of the 1959 series with the British Isles by six penalties to four tries, a conversion and a penalty. The British supporters screamed injustice, yet the New Zealanders played within the laws, and avenged earlier defeats of similar style. The British Lions should certainly have put the game beyond doubt when they were well in control at 17–9 with just 13 minutes left, particularly as All Blacks Finlay and Jones were carrying bad injuries.

Don Clarke opened the scoring for New Zealand with the first of his penalties after 20 minutes following a scrum infringement. Faull went offside two minutes later, Clarke adding another three points. The Lions continued this kicking duel with a Hewitt penalty on the half hour to open their account. In the last ten minutes before the interval the Lions forged ahead with tries from O'Reilly – set up by Risman with a break from the 25 – and Price, who anticipated a bouncing ball better than both Clarke and Jackson in the in-goal area.

Five minutes into the second half the Lions scored again, when the flanker Smith fed Jackson for the third try. With 13 minutes left the Lions scored a fourth after poor New Zealand defence had given Price and Scotland room to interpass. Price took the scoring pass, and this time Risman converted.

Clarke, who in the meantime had kicked his third penalty, reduced the leeway with a 50-yard (45 m) penalty after 70 minutes. With seven minutes left, Clarke thundered over another from 45 yards (41 m), and finally, with only two minutes remaining, he slotted the 'pressure kick'. Even then the Lions came desperately close to a fifth try, only to be penalized.

So to the central figure. Don Clarke, born 10 November 1933, was wrongly believed just to be a place kicker. For a man of 6 ft 2 in (1.88 m) and up to 17½ stones (111 kg) he was surprisingly agile, with fine positional sense. He played 31 times for New Zealand between 1956 and 1964 and scored 207 points in internationals, still a New Zealand record. Educated at Te Aroha College, he first played for Waikato at the age of 17. Clarke, whose brother Ian was a prop in the same international team, played Plunkett Shield cricket as a medium pacer for Auckland and Northern Districts in the 1950s. A farmer and a sales representative, he later emigrated to South Africa. He certainly made an indelible impression with his massive, slide-rule place-kicking.

NEW ZEALAND: D. B. Clarke (Waikato); B. E. McPhail (Canterbury), T. R. Lineen (Auckland), R. F. McMullen (Auckland), P. T. Walsh (Counties); R. H. Brown (Taranaki), R. J. Urbahn (Taranaki); I. J. Clarke (Waikato), R. C. Hemi (Waikato), W. J. Whineray (Auckland, capt.); S. F. Hill (Canterbury), I. N. MacEwan (Wellington); B. E. L. Finlay (Manawatu), E. A. R. Pickering (Waikato), P. F. H. Jones (North Auckland)

BRITISH ISLES: K. J. F. Scotland (Scotland); P. B. Jackson (England), D. Hewitt (Ireland), M. J. Price (Wales), A. J. F. O'Reilly (Ireland); A. B. W. Risman (England), R. E. G. Jeeps (England); H. F. McLeod (Scotland), A. R. Dawson (Ireland, capt.), B. G. M. Wood (Ireland); W. R. Evans (Wales), R. H. Williams (Wales); G. K. Smith (Scotland), N. A. A. Murphy (Ireland), J. Faull (Wales)
Referee: A. L. Fleury (Otago)

Springboks' Forward March

24 November 1951, Murrayfield, Edinburgh
SCOTLAND   0   SOUTH AFRICA   44

The finest hour on arguably the Springboks' finest tour. They played 31 matches in Britain and France, won 30 and lost just once – to London Counties 11–9, a defeat that probably did more good than harm.

Like many touring teams, the Springboks were described in their own country as not being the equal of others. Yet a touring team has advantages of living and training together, and despite losing their captain early in the tour, left behind the legacy of a world record at

Murrayfield that still survives (as at 1987).

Basil Kenyon, the tour captain, suffered eye damage as early as the fifth game, an injury that forced him into early retirement. His manager, Danie Craven, former international and future head of South African rugby, described him as one of the best captains he had seen. After Kenyon's mishap, sustained at Pontypool, the other number 8 in the party, Hennie Muller, took over.

Under today's points values, Scotland would have been beaten 53–0. Scotland held their own for 15 minutes, before the roof fell in. George Burrell, the Gala full-back, was deceived by a high kick, and Du Rand finished off a rush and exchange of passes. Van Schoor, another Rhodesian, added the second which the prop Geffin converted. Cameron missed Scotland's best chance with a penalty and Elliot went close, before Koch, steaming upfield, took advantage of non-existent cover to score the third try, converted by Geffin. Brewis had a hand in the next two scores, beginning with a drop goal, then creating space for Koch to score his second try in a movement again featuring Du Rand. At halftime the Springboks led 19–0.

Shortly after the break another forward – Delport, the hooker – scored a breakaway try after the Scots had been pressing. The rampaging forwards were again involved in the next scores: Van Wyk grabbed a try, then created a gap, Du Rand crosskicked (who ever heard of a lock crosskicking?) and Muller went over. Next, Lategan broke away from halfway to restore the threequarters' pride. Finally, Dinkelmann, the other lock, trundled over in the left-hand corner. Geffin converted all five in the second half.

The Springbok forwards had scored seven tries and converted seven. A simple and crushing statistic. And it was from this match that the phrase 'we were lucky to get nothing' was coined.

SCOTLAND: G. Burrell (Gala); J. G. M. Hart (London Scottish), D. M. Scott (London Scottish), F. O. Turnbull (Kelso), D. M. Rose (Jedforest); A. Cameron (Glasgow HSFP, capt.), A. F. Dorward (Gala); J. C. Dawson (Glasgow Acads), J. A. R. Macphail (Edinburgh Acads), R. L. Wilson (Gala); H. M. Inglis (Edinburgh Acads), J. Johnston (Melrose); W. I. D. Elliot (Edinburgh Acads), P. W. Kininmonth (Richmond), R. C. Taylor (Kelvinside Acads)

SOUTH AFRICA: J. Buchler (Transvaal); F. Marais (Boland), R. Van Schoor (Rhodesia), M. T. Lategan (Western Province), P. Johnstone (Western Province); J. D. Brewis (Northern Transvaal), P. W. du Toit (Western Province); A. Geffin (Transvaal), W. Delport (Eastern Province), C. Koch (Boland); J. Du Rand (Rhodesia), E. Dinkelmann (Northern Transvaal); C. J. Van Wyk (Transvaal), S. P. Fry (Western Province), H. Muller (Transvaal, capt.)
Referee: M. J. Dowling (Ireland)

THE RECORDS
Biggest winning margin
44–0 is the biggest winning margin between International Board countries

Most tries by forwards in an international
7   Koch (2), Du Rand, Dinkelmann, Van Wyk, Muller, Delport

Most conversions by a forward in an international
7   A. Geffin (prop)

Most points by front five
29   Koch (2T), Delport (1T), Geffin (7C), Du Rand (1T), Dinkelmann (1T) Total 5T 7C.

Dropped for next international after 44–0 win
F. Marais

All Blacks Bow to Barbarians' Brilliance

27 January 1973, Cardiff Arms Park
BARBARIANS   23   NEW ZEALAND   11

The traditional end-of-tour showpiece game at the National Stadium was of particular significance. It proved that for the time being British rugby was going in the right direction, and it contained *The Try*. Quite simply, it was one of those games where a video of the entire match should have been required viewing for every school in the world to show youngsters how the game can be played. The All Blacks decided to perform the Haka for the first time before this 28th match of a long and strenuous tour, and they contributed handsomely to the exhibition, especially after being a record 17 points adrift at halftime.

The Barbarians, true to its tradition as a club side, had chosen an uncapped player in the team – Bob Wilkinson, the promising Bedford and Cambridge University lock. The remainder of the team was on duty several months

earlier as the first British Lions team to win a series in New Zealand, except for Tom David, Phil Bennett and Sandy Carmichael, the last named coming home early after the brawl against Canterbury.

The Try was scored after just two minutes. As every Welshman will tell, only one player from outside the Principality was involved in the move which began innocuously enough with Phil Bennett fielding a deep kick just outside his own line. He sidestepped Scown and two others and passed to J. P. R. Williams (who held off a head high tackle from his namesake), from whom the ball went to Pullin, Dawes, David, Quinnell and Edwards, though the final pass was intended for Bevan. The Cardiff scrum-half dived triumphantly into the left-hand corner. John Pullin is involved in more quiz questions about his involvement in that piece of history than about his 42 caps for England.

By halftime the score had reached rout proportions. Bennett had added a penalty after seven minutes, and

Slattery and Bevan scored tries in which they towed a posse of defenders over the line with them. Bennett converted the Irish flanker's try.

After five minutes of the second half a Karam penalty put the New Zealanders on their way. Then Bryan Williams cut clean through between his threequarters to set up an overlap for Batty. The tourists brought the score back to 17–11 with another try from Batty who had correctly worked out that the only way to beat J. P. R. Williams in a one-to-one confrontation was to boot the ball over his head and beat the full-back on the turn. Batty, jeered following an altercation with David, was the find of the tour.

The Barbarians, though, had the last word when the outstanding Duckham and Gibson set up a try for J. P. R. Williams who, like Edwards before, had to avoid a last-ditch, head-hunting tackle from Batty. Bennett sealed the victory with a superb conversion from his 'wrong' side.

This was certainly the Barbarians' finest victory and probably the best performance by a British team on their own soil.

BARBARIANS: J. P. R. Williams (London Welsh); D. J. Duckham (Coventry), S. J. Dawes (London Welsh, capt.), C. M. H. Gibson (NIFC), J. C. Bevan (Cardiff); P. Bennett (Llanelli), G. O. Edwards (Cardiff); A. B. Carmichael (West of Scotland), J. V. Pullin (Bristol), R. J. McLoughlin (Blackrock College); R. M. Wilkinson (Cambridge University), W. J. McBride (Ballymena); J. F. Slattery (Blackrock College), T. P. David (Pontypridd), D. L. Quinnell (Llanelli)

'The Try' *in progress. Barbarians' captain John Dawes passes inside to Tommy David. Scorer Gareth Edwards lurks in the distance (second from right) as New Zealand's scrum-half Sid Going (No 9) tries to disrupt the move.*

NEW ZEALAND: J. F. Karam (Wellington); B. G. Williams (Auckland), B. J. Robertson (Counties), I. A. Hurst (Canterbury), G. B. Batty (Wellington); R. E. Burgess (Manawatu), S. M. Going (North Auckland); G. J. Whiting (King Country), R. A. Urlich (Auckland), K. K. Lambert (Manawatu); H. H. Macdonald (Canterbury), P. J. Whiting (Auckland); I. A. Kirkpatrick (Poverty Bay, capt.), A. J. Wyllie (Canterbury), A. I. Scown (Taranaki)
Referee: G. Domercq (France)

5 THE WORLD CUP'S JUNIOR NATIONS

Nine emerging nations took part in the 1987 World Cup – Romania and Italy from Europe; Canada, the USA and Argentina from the Americas; Japan; the Pacific Islands of Fiji and Tonga, with Zimbabwe, Africa's sole representative.

This chapter traces the development of the game in these countries and, where possible, the current structure and domestic competitions within these nations. Interestingly, several of the national organizations are the envy of many of the more established International Board countries.

Argentina

Number of clubs 205
Number of players 21 000
Colours Blue and white hooped shirts
Foundation (Union) 1886 (League) 1899
Headquarters UAR, Pacheco de Melo 2120, Buenos Aires
Principal Stadiums Velez Sarsfield, Buenos Aires (cap. 55 000), Oeste Stadium, Buenos Aires (cap. 38 000)

ARGENTINA – NATIONAL CHAMPIONS

1899	Lomas	1953	Obrias Sanitarias
1900–4	Buenos Aires	1954–7	Atletico San Isidro
1905–6	Rosario Athletic	1958–9	Buenos Aires
1907	Belgrano	1960	Not held
1908–9	Buenos Aires	1961–2	Atletico San Isidro
1910	Belgrano	1963	Belgrano
1911–12	Gymnasia y Escrima	1964	Atletico San Isidro
1913	Lomas	1965	Not held
1914	Belgrano	1966	Belgrano
1915	Buenos Aires	1967	Atletico San Isidro &
1916	Not held		Belgrano
1917–18	Atletico San Isidro	1968	Universitario & San Isidro
1919	Not held	1969	Universitario
1920–30	Atletico San Isidro	1970	San Isidro Club &
1931	Universitario		Universitario
1932	Gymnasia y Escrima	1971–3	San Isidro Club
1933–4	Atletico San Isidro	1974–6	Atletico San Isidro
1935	Rosario Athletic	1977–80	San Isidro Club
1936–40	Not held	1981–2	Atletico San Isidro
1941	San Isidro Club	1983–4	San Isidro Club
1942	Universitario	1985	Atletico San Isidro
1943	Atletico San Isidro	1986	Banco Naçion & San Isidro
1944–5	Universitario		Club
1946	Pucara		
1947	Universitario		
1948	San Isidro Club		
1949	Atletico San Isidro &		
	Universitario		
1950	Universitario & Pucara		
1951–2	Universitario		

Martin Sansot, one of Argentina's finest players, one of the top full-backs in the world during the 1970s.

Rugby was first introduced into Argentina probably in 1873. A local newspaper records that the 'Banks' played the 'City' at the Buenos Aires Cricket Club at Palmermo on the outskirts of the capital. However, the first game under proper laws was probably played on 18 May 1874. Both were well-known local families of British stock.

The Buenos Aires RFC was formed in 1886 when the two oldest clubs in each code merged to form the Buenos Aires Cricket and Football Club. The rugby section still play in the local league. The first league started in 1899, four clubs – Buenos Aires FC, Lomas (the first winners), Rosario and Belgrano – taking part. All had just been affiliated to the River Plate Rugby Union, the Argentine RU as we know it today.

The first all-Argentine side made its first appearance in 1904. Formed by students from Buenos Aires University, they played in the championship under the name of the School of Engineering. A year later the bulk of the School of Engineering XV represented the Argentines in a match against those of British stock. The locals won 21–5. Three British teams visited before the war – 1910, 1927 and 1936. After the war, tours from Britain were again popular, but the sphere of influence had moved to South Africa. As threats of isolation set in, the South Africans sent representative teams and coaches to the Argentine in increasing numbers. Izak Van Heerden became the first Argentine coach in 1965, bringing with him new methods and organization. This helped the development and improvement of rugby, and Argentina made strides towards world class with wins against Wales and Scotland and, more recently, France, Australia and South Africa, as well as drawing with New Zealand.

Canada

Number of clubs 207
Number of players 10 500
Colours Red jerseys with white maple leaf, white shorts
Foundation 1929
Headquarters 333 River Road, Ontario K1L 8B9
Principal Stadium Burnaby (cap. 20 000)

Though rugby was introduced into Canada by British military stationed in the country, and by members of the Royal Navy based at Halifax and Esquimault, the major credit for the embryonic Canadian game lies with the international A. St G. Hammersley. Shortly after playing for England in the very first international against Scotland in 1871, he took the game to British Columbia, which with its influx of British professional people during the 1960s, including many PE teachers, continues to dominate the scene. New Zealand touring teams frequently stop over on the way to or from Britain, and the results of British Columbian sides have been far superior to those of the full national team.

Canadian rugby is split East–West, or British Columbia versus the Rest. In the East the game developed

Rugby in Canada in 1907. Note the eccentric headgear.

Canada and Japan (hooped shirts) dispute possession during the 1986 match at Vancouver, which the Japanese won by 26–21.

earlier, with reports of a match in 1863 between an English Army XV and students from McGill University. Montreal Football Club is amongst the oldest in the world, dating from 1865. The Canadian RU was formed in 1929 when six Provinces met in Winnipeg to draw up the constitution. After folding in 1939 at the outset of World War II, the CRU was reformed in 1965, this time with government finance.

CURRENT STRUCTURE

The Inter Provincial Competition is the backbone of the country's rugby. Another nationwide competition is held for the smaller Unions. Each Union runs its own club competition. Ontario and Eastern Ontario have two divisions each, Niagara and Quebec three each, and Toronto has four.

Travel proves a handicap. Climate can also cause problems. In the East matches take place in the spring and autumn – May to October. In British Columbia the Northern Hemisphere season – from September to April – is the norm, being the only climate suitable for winter competition.

INTERNATIONAL TOURS

		P	W	D	L	F	A
1902–3	British Isles	23	8	2	13	114	243
1932	Japan	7	5	0	2	150	82
1962	British Isles	16	1	1	14	89	290
1971	Wales	5	2	0	3	66	141
1979	Britain/France	6	3	1	2	68	75
1981	Argentina	5	4	0	1	132	71
1982	Japan	6	4	0	2	145	67
1983	England	5	2	0	3	51	82
1985	Australia	9	4	0	5	144	230
1986	France	3	1	0	2	29	45
1986	Ireland	4	0	0	4	63	98

CANADIAN VICTORIES OVER TOURING TEAMS

British Columbia
1912   Australia   W 15–0
1958   Australia   W 11–8
Vancouver
1912   Australia   W 6–3
Victoria
1912   Australia   W 13–11

OTHER INTERNATIONALS

1966   Canada 8, British Lions 19
1976   Canada 4, Barbarians 29

CANADA – INTER-PROVINCIAL CHAMPIONSHIP

1958	British Columbia 18, E. Canada 9
1959	British Columbia 24, E. Canada 3
1960–5	Not played
1966	British Columbia 50, Ontario 3
1967	British Columbia 27, Quebec 6
1968	British Columbia 13, Quebec 3
1969	British Columbia 21, Quebec 9
1970	British Columbia 26, Ontario 6
1971	Ontario 27, British Columbia 17
1972	Ontario 7, Alberta 3
1973	Ontario 17, Alberta 7
1974	British Columbia 48, Newfoundland 3
1975	British Columbia 43, Ontario 6
1976	British Columbia 35, Ontario 6
1977	British Columbia 7, Ontario 3
1978	British Columbia 41, Quebec 3
1979	British Columbia 36, Ontario 7
1980	British Columbia 48, Ontario 7
1981	British Columbia 9, Ontario 3
1982	Ontario 21, British Columbia 9
1983	British Columbia 25, Ontario 9
1984	British Columbia 16, Ontario 9
1985	British Columbia 31, Ontario 11
1986	British Columbia 29, Ontario 12

INTER BRANCH CHAMPIONSHIP

1985   Vancouver Island 10, Toronto 6
1986   Edmonton 17, Vancouver Island 12

Fiji

Number of clubs 600
Number of players 12 500
Colours White shirts, blue
  shorts
Foundation 1913
Headquarters FRU, PO
  Box 1234, Suva
Principal Stadium FRU
  Stadium, Suva (cap.
  30 000)

Top *Team talk Fijian style.* Centre *Fiji enter the Rugby Stadium, then* (above) *cause one of rugby's major surprises by beating the British Isles 25–21 at Suva in 1977.*

Fiji are fairly certain that the first rugby match was played in Ba round about 1884 by European and Fijian soldiers of the Native Constabulary led by a Major Thurston. In fact, in the early days of Fiji's life as a colony the majority of Fijians played soccer, though even more played cricket.

By 1900 reports of games were beginning to appear in the press and a club competition began in 1904. Two of the earliest clubs were Civil Service and Constabulary under the guidance of Messrs Pennefather and Judd.

In 1905, Ratu Jone Tabaiwalu returned from school at Wanganui, New Zealand, and introduced rugby to Fijians at Naililili, Rewa. In fact at that time Fijians described rugby as 'Veicaqe vaka-Naililili', or more commonly 'Veicaqe vaka-Peritania' (football Naililili or British style). Regular matches were being played against visiting warships and by 1911 the first regular Fijian Club (Davies) had also been formed.

In 1913 a group of New Zealanders came to Suva to build the Grand Pacific Hotel. One of them was a plumber named Paddy Sheehan. Paddy was a mighty forward for Southern Club, Dunedin. Paddy saw the need for organizing all this casual rugby, so he formed the Pacific Club. Three more clubs were planned by the end of the first meeting: the Cadets Club (mainly bank staff), the United Services Club and Imperial. Later The Colonial Sugar Refining Company Ltd staff played under the name Rewa. Together these clubs formed the Fiji Rugby Football Union.

The Governor at the time, Sir Ernest Bickham Sweet-Escott, donated the Escott shield for the club championship which was first won by the Pacific Club and, 60 years later, is still competed for by Suva Union clubs.

Fiji's first overseas match was in Apia, Samoa, in August 1924 while the team was on its way to Tonga on a tour organized by A. S. Farebrother, a stalwart of Fiji rugby until his death in 1945. The match was played at 7.00 a.m. to allow their Samoan/New Zealander opponents time to get to work after the game and took place on a pitch with a large tree in the centre. Fiji played in all black and won 6–0. All the players paid their own fares.

The first visit by an overseas side was by Auckland University College in 1926. Their record was P4 W1 D1 L2. Tonga also visited Fiji for the first time and Fiji played in its present uniform of white jersey, blue shorts and palm tree badge for the first time.

In 1937 the Lomaiviti Rugby Union at Levuka was formed, although occasional matches between Lautoka and Vatukoula are on record in 1937. There was probably a healthy competition at Vatukoula from the mid-1930s and the Northern Union was formed in 1938.

Nineteen thirty-eight was also notable because Fijians played in boots for the first time – in honour of the first Maori team to visit Fiji – though there was still a regrettable tendency to throw discarded boots to the touchline during matches!

During the war there was less organized rugby but far more matches were in fact played by a large number of service teams including New Zealanders and Australians in Fiji. In many ways this period, following the unbeaten tour of New Zealand in 1939, may have been the take-off point of modern Fiji rugby.

WORLD RECORD

Fiji took part in the 1969 South Pacific Games in Port Moresby. On successive days they set a 'world' scoring record for 'internationals'. The full results from that championship were:

16 August   Fiji 84, Wallis and Futuna 8
18 August   Fiji 79, Papua New Guinea 0
21 August   Fiji 113, Solomon Islands 13
22 August   Fiji 113, New Caledonia 3
23 August   Fiji 88, Papua New Guinea 3

Fiji scored 457 points in eight days. Most official records do not include these results in their official lists due to the quality of the opposition.

For the 'Pacific Derby' (Tonga v Fiji), see Tonga page 126.

Two of the most famous victories in Fijian rugby have come at the expense of British teams – the Barbarians and the British Lions. The full scores:

24 October 1970, Gosforth

BARBARIANS	9	T: Duckham, J. S. Spencer
		PG: J. P. R. Williams
FIJI	29	T: Batibasaga, Nasave, Visei, Qoro, Racike, Tuese, Ravouvou
		C: Batibasaga (4)

16 August 1977, Suva

FIJI	25	T: Narasia (2), Racika (2), Kuinikoro
		C: Racika
		DG: Tikoisuva
BRITISH LIONS	21	T: Bennett, Beaumont, Burcher
		C: Bennett (3)
		PG: Bennett

Italy

Number of clubs 314
Number of players 25 772
Colours Blue shirts, white shorts
Foundation 1928
Headquarters 2 Via Leopoldo Franchetti, 00194 Rome

The speed with which Italy organized their Union and then their league is a lesson for other aspiring nations. Though the game had infiltrated through France in 1910, the war years brought a halt to development. By 1927 there was a revival, with a dozen clubs playing the game regularly. A year later the Italian Rugby Federation was formed, and in 1929 Ambrosiana Milano won the first championship.

Italy were founder members of the FIRA championship. Their initial growth and development was hindered by the refusal of many schools to accept rugby on the curriculum. But with the influx of overseas coaches and players, many educationalists are now keen to include the game. So much so that the Italians won the FIRA title in 1985, beating the pride of French youth 8–4 in the final. They underlined this with a win over England.

CURRENT STRUCTURE

Italy is now beginning to reap the benefit of the influx of outstanding coaches such as Pierre Villepreux, the former French full-back, and the late Carwyn James, the best coach of his generation. International players of the highest quality have also graced the first division – Rob Louw and Rudi Visagie (South Africa), David Campese and Roger Gould (Australia) and John Kirwan (New Zealand) have been amongst several recent internationals to play in Italy. The championship is run on a league basis. There is a first division, a second division, and two regional third divisions. Promotion into the third division is via the regional leagues. Sponsorship plays an integral part of the club scene: all the major clubs (and most of the smaller clubs) are sponsored and in 1986 the first division contained names such as Bennetton Treviso, Brunelleschi Brescia, Deltalat Rovigo, Eurobags Casale, Fracasso San Dona, Maa Milan and Rolly Go Roma.

ITALY – INTERNATIONAL RECORDS
TEAM RECORDS
Most points scored
49 v Czechoslovakia 1975 (49–9)
Biggest winning margin
45 v Belgium 1937 (45–0)
Heaviest defeat
Romania 69, Italy 0 1977, New Zealand 70, Italy 6 1987
Most tries scored
10 v Belgium 1937
Most tries conceded
13 v Romania, 12 v New Zealand 1987

INDIVIDUAL RECORDS
Most internationals
Bona 50 1972–81
Most points
Stefano Bettarello 405 1979–86
Most points in a match
Stefano Bettarello 29 v Canada 1983
Most tries in a match
Cova 4 v Belgium 1937
Most penalty goals in a match
Stefano Bettarello 5 v Canada 1983 and 5 v Morocco 1983

ITALY – NATIONAL CHAMPIONS

1929	Ambrosiana Milano	1941	Amatori Milano
1930	Amatori Milano	1942	Amatori Milano
1931	Amatori Milano	1943	Amatori Milano
1932	Amatori Milano	1944–5	Not held
1933	Amatori Milano	1946	Amatori Milano
1934	Amatori Milano	1947	Ginnastica Torino
1935	Roma	1948	Roma
1936	Amatori Milano	1949	Roma
1937	Roma	1950	Parma
1938	Amatori Milano	1951	Rovigo
1939	Amatori Milano	1952	Rovigo
1940	Amatori Milano	1953	Rovigo

1954	Rovigo	1972	Petrarca Padova
1955	Parma	1973	Petrarca Padova
1956	*Faema* Treviso	1974	Petrarca Padova
1957	Parma	1975	*La Concordia* Brescia
1958	Fiamme Oro Padova	1976	*Sanson* Rovigo
1959	Fiamme Oro Padova	1977	Petrarca Padova
1960	Fiamme Oro Padova	1978	*Metalcrom* Treviso
1961	Fiamme Oro Padova	1979	*Sanson* Rovigo
1962	Rovigo	1980	Petrarca Padova
1963	Rovigo	1981	*Mael* L'Aquila
1964	Rovigo	1982	*Scavolini* L'Aquila
1965	Partenope Napoli	1983	*Benetton* Treviso
1966	Partenope Napoli	1984	Petrarca Padova
1967	L'Aquila	1985	Petrarca Padova
1968	Fiamme Oro Padova	1986	Petrarca Padova
1969	L'Aquila	1987	Petrarca Padova
1970	Petrarca Padova		
1971	Petrarca Padova		

Italy's first visit to Twickenham in 1984/5, where they lost 21–9 to England 'B'. Italy (dark shirts) took part in the 1987 World Cup.

Japan

Number of clubs 3000
Number of players 175 000
Colours Red and white hooped shirts, white shorts
Foundation 1926
HQ and Principal Stadium Chichibu Stadium, Tokyo (cap. 60 000)

Rugby was introduced into Japan by Edward Clark, a graduate of Cambridge University, who with Ginnosuke Tanaka introduced the game to Keio University in 1899.

In 1900 Keio played their first match against Yokohama Country and Athletic Club (YCAC), a club formed among the British residents in Yokohama. This was to become an annual encounter. In the same year an annual match was also arranged between Keio and KRAC, a similar club in Kobe.

In 1926 the Japan Rugby Football Union was formed with the co-operation of the Kanto and Seibu (now Kansai) Unions. At this time rugby was still limited to universities and schools, but the standard of rugby steadily improved.

In 1936 the first New Zealand Universities team toured Japan, winning six out of the seven games but drawing the last against Japan Universities.

However, in World War II rugby came to a complete halt. During the immediate post-war period rugby had lost its impact, and the players were far below the standards of the pre-war days. Also professional baseball dominated the interest and support of the general sport fans. The majority of the young, promising athletes took up baseball which also affected the popularity and development of the game.

Japan's first major club team, the 1903 Keiogijuku University team (left above) and in action (below).

CURRENT STRUCTURE

Top-level rugby today in Japan is played mostly among universities and company teams rather than club teams. After graduating from universities, players can seriously continue their rugby activities only if they enter companies which run rugby teams.

The main attraction in Tokyo, however, is still the fixtures between the universities, although a higher standard of rugby can often be seen between company teams. During the New Year holidays a national inter-company tournament is held in Tokyo or Osaka, at which the champion among company teams is decided. Also during the same period the All Japan University

Japanese winger Itoh, scorer of two tries against Wales in 1973, shows understandable anguish as he is thwarted by the corner flag in his search for a third touchdown.

Championship is held and in the middle of January a match between the champion company team and the champion university team takes place to decide the best team of the year.

The Japan Rugby Football Union has headquarters in Tokyo and administers the game through three district unions: Kanto, Kansai and Kyushu. There are over 3000 teams affiliated with the Japan RFU and rugby is now played in almost every university and school. Japan's one great handicap is the scarcity of grounds. Tokyo's only ground with stands is the Chichibu Rugby Ground which is used for too many games; this lovely pitch is reduced by November to bare dirt. This scarcity also makes it difficult to arrange steady fixture schedules.

JAPAN – CLUB CHAMPIONSHIP
Nippon Steel Kamaishi have won the club title 1979–86, a record, beating the previous record three wins by Nippon Steel Yawata and Kintetsu Rail.

WORLD RECORD
A crowd of 60000 watched the 1985 Japanese club championship final when Nippon Steel beat Doshisha University 31–17. The previous record for a club match was the 48000 that witnessed the Cardiff v Newport match in 1948.

Romania

Number of clubs 209
Number of players 17 200
Colours Yellow shirts, blue shorts
Foundation 1914
Headquarters Str. Vasile Conta 16, Bucharest
Principal Stadium 23rd August Stadium, Bucharest (cap. 90 000)

Early ties with France stimulated development in Romania. Several students had been educated in Paris – the Romanians are the most Latin of the Iron Curtain peoples – and on their return had taken the game into the existing sports clubs. The first club was the Romanian Tennis Club of Bucharest, founded in 1914. The Tennis Clubs' foresight in organizing a national competition aided the formation of the Federatia Romana di Rugbi. The early clubs – Viforul Dacia, Post and Telecommunications, Stadiul Roman, Sporting Club, Educatzia Fizica and Sportulul Studentesc – formed a solid base.

Club rugby was, and still is, centred around Bucharest, the first provincial club to win the championship being Universitea Timisoara in 1972. Three years later Farul Constanta also took the title out of the capital.

The national side has always been amongst the pioneers. Romania took part in the early Olympics, their game then benefited by regular contact with the French, the Communist Youth festivals featured rugby, and Romania are the only country other than France to win the FIRA Championship.

The last decade has seen contact with all the world's leading rugby-playing countries except for Australia and South Africa.

CURRENT STRUCTURE
The first division has 16 teams, with 42 in regionalized second divisions. Entry to these divisions is through local leagues. The top clubs are Farul Constanta and Steaua Bucharest, the army team.

ROMANIA v FRANCE
Traditionally the highlight of the Romanian season, when France honour Romania by playing their full international XV. On 19 May 1957 in the August 23rd Stadium, Bucharest, over 95000 spectators saw France beat Romania 18–15. It was part of a 'double header' – but the Romanian Football Annual records only a 1–1 draw with Poland in a 'B' soccer international on that day, so the crowd would have primarily been rugby supporters.

The full list of France v Romania matches is as follows (up to 1979, when the games appear in the Romania v International Board countries section):

Year	Venue	Winner	
1919	Paris	France	48–5
1924	Paris	France	59–3
1936	Berlin	France	26–5

Year	Venue	Winner		Year	Venue	Winner	
1937	Paris	France	27–11	1968	Bucharest	Romania	15–14
1938	Bucharest	France	11–8	1969	Tarbes	France	14–9
1957	Bucharest	France	18–15	1970	Bucharest	France	14–3
1957	Bordeaux	France	39–0	1971	Beziers	France	31–12
1960	Bucharest	Romania	11–5	1972	Constanta	France	15–6
1961	Bayonne	Drawn	5–5	1973	Valencia	France	7–6
1962	Bucharest	Romania	3–0	1974	Bucharest	Romania	15–10
1963	Toulouse	Drawn	6–6	1975	Bordeaux	France	36–12
1964	Bucharest	France	9–6	1976	Bucharest	Romania	15–12
1965	Lyon	France	8–3	1977	C-Ferrand	France	9–6
1966	Bucharest	France	9–3	1978	Bucharest	France	9–6
1967	Nantes	France	11–3				

ROMANIA VERSUS INTERNATIONAL BOARD COUNTRIES
Since 1979 (prior to 1987 World Cup)

1979 Wales 13, Romania 12
      France 30, Romania 12
1980 Ireland 13, Romania 13
      Romania 15, France 0
1981 Scotland 12, Romania 6
      Romania 6, New Zealand 14
      France 17, Romania 9
1982 Romania 13, France 9
1983 Romania 24, Wales 6
      France 26, Romania 15
1984 Romania 28, Scotland 22
      Romania 3, France 18
1985 England 22, Romania 15
      France 25, Romania 13
1986 Ireland 60, Romania 0
      Romania 3, France 20

Biggest crowd
95 000, Romania 15, France 18 (23rd August Stadium, Bucharest, 19 May 1957)

Romania's first visit to Twickenham resulted in a 22–15 defeat by England in 1985. Here Mircea Paraschiv attempts to round the England flanker John Hall.

CLUB CHAMPIONS

1914	Tennis Club Roman Bucharest	1929	Sportul Studentesc Bucharest	1943	Viforul Dacia Bucharest
1915	Tennis Club Roman Bucharest	1930	Stadiul Roman Bucharest	1944	Viforul Dacia Bucharest
1916	Tennis Club Roman Bucharest	1931	Stadiul Roman Bucharest	1945	Viforul Dacia Bucharest
1919	Stadiul Roman Bucharest	1932	Sportul Studentesc Bucharest	1946	Sportul Studentesc Bucharest
1920	Educatia Fizica Bucharest	1933	PTT Bucharest	1947	Stadiul Roman Bucharest
1921	Tennis Club Roman Bucharest	1934	PTT Bucharest	1948	CFR Bucharest
1922	Tennis Club Roman Bucharest	1935	Sportul Studentesc Bucharest	1949	CCA Bucharest
1923	Tennis Club Roman Bucharest	1936	Sportul Studentesc Bucharest	1950	CFR Bucharest
1924	Stadiul Roman Bucharest	1938	Tennis Club Roman Bucharest	1951	Dinamo Bucharest
1925	Sportul Studentesc Bucharest	1939	Sportul Studentesc Bucharest	1952	Dinamo Bucharest
1926	Stadiul Roman Bucharest	1940	Tennis Club Roman Bucharest	1953	CCA Bucharest
1927	Tennis Club Roman Bucharest	1941	Viforul Dacia Bucharest	1954	CCA Bucharest
1928	Stadiul Roman Bucharest	1942	Tennis Club Roman Bucharest	1955	Locomotiva Grivitza Rosie
				1956	Dinamo Bucharest
				1957	Locomotiva Grivitza Rosie
				1958	CFR Grivitza Rosie Bucharest
				1959	CFR Grivitza Rosie Bucharest

1960	CFR Grivitza Rosie Bucharest
1961	Steaua Bucharest
1962	Grivitza Rosie Bucharest
1963	Steaua Bucharest
1964	Steaua Bucharest
1965	Dinamo Bucharest
1966	Grivitza Rosie Bucharest
1967	Grivitza Rosie Bucharest
1968–9	Dinamo Bucharest
1970	Grivitza Rosie Bucharest
1971	Steaua Bucharest
1972	Universitea Timisoara
1973	Steaua Bucharest
1974	Steaua Bucharest
1975	Farul Constanta
1976	Farul Constanta
1977	Steaua Bucharest
1978	Farul Constanta
1979	Steaua Bucharest
1980	Steaua Bucharest
1981	Steaua Bucharest
1982	Dinamo Bucharest
1983	Steaua Bucharest
1984	Steaua Bucharest
1985	Steaua Bucharest
1986	Farul Constanta

Tonga

Number of clubs 85
Number of players 4000
Colours Scarlet shirts, white shorts
Foundation 1923
Headquarters PO Box 369, Nuku'Alofa
Principal Stadium Teufaiva Park, Nuku'Alofa (cap. 19 000)

The game was first played in Tonga in 1900, and organized rugby began in 1924. While Fiji's relations with other overseas unions built up, it was not until the mid-1970s, with tours to Australia, New Zealand and the United Kingdom, that Tonga ventured onto the international scene.

Fiji is Tonga's oldest and greatest rival and Tonga won their first encounter. Harmony on the pitch between the two has not always been evident, with 1928, 1934 and 1963 proving particularly sad occasions. But the current climate is very healthy, and both benefit from the competition in the Pacific championship, which now includes Western Samoa.

CURRENT STRUCTURE
The Tongan Union was founded in 1923 and oversees a complex system of schools, provincial and seven-a-side rugby. The Jubilee tour to Australia in 1973 provided the country with their most significant win to date, a 16–11 win against Australia at the Sydney Cricket Ground, a result that may have taken them above their station in world terms.

TONGA v FIJI
The 'Pacific derby', first played in 1924. Below is a list of the results, but do not include the Triangular Tournament results (also called Pacific Championship). Matches in Tonga appear as H (game played at Nuku'Alofa) and matches in Fiji as A (played at Suva).

Year		Result	
1924	H	Tonga	9–6
1924	H	Fiji	14–3
1924	H	Drawn	0–0
1926	A	Fiji	10–3
1926	A	Tonga	13–8
1926	A	Tonga	6–3
1928	H	Tonga	9–6

Year		Result	
1928	H	Fiji	9–5
1928	H	Tonga	11–8
1932	A	Fiji	11–0
1932	A	Fiji	24–5
1932	A	Fiji	30–0
1934	H	Fiji	16–6
1934	H	Tonga	6–5
1934	H	Fiji	30–8
1947	A	Fiji	25–3
1947	A	Fiji	19–9
1958	H	Fiji	17–14
1958	H	Fiji	11–10
1958	H	Tonga	16–11
1959	A	Tonga	14–11
1963	A	Fiji	8–5
1963	A	Fiji	25–9
1967	H	Fiji	18–6
1967	H	Drawn	6–6
1967	H	Fiji	9–6
1968	A	Tonga	8–6
1968	A	Fiji	12–10
1968	A	Fiji	11–6
1972	H	Fiji	12–6
1972	H	Fiji	15–8
1972	H	Fiji	16–6
1977	A	Fiji	13–9
1977	A	Fiji	33–7
1977	A	Fiji	43–9
1979	A	Tonga	6–3*
1981	H	Tonga	10–4
1981	H	Fiji	10–8
1981	H	Fiji	18–8
1984	A	Fiji	22–12
1986	A	Fiji	18–3

Final of South Pacific Games

TONGA – NATIONAL CHAMPIONS SINCE 1977
In 1986 there were seven competitions for the Shield – A1 (championship), A2, B1, B2, C1, C2, C3 Divisions; the same divisions also applied for the Cup competition.

	Shield	Cup
1977	Hihifo and Kolomotu'a	
1978	Hihifo	
1979	Hihifo and Kolomotu'a	
1980	Polisi	
1981	Hihifo	
1982	Tavatu'utolu	
1983	Hihifo	
1984	Hihifo	Kolomotu'a
1985	Hihifo	Hihifo
1986	Polisi	Polisi and Hihifo

United States

Number of clubs *c.* 1200
Number of players *c.* 75 000
Colours Red, white and
blue shirts, white shorts
Foundation 1975
Headquarters 525 Mason
Av, St Louis, Missouri
63119

Though mention of United States prowess crops up throughout rugby history with the meetings of touring teams returning from Britain to the Antipodes, and the amazing victories in the Olympic Games, the United States Rugby Union was formed as recently as 7 June 1975. But the American game was fragmented, with enthusiasts playing in the Californian universities, the Pacific Coast and New York.

Following that extraordinary retention of the Olympic title in 1924, rugby entered a state of decline. Colleges and universities concentrated on American football, newspapers ignored rugby, and despite a fairly solid base in California, in world terms the country was a nonentity. Individual enthusiasm foundered on vast distances and the lack of finance to break down the travel barriers. Local unions struggled on until 1968, when three Unions, Eastern, Pacific Coast and Midwest, met in Chicago and tried in vain to form a national union. The next opportunity arose at the 1970 World Congress at Cambridge, where the four Unions in attendance used the Congress to plan further moves. Another five years of discussion, paperwork and correspondence took place before the Midwest Union decided at their meeting in 1975 to invite all the other Unions.

Since 1968 the game had flourished in the various clubs. Over 700 now existed. Unions were beginning to challenge other Unions. Players were being recruited from established American football centres. Travel had become easier. Europeans had moved into America. It is estimated that United States' rugby will be a force by the end of the century once techniques have been ingrained and travel problems overcome. With the advent of the World Cup, several things were certain – a rugby market in the United States does exist; United States' rugby was united under one ruling body; and, most importantly, rugby was there to stay. In 1986 there were no fewer than 161 tournaments in the country. To mitigate travel problems, teams plays weekend festivals which are proving very popular.

The 1912 Australians were the only major touring team of the era specifically to visit the United States. Details of the tour, giving an indication of the teams in California at the time, are listed below.

Barbarians 8, Australians 29
Santa Clara 8, Australians 20
Stanford University 0, Australians 6
Stanford University 13, Australians 12
Olympic 0, Australians 20
University of California 0, Australians 18
St Mary's High School 0, Australians 27
University of California 6, Australians 5
University of California 3, Australians 23
University of Nevada 6, Australians 56
Santa Clara 8, Australians 19
University of S. California 0, Australians 41

UNITED STATES	8	T: Harrigan
		C: Erb
		PG: Erb
AUSTRALIA	12	T: Meibusch (2), Carroll
		PG: Prentice

Australia moved on to Canada where they lost all three matches in British Columbia.

UNITED STATES v CANADA

1977 Vancouver

CANADA	17	T: Bower, Greig, de Goede
		C: Gonis
		PG: Hindson
UNITED STATES	6	PG: Jablonski (2)

1978 Towson

UNITED STATES	12	T: Klein
		C: Jablonski
		PG: Jablonski (2)
CANADA	7	T: McTavish
		PG: Gonis

1979 Toronto

CANADA	19	T: McTavish
		PG: Wiley (4), Billingsley
UNITED STATES	12	PG: Jablonski (4)

1980 Saranac Lake

UNITED STATES	0	
CANADA	16	T: McTavish (2)
		C: Shiefler
		PG: Shiefler
		DG: Shiefler

Rugby Football in the United States in 1897. The photograph by John Burton of New York clearly states that the match in progress is Rugby Football as opposed to American Football.

1981 Calgary
CANADA	6	PG: Shiefler (2)
UNITED STATES	3	PG: Cooke

1982 Albany
UNITED STATES	3	PG : Halliday
CANADA	3	PG: Wyatt

1983 Vancouver
CANADA	15	T: Billingsley
		C: Wyatt
		PG: Wyatt (2), Shiefler
UNITED STATES	9	T: Helu
		C: Nelson
		PG: Nelson

1984 Chicago
UNITED STATES	21	T: Hartman
		C: Nelson
		PG: Nelson (5)
CANADA	13	T: Wyatt
		PG: Wyatt (3)

1985 Vancouver
CANADA	21	PG: Wyatt (6)
		DG: Wyatt
UNITED STATES	10	T: Caulder
		PG: Inns (2)

1986 Tucson
UNITED STATES	16	T: Crivellone, W. Everett, Jefferson C: Inns (2)
CANADA	27	T: Ennis, Lecky
		C: Wyatt (2)
		PG: Wyatt (3)
		DG: Wyatt, Rees

1987 Vancouver
CANADA	33	T: Gray (3), Ennis, de Goede, Evans C: Rees (3)
		PG: Rees
UNITED STATES	9	T: Helu
		C: Nelson PG: Nelson

Canada's Ron McInness prepares to release the ball to team-mate Hans de Goede (No 5) during the 1985 game against the United States at Vancouver. Canada have taken a handy lead in the annual matches between the two countries which began in 1974.

ALL OTHER INTERNATIONALS (pre-World Cup)
1976	L	v	Australia	12–24
1976	L	v	France	14–33
1977	L	v	England	11–37
1980	L	v	Wales	18–24
1980	L	v	New Zealand	6–53
1981	L	v	South Africa	7–38
1982	L	v	England	0–59
1983	L	v	Australia	3–49
1985	W	v	Japan	16–15
1986	D	v	Japan	9–9
1987	W	v	Tunisia	47–13

NATIONAL CLUB CHAMPIONSHIP FINALS
1983   Old Blues 23, Dallas Harlequins 0
1984   Dallas Harlequins 31, Los Angeles 12
1985   Milwaukee 10, Denver Barbarians 4
1986   Old Blues 20, Old Blue 0
1987   Old Blues 28, Pittsburgh 10
N.B. Old Blues are from California, Old Blue are from New York. The highest individual score is 19 points by the Springbok Naas Botha in the 1984 final.

Zimbabwe

Number of clubs 35
Number of players 1650
Colours Olive green and white hooped shirts
Foundation 1980
Headquarters PO Box 1129, Harare
Principal Stadium National Stadium, Harare (cap. 20 000)

Though the history of Zimbabwe rugby only dates from 1980, the country as Rhodesia has a proud and at times famous history, stretching back to Pioneer days. As hosts – occasionally successfully – of many major touring teams and with a solid position in the highly competitive South African Currie Cup, when affiliated to that country, Zimbabwean rugby has a proud tradition.

In 1890 the Pioneers stopped at the Shaski River, and in the sandy bed of the river challenged the local police to a game. The Pioneers soon settled and organized themselves into a playing unit. The Rhodesian Rugby Union was born in 1895, with five clubs, Kopje and Causeway from Salisbury (Harare) and BAC, Queens and Matabele Police in Bulawayo. There were at this stage some 10 000 European males in the country. The provincial teams had fun. When Selukwe were visited by Gwelo, and were on the wrong end of a hiding in 1899, they were rescued by the local referee who pulled a penknife out of his pocket and cut the ball!

By 1901 the first provincial game between Matabeleland (Bulawayo) and Mashonaland (Salisbury) was played. The first match was won by Matabeleland 16–0. At this stage Bulawayo had 2681 Europeans to 965 in Salisbury. Two years later with Sir William Milton, the England international at the helm, Mashonaland won both return games 9–3 and 11–9. After the creation of

North and South Rhodesia, the rugby stronghold was still in the South, until the 1930s when the North produced fine players in the Copperbelt region, which were lost in the 1960s with Zambia's independence.

Of all the years in Rhodesian rugby, 1949 is the season which stands out. Within a few days they beat Northern Transvaal 15–14 and then met the All Blacks twice. On 27 April 1949 – the greatest day in Rhodesia's history – they beat the might of New Zealand 10–8. A few days later the teams drew 3–3.

In 1973–4 there were 49 clubs in the country, but the early ravages of war and uncertainty towards the future had reduced that figure to 32 in 1978. Provincial rugby suffered from the atrocities. Yet the country produced quality players to the end. After independence, two Zimbabwean players were in the Springbok team which beat the 1980 British Lions – the centre David Smith and world-class wing Ray Mordt. Hooker Chris Rogers was then to play for South Africa. Allan Sunderland and Kevin Eveleigh, the New Zealand back-row players, coached in the country. It is hoped that the excellent standards set by their predecessors can be maintained in today's changed circumstances. The Pioneer spirit may be necessary again.

RHODESIAN SPRINGBOKS
The following players represented South Africa whilst playing for Rhodesia.

	Year	*Caps*
J. A. Du Rand	1949–56	21
R. A. Hill	1960–3	7
A. W. McDonald	1965	5
R. H. Mordt	1979–81	14
I. W. Robertson	1974–6	5
D. J. Smith	1980	4
D. C. Van Jaarsveldt	1960	1
R. A. M. Van Schoor	1949–53	12

Van Jaarsveldt is the only Rhodesian to have captained South Africa (v Scotland 1960). Du Rand's 21 caps were a record at the time. Mordt scored nine tries which was then second on the all-time list. MacDonald's caps were against Australia and New Zealand on tour. Smith's caps were all against Bill Beaumont's British Lions.

ZIMBABWE – NATIONAL CLUB RUGBY CHALLENGE
1983 Old Georgians
1984 Old Georgians
1985 Alexandra
1986 Harare Sports Club

INTER CITY LEAGUE
1980 Old Harareans/Salisbury Sports Club (shared)
1981 Salisbury Sports Club
1982 Harare Sports Club
1983 Old Harareans
1984 Harare Sports Club
1985 No competition
1986 Old Georgians

ZIMBABWE INTERNATIONAL RESULTS 1980–7
1982	Zimbabwe 23, Romania 25	
	Zimbabwe 24, Romania 25	
	Zambia 4, Zimbabwe 54	
	Zimbabwe 15, Kenya 12	
1983	Spain 8, Zimbabwe 17	
1984	Zimbabwe 22, Spain 13	
	Zimbabwe 18, Spain 30	
1985	Zimbabwe 15, Kenya 13	
	Zimbabwe 6, Italy 10	
	Zimbabwe 10, Italy 12	
	Spain 13, Zimbabwe 12	
	Portugal 18, Zimbabwe 17	
	Spain 13, Zimbabwe 12	
1986	Zimbabwe 26, USSR 19	
	Zimbabwe 9, USSR 31	
1987	Zimbabwe 35, Portugal 9	

RHODESIA AGAINST TOURING TEAMS

v British Lions				v Australia		
1910	L	11–24		1933	L	5–24
1924	L	3–16		1933	L	0–33
1938	L	11–25		1953	L	15–18
1938	L	11–45		1953	D	8–8
1955	L	14–27		1953	L	11–31
1955	L	12–16		1963	L	11–22
1962	L	9–38		1969	L	11–16
1968	L	6–32				
1974	L	6–42		**v Ireland**		
				1961	L	0–24

v New Zealand				v Argentina		
1928	L	8–44		1965	W	17–12
1949	W	10–8				
1949	D	3–3		**v Italy**		
1960	L	9–13		1973	W	42–4
1960	L	14–29				
1970	L	14–27		**v USA***		

v France				v USA*		
1958	L	0–19		1978	W	32–15
1964	L	11–34				
1967	L	13–36				

Not considered as an international by USA

A feature of Zimbabwean rugby during recent times has been the influx of quality players in coaching roles. Kevin Eveleigh, the All Black flanker, feeds the ball back against Surrey in 1980 during Zimbabwe's tour to Britain.

6 THE GROUNDS

The world's major rugby-playing centres fall into distinct categories. In Britain, the international centres are steeped in history. In the Antipodes, at cities like Sydney, Christchurch, Auckland and formerly Dunedin and Wellington, the rugby grounds share with cricket for alternate summer and winter use. In the emerging nations, football grounds are used, while other smaller countries have their own compact national stadia, which in most cases house the offices of their Union. The grounds described here are rugby venues only today.

Twickenham

Many who have never even seen a game of rugby know what the name Twickenham means in a sporting sense. It has become one of the stately homes of British sport. Twickenham is not only a fine, spacious stadium, but also the home of Rugby Union, from where the game is administered throughout the world.

The first 10¼ acres of the Twickenham ground were selected in 1907, picked out by a fine local sportsman, Billy Williams, in a patch of open land south of Hounslow and north of Twickenham and Whitton. Endearingly known as 'Billy Williams's Cabbage Patch' in its early days, cabbages and other vegetables grew there, along with fruit trees and mushrooms.

The purchase price of the original ground was £5572 12s 6d, with most of the business details in the hands of the Hon. Treasurer of the RFU, William Cail, then in his fourteenth year in office. At the time, the RFU had no ground, and their office was a small room in Surrey Street, just off the Strand. A further £1606 9s 4d was added to the bill for legal fees, architects' reports and the purchase of materials.

The following year, 1908, another £8812 15s was spent on the construction of mounds for the stands, roads, a groundsman's cottage, stands and entrances. The original ground, when complete, had a capacity of 30 000 with 6000 seats. The capacity of 75 000 was reached in 1949-50 but is now controlled by the Government's crowd-safety regulations.

The first match at Twickenham was held on 2 October 1910, when the host club Harlequins, inspired by Adrian Stoop, beat Richmond 14–10.

The first international was played on 15 January 1910, when England beat Wales 11–6. The first score came after one minute with a try by F. E. Chapman, the Westoe winger, who was making his international debut.

South Africa was the first team to beat England at Twickenham, by 6–0 in 1913.

The Rowland Hill Memorial Gates were erected in 1929 at a cost of £6316.

The weather vane on the South Stand was erected in 1950, and took the place of the old clock. The vane was designed by one Kenny Dalgleish and depicted Hermes passing a rugby ball.

TWICKENHAM DURING THE WAR YEARS

1914. Became a grazing ground for horses and sheep.
1939. The East Car Park was turned into allotments, and the iron fencing turned into scrap. The RFU offices, changing rooms and restaurants were occupied by the Civil Defence. The stands became garages for fire engines and lorries. The West Car Park became a coal dump. On 1 July 1944, a 'V' bomb landed in nearby Talma Gardens, damaging the West Stand.

The ground capacity has now been reduced to 54 500 after the construction of hospitality boxes, a museum and shops in the South Stand, at a cost of nearly £5 million.

Most pts (home team):
37–0 v France, 1911
Most pts (away team):
27–20 by France, 1975
Biggest winning margin:
37 (37–0) v France, 1911
Biggest losing margin:
16 (3–19) by Australia, 1984

The new South Stand at Twickenham, completed in 1984.

Lansdowne Road

The oldest of the world's rugby grounds, Lansdowne Road has housed internationals since 1878, Ireland's second match (the first was on Leinster's cricket ground at Rathmines). Apart from occasional sorties to Cork and to Ravenhill, Belfast, the stadium has played host to all Ireland's games.

William Henry Dunlop, the key figure in the embryonic Lansdowne Road, bought a plot of land in the outskirts of Dublin between the River Dodder and Lansdowne Road station from the Earl of Pembroke for use as a multi-sport centre, including rugby. The club, named Lansdowne, built a clubhouse which remains today as the cottage in the ground, and from 1880 shared the facilities with a new club, Wanderers. Unlike Cardiff, where the Welsh team use the main stadium and Cardiff have the adjacent ground, except for major games, the two clubs and Ireland use the ground constantly.

Lansdowne Road's proud new stand, the Triple Crown Stand, was completed in 1984, while in the 1985-6 season the ground became the first in world rugby to stage 150 internationals. Dublin's 'anthem', *Cockles and Mussels*, issuing from thousands of Irish throats, provides an inspiring refrain for any man wearing a green jersey.

Most pts (home team): 25–15 v England, 1983;
25–6 v France, 1975
Most pts (away team): 38–0 by South Africa, 1912
Biggest winning margin: 22 (22–0) v England, 1947
Biggest losing margin: 38 (0–38) by South Africa, 1912

Murrayfield

The youngest of the Five Nations' grounds, Murrayfield was first used on 21 March 1925, against England who were going for the Grand Slam. The Scots celebrated the new stadium with a 14–11 win in front of 70 000 people. Youngest it may be, but foresight has put Murrayfield in advance of other stadia in one important respect: the installation in 1959 by Sir Charles Hepburn of undersoil heating, enabling every game to be played in perfect conditions.

Scotland moved around Edinburgh in the early days, each new ground proving too small. International rugby's first ever game took place at the Edinburgh Academicals ground in 1871. The nomadic national team moved on to Glasgow and Powderhall, before stopping at Inverleith. Then, in 1922, the purchase of the old Edinburgh Polo Ground at Murrays Field was announced, and within three years the new ground was complete. The West Stand was added in the mid 1930s, and fifty years later another was added to the other side of the ground.

WORLD RECORD CROWD
104 000 (approx) Scotland v Wales, 1 March 1975.

Most pts (home team): 33–6 v England, 1986
Most pts (away team): 44–0 by South Africa, 1951
Biggest winning margin: 27 (33–6) v England, 1986
Biggest losing margin: 44 (0–44) by South Africa, 1951

National Stadium, Cardiff

The National Stadium is its official name, but Cardiff Arms Park it still is to a whole generation of rugby followers. The name Arms Park comes from the early days. In 1845 Cardiff Cricket Club had established one of the first cricket clubs in the country. It was on a piece of land at the back of the Cardiff Arms Coaching Inn. In

The shell of the new National Stadium, Cardiff, is evident as Brian Thomas (centre) leaves the field after Wales' 24–11 win against Ireland in 1969. The commentators' box is visible at the top right of the photo.

Left *Murrayfield as it looked in 1925. Note the early crush barriers erected for crowds in excess of 90 000. England were the first visitors to the new stadium and were beaten 14–11.*

1876 Cardiff rugby team joined forces with the Cricket Club for alternate summer and winter facilities.

The ground has undergone enormous changes until today, when 64 500 spectators cram into a horseshoe-shaped stand with just one open end. Originally all four of the major Welsh rugby grounds were used: Cardiff, Swansea, Newport and Llanelli, then just Cardiff and Swansea. Finally in 1954 Cardiff became the sole international ground, because the Welsh RFU owned the ground, and was in the country's major population centre.

The National Stadium complex began in thought and word in the 1960s and in deed from 1968. The first move was by Glamorgan County Cricket Club from the adjacent ground to nearby Sophia Gardens. That allowed Cardiff RFC to play their home matches on the pitch, to build a stadium with a capacity of 22 000, and for the surrounding area to house tennis and bowls clubs.

In 1970 the first part of the stadium was complete and by 1984 the remainder of the ground had been constructed at a total cost of £9 million, with 36 000 seats. It stands as a monument to Welsh rugby heritage, and at only 200 metres from the city centre, it is truly part of the community.

Most pts (home team): 36–4 v France, 1908
Most pts (away team): 34–18 by Scotland, 1982
Biggest winning margin: 32 (36–4) v France, 1908
Biggest losing margin: 20 (3–23) by New Zealand, 1980.

Parc des Princes

The Parc des Princes is a mixture of Twickenham and Wembley, in that both rugby and football are played there. The French rugby team use the facilities for internationals and the club championship final. The two Paris First Division football clubs, Paris St Germain and Racing Club, play their home matches there, as well as European Cup finals and internationals.

International rugby has been played at the Parc in two different eras. The old Parc des Princes staged France's very first international – a crushing 38–8 loss to the 1905-6 New Zealanders. From then France played 28 times up to World War 1, won one (at the neighbouring Colombes Stadium) and lost the others. The old Parc had become outdated and too small, and after the war all fixtures were switched to Colombes. But a true international stadium was required, and attention reverted to the Parc, which had been a shell since 1920. A concrete bowl seating 48 500 was built on the old site and was ready for use again on 12 January 1973 against Scotland. Since then France have become very hard to beat at home (see below). Close to the Metros of Porte d'Auteuil and St Cloud, the new Parc again has a problem of size. At least five football grounds – including the Beaujoire at Nantes where France beat New Zealand in 1986 – are larger. But again, as long as the pilgrimage from the South to Paris continues – town bands, cockerels and all – the Parc will survive.

THE RECORDS
Home defeats by France since 12 Jan 1973:
v England   13–17   1980
                 15–27   1982
v Wales   10–25   1975
v New Zealand   3–15   1977
                          6–18   1981
v South Africa   8–10   1974

Most pts (home team): 34–6 v Australia, 1976
Most pts (away team): 47–5 by Wales, 1909
Biggest winning margin: 28 (34–6) v Australia, 1976
Biggest losing margin: 42 (47–5) by Wales, 1909

Ballymore

Many Australian experts reckon that the reason that Queensland rugby has improved so markedly in recent seasons, has been the acquisition of the Ballymore Oval. Thanks to a more clement winter, in many Southern Hemisphere countries state and international matches were played on cricket grounds. However, Ballymore is unusual in that it is exclusively a rugby venue, with stands like those on British grounds.

The Queensland RU first moved in during 1967, when the McLean stand – named after the country's most famous rugby family – was constructed, and Queensland took on New South Wales in the first game. Ballymore quickly received international status, with a match against France in 1968. While the Sydney Cricket Ground is still Australia's premier ground, Ballymore hosts an almost equal number of international matches. It boasts a quaint part of the ground – the Breakfast Creek End!

Most pts (home team): 30–21 v England, 1975
Most pts (away team): 27–12 by Ireland, 1979
Biggest winning margin: 10 (18–8) v Wales, 1978
Biggest losing margin: 15 (12–27) by Ireland, 1979

South Africa

Many of the early grounds followed the Southern Hemisphere vogue of doubling as cricket and rugby grounds, but the enthusiasm generated by the Currie Cup, where crowds of 40 000 are the norm and 60 000 are common, has enabled some of the provinces to build their own rugby stadia. These are the playing grounds.

JOHANNESBURG

The Ellis Park Stadium, near the business centre of Dornfontein, is the largest rugby ground in the world – capacity 100 000, with everyone seated. During the reconstruction of the stadium (completed in the early

1980s) the Wanderers stadium (capacity 45 000) was used. Ellis Park almost bankrupted the Transvaal Union who were some £5 million in debt at one stage. The former white elephant is now home to two black soccer teams – Kaiser Chiefs and Orlando Pirates from Soweto with their 40 000 support – pop concerts, and other events.

Most pts (home team): 35–9 v England, 1984
Most pts (away team): 19–14 by France, 1967
Biggest winning margin: 26 (35–9) v England, 1984
Biggest losing margin: 9 (9–18) by England, 1972

CAPE TOWN

Very probably the world's most picturesque ground with Table Mountain as a backdrop, **Newlands** houses the offices of the South African and Western Province Rugby Boards. Recently reconstructed to house 54 500, Newlands is separated from the cricket ground by about 800 metres of other sports grounds. The complex includes restaurants and a museum.

Most pts (home team): 24–8 v Ireland, 1961
Most pts (away team): 18–14 by Australia, 1953
Biggest winning margin: 16 (24–8) v Ireland, 1961
Biggest losing margin: 8 (5–13) by New Zealand, 1928; (3–11) by New Zealand, 1960

PRETORIA

The **Loftus Versveld** (named after a player and administrator, one of the men who faced the 1891 first British tour), home of Northern Transvaal, is an open bowl accommodating over 65 000. The stadium opened in 1938, the year before Versveld's death.

Most pts (home team): 33–18 v France, 1975
Most pts (away team): 18–33 by France, 1975
Biggest winning margin: 22 (37–15) v France, 1980
Biggest losing margin: Not lost

Right Flimsy scaffolding supports a vast bank of supporters in July 1974 at Ellis Park.

The finished article – the 104 000 capacity Ellis Park stadium in Johannesburg, where everyone is seated.

OTHER SOUTH AFRICAN GROUNDS

The **Free State Stadium**, **Bloemfontein**, holds 45 000, and is situated just outside the city centre. It is a largely open complex, built on the side of a park.

The **Boet Erasmus Stadium**, **Port Elizabeth** is the home of Eastern Province, and holds 50 000. Named after J. C. K. Erasmus (a mayor of the town), rugby was played at the Crusader ground until 1960.

In **Durban**, for cricket read Kingsmead, for rugby read **Kings Park**, just a mile further north, and close to the sea. The capacity was increased in 1985 to 48 500 with a new £3 million west stand, and major football matches are also staged there.

Andy Irvine

Heriot's F.P. and Scotland

Andrew Robertson Irvine has scored more points than anyone else in the history of international rugby. With 273 points for Scotland and another 28 for the British Isles in test matches, his total stands at 301 – if you include an obvious penalty try against Wales and 12 points against Romania. He holds the world record number of tries for a full back – nine, or ten if that penalty try is included. And, for good measure, if British Isles caps are included he is Scotland's most capped player, with 60.

He ws born on 12 September 1951 and was educated at George Heriot's School and Edinburgh University. He played all his club rugby for the school Old Boys – Heriot's Former Pupils, whom he steered to the Scottish championship in 1979. As a schoolboy he made four appearances for Scotland Schools in the centre but was first given representative honours for Edinburgh as a winger. Irvine made his international debut in 1972 against New Zealand, and spent most of his career at full-back, with the occasional return to the wing.

Blessed with a superb attacking sense which often compensated for lapses in defensive duties, Irvine made three Lions tours. In 1974 he was with Willie John McBride's team to South Africa, where he played in two tests on the wing because Phil Bennett had cut his foot. Irvine was leading points scorer on the tour with 156, and three years later was top scorer again in New Zealand with 87, which included the remarkable haul of five tries against King Country-Wanganui at Taumaruni. Finally in 1980 he was selected for the South African trip, but initially had to drop out. When Mike Slemen was forced to return

home, Irvine went out as replacement.

Two siege-gun kicks live in the memory. Both were in the final seconds and both were against England. In 1974, his 45-yard (41m) blast from the 'wrong' side of the field sealed a victory, while in 1982 a 55-yarder (50m) forced a draw. A ten-year international career ended in 1982, sadly just a couple of seasons before Scotland's Grand Slam, which would have been a fitting reward for a player who, at times, was not even Scotland's recognized kicker – Doug Morgan and Jim Renwick both had spells as number one kicker. In 1987 Andy Irvine was still turning out for Heriot's FP, and still in the first team.

Andy Irvine (with ball) sweeps past Bobby Windsor (second from right), the Welsh hooker, to score one of his ten international tries during Scotland's 18–9 defeat by Wales at Murrayfield in 1977.

THE WORLD RECORD

FOR SCOTLAND
Tries: 10
Conversions: 25
Penalty Goals: 61   Total: 273

FOR BRITISH ISLES
Tries: 2 (both as a wing)
Conversions: 1
Penalty Goals: 6   Total: 28

GRAND TOTAL: 301

Hugo Porta

Banco Naçion and Argentina

The finest player ever produced outside the International Board countries, Hugo Porta, an architect from Buenos Aires, has an astonishing international record. Almost singlehandedly he has dismantled lofty reputations in the major rugby

nations. Born on 11 September 1951, Porta was educated at La Salle College and Buenos Aires University. He plays for Banco Naçion of Buenos Aires and has over 40 international appearances for Argentina to his credit.

He made his international debut against Romania in 1973. Over the next decade and a half, Argentina – inspired by Porta, but including several other players of true world class – beat or severely embarrassed all the world's major teams. If Porta was not playing then the Pumas seemed lost. An example was in 1986 when Porta, injured against New South Wales, hobbled out of the first test with the net result that the team became rudderless and lost heart.

His highest points tally is 23 against France in 1974, seven penalties and a conversion, but the Pumas still lost 31–27. Porta was still around in 1985 when he scored 16 points in Argentina's 24–16 win against the French and added a further 11 points when France succumbed again 15–13 in 1986. He has scored 130 points in all against the French. In 1982 at Bloemfontein Porta again excelled. After South America (all Argentines) had lost the first test 50–18, Porta rattled up 21 points – a goal, a drop goal and four penalties – in an amazing turn around as South America won 21–12. The next 21-point bonanza was equally extraordinary. In 1985 New Zealand came to Buenos Aires, won the first test but had to settle for a 21-21 draw in the second – courtesy of four penalties and three drop goals from Porta. During his career Argentina have twice beaten Australia, twice drawn with England, and lost by a single point to Wales and Scotland.

It seems appropriate to end with Porta's world record points total: 359 in 40 matches against IB opposition (compare with Andy Irvine's 301), to which must be added a further 76 points

Hugo Porta demonstrates the classical kicking technique which made the Argentinian fly-half the most prolific scorer in international rugby history.

in 7 games against non-Board sides – not bad for an accountant!

Frik Du Preez

Northern Transvaal and South Africa

In an international career that lasted throughout the 1960s, Frik Du Preez played in a record 38 tests for South Africa, the same number as his Springbok colleague Jan Ellis. With that country's present international isolation it is a record that is likely to stand for some time.

Du Preez, born on 28 November 1935, was a typical Afrikaaner forward from the Northern Transvaal. He was 6ft 3in (1.87m) and 16 stones (101kg), was unhealthily fast for one so large, could play in the back row or more preferably at lock, and was a surprisingly deft place kicker. As a lock-forward he ranked with Colin Meads as

Frik du Preez prepares to brush aside covering England defenders Tony Neary (left) and Nigel Starmer-Smith during the President's XV v England Centenary match at Twickenham in 1971. The President's XV won 28–11.

the best in the game's history, and a living legend in his own country.

He was picked for his first tour in 1960–1 (to Britain) after a successful season with Northern Transvaal. Du Preez was drafted in for his first international cap at Twickenham on the flank, when Martin Pelser was injured. He celebrated with the conversion of the game's only try by Hopwood. In all he was to win seven caps on the flank. An Air Force officer at the time, he was one of the successes of the tour, notching up some 58 points. During the increasingly turbulent years of the 1960s, Du Preez had eight different partners at lock forward.

He scored 11 points (one try, a conversion, two penalties) for South Africa in test matches and 87 points in a record 87 appearances for the Springboks in all matches – a fine tally for someone who was not the regular kicker. The try was one of the most talked about in rugby circles. Playing against the 1968 Lions in the first test on his home ground in Pretoria, he won a lineout ball on halfway, bolted around the front of the lineout, and set off for the line, outstripping any vestige of covering defence before bowling Lions full-back Tom Kiernan out of play and diving over.

At 36, Frederik Christoffel Hendrik Du Preez announced his retirement after the 1971 tour to Australia, his sixth in all. He led the team onto the field for his last international after which speeches were made by fellow tourists. Du Preez declined to speak in reply – in the eyes of a witness, 'it was the most eloquent non-speech ever heard'.

Colin Meads, with ball, leads an All Black charge during the 1967 tourists' match against North of England. The All Blacks won 33–3 at Manchester's White City Stadium.

Colin Meads

King Country and New Zealand

Colin Meads is the epitome of New Zealand rugby, the large, raw-boned forward, fierce and uncompromising on the field, polite and courteous off it. Born on 3 June 1936 at Cambridge, Waikato, Meads won 55 caps between 1957 and 1971. He wore the All Black jersey on 133 occasions; both are records. He was always the first player to be selected for any World XV, and the first to be invited to the series of centenary games throughout the world which coincided with his retirement.

Meads took up rugby at the age of eight at prep school. He moved through the well-structured New Zealand schools system to the King Country XV. His international debut came in the 25–11 win over Australia in 1957. Like many outstanding players, Meads took a little while to settle into the New Zealand team, with some doubts surrounding his best position. At 6ft 4in (1.90m) and over 15 stones (95kg) he could play at flanker (where he was first capped), number 8 and lock. In his second game against Australia, a week later, he scored the first of seven

international tries. He was deputizing on the wing!

Meads was dropped after the famous 18–17 win over the 1959 Lions when six penalties overruled four tries (see p. 116). He was also omitted after a poor draw with Australia in 1962. For his last nine years, though, he was the automatic selection at lock, obviously his best position.

As a farmer and fitness fanatic, Meads found his job was perfect for keeping fit. He used to carry sheep on his shoulders as unwilling partners in weight training exercises. His brother Stan was also a fine player. Between 1961 and 1966 he played alongside Colin, locking the New Zealand second row. Stan played 15 times for his country, then retired prematurely to manage the family farm.

There were three major disappointments in the rugby career of Colin Meads. He was sent off for aiming a kick at Scotland's fly-half Chisholm in the 1967 match at Murrayfield. He was captain of the ill-fated New Zealand team which lost the test series (for the first time) to the Lions in 1971. And, more recently, he received criticism for

going with the rebel Cavaliers to South Africa as coach.

Nicknamed 'Pinetree', Colin Meads is held in no higher esteem than by fellow members of the lock-forwards union. Even now legions of up-and-coming players wanting to wear the black shirt with the white fern, are told to model themselves on his style of play. They would do so without being told.

THE RECORDS
Record number of New Zealand caps 55

Record number of New Zealand representative appearances 133

World record number of international appearances by brothers Stan Meads (15 caps), Colin Meads (55): Total 70

Mark Ella

Randwick, New South Wales and Australia

Mark Ella has joined that list of Australian super-heroes, Don Bradman, the tennis players Laver, Hoad, Rosewall, Court and Goolagong, Lillee and Thomson, Dawn Fraser and the swimmers. But, after an apparent lull in their sporting triumphs, Australians have a new generation of idols: Greg Norman dominated the golf world, Australia won the America's Cup and the Davis Cup, and produced two of the finest rugby teams in either code ever to visit Britain.

The Union side, though, has never had the acclaim that it might have received in the fanatical regions of Wales, South Africa and New Zealand. An underrated pack of forwards, the quiet authority of Andrew Slack, the all round skills of David Campese, and the genius of Mark Ella.

While it may seem churlish to select one player from the 1984 Australians, there is no doubt that Ella's skills and charisma made him *the* personality of the tour. One of 14 children, he was born into a poor aboriginal family with Rugby League loyalties, so it seemed certain that sooner rather than later he would leave the amateur ranks. Yet somehow tours to England with the Australian schools, and

a period with his successful club side Randwick, playing almost telepathic rugby alongside brothers Gary and Glen, helped his decision to remain in the amateur code. Randwick played open rugby under national coach Bob Dwyer, and frequent tours stimulated the appetite.

The road into the national team, however, was not clear cut. Paul McLean, from the heavily backed Queensland side and record points scorer, was the custodian of the outside-half berth. It took a little while for Mark's different style to be harnessed by the national team. After McLean's retirement, Mark took over the captaincy until the shock arrival of Queensland's Andrew Slack, who turned out a wise tour captain to the United Kingdom. Watched in the middle of the night throughout Australia, the Wallabies powered towards the Grand Slam with Ella's silky skills flourishing.

He had a lot in his favour – a

scrum-half in Nick Farr-Jones who protected him with a long pass, and took on much of the covering chores himself. Like Gareth Edwards, he thrived after being relieved of the burdensome task of captaincy. He received ample possession from a huge pack. All this stimulated his natural talents: his handling and ability to read a game, his instinctive linkage between backs and forwards. He played like a typical American quarterback, calling the shots. To cap it all, he scored a try in all four tests in the 1984 sreies. He retired almost immediately after to start a new career with a tobacco company.

By international fly-half standards Mark Ella was an average kicker both out of the hand and place kicking. It meant simply that he had to become more adaptable, more inventive, and would have to settle for skill to beat an opponent, to open up the game. Rugby was the beneficiary.

Three England defenders halt Mark Ella during the 1982 England v Australia international at Twickenham, but the Australian fly-half still manages to make the ball available.

7 INTERNATIONAL BOARD COUNTRIES v WORLD CUP JUNIOR NATIONS

MATCH RECORDS

It has become policy now for several of the International Board countries to award caps for 'internationals' against nations who appeared in the World Cup. However, there is a certain lack of uniformity; each country decides itself whether or not to classify a game as a full international, and whether the points scorers should be credited.

This section traces the matches and tours between the IB countries and their emerging counterparts (prior to 1987 World Cup). Full scorecards have been found in all but a few instances, making this the fullest possible set of rugby records, plus statistics arising from these matches. Finally, there are results of matches between the non-IB nations invited to the World Cup.

ENGLAND V ARGENTINA

14 Oct 1978, Twickenham
ENGLAND	13	T: Gifford, Squires
		C: Bushell
		DG: Horton
ARGENTINA	13	T: Campo, Passaglia
		C: Porta
		PG: Porta

30 May 1981, Buenos Aires
ARGENTINA	19	T: Campo (2)
		C: Porta
		PG: Porta
		DG: Porta, Landejo
ENGLAND	19	T: Woodward (2), H. Davies
		C: Hare (2)
		PG: Hare

6 Jun 1981, Buenos Aires
ARGENTINA	6	T: Travaglini
		C: Porta
ENGLAND	12	T: H. Davies
		C: Hare
		PG: Hare (2)

ENGLAND v CANADA

1964, Vancouver
CANADA	0
ENGLAND	29

29 Jun 1982, Vancouver
CANADA	6	PG: Shiefler (2)
ENGLAND	43	T: Swift (2), Scott,
		S. J. Smith, Carleton (2),
		Cusworth
		C: Hare (3)
		PG: Hare(3)

15 Oct 1983, Twickenham
ENGLAND	27	T: Youngs, Winterbottom,
		penalty try
		C: Hare (3)
		PG: Hare (3)
CANADA	0	

ENGLAND v FIJI

28 Aug 1973, Suva
FIJI	12	T: Kurisaru, Latilevu
		C: Ratudina, Batisbasaga
ENGLAND	13	T: Evans, Squires
		C: Jorden
		PG: Jorden

29 May 1979, Suva
FIJI	7	T: Nayate
		PG: Musunamasi
ENGLAND	19	T: Cardus, Beaumont,
		Squires
		C: H. Davies
		PG: H. Davies

16 Oct 1982, Twickenham
ENGLAND	60	T: Trick (3), Swift (2), Gadd
		(2), Scott, S. J. Smith,
		Cusworth, Dodge,
		Colclough
		C: Hare (6)
FIJI	19	T: Tamata, Politini, Namoro
		C: Sevaro (2)
		PG: Sevaro

ENGLAND v JAPAN

24 Sep 1971, Osaka
JAPAN	19	T: Mizutani, Murata
		C: Yamaguchi
		PG: Yamaguchi (3)

ENGLAND	27	T: Cowman (2), Webb, Glover, Janion C: Cowman, Rossborough PG: Cowman

28 Sep 1971, Tokyo
JAPAN	3	PG: Yamaguchi
ENGLAND	6	PG: Rossborough (2)

13 May 1979, Osaka
JAPAN	19	T: Kobayashi, Mori C: Matsuo PG: Matsuo (2) DG: Matsuo
ENGLAND	21	T: Wheeler, Squires C: Hare (2) PG: Hare (3)

20 May 1979, Tokyo
JAPAN	18	T: Matsuo (3), Minawakawa C: Matsuo
ENGLAND	38	T: Dodge (2), Carleton (2), Pomphrey (2) C: H. Davies (4) PG: H. Davies (2)

11 Oct 1986, Twickenham
ENGLAND	39	T: Underwood, Hall, Bailey, Richards, Rees, Salmon C: Rose (6) PG: Rose
JAPAN	12	T: Konishi C: Matsuo PG: Matsuo (2)

ENGLAND v TONGA

1 Jun 1979, Nuku'Alofa
TONGA	17	T: Finau, Valu (2) C: Ma'ake PG: Ma'ake
ENGLAND	37	T: Slemen (2), Allchurch, Scott, Carleton C: H. Davies (4) PG: H. Davies (3)

ENGLAND v UNITED STATES

15 Oct 1977, Twickenham
ENGLAND	37	T: Wyatt (4), Scott, Carleton C: Hare (5) PG: Hare
UNITED STATES	11	T: Kelso, Duncanson PG: Halliday

19 Jun 1982, Hartford
UNITED STATES	0	
ENGLAND	59	T: S. J. Smith (2), Swift (2), Scott (2), Carleton, Rendall, Wheeler C: Hare (7) PG: Hare (2) DG: Cusworth

IRELAND v ARGENTINA

10 Nov 1973, Dublin
IRELAND	21	T: Slattery, Quinn, Grace, McMaster C: Ensor DG: Quinn
ARGENTINA	8	T: Leiros, Porta

IRELAND v FIJI

8 Jun 1976, Suva
FIJI	0	
IRELAND	8	T: Grace, Clegg

19 Oct 1985, Lansdowne Road, Dublin
IRELAND	16	T: Bradley PG: Kiernan (4)
FIJI	15	T: Laulau, Tuvula C: Damu (2) PG: Damu

IRELAND v JAPAN

26 May 1985, Osaka
JAPAN	13	T: Ishiyama, Konishi C: Honjo PG: Honjo
IRELAND	48	T: Ringland (3), Matthews (2), Kiernan, MacNeill, Fitzgerald C: Kiernan (5) PG: Kiernan (2)

2 Jun 1985, Tokyo
JAPAN	15	T: Onuki, Murai C: Kobayashi (2) PG: Kobayashi
IRELAND	33	T: Kiernan (2), Mullin, Anderson C: Kiernan (4) PG: Kiernan (3)

IRELAND v ROMANIA

18 Oct 1980, Lansdowne Road, Dublin
IRELAND	13	T: F. P. Quinn PG: Campbell (3)
ROMANIA	13	T: Parachiv PG: Constantin (3)

1 Nov 1986, Lansdowne Road, Dublin
IRELAND	60	T: Crossan (3), Mullin (2), Dean (2), Anderson, Bradley, McNeill C: Kiernan (7) PG: Kiernan (2)
ROMANIA	0	

SCOTLAND v ARGENTINA

13 Sep 1969, Buenos Aires
ARGENTINA	20	T: A. Travaglini (2), Walther
		C: Harris-Smith
		PG: Harris-Smith
		DG: Harris-Smith (2)
SCOTLAND	3	T: M. A. Smith

27 Sep 1969, Buenos Aires
ARGENTINA	3	T: Otano
SCOTLAND	6	T: Carmichael
		PG: Blaikie

24 Nov 1973, Murrayfield
SCOTLAND	12	PG: Morgan (3)
		DG: Telfer
ARGENTINA	11	T: A. Travaglini, Porta
		DG: Porta

SCOTLAND v FIJI

25 Sep 1982, Murrayfield
SCOTLAND	32	T: Dods (2), Johnston, F. Calder, Beattie
		C: Dods (3)
		PG: Dods
		DG: Rutherford
FIJI	12	T: Nadruka
		C: Sevaro
		PG: Sevaro (2)

SCOTLAND v JAPAN

25 Sep 1976, Murrayfield
SCOTLAND	34	T: Gammell (2), McGeechan, Ashton, Lawson, Irvine, Fisher
		C: Irvine (3)
JAPAN	9	T: Fujiwara
		C: Tanaka
		PG: Tanaka

18 Sep 1977, Tokyo
JAPAN	9	T: Ujino
		C: Tanaka
		PG: Matsuo
SCOTLAND	74	T: Gammell (4), Laidlaw (2), Cranston, Dickson, Moffat, McGuiness, Wilson
		C: Mair (9)
		PG: Mair (4)

27 Sep 1986, Murrayfield
SCOTLAND	33	T: Tukalo (4), Duncan, Campbell
		C: Dods (3)
		PG: Dods
JAPAN	18	T: Onuki, Chida, Katsuki
		PG: Matsuo
		DG: Matsuo

SCOTLAND v ROMANIA

26 Sep 1981, Murrayfield
SCOTLAND	12	PG: Irvine (4)
ROMANIA	6	PG: Constantin (2)

12 May 1984, Stadium August 23rd, Bucharest
ROMANIA	28	T: Dumitru, Parachiv, Radulescu
		C: Alexandru (2)
		PG: Alexandru (3)
		DG: Alexandru
SCOTLAND	22	T: Leslie, Dods
		C: Dods
		PG: Dods (3)
		DG: Robertson

30 Mar 1986, Stadium August 23rd, Bucharest
ROMANIA	18	PG: Ignat (5)
		DG: Ignat
SCOTLAND	33	T: Jeffrey, S. Hastings, Deans
		C: G. Hastings (3)
		PG: G. Hastings (5)

SCOTLAND v TONGA

28 Sep 1974, Murrayfield
SCOTLAND	44	T: Steele (4), Dick, Lauder, MacLauchlan
		C: Irvine (5)
		PG: Irvine (2)
TONGA	8	T: Fifita, 'Iskeli

WALES v ARGENTINA

14 Aug 1968, Buenos Aires
ARGENTINA	9	*
WALES	5	T: Turner
		C: Dawes

28 Aug 1968, Buenos Aires
ARGENTINA	9	*
WALES	9	T: Ferguson
		PG: Ferguson (2)

16 Oct 1976, Cardiff Arms Park
WALES	20	T: T. G. R. Davies, Edwards
		PG: Bennett (4)
ARGENTINA	19	T: Gauweloose, Beccar-Varela
		C: Porta
		PG: Porta, Beccar-Varela (2)

*Details not available

WALES v CANADA

2 Oct 1971, Cardiff Arms Park
WALES	56	T: Mathias (3), David (2), K. Hughes (2), Morris,

Tovey, B. Llewellyn
C: R. Williams (5)
PG: R. Williams
DG: R. Williams

CANADA 10 T: McTavish (2)
C: Burnham

9 Jun 1973, Toronto
CANADA 20 T: Wyndham (2), Docherty
C: Deacy
PG: Deacy (2)

WALES 58 T: David (2), K. Hughes (2)
J. D. Bevan, J. J. Williams,
Bennett, B. Llewellyn,
Taylor
C: Bennett (7), Taylor
PG: Bennett (2)

WALES v FIJI

26 Sep 1964, Cardiff Arms Park
WALES 28 T: Bebb (2), D. Thomas (2),
Pask, Weaver, Prothero
C: T. Price (2)
PG: Watkins

FIJI 22 T: Walisoliso (3), Soqosoqo,
Mucunabitu, Robe
C: Nawase (2)

25 Jun 1969, Suva
FIJI 11 T: Turagoka, Sikivou
C: Raitilava
PG: Raitilava

WALES 31 T: D. Hughes (3), Taylor
(2), Richards
C: Jarrett (5)
DG: J. P. R. Williams

9 Nov 1985, Cardiff Arms Park
WALES 40 T: P. T. Davies (2), Titley,
Holmes, Hadley, Pickering,
James
C: Thorburn (3)
PG: Thorburn (2)

FIJI 3 PG: Damu

31 May 1986, Suva
FIJI 15 T: Niuqila, Tuvula
C: Kubu (2)
PG: Lovokuru

WALES 22 T: J. Davies, Bowen
C: Bowen
PG: Dacey (3)
DG: J. Davies

WALES v JAPAN

6 Oct 1973, Cardiff Arms Park
WALES 62 T: Bennett (2), K. Hughes
(2), J. J. Williams, Bergiers,
Shell, Taylor, J. P. R.
Williams, T. G. R. Davies,

Windsor
C: Bennett (9)
JAPAN 14 T: Itoh (2)
PG: Yamamoto (2)

21 Sep 1975, Osaka
JAPAN 12 PG: Ueyama (4)
WALES 56 T: J. J. Williams (2), T. G. R.
Davies (2), Gravell (2),
T. P. Evans (2), Shell,
J. D. Bevan
C: Fenwick (5)
PG: Fenwick (2)

24 Sep 1975, Tokyo
JAPAN 6 PG: Ueyama (2)
WALES 82 T: J. P. R. Williams (3),
Bennett (2), T. G. R. Davies
(2), Price (2), J. J. Williams
(2), T. M. Davies, Gravell,
Faulkner
C: Bennett (10)
PG: Bennett (2)

22 Oct 1983, Cardiff Arms Park
WALES 29 T: Hadley, Brown, Dacey,
Bowen, Giles
C: Wyatt (3)
PG: Wyatt

JAPAN 24 T: Konishi, Tanifuji, Chida,
Fujita
C: Kobayashi
PG: Kobayashi (2)

WALES v ROMANIA

6 Oct 1979, Cardiff Arms Park
WALES 13 T: Griffiths
PG: Fenwick
DG: G. Davies (2)

ROMANIA 12 T: Ionescu
C: Bucos
PG: Constantin (2)

12 Nov 1983, Bucharest
ROMANIA 24 T: Caraguea, Muriaru,
Aldea, Lungu
C: Alexandru
PG: Alexandru (2)

WALES 6 PG: G. Evans (2)

WALES v TONGA

19 Oct 1974, Cardiff Arms Park
WALES 26 T: Finlayson (2), Fenwick,
J. D. Bevan, Cobner
PG: Martin (2)

TONGA 7 T: Talilotu
PG: Valita

10 Jun 1986, Nuku'Alofa
TONGA 7 T: Fifita
PG: Lovo

WALES	15	T: P. Moriarty C: Dacey PG: Bowen (2), Dacey

FRANCE v ARGENTINA

1949, Buenos Aires
ARGENTINA	0	
FRANCE	5	T: Caron C: J. Prat

1949, Buenos Aires
ARGENTINA	3	PG: Rene
FRANCE	12	T: Pomathios (2) C: J. Prat DG: J. Prat

1954, Buenos Aires
ARGENTINA	8	T: Hugues C: Ehrmann PG: Bernacci
FRANCE	22	T: Bienes (2), Murillo C: Vannier (2) PG: Vannier (2) DG: Danos

1954, Buenos Aires
ARGENTINA	3	PG: Bernacci
FRANCE	30	T: Bienes, A. Boniface (2), Roge, Morel C: Vannier (3) PG: Vannier DG: Vannier (2)

1960, Buenos Aires
ARGENTINA	3	PG: Devoto
FRANCE	37	T: Domenech (2), De Gregorio, Dizabo, Larrue, Celeya (2), Lacroix C: Vannier (5) PG: Vannier

1960, Buenos Aires
ARGENTINA	3	PG: Karplus
FRANCE	12	T: G. Boniface (2) PG: Brethes DG: Dizabo

1960, Buenos Aires
ARGENTINA	6	PG: Rios (2)
FRANCE	29	T: Lacroix, G. Boniface, Dupuy (2), Crancee, Dizabo C: Vannier (4) DG: Vannier

1974, Buenos Aires
ARGENTINA	15	T: Jurado C: Porta PG: Porta PG: Porta (3)
FRANCE	20	T: Dourthe, Bertranne, Fouroux C: Fouroux PG: Romeu (2)

1974, Buenos Aires
ARGENTINA	27	T: Walther C: Porta

		PG: Porta (7)
FRANCE	31	T: Gourdon (2), Bertranne, Dourthe C: Romeu (3) PG: Romeu (3)

19 Oct 1975, Lyon
FRANCE	29	T: Pecune (2), Skrela, Fouroux, Rives, Droitcourt C: Romeu PG: Romeu
ARGENTINA	6	PG: Porta (2)

25 Oct 1975, Paris
FRANCE	36	T: Bertranne, Skrela, Droitcourt, Romeu, Astre C: Romeu (2) PG: Romeu (4)
ARGENTINA	21	T: Gauweloose C: Porta PG: Porta

25 Jun 1977, Buenos Aires
ARGENTINA	3	PG: Porta
FRANCE	26	T: Bustaffa, Bertranne PG: Romeu (4), Aguirre DG: Romeu

2 Jul 1977, Buenos Aires
ARGENTINA	18	PG: Porta (6)
FRANCE	18	PG: Aguirre (6)

14 Nov 1982, Toulouse
FRANCE	25	T: Sella (2), Estève, Blanco PG: Blanco, Camberabero DG: Camberabero
ARGENTINA	12	T: G. Travaglini C: Porta PG: Porta (2)

20 Nov 1982, Paris
FRANCE	13	T: Begu, Blanco C: Camberabero PG: Camberabero
ARGENTINA	6	PG: Porta (2)

22 Jun 1985, Buenos Aires
ARGENTINA	24	T: Ure, Turnes C: Porta (2) PG: Porta (3) DG: Porta
FRANCE	16	T: Blanco, Bonneval C: Lescarboura PG: Lescarboura (2)

29 Jun 1985, Buenos Aires
ARGENTINA	15	T: Cuesta-Silva C: Porta PG: Porta (3)
FRANCE	23	T: Codorniou, Erbani, Berbizier, Blanco C: Lescarboura (2) PG: Lescarboura

31 May 1986, Buenos Aires
ARGENTINA	15	T: Ure C: Porta PG: Porta (3)
FRANCE	13	T: Bonneval PG: Laporte (3)

7 Jun 1986, Buenos Aires

ARGENTINA	9	PG: Porta (3)
FRANCE	22	T: Lescarboura, Sella, Dubroca
		C: Lescarboura (2)
		PG: Lescarboura (2)

FRANCE v CANADA

30 Sep 1978, Calgary

CANADA	9	T: Peace
		C: Wiley
		PG: Wiley
FRANCE	24	T: Bilbao, Belascain, Noves, Rives
		C: Aguirre
		PG: Aguirre, Vivies

29 Sep 1979, Charlety, Paris

FRANCE	34	T: Gallion, Blanco, Belascain, Gourdon
		C: Caussade (3)
		PG: Caussade (3)
		DG: Caussade
CANADA	15	T: Greig
		C: Taylor
		PG: Taylor (2)
		DG: Bibby

FRANCE v JAPAN

27 Oct 1973, Bordeaux

FRANCE	30	T: Delaigue, Barrau, Bertranne, Saisset, Skrela
		C: Cabrol (3)
JAPAN	18	T: Ohigashi, Shimazaki, Sakata
		PG: Ueyama, Shimazaki

23 Sep 1979, Tokyo

JAPAN	16	T: Ujino, Sakamoto, Fujiwara
		C: Ueyama, Minawakara
FRANCE	55	T: Noves (3), Paparemborde, Maleig, Beguerie, Cholley, Bastiat, Bilbao
		C: Aguirre (8)
		PG: Aguirre

19 Oct 1985, Dax

FRANCE	50	T: Lafond (4), Fabre, Cassagne, Codorniou, Rodriguez, Detrez, Dubroca
		C: D. Camberabero (5)
JAPAN	0	

26 Oct 1985, Nantes

FRANCE	52	T: D. Camberabero (2), Lafond (2), Charvet (2), Dintrans (2), Fabre, Rodriguez
		C: D. Camberabero (6)
JAPAN	0	

AUSTRALIA v ARGENTINA

27 Oct 1979, Buenos Aires

ARGENTINA	24	T: Madero (2)
		C: Porta
		PG: Porta
		DG: Porta (3)
AUSTRALIA	13	T: Crowe
		PG: P. McLean (2)
		DG: Melrose

3 Nov 1979, Buenos Aires

ARGENTINA	12	T: Petersen
		C: Porta
		PG: Porta
		DG: Porta
AUSTRALIA	17	T: Moon (2), Batch
		C: P. McLean
		PG: McLean

31 Jul 1983, Brisbane

AUSTRALIA	3	DG: Campese
ARGENTINA	18	T: Miguens, Petersen
		C: Porta (2)
		PG: Porta
		DG: Porta

8 Aug 1983, Sydney

AUSTRALIA	29	T: Moon (2), Roche, Campese, penalty try
		C: Campese (3)
		PG: Campese
ARGENTINA	13	T: Milano
		PG: Porta (2)
		DG: Porta

6 Jul 1986, Brisbane

AUSTRALIA	39	T: Papworth (2), Grigg, Campese
		C: Lynagh (4)
		PG: Lynagh (5)
ARGENTINA	19	T: Cuesta-Silva, J. Lanza, Turnes
		C: Porta, Madero
		PG: Porta

12 Jul 1986, Sydney

AUSTRALIA	26	T: Campese (2), Tuynman
		C: Lynagh
		PG: Lynagh (4)
ARGENTINA	0	

AUSTRALIA v CANADA

15 Jun 1985, Sydney

AUSTRALIA	59	T: Burke (2), Lane (2), Grigg (2), Calcraft, Farr-Jones, Kassulke
		C: Lynagh (7)
		PG: Lynagh (3)
CANADA	3	DG: Wyatt

23 Jun 1985, Brisbane
AUSTRALIA   43   T: Burke (3), Grigg, Cutler,
                  Tuynman, Farr-Jones
                  C: Lynagh (3)
                  PG: Lynagh (2)
                  DG: Lynagh
CANADA   15   T: Tucker
                  C: Wyatt
                  PG: Wyatt (3)

AUSTRALIA v FIJI

26 Jul 1952, Sydney
AUSTRALIA   15   T: Jones, Stapleton,
                  Johnson, Solomon
                  PG: Baker
FIJI   9   T: Valewai, Ranavue
                  PG: Ranavue

9 Aug 1952, Sydney
AUSTRALIA   15   T: Stapleton, Cox,
                  Shehadie, Windon
                  DG: Solomon
FIJI   17   T: Salabogi, Ralagi
                  C: Vatabua, Ranavue
                  PG: Vatabua, Ranavue

5 Jun 1954, Brisbane
AUSTRALIA   22   T: Cameron, Jones, Phipps,
                  Cross, Tate
                  C: Barker, Tooth
                  PG: Barker
FIJI   19   T: Naborisi, Cavalevu,
                  Domoni, Buroglevu
                  C: Vatebua (2)
                  PG: Vatebua

26 Jun 1954, Sydney
AUSTRALIA   16   T: Cross, Shehadie
                  C: Barker (2)
                  PG: Barker (2)
FIJI   18   T: Seruvatu, Sankuru
                  PG: Ranavue (3), Nawalu

10 Jun 1961, Brisbane
AUSTRALIA   24   T: Lisle, R. Thornett,
                  Magrath, Cleary, Phelps,
                  Catchpole
                  C: Dowse (3)
FIJI   6   PG: Bose (2)

17 Jun 1961, Sydney
AUSTRALIA   20   T: Cleary (2), Ellwood, Reid
                  C: Dowse
                  PG: Dowse (2)
FIJI   14   T: Nabou, Rasou, Lovodua
                  C: Bose
                  PG: Tawase

1 Jul 1961, Melbourne
AUSTRALIA   3   T: Lisle
FIJI   3   T: Levula

19 Sep 1972, Suva
FIJI   19   T: Varo (2)
                  C: Batisbasaga
                  PG: Batisbasaga (3)
AUSTRALIA   21   T: Thompson, Sullivan,
                  Burnett, Stumbles
                  C: Thompson
                  DG: Fairfax

12 Jun 1976, Sydney
AUSTRALIA   22   T: Batch (2), Ryan, Pearse
                  PG: P. McLean (2)
FIJI   6   T: Tuiese
                  C: Naituyaga

19 Jun 1976, Brisbane
AUSTRALIA   21   T: Ryan (2)
                  C: P. McLean (2)
                  PG: P. McLean (2)
                  DG: McLean
FIJI   9   PG: Raitilava (3)

26 Jun 1976, Sydney
AUSTRALIA   27   T: Batch, Pearse, Ryan
                  PG: P. McLean (5)
FIJI   17   T: Nasave, Matalau, Viriviri
                  C: Nasave
                  PG: Nasave

24 May 1980, Suva
FIJI   9   PG: Vinetaki, Waiseke
                  DG: Radrodo
AUSTRALIA   22   T: Martin, Moon
                  C: P. McLean
                  PG: P. McLean
                  DG: P. McLean

August 1983, Suva
FIJI   3   PG: Turuva
AUSTRALIA   16   T: Campese
                  PG: Lynagh (4)

10 Aug 1985, Brisbane
AUSTRALIA   52   T: Farr-Jones (2), Reynolds,
                  Cutler, Lawton, Papworth,
                  Grigg
                  C: Knox (3)
                  PG: Knox (3)
                  DG: Knox (2), Campese
FIJI   28   T: Nawalu, Niuqila, Cama,
                  Talawadua
                  C: Koroduadua (3)
                  PG: Koroduadua (2)

17 Aug 1985, Sydney
AUSTRALIA   31   T: Campese (2), Grigg,
                  McIntyre, Cutler
                  C: Knox
                  PG: Knox (3)
FIJI   9   PG: Koroduadua
                  DG: Koroduadua

AUSTRALIA v ITALY

4 Nov 1975, Milan

ITALY	15	T: Manni
		C: Ponzi
		PG: Ponzi (3)
AUSTRALIA	16	T: Crowe, Loane, Batch
		C: P. Mclean (2)

1 Jun 1986, Brisbane

AUSTRALIA	39	T: Campese (2), Tuynman, McIntyre, Moon, Burke
		C: Lynagh (6)
		PG: Lynagh
ITALY	18	T: Barba, Gaetaniello
		C: Bettarello, Troiani
		PG: Bettarello (2)

AUSTRALIA v JAPAN

2 Aug 1975, Sydney

AUSTRALIA	37	T: P. McLean (2), Robertson (2), Osborne, Wright
		C: P. McLean (5)
		PG: P. McLean
JAPAN	7	T: Aruga
		PG: Ueyama

17 Aug 1975, Brisbane

AUSTRALIA	50	T: Ryan (3), G. Shaw (2), A. Shaw, Hauser, Price
		C: P. McLean (6)
		PG: P. McLean (2)
JAPAN	25	T: Fujiwara (2), Aruga, Yoshida, Ishizuka
		C: Tanaka
		PG: Ueyama

AUSTRALIA v TONGA

23 Jun 1973, Sydney

AUSTRALIA	30	T: Stephens (2), Richardson, Cole, Hipwell, penalty try
		C: McGill (2), Richardson
TONGA	12	T: Tupi, Latu
		C: Ma'ake (2)

30 Jul 1973, Brisbane

AUSTRALIA	11	T: Cole, Tindall
		PG: McGill
TONGA	16	T: Vave, Latu, Kavapulu, Mafi

AUSTRALIA v UNITED STATES

16 Nov 1912, Berkeley

UNITED STATES	8	T: Harrigan
		C: Erb
		PG: Erb

AUSTRALIA	12	T: Meibusch (2), Carroll
		PG: Prentice

31 Jan 1976, Anaheim

UNITED STATES	12	PG: Oxman (4)
AUSTRALIA	24	T: Ryan, Price, Pearse
		C: Hindmarsh (3)
		PG: Hindmarsh (2)

9 Jul 1983, Sydney

AUSTRALIA	49	T: Campese (4), Slack (2), Ross, Roche, Hanley
		C: Gould (4), Campese
		DG: M. Ella
UNITED STATES	3	PG: Meyerseick

NEW ZEALAND v ARGENTINA

30 Oct 1976, Buenos Aires

ARGENTINA	9	PG: Beccar-Varela (2)
		DG: Porta
NEW ZEALAND	21	T: S. Wilson, Sloane
		C: Rowlands (2)
		PG: Rowlands (3)

6 Nov 1976, Buenos Aires

ARGENTINA	6	PG: Sansot, Porta
NEW ZEALAND	26	T: Rollerson, Cron, M. B. Taylor, N. M. Taylor
		C: Rowlands (2)
		PG: Rowlands (2)

8 Sep 1979, Dunedin

NEW ZEALAND	18	PG: R. Wilson (5)
		DG: Dunn
ARGENTINA	9	PG: Porta
		DG: Porta (2)

15 Sep 1979, Wellington

NEW ZEALAND	15	T: Cunningham, Loveridge
		C: R. Wilson (2)
		PG: R. Wilson
ARGENTINA	6	PG: Porta (2)

27 Oct 1985, Buenos Aires

ARGENTINA	20	T: J. Lanza, Cuesta-Silva
		PG: Porta (3)
		DG: Porta
NEW ZEALAND	33	T: Kirwan (2), Crowley, Hobbs
		C: Crowley
		PG: Crowley (4)
		DG: Crowley

3 Nov 1985, Buenos Aires

ARGENTINA	21	PG: Porta (4)
		DG: Porta (3)
NEW ZEALAND	21	T: Kirwan (2), Mexted, Green
		C: Crowley
		PG: Crowley

Willie John McBride

Ballymena and Ireland

Willie John McBride is the world's most capped forward. His 63 Irish caps and 17 appearances in test matches for the British Lions give a total of 80 international appearances, which was the all-time record before being overtaken (by one) by his neighbour and friend Mike Gibson (see p. 147). But just as important was that during his era between 1962 and 1975 he was the catalyst in the development of forward play in the British Isles from something akin to light comedy to a force that commanded total respect. Too often the British Lions had gone to South Africa and New Zealand with talented backs but with forwards incapable of matching the physical presence of the opposition or providing enough possession to win a test series.

After winning just three Irish caps, McBride was pitched into the 1962 tour to South Africa, playing in two tests. In 1966 he played in three tests in New Zealand. Two years later, back on the High Veld, McBride appeared in all four internationals. At the end of that tour the genial Irish lock-forward's tally was played 9 drawn 1 lost 8 – only a try in the first test in Pretoria providing a semblance of consolation. It was the only test try the Lions scored in that series.

He continued to give yeoman service to the Ireland pack. After playing in 11 consecutive internationals he was dropped. When recalled he played another 52 off the reel and was never dropped again. Only Gareth Edwards has played more times in succession for his country.

The 1968 tour may have been the end of tour frivolities. Beds came floating out of hotel windows, trees were set alight –

the 'Wreckers' created havoc wherever they went, led by a certain giant Irish lock-forward. But by 1971 McBride was one of the senior and more responsible members of the tour party. As father figure to the forwards, he was asked for 40 per cent possession from the pack by coach Carwyn James. The pack supplied 40 per cent plus, and the Lions won the series 2–1 with one drawn. Three years later he was appointed captain for his third visit to South Africa with the Lions and a record fifth tour (later equalled by Gibson).

Quite simply, the 1974 Lions were the best British Isles side ever, and McBride was the keystone. They won every game bar the last test match which was drawn 13–13 controversially, with a late Lions try disallowed. A party which had set off fearing the consequences of the unavailability of Duckham, Gibson and Gerald Davies for business reasons, returned home heroes.

Willie John McBride emerges from the Durban surf on a rare day off during the all-conquering British Lions tour to South Africa in 1974.

Captain in Ireland's centenary season and with his club having won the Ulster Senior Cup, McBride called it a day in 1975. He was born, educated and still works (in banking) in Ballymena, and played for the club side.

Like Mike Gibson, Mary Peters, Barry McGuigan and the Northern Ireland football team, Willie John McBride had his greatest hours in Ireland's darkest times. He brought sporting peace to a troubled land.

Jean-Pierre Rives

Toulouse, Racing Club de Paris and France

An international match programme recorded the following facts about the career of Jean-Pierre Rives: 'Flanker. Born 31/12/52 at Toulouse. 5ft 10in (1.75m), 13 stones (82.5kg). He was a schoolboy international, then played for French Universities and France 'B'. Made his international debut for France against England in 1975, France winning 27–20. Succeeded Jean-Pierre Bastiat as captain of France in 1977, and captained his country on a world record 34 occasions against major nations.

He led France to the Grand Slam in 1981. Formerly played for Toulouse before moving to Racing Club Paris during the latter part of his career. Won 47 caps against major nations and 59 in all internationals.'

Impressive reading, but it fails to chronicle the remarkable contribution to the game of rugby in France. Flaxen haired, often flecked with blood (his own), and heavily bandaged, he gave the appearance of a boxer who refused to quit. But he was a winner. A former law graduate from Toulouse, he wa a captain who led by example, not by force. In doing so he allowed the national team to exhibit its natural flair, while instilling the steel of discipline often lacking in earlier French teams.

Most of the sides he was involved with got the winning habit. Toulouse, the slumbering giant of French club rugby, woke up to win the championship. France won the Grand Slam, and won a memorable Bastille Day encounter in New Zealand by 24–19. And, in the twilight of his career, he forsook the south and joined Racing Club, not so much a slumbering giant as a dead one, turning them into a first division outfit.

The essence of Rives' play was to be in proximity to the ball. Never the sprinter, the scorer of flamboyant tries or the floater, but always harrying opposing threequarters, getting into the thick of the action, smothering, tidying up – infuriating the opposition by his omnipresence. He could pass like a threequarter too.

The previous world record number of appearances as captain was held by Wilson Whineray of New Zealand with 30. Rives led his side 30 times too, but another four appearances against the likes of Romania were sometimes more difficult than a frolic in the spring sunshine against England. It is a record that may stand for only a short time, and when it eventually falls, we can only hope that the next incumbent offers as much for the general good of the game as Jean-Pierre Rives.

See page 1 for picture.

Mike Gibson, captain for the match, probes for an opening against the New Zealand Maoris on the 1971 British Lions tour to New Zealand. The Lions beat the Maoris 23–11.

Mike Gibson

Northern Ireland Football Club and Ireland

The world's most capped player, Cameron Michael Henderson Gibson played in 69 internationals for Ireland and another 12 for the British Isles, a grand total of 81 appearances. His tally beats by one that of his Irish colleague and friend Willie John McBride (see p. 146).

Mike Gibson, a Belfast solicitor, began his international career in 1964 when still a student at Cambridge University. It started a career that was to achieve world stature at fly-half and then again at centre. He remained a permanent fixture in the Irish team until 1979 and made a record five tours with the British Isles in 1966, 1971 and 1977 to New Zealand, and 1968 and 1974 to South Africa.

He was involved in British rugby's finest hours in New Zealand, in a back line that read Edwards, John, Bevan, Gibson, Dawes, Gerald Davies and J. P. R. Williams. In 1974 he joined Willie John's team in South Africa as a replacement for the injured Alan Old, and although not playing in the tests, was an integral member of the 'gin and tonic XV' and as any tourist will confirm, a strong reserve XV is essential for a successful tour. In 1974 Ireland broke the Welsh monopoly by winning the Five Nations Championship.

Mike Gibson kept his head when all around him were losing theirs. A gifted natural footballer in both positions, he was highly versatile: in his 69 appearances for Ireland, he scored 9 tries, kicked 7 conversions, 6 dropped goals and 17 penalties. He played all his club rugby for NIFC – Northern Ireland Football Club – and broke Willie John's record on the 1979 tour to Australia.

Gibson's ability was best summed up by Wilson Whineray, the legendary All Black captain, who, when asked for his opinion of the 1971 British Lions – the only British team to win a series in New Zealand – replied, 'the Lions' greatest strength was in their backs, and unquestionably the finest back was Mike Gibson'.

NEW ZEALAND v CANADA

11 Oct 1980, Vancouver
CANADA	10	T: Bibby
		PG: Shiefler
NEW ZEALAND	43	T: M. Shaw (3), Mourie, Haden, Osborne, S. Wilson, Fraser
		C: Rollerson (4)
		PG: Rollerson

NEW ZEALAND v FIJI

14 Jun 1974, Suva
FIJI	13	T: Latilevu, Cavuitati
		C: Naituyaga
		PG: Naituyaga
NEW ZEALAND	14	T: Batty, Williams, Hurst
		C: Karam

23 Jul 1980, Suva
FIJI	6	T: Kunikoro
		C: Gavidi
NEW ZEALAND	30	T: Fraser (3), Allen, B. Robertson
		C: Codlin (2)
		PG: Codlin (2)

13 Sep 1980, Auckland
NEW ZEALAND	33	T: Osborne (2), K. J. Taylor (2), Wylie, Woodman
		C: Valli (3)
		PG: Valli
FIJI	0	

NEW ZEALAND v ITALY

28 Nov 1979, Rovigo
ITALY	12	T: N. Francescato
		C: Bettarello
		PG: Bettarello (2)
NEW ZEALAND	18	T: Mexted, Fraser
		C: Hewson (2)
		PG: Hewson, R. Wilson

NEW ZEALAND v ROMANIA

24 Oct 1981, Bucharest
ROMANIA	6	PG: Constantin
		DG: Alexandru
NEW ZEALAND	14	T: Salmon, Dalton
		PG: Hewson
		DG: Hewson

NEW ZEALAND v UNITED STATES

15 Nov 1913, Berkeley
UNITED STATES	3	PG: Peart

NEW ZEALAND	51	T: Roberts (3), McKenzie (2), Gray (2), Murray (2), McDonald (2), Wylie, McGregor
		C: Graham (4), McDonald, Mitchinson

1980, San Diego
UNITED STATES	6	PG: Cooke (2)
NEW ZEALAND	53	T: Woodman (3), Osborne (2), Wilson, Allen, Old
		C: Codlin (6)
		PG: Codlin (3)

SOUTH AFRICA v SOUTH AMERICA (ARGENTINA)

26 Apr 1980, Johannesburg
SOUTH AFRICA	24	T: T. du Plessis, Mordt, Germishuys
		C: Botha (3)
		PG: Botha
		DG: Botha
SOUTH AMERICA	9	T: Travaglini
		C: Porta
		PG: Porta

3 May 1980, Durban
SOUTH AFRICA	18	T: M. du Plessis
		C: Botha
		PG: Botha
		DG: Botha (3)
SOUTH AMERICA	9	PG: Piccardo (3)

18 Oct 1980, Montevideo
SOUTH AMERICA	13	T: Cubelli, Madero
		C: Porta
		DG: Landejo
SOUTH AFRICA	22	T: Stofberg, Gerber, Berger
		C: Botha (2)
		PG: Botha
		DG: Botha

26 Oct 1980, Santiago
SOUTH AMERICA	16	T: Campo, Iachetti
		C: Porta
		PG: Porta
		DG: Porta
SOUTH AFRICA	30	T: Mordt (2), Germishuys (2), Gerber, M. du Plessis
		C: Botha (3)

27 Mar 1982, Pretoria
SOUTH AFRICA	50	T: Gerber (3), Mordt (2), Oosthuizen, C. du Plessis, W. du Plessis
		C: Botha (6)
		PG: Heunis
		DG: Botha
SOUTH AMERICA	18	T: Puccio
		C: Porta
		PG: Porta (4)

3 Apr 1982, Bloemfontein

SOUTH AFRICA	12	T: Gerber
		C: Botha
		PG: Botha (2)
SOUTH AMERICA	21	T: Porta
		C: Porta
		PG: Porta (4)
		DG: Porta

20 Oct 1984, Pretoria

SOUTH AFRICA	32	T: Louw, Gerber, Serfontein, Heunis, Mallett
		C: Tobias (2), Gerber
		PG: Tobias (2)
SOUTH AMERICA	15	T: Palma, de Vedia
		C: Porta (2)
		PG: Porta

27 Oct 1984, Cape Town

SOUTH AFRICA	22	T: C. du Plessis, Ferreira, Mordt, Gerber
		PG: Tobias (2)
SOUTH AMERICA	13	T: Sansot
		PG: Porta (3)

SOUTH AFRICA v UNITED STATES

1981, Glenville

UNITED STATES	7	T: Walton
		PG: Smith
SOUTH AFRICA	38	T: Mordt (3), Geldenhuys, Germishuys (2), Beck, Berger
		C: Botha (3)

RECORDS

INTERNATIONAL BOARD COUNTRIES v WORLD CUP JUNIOR NATIONS

Four tries in a match
W. C. C. Steele (Scotland) v Tonga 1974
W. B. Gammell (Scotland) v Japan 1976
D. M. Wyatt (England) v USA 1977
J.-B. Lafond (France) v Japan 1985
D. I. Campese (Australia) v USA 1986
I. Tukalo (Scotland) v Japan 1986
I. Evans (Wales) v Canada 1987 (World Cup)
C. Green (New Zealand) v Fiji 1987 (World Cup)
J. Gallagher (New Zealand) v Fiji 1987 (World Cup)

20 points in a match
34 P. Bennett (Wales) v Japan 1975
30 C. D. R. Mair (Scotland) v Japan 1976
30 D. Camberabero (France) v Zimbabwe 1987 (World Cup)
27 A. G. Hastings (Scotland) v Romania 1987 (World Cup)
26 G. Fox (New Zealand) v Fiji 1987 (World Cup)

Match aggregates over 75 points*
88 Wales (82) v Japan (6) 1975
83 Scotland (74) v Japan (6) 1976
80 Australia (52) v Fiji (28) 1985
79 England (60) v Fiji (19) 1982
78 Wales (58) v Canada (20) 1971
76 Wales (62) v Japan (14) 1973

Most tries in a match*
14 Wales v Japan 1975 (82–6)

11 Wales v Japan 1973 (62–14)
11 Scotland v Japan 1976 (74–9)

Most penalties in a match*
6 J. M. Aguirre (France) v Argentina 1977
(H. Porta kicked six in the same match: world record score draw of 18–18).
*For additions see Chapter 1.

WORLD CUP JUNIOR NATIONS v INTERNATIONAL BOARD COUNTRIES

Three tries in a match
Y. Matsuo (Japan – fly-half) v England 1979
S. Walisoliso (Fiji – prop) v Wales 1964

Most points in a match
23 H. Porta (Argentina) v France 1974
21 H. Porta (S. America) v South Africa 1984
21 H. Porta (Argentina) v New Zealand 1985

Most penalties in a match
7 H. Porta (Argentina) v France 1974
6 H. Porta (Argentina) v France 1977

TOURS – WORLD CUP JUNIOR NATIONS AND IB COUNTRIES

ARGENTINA IN AUSTRALIA
16 July–7 August 1983

W v New South Wales		19–7
L v Capital Territory		9–35
W v Queensland		34–28
W v NSW Country		46–3
W v **Australia**		18–3
W v Queensland Country		22–12

L v **Australia**		13–29

22 June–12 July 1986

W v NSW Country		39–7
W v South Australian XV		38–19
L v New South Wales		18–30
L v Queensland		9–59
L v **Australia**		19–39
W v Queensland Country		41–3
L v **Australia**		0–26

AUSTRALIA IN ARGENTINA
13 October–3 November 1979

W v San Isidro		17–12
W v Interior Select		47–12
W v Buenos Aires XV		22–6
W v Rosario		21–13
L v **Argentina**		13–24
W v Cuyo		43–4
W v **Argentina**		17–12

ENGLAND IN ARGENTINA
16 May–6 June 1981

W v San Isidro		20–14
W v Northern Region		36–12
W v Buenos Aires XV		34–25
W v Southern Region		47–3
D v **Argentina**		19–19
W v Littoral		25–21
W v **Argentina**		12–6

ARGENTINA IN IRELAND AND SCOTLAND
31 October–24 November 1973

D v Munster		12–12
L v Ulster		13–23
W v Connaught		16–7
L v **Ireland**		8–21
L v Glasgow and Edinburgh		13–18
D v South of Scotland		16–16
W v North and Midlands		28–23
L v **Scotland**		11–12

ARGENTINA IN FRANCE
8 October–29 October 1975

L v Regional XV	14–27
W v Second Division XV	10–3
W v Regional XV	9–3
L v **France**	6–29
L v Regional XV	18–21
L v **France**	21–36
W v Regional XV	17–16

1982

W v French Selection	38–15
L v French Selection	15–25
L v French Army	9–27
W v French Barbarians	22–8
L v **France**	12–25
W v French Selection	12–9
L v **France**	6–13
W v **Spain**	28–19

FRANCE IN ARGENTINA
1949

W v Provincia	21–3
W v San Isidro	19–3
W v President's XV	21–3
W v La Plata	21–3
W v Pucara	16–0
W v Capital	20–3
W v Parana	14–0
W v **Argentina**	5–0
W v **Argentina**	12–3

1954

W v Belgrano	29–14
W v Combinado	32–3
W v Provincia	16–3
W v San Isidro	6–0
W v Capital	15–6
W v RFC Eva Peron	22–0
W v **Argentina**	22–8
W v Provincia	3–0
W v Pucara	12–3
W v Capital	8–3
W v **Argentina**	30–3

1960

W v A.S. Francaise	14–3
W v Gymnasia y Escrima	40–6
W v Buenos Aires University	26–3
W v Puyerredon	26–0
W v **Argentina**	37–3
W v San Fernando	60–5
W v San Isidro	65–5
W v Cordoba	69–8
W v **Argentina**	12–3
W v Pucara	27–9
W v **Argentina**	29–6
W v **Chile**	55–6

1974

W v **Brazil**	99–7
W v C.A. San Isidro	34–10
W v Cuyo	59–4
W v Buenos Aires	31–9
W v Rosario	21–10
W v Interior XV	61–12
W v **Argentina**	20–15
W v **Argentina**	31–27

11 June–2 July 1977

W v Buenos Aires Selection	38–4
W v Interior Selection	28–12
W v Combined Clubs	23–6
W v Cuyo	25–4
W v **Argentina**	26–3
W v Santa Fe	34–6
D v **Argentina**	18–18

8–29 June 1985

W v San Isidro	41–18
W v Cuyo	64–6
W v Buenos Aires XV	50–15
W v Tucuman	24–7
L v **Argentina**	16–24
W v Santa Fe	82–7
W v **Argentina**	23–15

31 May–7 June 1986

L v **Argentina**	13–15
W v Argentina 'B'	45–24
W v **Argentina**	22–9

IRELAND IN ARGENTINA AND CHILE
1952

W v Chilean All Stars	30–0
W v Capital	12–6
L v Pucara	6–11
D v Provincial XV	6–6
W v Argentina 'A'	19–3
D v **Argentina**	3–3
W v Argentina 'B'	25–3
W v **Argentina**	6–0
W v Buenos Aires Past and Present	19–11

IRELAND IN ARGENTINA
1970

W v Interior XV	33–11
W v Argentina 'B'	9–6
W v Rosario	11–6
W v Argentina 'D'	14–3
L v **Argentina**	3–8
L v Argentina 'C'	0–17
L v **Argentina**	3–6

SCOTLAND IN ARGENTINA
6–27 September 1969

W v Pumas 'C'	19–9
W v Provincial XV	11–3
L v **Argentina**	3–20
W v Rosario Province	20–6
W v Pumas 'B'	9–5
W v **Argentina**	6–3

NEW ZEALAND IN ARGENTINA AND URUGUAY
12 October–9 November 1976

W v **Uruguay**	64–3
W v Buenos Aires Selection	24–13
W v Interior Selection	30–13
W v Casi	37–3
W v Tucuman	51–15
W v **Argentina**	21–9
W v Rosario	43–4
W v **Argentina**	26–6

W v Mendoza	25–6

13 October–3 November 1985

W v San Isidro	22–9
W v Rosario	28–9
W v Buenos Aires XV	31–13
W v Cordoba	72–9
W v **Argentina**	33–20
W v Mar del Plata	56–6
D v **Argentina**	21–21

ARGENTINA IN NEW ZEALAND
1979

W v Poverty Bay	26–3
W v Auckland	18–13
W v Manawatu	21–10
W v Bay of Plenty	32–12
W v Taranaki	19–9
L v **New Zealand**	9–18
W v South Canterbury	23–13
L v **New Zealand**	6–15
L v Counties	11–18

WALES IN ARGENTINA
7–28 September 1968

W v Belgrano	24–11
W v Provincial XV	14–3
L v **Argentina**	5–9
D v Argentine Juniors	8–8
W v Combined XV	9–6
D v **Argentina**	9–9

ARGENTINA IN WALES AND ENGLAND
29 September–16 October 1976

W v East Wales	25–22
W v Cardiff	29–25
W v Aberavon	18–6
L v North and Midlands (England)	9–24
L v West Wales	12–24
L v **Wales**	19–20

ARGENTINA IN BRITAIN, IRELAND AND ITALY
27 September–24 October 1978

W v Southern Counties	39–9
L v London Division	15–22
L v Northern Division	6–20
W v North Midlands	22–14
W v English Students	15–9
D v **England**	13–13
W v Wales 'B'	17–14
W v Leinster	24–13
L v **Italy**	6–19

CANADA IN AUSTRALIA
25 May–23 June 1985

W v Queensland Country	13–6
W v Northern Territory	30–12
L v Western Australia	6–16
W v South Australia	24–16
L v New South Wales	6–31
L v New South Wales Country	23–31
L v **Australia**	3–59

W v Brisbane	24–16
L v **Australia**	15–43

CANADA IN ENGLAND
1–15 October 1983

W v Combined Services	17–14
L v Headingley	9–16
W v Oxford University	16–9
L v Sussex	9–16
L v **England**	0–27

ENGLAND IN CANADA AND USA
24 May–19 June 1982

W v Eastern Canada	52–3
W v **Canada**	43–6
W v Cougars	26–6
W v Pacific Coast	28–6
W v Western	45–6
W v Mid-West	58–7
W v Eastern	41–0
W v **United States**	59–0

CANADA IN WALES
18 September–2 October 1971

W v Monmouthshire Under-25	17–15
W v Western Counties	15–10
L v Wales 'B'	10–38
L v Glamorgan Under-25	14–22
L v **Wales**	10–56

WALES IN CANADA
26 May–9 June 1973

W v British Columbia	31–6
W v Alberta	76–6
W v Quebec and Maritimes	44–9
W v Ontario	79–0
W v **Canada**	58–20

CANADA IN BRITISH ISLES
13 October–8 December 1962

L v Western Counties	8–30
L v Irish Universities	8–32
L v Munster	8–11
L v EbbwVale/Newbridge	8–16
L v Bridgend/Maesteg	3–17
L v Oxford University	0–56
L v London Clubs	0–14
L v Cambridge University	11–16
L v Midland Clubs	3–8
D v Barbarians	3–3
L v Edinburgh	3–22
L v North/South of Scotland	12–24
L v Welsh Under-23	0–8
W v Western Counties	8–3
L v Combined Services	8–11

CANADA IN BRITAIN AND FRANCE
12–29 September 1979

W v Somerset	15–6
W v Cornwall	10–6
L v Cardiff	8–19

D v Southern Counties	6–6
W v France 'B'	14–4
L v **France**	15–34

FIJI IN AUSTRALIA
1952

W v North Harbour	21–9
W v City XV	28–9
D v New South Wales	14–14
W v New England	30–18
W v Queensland	24–17
W v United Services	33–14
L v **Australia**	9–15
W v Western Districts	50–8
W v Newcastle	28–24
W v **Australia**	17–15

1954

W v South Harbour	24–11
W v Metropolitan	11–8
W v Newcastle	28–15
W v Southern Districts	64–0
L v New South Wales	13–16
W v Toowoomba	69–5
W v Queensland	53–16
W v Brisbane	34–9
L v **Australia**	19–22
W v New England	37–14
W v Riverina	29–6
W v Victoria	42–12
W v South Australia	21–8
W v New South Wales	24–19
W v Combined Services	27–16
W v **Australia**	18–16
W v Central Western	17–14

1961

W v North Harbour	25–12
L v South Harbour	11–16
L v New South Wales	13–17
W v Central Western	17–6
W v Newcastle	17–8
W v Queensland	13–9
L v **Australia**	6–24
W v Northern NSW	25–14
L v **Australia**	14–20
L v Southern NSW	14–16
W v South Australia	56–17
W v Victoria	26–12
D v **Australia**	3–3
W v Barbarians	43–17

1969

W v Victoria	40–8
W v ACT	17–12
W v Sydney	31–16
W v NSW Country	22–9
L v New South Wales	5–6
L v Queensland	16–17
W v **Australia**	26–3
W v Queensland Country	40–21
W v North Queensland	45–12

15 May–26 June 1976

L v Sydney	4–12
W v Tasmania	48–8
W v Western Australia	47–3
L v South Australia	7–10
W v Victoria	27–4

L v NSW Country	11–13
L v New South Wales	6–37
W v Capital Teritory	28–12
L v **Australia**	6–22
L v Queensland	16–28
L v **Australia**	9–21
W v Queensland Country	24–4
L v **Australia**	17–27

13 July–17 August 1985

D v Sydney	27–27
W v Australian Universities	26–24
L v Queensland	6–47
W v Queensland Country	39–10
W v NSW Country	36–12
L v Capital Territory	23–34
L v New South Wales	10–43
W v New South Wales 'B'	36–16
L v **Australia**	28–52
L v **Australia**	9–31

AUSTRALIA IN FIJI
17–24 May 1980

W v Nadi	25–11
W v Rewa	46–14
W v **Fiji**	22–9

FIJI IN NEW ZEALAND
1939

W v Bay of Plenty Maori XV	11–0
W v North Auckland	12–11
W v King Country	14–9
W v Auckland	17–11
D v Nelson-Golden Bay-Motueka	6–6
W v Buller	9–4
W v Ashburton County	10–4
W v NZ Maoris	14–4

1951

L v Thames Valley	6–16
W v Bay of Plenty	32–23
W v Poverty Bay	14–11
W v Hawke's Bay	23–14
W v Marlborough	28–16
W v Buller	6–3
W v South Canterbury	24–14
L v Otago	5–26
D v Southland	11–11
L v Canterbury	22–24
W v Bush	9–6
L v Wanganui	11–14
W v NZ Maoris	21–14
D v Waikato	11–11
L v Auckland	16–29

1954

L v Auckland	3–39

1957

D v Poverty Bay	14–14
W v Bay of Plenty	22–3
W v Auckland	38–17
W v North Auckland	6–3
D v Taranaki	8–8
L v King Country	14–26
W v Manawatu	30–12
W v Wairarapa	27–8

W v NZ Maoris	36–13
W v Marlborough	39–9
W v West Coast	23–17
L v Southland	8–13
W v NZ Maoris	17–8
W v Mid-Canterbury	16–9
L v Canterbury	16–22

1974

W v Buller	25–3
L v Canterbury	4–9
W v North Otago	14–11
W v Otago	9–7
L v Marlborough	13–21
L v Waikato	7–13
W v King Country	38–3
L v NZ Maoris	9–24
W v Hawke's Bay	28–21
W v North Auckland	21–8
W v Wanganui	28–9
L v NZ Maoris	25–39
W v Auckland Invitation XV	31–20

1980

L v Wanganui	11–16
L v Wellington	8–24
W v West Coast	28–12
L v Canterbury	4–10
W v Southland	22–21
L v Otago	10–18
W v Hawke's Bay	28–19
W v King Country	31–22
L v Counties	10–35
L v North Auckland	4–38
L v NZ Maoris	9–22
L v **New Zealand**	0–33

FIJI IN SCOTLAND AND ENGLAND
15 September–10 October 1982

L v Edinburgh	12–47
L v South of Scotland	17–23
L v Anglo-Scots	19–29
L v **Scotland**	12–32
L v North of England	4–19
L v South and South West	6–36
L v Midlands	16–25
L v Cambridge University	12–30
L v English Students	9–26
L v **England**	19–60

FIJI IN ENGLAND AND WALES
7 October–21 November 1970

W v Devon and Cornwall	17–3
L v Glos. and Somerset	13–25
D v Midland Counties West	16–16
W v North West Counties	11–6
L v North East Counties	6–14
W v Barbarians	29–9
L v Cambridge University	8–12
L v London Counties	0–22
W v Oxford University	8–3
W v Midland Counties East	24–14
L v South	8–10
L v England Under-25	11–15
W v Combined Services	11–6

L v Wales Under-25	6–8

FIJI IN WALES
12–29 September 1964

W v Bridgend and Maesteg	23–12
L v Glamorgan and Monmouth	22–23
W v Western Counties	12–6
L v **Wales**	22–28
D v Abertillery and Newbridge	11–11

FIJI IN WALES AND IRELAND
9 October–9 November 1985

W v Cross Keys	26–12
L v Cardiff	15–31
W v Swansea	23–14
L v **Ireland**	15–16
L v Ulster	9–23
W v Connaught	7–6
W v Newport	7–6
W v London Welsh	22–9
L v Llanelli	28–31
L v **Wales**	3–40

WALES IN FIJI, TONGA AND WESTERN SAMOA
24 May–14 June 1986

L v Eastern Fiji	13–29
W v Western Fiji	19–14
W v **Fiji**	22–15
W v Tongan Presidents XV	13–9
W v **Tonga**	15–7
W v **Western Samoa**	32–14

ITALY IN AUSTRALIA
1981

W v Central Queensland	27–8
W v Mount Isa	38–3
W v Townsville	30–13
W v Cairns	29–0
L v Queensland	11–68
W v NSW Country	18–13
L v ACT	18–19
W v South Australia	22–3
W v Victoria	23–6

17 May–1 June 1986

L v NSW Country	9–22
L v Brisbane	19–37
W v North Queensland	28–15
W v Queensland Country	25–23
L v **Australia**	18–39

ITALY IN NEW ZEALAND
1980

L v Nelson Bays	9–13
W v Wairarapa-Bush	13–9
L v Taranaki	9–30
W v Horowhenua	21–12
L v NZ Juniors	13–30

JAPAN IN AUSTRALIA
1975

W v Western Australia	14–10
W v South Australia	21–17

W v Victoria	20–16
L v Sydney	22–38
L v **Australia**	7–37
L v NSW Country	20–97
L v Queensland	23–64
W v Queensland Country	33–12
L v **Australia**	25–50

JAPAN IN ENGLAND AND SCOTLAND
17 September–11 October 1986

L v South of Scotland	12–45
W v Scottish North– Midlands	27–19
L v Edinburgh	14–26
L v **Scotland**	18–33
L v Leicestershire	22–33
W v Cornwall	36–15
L v Combined England Students	4–43
L v **England**	12–39

ENGLAND IN THE FAR EAST
21 September–8 October 1971

W v Waseda University	56–4
W v **Japan**	27–19
W v **Japan**	6–3
W v Hong Kong	26–0
W v Singapore	39–9
W v Ceylon	40–11
W v Ceylon	34–6

ENGLAND IN JAPAN, FIJI AND TONGA
10 May–1 June 1979

W v Japan 'B'	36–7
W v **Japan**	21–19
W v Kyushu	80–3
W v **Japan**	38–18
W v Fiji Juniors	39–22
W v **Fiji**	19–7
W v **Tonga**	37–17

JAPAN IN FRANCE
9–26 October 1985

L v French Selection	17–44
L v Borgogne	8–48
L v Littoral	11–37
L v **France**	0–50
L v French Barbarians	4–45
L v **France**	0–52

FRANCE IN THE FAR EAST AND CANADA
9–30 September 1978

W v Hong Kong	26–6
W v Japan Select	61–10
W v Western Japan	90–18
W v Kyushu	37–3
W v **Japan**	55–16
W v British Columbia	17–10
W v **Canada**	24–9

IRELAND IN JAPAN
19 May–2 June 1985

W	v	East Japan	42–15
W	v	Japan 'B'	34–10
W	v	**Japan**	48–13
W	v	West Japan	44–13
W	v	**Japan**	33–15

JAPAN IN NEW ZEALAND
1974

L	v	Counties	23–42
W	v	Taranaki	19–15
D	v	Poverty Bay	13–13
W	v	South Canterbury	23–18
L	v	NZ Universities	31–40
L	v	Southland	20–39
L	v	NZ Juniors	31–55
W	v	NZ Universities	24–21

SCOTLAND IN THE FAR EAST
4–18 September 1977

W	v	Thailand	82–3
W	v	Hong Kong	42–6
W	v	Combined Universities (Japan)	59–13
W	v	Japanese Selection	50–16
W	v	**Japan**	74–9

JAPAN IN WALES
8–22 October 1983

W	v	Abertillery	17–13
L	v	Pembrokeshire	15–28
D	v	Neath	21–21
W	v	Newbridge	19–14
L	v	**Wales**	24–29

JAPAN IN WALES, ENGLAND AND FRANCE
22 September–27 October 1973

L	v	East Glamorgan	11–23
L	v	Monmouthshire	16–26
L	v	West Glamorgan	6–19
W	v	Western Counties (Wales)	12–9
L	v	**Wales**	14–62
L	v	Midland Counties	6–10
L	v	England Under-23	10–19
L	v	French Regional XV	19–51
L	v	French Regional XV	18–29
W	v	French Regional XV	19–8
L	v	**France**	18–30

WALES IN HONG KONG AND JAPAN
10–24 September 1975

W	v	Hong Kong	57–3
W	v	Combined XV	32–3
W	v	Japan 'B'	34–7
W	v	**Japan**	56–12
W	v	**Japan**	82–6

JAPAN IN BRITAIN AND ITALY
22 September–21 October 1976

L	v	Gloucestershire	10–62
L	v	**Scottish XV**	9–34

W	v	English Students	21–16
L	v	Combined Services	21–23
W	v	Cambridge University	38–35
L	v	Combined Welsh Clubs	9–63
W	v	Oxford University	37–0
L	v	England Under-23	15–58
L	v	Italy Under-21	30–31
L	v	**Italy**	3–25

JAPAN IN UNITED STATES AND CANADA
1986

L	v	Eastern	21–35
L	v	Midwest	6–24
W	v	Western	23–13
W	v	Junior Eagles	21–10
W	v	Pacific Coast	24–3
D	v	**United States**	9–9
L	v	Canada 'A'	21–50
W	v	**Canada**	26–21

ROMANIA IN ENGLAND
29 December 1984–5 January 1985

L	v	Northern Division	8–17
L	v	South and South West	3–15
L	v	**England**	15–22

ROMANIA IN IRELAND
4–22 October 1980

W	v	Munster	32–9
L	v	Leinster	10–24
W	v	Ulster	15–13
W	v	Connaught	28–9
D	v	**Ireland**	13–13

ROMANIA IN NEW ZEALAND
6–30 August 1975

W	v	Poverty Bay	19–12
W	v	Waikato	14–9
L	v	Manawatu	9–28
L	v	North Auckland	0–3
W	v	Marlborough	21–6
W	v	Southlands	12–9
L	v	South Canterbury	4–12
D	v	NZ Juniors	10–10

ROMANIA IN SCOTLAND
19–26 September 1981

W	v	Edinburgh	18–13
W	v	South of Scotland	18–10
L	v	**Scotland**	6–12

ROMANIA IN WALES
22 September–6 October 1979

W	v	Ebbw Vale	12–0
W	v	Pontypridd	9–3
W	v	North Wales	38–15
W	v	West Wales	15–11
L	v	**Wales**	12–13

TONGA IN AUSTRALIA
6 June–7 July 1973

W	v	South Australia	29–6
L	v	Victoria	10–13
W	v	Sydney	19–14

L	v	New South Wales	0–18
L	v	ACT	6–17
L	v	**Australia**	12–30
L	v	NSW Country	11–22
W	v	**Australia**	16–11
L	v	Queensland	10–18
W	v	Darling Downs	12–9

TONGA IN ENGLAND AND WALES
14 September–19 October 1974

W	v	East Wales	18–13
L	v	Llanelli	15–24
L	v	North Wales	3–12
L	v	Glasgow	16–33
L	v	**Scotland**	8–44
L	v	Northern Counties (England)	12–17
L	v	England Under-23	4–40
L	v	Newport	6–14
L	v	West Wales	6–14
L	v	**Wales**	7–26

TONGA IN NEW ZEALAND
1969

L	v	Nelson Bays	21–22
W	v	South Canterbury	25–14
W	v	Buller	40–8
W	v	NZ Maoris	26–19
L	v	Horowhenua	10–22
L	v	NZ Juniors	3–43
W	v	East Coast	28–19
L	v	North Auckland	5–47
L	v	Thames Valley	10–12
W	v	NZ Maoris	19–6
D	v	Bay of Plenty	0–0

1975

W	v	Wairarapa-Bush	13–12
W	v	West Coast	21–17
L	v	North Otago	18–30
L	v	Canterbury	20–31
W	v	Mid-Canterbury	22–19
W	v	Wanganui	28–15
W	v	East Coast	47–6
L	v	NZ Maoris	16–23
W	v	King Country	18–13
W	v	Counties	17–12
W	v	Thames Valley	41–16
L	v	NZ Maoris	7–37

UNITED STATES IN AUSTRALIA
1983

W	v	Western Australia	25–18
W	v	Victoria	13–8
L	v	Sydney	9–13
L	v	Queensland	10–14
W	v	South Australia	34–15
W	v	NSW Country	26–3
L	v	**Australia**	3–49

UNITED STATES IN ENGLAND
28 September–15 October 1977

W	v	Civil Service	15–6
L	v	Cornwall	11–12
L	v	Coventry	6–33

L v Gosforth	12–18	W v San Francisco	
W v Cambridge University	20–18	Barbarian Club	30–0
L v **England**	11–37	W v Leland Stanford	

L v Gosforth	12–18
W v Cambridge University	20–18
L v **England**	11–37

FRANCE IN UNITED STATES
6–12 June 1976

W v Eastern	16–12
W v New York Selection	71–7
W v **United States**	33–14

NEW ZEALAND IN USA
4 October–25 November 1913

W v Olympic Club	19–0
W v University of California	31–0

W v San Francisco Barbarian Club	30–0
W v Leland Stanford University	54–0
W v Leland Stanford University	56–0
W v University of Santa Clara	42–0
W v University of California	38–3
W v University of Nevada	55–0
W v University of California	33–0
W v St Mary's College	26–0
W v University of Southern	

California	40–0
W v University of Santa Clara	33–0
W v All-America	51–3
W v Victoria	23–0
W v Victoria	35–0
W v Vancouver	44–0

SCOTLAND IN USA AND CANADA
8–22 May 1985

W v Vancouver Island	20–10
L v British Columbia	13–22
W v Grizzlies	32–6
W v Wolverines	62–6
W v Alberta	79–0

INTERNATIONALS BETWEEN WORLD CUP JUNIOR COUNTRIES

ARGENTINA v CANADA
1981   Argentina 35, Canada 0

ARGENTINA v FIJI
1980   Argentina 34, Fiji 22
1980   Argentina 38, Fiji 16

ARGENTINA v ITALY
1978   Italy 19, Argentina 6

ARGENTINA v ROMANIA
1973   Argentina 15, Romania 9
1973   Argentina 24, Romania 3

CANADA v FIJI
1970   Canada 17, Fiji 35

CANADA v JAPAN
1932   Japan 9, Canada 8
1932   Japan 38, Canada 5
1982   Japan 24, Canada 18
1982   Japan 16, Canada 6
1986   Canada 21, Japan 26

CANADA v TONGA
1974   Canada 14, Tonga 40

JAPAN v ITALY
1976   Italy 25, Japan 3

JAPAN v UNITED STATES
1985   Japan 15, United States 16
1986   United States 9, Japan 9

8 INTERNATIONAL RUGBY RECORDS

I: World Records   II: International Championship
III: British Lions   IV: Barbarians

Keeping accurate statistics on what constitutes an international and the subsequent awarding of international caps has become a problem. In previous years, caps were awarded only in matches between International Board countries – the Five Nations, New Zealand, Australia and South Africa.

With the arrival in the late 1960s of Argentina and in the 1950s of Romania onto the world scene, IB countries began to accept their ability and gave the internationals full status. (France had already done so for years.) But in the last couple of years the lack of continuity has increased.

Take May and June 1986, for example. Wales awarded caps against Fiji and Tonga who competed in the World Cup, and Western Samoa who did not. South Africa will award caps for those who played against the 'rebel' New Zealand Cavaliers, who would not have been honoured by their Union. France awarded caps against non-IB Argentina, as they have always done against Romania.

Rugby is unlike soccer where the ruling is to award

international caps against other countries affiliated to FIFA, their governing body. Will rugby authorities now decree that *all* World Cup competitors be given full status?

The author respects each country's decision to award caps to opposition considered worthy of international status. If some statistics differ from those in another book, it is for that reason.

I: WORLD RECORDS

Records for matches between IB countries, plus British Isles, from 1890.

TEAM RECORDS

Highest score
49 Wales (49–14) v France 1910 Swansea
49 New Zealand (49–6) v Wales 1987 Brisbane (World Cup)

Biggest winning margin
44 South Africa (44–0) v Scotland 1951 Murrayfield

Most tries in an international
11 Wales (47–5) v France 1909 Paris (Colombes)

Most points on an overseas tour (all matches)
868 New Zealand to B. Isles/France (33 matches) 1905–6

Most tries on an overseas tour (all matches)
215 New Zealand to B. Isles/France (33 matches) 1905–6

Most points in an international series
97 New Zealand v Australia (3 matches) 1972 in NZ

Most tries in an international series
16 South Africa v B. Isles (4 matches) 1955 in SA
16 New Zealand v Australia (3 matches) 1972 in NZ

Most points in Five Nations Championship in a season
102 Wales 1975–6

Most tries in Five Nations Championship in a season
21 Wales 1909–10

Biggest win on a major tour (all matches)
117–6 New Zealand v S. Australia 1974 Adelaide

Unbeaten teams on major tour
New Zealand to B. Isles 1924–5 P 32, W 32
B. Isles to S. Africa 1974 P 22, W 21, D 1
B. Isles to S. Africa 1891 P 19, W 19

INDIVIDUAL RECORDS
(including appearances for British Isles, shown in brackets)

Most capped player
Overall
C. M. H. Gibson (Ireland) 81(12)[1] 1964–79
in individual positions
Full-back
J. P. R. Williams (Wales) 62(8)[2] 1969–81
Wing
K. J. Jones (Wales) 47(3)[3] 1947–57
Centre (includes 2nd five-eighth)
J. M. Renwick (Scotland) 52(1)[4] 1972–84
Fly-half (includes 1st five-eighth)
J. W. Kyle (Ireland) 52(6) 1947–58
Scrum-half
G. O. Edwards (Wales) 63(10) 1967–78
Prop
P. A. Orr (Ireland) 59(1) 1976–87
Hooker
C. T. Deans (Scotland) 53 1978–87
J. V. Pullin (England) 49(7) 1966–76
Lock
W. J. McBride (Ireland) 80(17) 1962–75
Flanker
J. F. Slattery (Ireland) 65(4) 1970–84
No 8
T. M. Davies (Wales) 46(8)[5] 1969–76

[1]*Gibson made 40 appearances for Ireland as a centre and 8 for the Lions, making 48 at centre in all. As a fly-half he made 25 appearances for Ireland and 4 for the Lions, making 29 in all. He also made four appearances for Ireland on the wing. His 69 caps for Ireland, out of 81 in all, are the record for an individual country.*
[2]*Williams won 63 caps in all, but was chosen once for Wales as a flanker.*
[3]*T. G. R. Davies (Wales), 51(5), won 39 caps as a wing and 12 as a centre, one of them for the Lions.*
[4]*R. Bertranne (France) has made most appearances, 52, for an individual country as a threequarter. He played 39 times in the centre and 13 on the wing.*
[5]*B. Dauga (France), 50 caps, won 21 at No 8 and 29 at lock.*

Most consecutive international appearances
53 W. J. McBride (Ireland)
53 G. O. Edwards (Wales)

Longest international career
17 seasons G. M. Cooke (Australia) 1932–48

Most internationals as captain
34 J.-P. Rives (France) 1979–84
30 W. J. Whineray (NZ) 1958–65

Most points in internationals
301* A. R. Irvine (Scotland) (59(9) appearances) 1972–82
261 points for Scotland, 28 for British Isles; includes one penalty try and 12 points v Romania.
H. Porta (Argentina) has scored 359 points v IB countries, 1974-87.

Most points in an international
26 A. R. Hewson (NZ) v Australia 1982 Auckland
D. Camberabero scored 30 points v Zimbabwe in 1987 (World Cup).

Most tries in internationals
25 D. I. Campese (Australia) (34 appearances) 1982–7

Most tries in an international
5* D. Lambert (England) v France 1907 London (Richmond)
on international debut.

Most penalty goals in an international
6 D. B. Clarke (NZ) v B. Isles 1959 Dunedin
6 G. R. Bosch (SA) v France 1975 Pretoria
6 G. Evans (Wales) v France 1982 Cardiff
6 S. O. Campbell (Ireland) v Scotland 1982 Dublin
6* K. J. Crowley (NZ) v England 1985 Christchurch
6 C. R. Andrew (England) v Wales 1986 Twickenham
6* A. G. Hastings (Scotland) v France 1986 Murrayfield
6 M. P. Lynagh (Australia) v France 1986 Brisbane
on international debut.
H. Porta kicked 7 goals v France in 1974.

Most conversions in an international
8   J. Bancroft (Wales) v France
1910 Swansea
G. Fox (NZ) converted 10 v Fiji in 1987 (World Cup).

Most dropped goals in an international
3   P. Albaladejo (France) v Ireland 1960 Paris (Colombes)
3   P. F. Hawthorne (Australia) v England 1967 Twickenham
3   H. E. Botha (SA) v Ireland 1981 Durban
3   J.-P. Lescarboura (France) v England 1985 Twickenham
3   J.-P. Lescarboura (France) v NZ 1986 Auckland

Most points in an International Championship season
54   J.-P. Lescarboura (France) (4 appearances) 1983–4

Most tries in an International Championship season
8   C. N. Lowe (England) (4 appearances) 1913–4
8   I. S. Smith (Scotland) (4 appearances) 1924–5

Tries in each International Championship matches
H. C. Catcheside (England) 1923–4

A. C. Wallace (Scotland) 1924–5
P. Estève (France) 1982–3
P. Sella (France) 1985–6

Most penalty goals in an International Championship season
16   P. H. Thorburn (Wales) (4 appearances) 1985–6

Most conversions in an International Championship season
11   J. Bancroft (Wales) (4 appearances) 1908–9

Most dropped goals in an International Championship season
5   G. Camberabero (France) (3 appearances) 1966–7
J.-P. Lescarboura (France) dropped a goal in each championship match 1983–4, a unique feat.

Most points on an overseas tour
230   W. J. Wallace (NZ) (25 appearances) in B. Isles/France 1905–6

Most tries on an overseas tour
42   J. Hunter (NZ) (23 appearances) in B. Isles/France 1905–6

Most points in any tour match
43   R. M. Deans (NZ) v South Australia 1984 Adelaide

Most tries in any tour match
T. R. Heeps (NZ) v Northern NSW 1962
P. Estève scored 8 for France v Japan in 1984, but this was not against an IB nation.

PARTNERSHIP RECORDS
(including appearances for British Isles shown in brackets)

Centre threequarters
A. Boniface and G. Boniface (France) 18
Half-backs
P. Bennett and G. O. Edwards (Wales) 29(4)
J. Y. Rutherford and R. J. Laidlaw (Scotland) 36
Front row
R. Paparemborde, A. Paco and G. Cholley (France) 21
Second row
A. J. Martin and G. A. D. Wheel (Wales) 27
Back row
J. Matheu, J. Basquet and J. Prat (France) 22

MOST CAPPED PLAYERS (at end of 1987 World Cup)
(Matches against IB countries; GB denotes played for British Isles; figures in brackets are caps for home country; figures in *italic* are caps v non-IB countries)

C. M. H. Gibson (Ireland, GB) (69) 81
W. J. McBride (Ireland, GB) (63) 80
J. F. Slattery (Ireland, GB) (61) 65
G. Edwards (Wales, GB) (53) 63
J. P. R. Williams (Wales, GB) (55) 63
P. A. Orr (Ireland, GB) (58) 59
T. J. Kiernan (Ireland, GB) (54) 59
A. R. Irvine (Scotland, GB) (50) 59   *1*
C. Meads (New Zealand) 55
S. Blanco (France) 54   *18*
G. Price (Wales, GB) (41) 53
C. T. Deans (Scotland) 53
J. Kyle (Ireland, GB) (46) 52
R. Bertranne (France) 52   *17*
M. Keane (Ireland, GB) (51) 52
T. G. R. Davies (Wales, GB) (46) 51
J. McLauchlan (Scotland, GB) (43) 51
J. Renwick (Scotland, GB) (50) 51   *1*
B. Dauga (France) 50   *13*
A. B. Carmichael (Scotland) 50
N. Murphy (Ireland, GB) (41) 49
K. Kennedy (Ireland, GB) (45) 49
J. Pullin (England, GB) (42) 49
P. Wheeler (England, GB) (41) 48
A. J. Tomes (Scotland) 48

K. Jones (Wales, GB) (44) 47
J.-P. Rives (France) 47   *12*
H. McLeod (Scotland, GB) (40) 46
S. Millar (Ireland, GB) (37) 46
T. M. Davies (Wales, GB) (38) 46
W. P. Duggan (Ireland, GB) (41) 45
S. P. Poidevin (Australia) 45
A. F. McHarg (Scotland) 44
A. Neary (England, GB) (43) 44
P. Sella (France) 44
R. J. McLoughlin (Ireland, GB) (40) 43
M. Crauste (France) 43   *19*
W. Spanghero (France) 42   *9*
G. V. Stephenson (Ireland) 42
B. Meredith (Wales, GB) (34) 42
D. Bebb (Wales, GB) (34) 42
R. Paparemborde (France) 42   *9*
W. Mulcahy (Ireland, GB) (35) 41
N. Henderson (Ireland, GB) (40) 41
D. Williams (Wales, GB) (36) 41
J. Condom (France) 41
D. Rollo (Scotland) 40
J.-P. Lux (France) 40   *7*
I. R. McGeechan (Scotland, GB) (32) 40

200 OR MORE POINTS IN INTERNATIONALS
(Points for individual countries, excluding British Lions tests)

	PTS	TESTS	T	C	DG	PG
H. Porta (Argentina)	359					
A. R. Irvine[1] (Scotland)	273	51	10	25	—	61
M. P. Lynagh (Australia)	270	20	2	47	5	51
J.-P. Romeu (France)	262	34	4	27	9	55
P. E. McLean (Australia)	257	30	2	27	3	62
H. E. Botha (South Africa)	242	21	1	41	14	38
W. H. Hare (England)	240	25	2	14	1	67
S. O. Campbell (Ireland)	217	22	1	15	7	54
D. B. Clarke (New Zealand)	207	31	2	33	5*	38
A. R. Hewson (New Zealand)	201	19	4	22	4	43

*(Plus 2 goals from a mark)

[1]*Also scored 28 points in 9 tests for the Lions, giving him a world record 301 points in all internationals.*

12 OR MORE TRIES IN INTERNATIONALS
(Tries for individual countries, excluding British Lions tests)

	TRIES	TESTS		TRIES	TESTS
D. I. Campese (Australia)	25	34	K. Jones (Wales)	17	44
I. S. Smith (Scotland)	24	32	R. Bertranne (France)	17	69
C. Darrouy (France)	23	40	W. Llewellyn (Wales)	16	20
T. G. R. Davies (Wales)	20	46	I. A. Kirkpatrick (New Zealand)	16	39
G. O. Edwards (Wales)	20	53	G. V. Stephenson (Ireland)	15	42
S. S. Wilson (New Zealand)	19	34	D. M. Gerber (South Africa)	15	15
J. Dupuy (France)	19	57	G. Boniface (France)	14	35
S. Blanco (France)	19	54	A. Jaureguy (France)	14	42
P. Sella (France)	19	44	B. J. Moon (Australia)	13	31
C. N. Lowe (England)	18	25	J. Germishuys (South Africa)	12	20
R. Gibbs (Wales)	17	16	J.-F. Gourdon (France)	12	22
J. L. Williams (Wales)	17	17	J. J. Williams (Wales)	12	30

TEN OR MORE DROP GOALS IN INTERNATIONALS

	TESTS
H. E. Botha (South Africa)	14
J.-P. Lescarboura (France)	14
G. Camberabero (France)	12
P. Albaladejo (France)	12
H. Porta (Argentina)	12

FASTEST TO 100 POINTS IN INTERNATIONALS

	TESTS
M. P. Lynagh (Australia)	8
H. E. Botha (South Africa)	11
A. R. Hewson (New Zealand)	11
F. McCormick (New Zealand)	12
D. B. Clarke (New Zealand)	12

II: INTERNATIONAL CHAMPIONSHIP RESULTS TABLE

	1910		1911		1912		1913		1914		1920		1921		1922		1923		1924		1925		1926		1927		1928		1929	
	Pts	Psn	Pts	Psn	Pts	Psn	Pts	Psn	Pts	Psn	Pts	Psn	Pts	Psn	Pts	Psn	Pts	Psn	Pts	Psn	Pts	Psn	Pts	Psn	Pts	Psn	Pts	Psn	Pts	Psn
ENGLAND	7	1	4	3	6	1=	8	1	8	1	6	1=	8	1	5	2	8	1	8	1	5	2=	3	4	4	3	8	1	4	4
FRANCE	0	5	2	4	0	5	0	5	0	4=	2	4	4	2=	2	4=	2	3=	2	4=	0	5	0	5	2	4=	2	3=	0	5
IRELAND	3	4	6	2	6	1=	2	4	4	3	0	5	2	4=	2	4=	2	3=	4	2=	5	2=	6	1=	6	1=	6	2	5	2=
SCOTLAND	4	3	0	5	4	3=	4	3	0	4=	6	1=	2	4=	4	3	6	2	4	2=	8	1	6	1=	6	1=	2	3=	6	1
WALES	6	2	8	1	4	3=	6	2	6	2	6	1=	4	2=	7	1	2	3=	2	4=	2	4	5	3	2	4=	2	3=	5	2=

(Values shown as "Pts Psn". Grand Slam years shown in bold.)

	1930	1931	1932	1933	1934	1935	1936	1937	1938	1939	1940	1947	1948	1949	1950
ENGLAND	5 1	1 5										6 1=	1 5	4 2=	2 5
FRANCE	4 2=	4 2=										4 3=	4 2=	4 2=	3 3=
IRELAND	4 2=	4 2=										4 3=	**8 1**	6 1	3 3=
SCOTLAND	3 5	4 2=										0 5	4 2=	4 2=	4 2
WALES	4 2	7 1										6 1=	3 4	2 5	**8 1**

	1951	1952	1953	1954	1955	1956	1957	1958	1959	1960	1961	1962	1963	1964	1965
ENGLAND	2 4=	6 2	7 1	6 1=	3 4	4 2=	**8 1**	6 1	4 2=	7 1=	3 4	4 3=	7 1	3 3=	3 4
FRANCE	6 2	2 4	2 4	6 1=	6 1=	4 2=	0 5	4 3	5 1	7 1=	7 1	6 1	4 2=	3 3=	5 2=
IRELAND	7 1	4 3	5 3	2 4	1 5	4 2=	2 2=	2 5	4 2=	0 5	2 5	0 5	3 4	2 5	5 2=
SCOTLAND	2 4=	0 5	0 5	0 5	4 3	2 5	2 2=	3 4	3 5	2 4	4 2=	5 2	4 2=	6 1=	1 5
WALES	3 3	**8 1**	6 2	6 1=	6 1=	6 1	2 2=	5 2	4 2=	4 3	4 2=	4 3=	2 5	6 1=	6 1

	1966	1967	1968	1969	1970	1971	1972	1973	1974	1975	1976	1977	1978	1979	1980
ENGLAND	1 5	4 2=	4 3	4 3	2 4=	3 3=		4 1=	3 5	2 5	0 5	4 3	4 3	3 4	**8 1**
FRANCE	5 2=	6 1	**8 1**	1 5	6 1=	4 2		4 1=	4 2=	4 2=	6 2	**8 1**	6 2	5 2	2 4=
IRELAND	3 4	4 2=	5 2	6 2	4 3	3 3=		4 1=	5 1	4 2=	2 4	0 5	2 4	4 3	4 2=
SCOTLAND	5 2=	4 2=	0 5	2 4	2 4=	2 5		4 1=	4 2=	4 2=	4 3	2 4	0 5	2 5	2 4=
WALES	6 1	2 5	3 4	7 1	6 1=	**8 1**		4 1=	4 2=	6 1	**8 1**	6 2	**8 1**	6 1	4 2=

	1981	1982	1983	1984	1985	1986	1987
ENGLAND	4 2=	5 2=	1 5	2 4	3 4	4 3=	2 4=
FRANCE	**8 1**	2 4=	6 1=	6 2	6 2	6 1=	**8 1**
IRELAND	0 5	6 1	6 1=	0 5	7 1	0 5	4 2=
SCOTLAND	4 2=	5 2=	2 4	**8 1**	0 5	6 1=	4 2=
WALES	4 2=	2 4=	5 3	4 3	4 3	4 3=	2 4=

8 1 = Grand Slam years.

INTERNATIONAL CHAMPIONSHIP

TEAM RECORDS

Title wins
Wales 27
England 24
Scotland 16
Ireland 13
France 10

Highest points aggregate
102 Wales 1976

Lowest points aggregate
15 Ireland 1894 (4 nations)
25 England 1930 (5 nations)

Fewest points against
0 England 1892 (4 nations)
4 England 1913 (5 nations)

Most points against
67 Ireland 1983

Most tries scored
20 England 1914

Most tries against
9 England 1914

Highest number of points
325 1983 (10 matches)
176 1938 (6 matches)

Lowest number of points
93 1959 (10 matches)
46 1893 (6 matches)

Highest number of tries
55 1911 (10 matches)
35 1938 (6 matches)

Lowest number of tries
12 1959 (10 matches)
10 1939 (6 matches)

Longest winning run
10 England 1883–6
10 England 1922–5

Longest losing run
17   France 1911–20

Longest run without defeat
13   England 1922–5

Longest run without victory
17   France 1911–20

Most consecutive titles
4   France 1959–62

Longest run without title win
30   France 1910–59

Most consecutive wooden spoons
4   France 1924–7
4   Ireland 1920–3

INDIVIDUAL RECORDS

Most points
54   J.-P. Lescarboura (France) 1984
52   S. O. Campbell (Ireland) 1983
52   P. L. Thorburn (Wales) 1986
52   G. Hastings (Scotland) 1986
50   P. W. Dods (Scotland) 1984
47   M. J. Kiernan (Ireland) 1985
46   S. O. Campbell (Ireland) 1980 and 1982

44   W. H. Hare (England) 1984
44   G. Laporte (France) 1986
42   W. H. Hare (England) 1983
41   M. Rose (England) 1987
39   H. Davies (Wales) 1984
38   R. W. Hosen (England) 1967
38   P. Bennett (Wales) 1976
38   A. P. Ward (Ireland) 1978
38   S. P. Fenwick (Wales) 1979

III: BRITISH ISLES RECORDS

The records of touring sides representing the four Home Unions, 1910–86.

TEAM RECORDS

Highest score
Overall
31 v Australia (31–0) 1966 Brisbane
v individual countries
28 v S. Africa (28–9) 1974 Pretoria
17 v New Zealand (17–18) 1959 Dunedin
31 v Australia (31–0) 1966 Brisbane

Biggest winning points margin
Overall
31 v Australia (31–0) 1966 Brisbane
v individual countries
19 v S. Africa (28–9) 1974 Pretoria
10 v New Zealand (13–3) 1971 Wellington
31 v Australia (31–0) 1966 Brisbane

Highest score by opposing team
Overall
38 New Zealand (6–38) 1983 Auckland
v individual countries
34 S. Africa (14–34) 1962 Bloemfontein
38 New Zealand (6–38) 1983 Auckland
8 Australia (11–8) 1966 Sydney

Biggest losing points margin
Overall
32 v New Zealand (6–38) 1983 Auckland
v individual countries
20 v S. Africa (14–34) 1962 Bloemfontein

32 v New Zealand (6–38) 1983 Auckland
1 v Australia (5–6) 1930 Sydney

Most tries by B. Isles in an international
5 v Australia (24–3) 1950 Sydney
5 v S. Africa (23–22) 1955 Johannesburg
5 v Australia (24–3) 1959 Sydney
5 v Australia (31–0) 1966 Brisbane
5 v S. Africa (28–9) 1974 Pretoria

Most tries against B. Isles in an international
7 by South Africa (9–25) 1955 Cape Town

Most points on overseas tour (all matches)
842 in Australia, New Zealand and Canada (33 matches) 1959
Includes 582 points in 25 matches in New Zealand.

Most tries on overseas tour (all matches)
165 in Australia, New Zealand and Canada (33 matches) 1959
Includes 113 tries in 25 matches in New Zealand.

INDIVIDUAL RECORDS

Most capped player
Overall
W. J. McBride 17 1962–74
in individual positions
Full-back
J. P. R. Williams 8[1] 1971–4
Wing
A. J. F. O'Reilly 9[2] 1955–9
Centre
C. M. H. Gibson 8[3] 1966–71
Fly-half
P. Bennett 8 1974–7
Scrum-half
R. E. G. Jeeps 13 1955–62
Prop
G. Price 12 1977–83
Hooker
B. V. Meredith 8 1955–62
Lock
W. J. McBride 17 1962–74
Flanker
N. A. A. Murphy 8 1959–66
No 8
T. M. Davies 8[4] 1971–4

[1] *A. R. Irvine, 9 tests, played 7 times at full-back and twice as a wing.*
[2] *O'Reilly, 10 tests in all, played once as a centre.*
[3] *Gibson, 12 tests in all, played 4 times as a fly-half. I. R. McGeechan, 8 tests, played 7 times as a centre and once, as a replacement, on the wing.*
[4] *Both A. E. I. Pask and J. W. Telfer (8 tests each), played 4 times at No 8 and 4 tests at flanker.*

Most internationals as captain
6   A. R. Dawson 1959

Most points in internationals
44   P. Bennett (8 appearances) 1974–7

Most points in an international
18   A. J. P. Ward v S. Africa 1980
     Cape Town

Most tries in internationals
6   A. J. F. O'Reilly (10
    appearances) 1955–9

Most tries in an international
2   C. D. Aarvold v New Zealand
    1930 Christchurch
2   J. E. Nelson v Australia   1950
    Sydney
2   M. J. Price v Australia   1959
    Sydney
2   M. J. Price v New Zealand 1959
    Dunedin
2   D. K. Jones v Australia 1966
    Brisbane
2   T. G. R. Davies v New Zealand
    1971 Christchurch
2   J. J. Williams v S. Africa 1974
    Pretoria
2   J. J. Williams v S. Africa 1974
    Port Elizabeth

Most conversions in an international
5   S. Wilson v Australia 1966
    Brisbane

Most points for B. Isles on overseas tour – 188
B. John (17 appearances) 1971
   Australia/N. Zealand
Includes 180 points in 16 appearances in New Zealand.

Most tries for B. Isles on overseas tour
22*   A. J. F. O'Reilly (23
      appearances) 1959 Australia/N.
      Zealand/Canada
Includes 17 tries in 17 appearances in New Zealand.*
**Includes one penalty try.*

Most points for B. Isles in international series
35   T. J. Kiernan (4 appearances)
     1968 S. Africa

Most tries for B. Isles in international series
4   J. J. Williams (4 appearances)
    1974 S. Africa

Most points for B. Isles in any tour match
37   A. G. B. Old v South Western
     Districts 1974 Mossel Bay, SA

Most tries for B. Isles in any tour match
6   D. J. Duckham v West Coast-
    Buller 1971 Greymouth, NZ
6   J. J. Williams v South Western
    Districts 1974 Mossel Bay, SA
A. R. Irvine scored 5 tries from full-back v King Country-Wanganui 1977 Taumarunui, NZ.

BRITISH LIONS – TOUR RECORDS

TO NEW ZEALAND

	P	W	D	L	F	A
1888	19	13	4	2	82	33
1904	5	2	1	2	22	33
1908	17	9	1	7	184	153
1930	21	15	—	6	420	205
1950	23	17	1	5	420	162
1959	25	20	—	5	582	266
1966	25	15	2	8	300	281
1971	24	22	1	1	555	204
1977	25	20	1	4	586	295
1983	18	12	0	6	478	266
	202	145	11	46	3629	1898

TO AUSTRALIA

	P	W	D	L	F	A
1888	16	14	2	0	210	65
1899	21	18	0	3	333	90
1904	14	14	0	0	265	51
1908	9	7	0	2	139	48
1930	7	5	0	2	204	113
1950	6	5	0	1	150	52
1959	6	5	0	1	174	70
1966	8	7	1	0	202	48
1971	2	1	0	1	25	27
	89	76	3	10	1702	564

TO SOUTH AFRICA

	P	W	D	L	F	A
1891	19	19	—	—	224	1
1896	21	19	1	1	310	45
1903	22	11	3	8	231	138
1910	24	13	3	8	290	236
1924	21	9	3	9	175	155
1938	23	17	—	6	407	272
1955	24	18	1	5	418	271
1962	24	15	4	5	351	208
1968	20	15	1	4	377	181
1974	22	21	1	0	729	207
1980	18	15	0	3	401	244
	238	172	17	49	3913	1958

Total Tour Records

Tours	P	W	D	L	F	A
21	529	393	31	1051	9244	4234

Highest scores on tour
97 v S.W. Districts, South Africa 1974 (97–0)
71 v Western Australia 1930 (71–3)
70 v Eastern Canada 1959 (70–6)
69 v Griqualand West 1974 (69–16)
64 v Marlborough-Nelson-Golden Bay-Motueka, New
   Zealand 1959 (64–5)
60 v Western Australia 1966 (60–3)
60 v King Country-Wanganui, New Zealand 1977 (60–9)

100 points on tour

188	B. John 1971	112	D. Hewitt 1959
156	A. R. Irvine 1974	110	R. Hiller 1971
127	J. F. Byrne 1896	104	R. Hiller 1968
125	P. Bennett 1977	104	T. J. Davies 1959
125	S. O. Campbell 1983	103	P. Bennett 1974

Most tours
5   W. J. McBride (Ireland)
5   C. M. H. Gibson (Ireland)

OTHER MATCHES

1950	W v Ceylon	44–6	
1959	W v British Columbia	16–11	
	W v Eastern Canada	70–6	
1962	W v East Africa	50–0	
1966	L v British Columbia	3–8
	W v Canada	19–8
1977	L v Fiji	21–25

IV: BARBARIANS

Offshoots of the Barbarians are now in most major countries. South Africa, France, New Zealand and Australia all have their own Barbarians, adhering to the same style of play. In 1977 the Australia-New Zealand Barbarians celebrated 21 years of opposition.

31 January 1948, at Cardiff
Barbarians 9 (3T), Australia 6 (1PG, 1T)
BARBARIANS: R. F. Trott; M. F. Turner, B. L. Williams, W. B. Cleaver, C. B. Holmes; T. A. Kemp, H. Tanner (capt); H. Walker, K. D. Mullen, I. C. Henderson, J. Mycock, W. E. Tamplin, W. I. D. Elliot, S. V. Perry, M. R. Steele-Bodger.
Scorers – Tries: Steele-Bodger, Holmes, Tanner
AUSTRALIA: B. J. Piper; A. E. J. Tonkin, T. Allan (capt), M. J. Howell, J. W. T. MacBride; E. G. Broad, C. T. Burke; E. Tweedale, W. L. Dawson, N. Shehadie, P. A. Hardcastle, G. M. Cooke, D. H. Kellar, A. J. Buchan, C. J. Windon.
Scorers – Try: Tonkin
            Penalty goal: Tonkin
Referee: A. S. Bean

26 January 1952, at Cardiff
Barbarians 3 (1T), South Africa 17 (1G, 3PG, 1T)
BARBARIANS: G. Williams; J. E. Woodward, B. L. Williams, L. B. Cannell, K. J. Jones; C. I. Morgan, W. R. Willis; R. V. Stirling, D. M. Davies, J. McG. K. Kendall-Carpenter, E. R. John, J. E. Nelson (capt), V. G. Roberts, J. R. G. Stephens, W. I. D. Elliot.
Scorer – Try: Elliot
SOUTH AFRICA: A. C. Keevy; F. P. Marais, R. A. M. Van Schoor, M. T. Lategan, J. K. Ochse; P. G. Johnstone, P. A. du Toit; F. E. van der Ryst, W. Delport, H. J. Bekker, E. Dinklemann, J. M. du Rand, S. P. Fry, H. S. V. Muller (capt), C. J. van Wyk.
Scorers – Tries: Ochse, van Wyk
            Conversion: Keevy
            Penalty goals: Keevy (2), Johnstone
Referee: M. J. Dowling

20 February 1954, at Cardiff
Barbarians 5 (1G), New Zealand 19 (2G, 1DG, 2T)
BARBARIANS: I. King; K. J. Jones, J. Butterfield, W. P. C. Davies, G. M. Griffiths; C. I. Morgan, W. R. Willis (capt); C. R. Jacobs, E. Evans, J. H. Smith, R. C. Hawkes, J. R. G. Stephens, R. C. C. Thomas, S. Judd, D. F. White.
Scorers – Try: Griffiths
            Conversions: King
NEW ZEALAND: R. W. H. Scott; M. J. Dixon, J. T. Fitzgerald, R. A. Jarden, B. B. J. Fitzpatrick, R. G. Bowers, K. Davis; K. L. Skinner, R. C. Hemi, H. L. White, D. O. Oliver, R. A. White, G. N. Dalzell,

R. C. Stuart (capt), W. A. McCaw.
Scorers – Tries: Davis, Dixon, White, Jarden
            Conversions: Jarden (2)
            Dropped goal: Scott
Referee: I. David

22 February 1958, at Cardiff
Barbarians 11 (1G, 2T), Australia 6 (2T)
BARBARIANS: R. W. T. Chisholm; A. R. Smith, G. T. Wells, M. S. Phillips, A. J. F. O'Reilly; C. I. Morgan (capt), A. A. Mulligan; N. Shehadie, A. R. Dawson, C. R. Jacobs, R. W. D. Marques, W. R. Evans, P. G. D. Robbins, J. Faull, A. Robson.
Scorers – Tries: Evans, Phillips, Dawson
            Conversion: Faull
AUSTRALIA: T. G. Curley; A. R. Morton, R. Phelps, J. K. Lenehan, K. J. Donald; R. M. Harvey, D. M. Connor; R. A. L. Davidson (capt), R. Meadows, G. N. Vaughan, D. M. Emanuel, A. R. Miller, J. E. Thornett, N. M. Hughes, W. J. Gunter.
Scorers – Tries: Emanuel, Donald
Referee: G. A. Walker
N.B. Australian prop forward Nick Shehadie who played for Australia v Barbarians in 1948 becomes the first player to appear both for and against the Barbarians in this fixture.

4 February 1961, at Cardiff
Barbarians 6 (2T), South Africa 0
BARBARIANS: H. J. Mainwaring; A. J. F. O'Reilly, H. M. Roberts, B. J. Jones, J. R. C. Young; R. A. W. Sharp, W. R. Watkins; B. G. M. Wood, A. R. Dawson (capt), S. Millar, W. R. E. Evans, B. Price, M. G. Culliton, W. G. D. Morgan, H. J. Morgan.
Scorers – Tries: W. G. D. Morgan, H. J. Morgan
SOUTH AFRICA: L. G. Wilson; B. P. van Zyl, J. P. Engelbrecht, J. L. Gainsford, M. J. G. Antelme; D. A. Stewart, P. de W. Uys; S. P. Kuhn, G. F. Malan, J. L. Myburgh, G. H. van Zyl, A. S. Malan (capt), P. J. van Zyl, H. J. M. Pelser, D. J. Hopwood.
Referee: M. F. Turner

15 February 1964, at Cardiff
Barbarians 3 (1DG), New Zealand 36 (6G, 2T)
BARBARIANS: S. Wilson; S. J. Watkins, M. S. Phillips, M. K. Flynn, C. P. Simpson; R. A. W. Sharpe, S. J. S. Clarke; L. J. Cunningham, A. R. Dawson (capt), I. J. Clarke, E. Jones, B. Price, M. G. Culliton, A. E. I. Pask, D. P. Rogers.
Scorers – Dropped goal: I. J. Clarke
NEW ZEALAND: D. B. Clarke; M. J. Dick, P. F. Little, D. A. Arnold, R. W. Caulton; B. A. Watt, C. R. Laidlaw; W. J. Whineray (capt), D. Young, K. F. Gray, A. J. Stewart, C. E. Meads, D. J. Graham, K. R. Tremain, W. J. Nathan.

Scorers – Tries: Nathan (2), Tremain, Meads, Graham, Dick, Caulton, Whineray
Conversions: Clarke (6)

Referee: D. G. Walters

N.B. Ian Clarke follows Nick Shehadie (1958) as a touring player to play for the Barbarians against his own side. Ian and Don, the All-Blacks full-back, are brothers.

28 January 1967, at Cardiff

Barbarians 11 (1G, 1PG, 1PT), Australia 17 (1G, 4T)

BARBARIANS: S. Wilson; S. J. Watkins, T. G. R. Davies, F. P. K. Bresnihan, P. B. Glover; D. Watkins, R. M. Young; N. Suddon, K. W. Kennedy, A. B. Carmichael, B. Price, W. J. McBride, N. A. Murphy (capt), J. W. Telfer, J. P. Fisher.

Scorers – Tries: Kennedy, Penalty try
Conversion: Wilson
Penalty goal: Wilson

AUSTRALIA: J. K. Lenehan; E. S. Boyce, R. J. Marks, J. E. Brass, R. Webb; P. F. Hawthorne, K. W. Catchpole; J. E. Thornett (capt), P. G. Johnson, A. R. Miller, R. G. Teitzel, M. Purcell, G. V. Davis, J. F. O'Gorman, J. Guerassimoff.

Scorers – Tries: Boyce (2), Hawthorne, O'Gorman, Webb
Conversion: Lenehan

Referee: R. W. Gilliland

16 December 1967, at Twickenham

Barbarians 6 (1DG, 1T), New Zealand 11 (1G, 1DG, 1T)

BARBARIANS: S. Wilson (capt); W. K. Jones, R. H. Lloyd, T. G. R. Davies, R. E. Webb; B. John, G. O. Edwards; C. H. Norris, F. A. Laidlaw, A. L. Horton, M. Wiltshire, P. J. Larter, D. Grant, G. A. Sherriff, R. B. Taylor.

Scorers – Try: Lloyd
Dropped goal: Wilson

NEW ZEALAND: W. F. McCormick; M. J. Dick, W. L. Davis, I. R. Macrae, A. G. Steel; E. W. Kirton, C. R. Laidlaw; B. L. Muller, B. E. McLeod, K. F. Gray, S. C. Strahan, C. E. Meads, K. R. Tremain, B. J. Lochore (capt), W. J. Nathan.

Scorers – Tries: Steel, Macrae
Conversion: McCormick
Dropped goal: Kirton

Referee: M. Joseph

31 January 1970, at Twickenham

Barbarians 12 (4T), South Africa 21 (3G, 1PG, 1DG)

BARBARIANS: J. P. R. Williams; A. T. A. Duggan, J. S. Spencer, C. M. H. Gibson, D. J. Duckham; B. John, G. O. Edwards (capt); K. E. Fairbrother, F. A. L. Laidlaw, D. B. Llewellyn, A. M. Davis, I. S. Gallacher, J. J. Jeffrey, R. J. Arneil, T. M. Davies.

Scorers – Tries: Arneil, Duckham, Duggan, Fairbrother

SOUTH AFRICA: H. O. de Villiers; S. H. Nomis, O. A. Roux, J. P. van der Merwe, A. E. van der Watt; M. J. Lawless, D. J. de Villiers (capt); J. F. K. Marais, C. H. Cockrell, J. L. Myburgh, F. C. H. du Preez, I. J. de Klerk, P. J. F. Greyling, J. H. Ellis, M. W. Jennings.

Scorers – Tries: Ellis (2), van der Watt
Conversions: D. J. de Villiers (3)
Dropped goal: Lawless
Penalty goal: D. J. de Villiers

Referee: G. C. Lamb

27 January 1973, at Cardiff

Barbarians 23 (2G, 1PG, 2T), New Zealand 11 (1PG, 2T)

BARBARIANS: J. P. R. Williams; D. J. Duckham, S. J. Dawes (capt), C. M. H. Gibson, J. C. Bevan; P. Bennett, G. O. Edwards; R. J. McLoughlin, J. V. Pullin, A. B. Carmichael, W. J. McBride, R. M. Wilkinson, T. P. David, J. F. Slattery, D. L. Quinnell.

Scorers – Tries: Edwards, Slattery, Bevan, Williams
Conversions: Bennett (2)
Penalty goal: Bennett

NEW ZEALAND: J. F. Karam; B. G. Williams, B. J. Robertson, I. A. Hurst, G. B. Batty; R. E. Burgess, S. M. Going; G. J. Whiting, R. A. Urlich, K. K. Lambert, H. H. MacDonald, P. J. Whiting, A. I. Scown, A. J. Wyllie, I. A. Kirkpatrick (capt).
Replacement: G. L. Colling (for Going after 60 mins)

Scorers – Tries: Batty (2)
Penalty goal: Karam

Referee: G. Domercq

30 November 1974, at Twickenham

Barbarians 13 (3PG, 1T), New Zealand 13 (1G, 1PG, 1T)

BARBARIANS: A. R. Irvine; T. G. R. Davies, P. J. Warfield, P. S. Preece, D. J. Duckham; J. D. Bevan, G. O. Edwards; J. McLauchlan, R. W. Windsor, F. E. Cotton, W. J. McBride (capt), G. L. Brown, R. M. Uttley, J. F. Slattery, T. M. Davies.

Scorers – Try: T. M. Davies
Penalty goals: Irvine (3)

NEW ZEALAND: J. F. Karam; B. G. Williams, B. J. Robertson, I. A. Hurst, G. B. Batty; D. J. Robertson, S. M. Going; K. K. Lambert, R. W. Norton, K. J. Tanner, P. J. Whiting, H. H. MacDonald, I. A. Kirkpatrick, K. W. Stewart, A. R. Leslie (capt).

Scorers – Tries: Leslie, Williams
Conversion: Karam
Penalty goal: Karam

Referee: G. Domercq

24 January 1976, at Cardiff

Barbarians 19 (2G, 1PG, 1T), Australia 7 (1PG, 1T)

BARBARIANS: A. R. Irvine; T. G. R. Davies, R. W. R. Gravell, C. M. H. Gibson, J. J. Williams; P. Bennett, G. O. Edwards; F. M. D. Knill, P. J. Wheeler, A. B. Carmichael, G. L. Brown, A. J. Martin, J. F. Slattery, T. P. Evans, T. M. Davies (capt).

Scorers – Tries: Bennett, Wheeler, J. J. Williams
Conversions: Bennett (2)
Penalty goal: Bennett

AUSTRALIA: J. C. Hindmarsh; J. R. Ryan, R. D. L'Estrange, G. A. Shaw (capt), L. E. Monaghan; L. J. Weatherstone, R. G. Hauser; J. E. C. Meadows, C. M. Carberry, R. Graham, G. Fay, R. A. Smith, G. K. Pearse, A. A. Shaw, M. E. Loane.
Replacements: W. A. McKid (for Monaghan), D. W. Hillhouse (for Loane)

Scorers – Try: Ryan
Penalty goal: Hindmarsh

Referee: G. Domercq

16 December 1978, at Cardiff

Barbarians 16 (1G, 2PG, 1T), New Zealand 18 (1PG, 1DG, 3T)

BARBARIANS: A. R. Irvine; H. E. Rees, R. N. Hutchings, J. M. Renwick, M. A. C. Slemen; P. Bennett, D. B. Williams; W. Dickinson, P. J. Wheeler, P. A. Orr, W. B. Beaumont, A. J. Martin, J.-P. Rives, J.-C. Skréla, D. L. Quinnell (capt).
Replacement: B. G. Nelmes (for Orr after 7 mins)
Scorers – Tries: Slemen (2)
               Conversion: Bennett
               Penalty goals: Bennett (2)
NEW ZEALAND: B. J. McKechnie; B. G. Williams, B. J. Robertson, W. M. Osborne, S. S. Wilson; E. J. Dunn, D. S. Loveridge; G. A. Knight, A. M. Dalton, B. R. Johnstone, A. M. Haden, F. J. Oliver, L. M. Rutledge, G. N. K. Mourie (capt), J. K. Fleming.
Replacement: J. C. Ashworth (for Johnstone after 40 mins)
Scorers – Tries: Johnstone, Rutledge, Williams
               Penalty goal: Rutledge
               Dropped goal: Dunn
Referee: N. R. Sanson

9 January 1982, at Cardiff
Barbarians v Australia
Match abandoned owing to heavy snow.

15 December 1984, at Cardiff
Barbarians 30 (2G, 2PG, 3T), Australia 37 (5G, 1PG, 1T)
BARBARIANS: S. Blanco; S. T. Smith, B. Mullin, R. A. Ackerman, R. Underwood; W. G. Davies (capt), J. Gallion; P. A. Orr, M. J. Watkins, I. G. Milne, R. L. Norster, D. G. Lenihan, S. McGaughey, G. Rees, W. Anderson.
Scorers – Tries: Milne, Smith, Underwood, Gallion, Blanco
               Conversions: Davies (2)
               Penalty goals: Davies (2)
AUSTRALIA: R. G. Gould; M. J. Hawker, A. G. Slack (capt), M. P. Lynagh, D. I. Campese; M. G. Ella, P. A. Cox; S. Pilecki, T. A. Lawton, A. J. McIntyre, S. A. G. Cutler, S. A. Williams, S. P. Poidevin, R. J. Reynolds, C. Roche.
Scorers – Tries: Poidevin (2), Williams, Hawker, Gould, Slack
               Conversions: Lynagh (5)
               Penalty goal: Lynagh
Referee: R. Hourquet
N.B. G. O. Edwards has appeared in a record 5 games between Barbarians and the tourists. B. G. Williams and B. J. Robertson (both New Zealand) have appeared in 3 games for the tourists against the Barbarians.

9 RUGBY ACHIEVEMENTS, OLYMPICS AND OTHER ODDITIES

RECORD SCORE

An amazing series of results punctuated the French third division in October 1984, featuring the small Dordogne town of Vergt (pop. 1500), who play in Group 9 of the French third division. The club fell foul of the French Federation, who banned four of their players for various misdemeanours. Vergt felt hard done by. The first fixture after the ban was against Lormont, and they arrived with just 11 players, the minimum number necessary for a game to take place.

Vergt kicked off, then stood still as Lormont ran through to score. Vergt kicked off again. The same happened. After ten minutes the score was 42–0, and the referee, who had seen enough, abandoned the game.

The following week the same happened again, except the game was played to a conclusion. Final score: Gujan Mestras 236, Vergt 0. New world record? Yet the glory of Gujan Mestras lasted just one week. Though Vergt were now a feared complement of 14, their differences with the FFR were still unresolved. The 'dummies of Vergt' proceeded to excel themselves against Lavardac. Final score here: Vergt 0, Lavardac 350 – 40 goals, 26 tries and two drop goals.

The games were regarded as official. The French third division is well structured, competitive, and totally bona fide. So should the record stand?

TWO RUGBY DYNASTIES

THE McLEANS

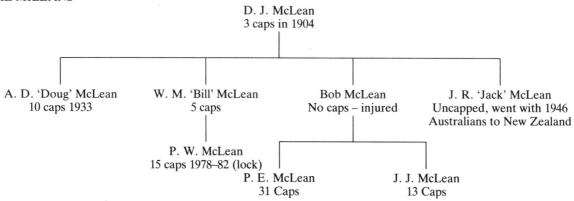

D. J. McLean
3 caps in 1904

A. D. 'Doug' McLean
10 caps 1933

W. M. 'Bill' McLean
5 caps

Bob McLean
No caps – injured

J. R. 'Jack' McLean
Uncapped, went with 1946
Australians to New Zealand

P. W. McLean
15 caps 1978–82 (lock)

P. E. McLean
31 Caps

J. J. McLean
13 Caps

R. A. McLean no relation.

*Paul McLean, youngest of the famous family, and
Australia's leading points scorer in internationals from
1980–7.*

THE MORKELS
Farmers from Somerset West, 40 miles from Cape Town.
Ten members of the family represented South Africa
1903-28.

The First: A. O. Morkel: Andrew Morkel, then studying
in Johannesburg, played against the 1903 British tourists.

A. O. Morkel, W. S. Morkel, D. F. T. Morkel: were on
Paul Roos' first Springbok tour to Britain. W. S. and
D. F. T. were brothers. W. S. gained four caps on that
tour, while D. F. T. 'Dougie' played nine times, 1906–13.

W. H. Morkel: was on the scene in 1910. In 1912 W. H.
'Boy', D. F. T. 'Dougie' and brothers J. W. H. 'Jackie'
and P. G. 'Gerhard' were on tour to Britain.

Five Morkels were on the 1921 tour to New Zealand:
H. J. 'Henry' and H. W. 'Harry' and J. A. 'Royal'
played in the tests.

The Last: P. K. Morkel v New Zealand 1928.

AUSTRALIAN FAMILIES
Dave Cowper, who won nine rugby caps for Australia
between 1931 and 1933 against the British Lions and
New Zealand, is the father of Bob Cowper, 27 cricket
tests for Australia, highest score 307 against England at
Melbourne in 1965–6. Test average 46.51.

Brothers Mitchell Cox (2 caps 1981–2) and Philip Cox
(16 caps 1979–84) followed father Brian Cox (8 caps
1952–7) into the Australian team.

GOOD START
Pieter Albertyn of Stellenbosch scored six tries in the
first 15 minutes of a game against Villagers in 1919.

BROTHERS IN ARMS
The only case of three brothers playing together in the
same international is when Freddie, Dick and John Luyt
– F. P., R. R., and J. D. – were all in the Springbok
teams which played Scotland, Wales and England on the
1912-13 tour. The Ellas were internationals at the same
time but never played all together in an international.

The only twins to play in the same international team
were Stewart and Jim Boyce, Australian wings against
New Zealand at Dunedin in 1964.

OLYMPIC RUGBY
Introduced by Baron Pierre de Coubertin (who refereed
the first ever French championship final), rugby was on
the Olympic programme at Paris in 1900, at London in
1908, Antwerp in 1920, and Paris again in 1924. In 1928
the International Olympic Committee turned down the
request to stage rugby at the Amsterdam Games. Three
factors were believed to be behind this: the IOC wanted
more emphasis on individual sports; women's athletics
had swollen the number of competitors; and the sport did
not receive the backing that it should have from the
British entries. Both the Soviet Union in 1980 and South
Korea in 1988 made attempts to have rugby readmitted,
and it should be pointed out that South Korea came
desperately close to achieving their aim.

THE RESULTS
1900 Paris
Three teams entered – France, Germany and Britain.

France won the gold, winning 27–17 against Germany, who were awarded the silver medal. Britain lost 27–8 to France in the only other match, and were awarded the bronze.

1908 London
Two teams entered – Britain, the hosts, and Australia. Just one match was played, a straight final, won by Australia 32–3.

1912 Stockholm
Not held

1920 Antwerp
Two teams entered – USA and France. The USA caused a shock by winning the only match 8–0 to take the gold medal.

1924 Paris
Three teams entered – France, USA and Romania. Each country played two games. Both France and USA beat Romania, who were awarded the bronze medal. France won 59–3, scoring 13 tries including four by the fine Stade Francais winger Adolphe Jaureguy. The USA then defeated Romania 39–0. The final was played at the Colombes Stadium, Paris on 18 May 1924 and the USA took the gold with a 17–3 victory before 30 000. The Americans, from Stanford University, scored five tries (Farrish (2), Patrick, Rogers and Manelli), with a conversion from Doe. Gallau scored the lone French try. The match finished in uproar, when Gideon Nelson, one of the reserves, was flattened by a walking stick. The American anthem was jeered, and rugby ceased at the Olympics.

Dual gold medallists
Daniel Carroll was a member of the Australian gold medal team in 1908, and won another gold for the USA in 1920.

Morris Kirksey, gold medallist in the sprint relay and silver medallist in the 100 metres on the track in 1920, was a member of the gold medal rugby team in 1920. Kirksey failed by 18 inches (46cm) to beat Charlie Paddock for the sprint gold.

TRY-SCORING FULL-BACKS

Two tries in an international*
J. P. R. Williams (Wales) v England, Twickenham 1976
A. R. Irvine (Scotland) v France, Murrayfield 1980
A. Hewson (New Zealand) v Scotland, Auckland 1981
R. Gould (Australia) v Scotland, Sydney 1982
S. Blanco (France) v Scotland, Paris 1985
S. Blanco (France) v Australia, Sydney 1986
J. Gallagher (New Zealand) scored 4 tries v Fiji 1987 (World Cup).

Most tries from full-back in internationals
13 S. Blanco (France)
10 A. R. Irvine (Scotland)
 7 D. I. Campese (Australia)
 6 J. P. R. Williams (Wales)
IB opposition only

PLAY STOPPED WAR
On 29 April 1902, a ceasefire was concluded between midday and sunset to enable the forces of Her Majesty and Paul Kruger to stage a rugby match. The Boer War, which had begun in 1899 between the Afrikaaners and Britain, finished a few months later. Sadly no details are available about the match.

YOU CAN'T TRUST THE POST
Roan Antelope's uprights on their ground at Luyansha, Zambia are 33.54 metres high (110ft ½in) and are the tallest in the world. Malcolm Phillips, the Malawi centre, had three penalty attempts and on each occasion the ball struck the same right-hand upright and stayed out! Happily for him, Malawi won 11–6.

KEEPING UP WITH THE JONESES
Mark Jones of Neath, capped by Wales in the 1987 Five Nations Championship against Scotland at Murrayfield, became the 54th with the surname Jones to wear the red jersey. Davies is second with 50, followed by Evans and Williams, each with 40.

Ivan Tukalo (Scotland) and Ivan Guerassimoff (Australia) are two internationals who are of Russian extraction.

Prince Alexander Obolensky was a Russian citizen at the time of his four caps for England in 1936.

RUGBY AND CRICKET INTERNATIONALS
A list of double internationals, now a rare breed.

Hornby was the first to captain England at both sports, followed by Stoddart. Castens was the first to captain South Africa at both sports.

Eric Tindall was not only a double international but enjoyed the unique distinction of refereeing international rugby and umpiring test cricket.

The most recent case worth mentioning is that of Brian McKechnie, the New Zealander who kicked the winning penalty against Wales in 1978, and who was the recipient of Trevor Chappell's notorious underarm delivery. McKechnie played eight rugby internationals, and several one-day cricket internationals, but never played test cricket.

	Rugby Caps	Cricket Test Matches
A. N. Hornby (E)	9	3
G. F. Vernon (E)	5	1
A. E. Stoddart (E)	11	16
W. H. Milton	2 (E)	3 (SA)
S. M. J. Woods	13 (E)	3 (E), 3 (A)
G. McGregor	13 (S)	8 (E)
H. H. Castens (SA)	1	N/A
A. R. Richards (SA)	1	1
F. Mitchell	6 (E)	2 (E), 3 (SA)
A. W. Powell (SA)	3	1
J. H. Anderson (SA)	3	1
P. S. T. Jones (SA)	3	1
J. H. Sinclair (SA)	1	25
R. H. Spooner (E)	1	10
R. O. Schwarz	3 (E)	20 (SA)
R. H. M. Hands	2 (E)	1 (SA)
G. R. Dickeson (NZ)	5	3
C. J. Oliver (NZ)	7	N/A
O. E. Nothling (A)	10	1

M. L. Page (NZ)	1	14
M. J. Turnbull	2 (W)	9 (E)
H. G. Owen-Smith	10 (E)	5 (SA)
E. W. T. Tindall (NZ)	5	1
W. N. Carson (NZ)	3	3
T. A. Harris (SA)	5	3
M. P. Donnelly	1 (E)	7 (NZ)
C. B. Van Ryneveld	4 (E)	19 (SA)
M. J. K. Smith (E)	1	50

N/A – number of caps not available though sources in that country confirm the player as a double international.

RUGBY AND ATHLETICS

Eric Liddell of *Chariots of Fire* fame is one of only two Olympic gold medallists in athletics events to be a rugby international. He won seven caps for Scotland and won the 400 metres gold medal at the 1924 Paris Olympics. (See Morris Kirksey in Olympic Rugby for the other instance.) Others to have won Olympic medals:

K. J. Jones (Wales) 44 caps – silver medal, 4 × 100 relay for Great Britain, 1948.
J. A. Gregory (England) one cap (1949), ran in the same relay as Jones.
Georges Andre (France) 7 caps, (1913–4) silver medal, High Jump, 1908. He competed in four Olympics.

Other notable achievements have been D. J. Whyte (Scotland) 13 caps (1965–7), 1959 AAA Long Jump champion . . . J. R. C. Young (England) nine caps (1958–61), AAA sprint champion . . . Pierre Faillot (France) eight caps, French 100, 200, 400 and 400 metres hurdles champion – he won the titles all on the same day!

RUGBY AND OTHER SPORTS

The 1908 Olympic middleweight final is one for the books. The gold medallist J. W. H. T. Douglas went on to captain England at cricket while the loser, somewhat controversially on points, was the Australian R. L. 'Snowy' Baker, who went on to win two rugby caps for Australia.

Arturo Rodrigues Jurado, the 1928 Olympic heavyweight boxing champion, played rugby for CA San Isidro, the champions, and for Argentina.

Tom Heeney, lock-forward for Hawke's Bay and Poverty Bay against South Africa in 1921, lost to Gene Tunney (USA) in a 1929 world heavyweight title bout.

John Freedman (four caps for Australia) crewed in the America's Cup for Australia on three occasions – in *Gretel 1* and *Gretel 2* and *Dame Pattie*. John Marques, Harlequins and England (23 caps), crewed for the British yacht *Sceptre* in the 1964 America's Cup challenge. Ron Jarden, New Zealand wing, crewed in the 1975 Admiral's Cup.

Alan Walker, the Australian centre (five caps), scored a memorable try for his country at Twickenham from the halfway line. As a cricketer he took four wickets in four balls for Notts against Leicestershire, and went with the Australians on tour to South Africa but did not play in a test.

NICKNAMES

WALLABIES

The first Australian tourists to Britain had a mascot, not a wallaby but a serpent called Bertie. Asked to find a name for their team, the players came up with two suggestions, Wallabies and Wolves. Voting in favour of the Wallabies was close.

SPRINGBOKS

South Africa had worn the green and gold since 1903. Three years later they undertook their first tour to Britain, a year after New Zealand's visit during which they had been nicknamed the 'All Blacks'. Tour manager J. C. Carden, the captain Paul Roos and vice-captain Paddy Caroline were brought together by the London press before the first training session, and asked to provide a nickname. Roos replied that the unanimous decision be *Der Springbokken*.

PUMAS

The crest on the Union Argentina de Rugby clearly depicts a jaguar. Yet on the 1965 tour to South Africa, the Argentinians stopped off in Salisbury to play Rhodesia. Local journalists and those from South Africa – strangely for a continent so full of wild life – mistook the jaguar for a puma. The nickname stuck, and to add salt to the wounds, Rhodesia won 17–12.

ALL BLACKS

The term was first used on the 1905–6 tour to Great Britain. The *Daily Mail* used the term 'Blacks' before the match with Northampton on 28 September, while the phrase 'All Blacks' appeared in the paper's columns following the 63–0 win against Hartlepool Clubs on 11 October. Ironically the 63–0 win remains the largest score by New Zealand on a tour of the British Isles.

COLOURS

SOUTH AFRICA

Barry Heatlie, South Africa's captain in their first international victory (5–0) against the British team in 1896, on that occasion brought the green shirts of the Diocesan Old Boys Club.

On 12 September 1903, for the third international against the next British team, Heatlie was recalled to the team, and again made captain. By this time the Diocesan Old Boys Club had ceased to exist, but the outfitters still had supplies of the club kit. So South Africa took the field in green shirts, white collars, black shorts and red socks borrowed from the Villagers club.

On 12 September 1906, three years to the day later, the South African Board settled on the colours – the green shirts had been worn for the country's first two major victories. In 1937 the shorts were changed to white, the collars became old gold, and the socks green.

AUSTRALIA

Australia's colours of gold shirts and green shorts were first used on the 1961 tour to South Africa, to avoid a clash with South Africa's more established green shirts with gold collars.

NEW ZEALAND

The first New Zealand team wore a dark blue jersey with a gold fern, when they went on tour to New South Wales in 1884. The New Zealand Rugby Union was formed in

1892, and for the first match under their jurisdiction, against New South Wales in 1894, the team was kitted out with a black jersey, white fern and white shorts by the Union. When New South Wales again visited New Zealand in 1901 photos of the match show the team wearing black shorts.

THE WORLD'S LARGEST CLUB

The world's largest rugby club is the Harlequin Football Club. Founded in 1866, the club has provided over 150 England players, 14 England captains and 10 RFU presidents.

In addition to the club which uses the RFU ground at Twickenham and the Adrian Stoop Memorial Ground in London, the following Harlequin clubs are affiliated throughout the world: Dallas Harlequins (USA), Pretoria Harlequins (South Africa), Tasmania Harlequins (Hobart, Australia), Harlequin club of Australia (Melbourne), Kenya Harlequins (Nairobi), and Harlequin club of New Zealand (Hamilton North).

Dallas Harlequins and Kenya Harlequins have both won their national club championship. Pretoria Harlequins have reached the final of the South African club championship, while the other three clubs have won their various provincial state competitions. The parent club in London has yet to reach the John Player Cup final (as of 1987) but has won the prestigious Middlesex Sevens on a record nine occasions.

REVOLUTIONARY WRITER

Che Guevara, the revolutionary killed in Bolivia by the army in 1967, had a passion for rugby. In 1950, his architect father started a rugby magazine called *Tackle* with Che's brother Roberto, some players from San Isidro, and the French correspondent in Argentina, Hugo de Condoleo. The weekly paper lasted for about three and a half months before folding. Che Guevara, under the pen name Chang-Cho, wrote a column in the magazine.

THE TALLEST, SHORTEST, HEAVIEST, LIGHTEST, OLDEST AND YOUNGEST INTERNATIONALS

Most appearances can be misleading, especially if the players want them to be! Here is a selection, drawn from the 'official' lists of extremes among International Board players.

Heaviest

Player	Country	lbs
P. R. Van der Merwe	South Africa	292
B. L. Muller	New Zealand	252
A. Estève	France	248

Lightest

Player	Country	lbs
G. McGhie	Australia	128
W. D. Sendin	South Africa	132
J. Gachassin	France	133
P. Reid	New Zealand	134

Tallest

Player	Country	ft in
P. K. Stagg	Scotland	6 10
A. Estève	France	6 9½

Alain Estève, the mountainous French lock forward, chooses two smaller New Zealanders including Sid Going (third left) as he makes his way towards the line during the 1973 France v New Zealand international. France won a famous victory 13–6.

S. A. G. Cutler	Australia	6 8
A. M. Haden	New Zealand	6 7
H. J. Bekker	South Africa	6 7

Shortest

Player	Country	ft in
G. McGhie	Australia	5 2
J. Gachassin	France	5 3
P. Tetzlaff, P. Reid	New Zealand	5 3
T. A. Gentles	South Africa	5 3

Oldest

Player	Country	Age
E. Hughes	New Zealand	40y 123d
L. E. Saxby	England	40y
A. R. Miller	Australia	38y 4m
J. McLauchlan	Scotland	37y 6m
J. A. Nel	South Africa	36y 1m

Youngest

Player	Country	Age
N. J. Finlay	Scotland	17y 36d
B. Ford	Australia	18y 3m
J. A. Loubser	South Africa	19y 1m
E. Wrigley	New Zealand	19y 79d

Left *Danie Craven, South African player, coach and administrator, played for his country in four different positions in four successive internationals – scrum-half, fly-half, centre and No 8.*

Centre *Ninian Finlay – is he or isn't he Scotland's youngest international?*

Right *Rugby – now a healthy mixture of World Cups, internationals, representative and club fixtures – still prides itself as one of the more light-hearted sports. A Groucho Marx/Erika Roe lookalike displays his credentials before the 1982 Wales v France match.*

A different shape of things to come? Women's rugby is now played seriously in some 20 countries, but this match at Richmond between the Actresses and Models seems to have captured public imagination.

10 THE OTHER RUGBY NATIONS

Federation Internationale de Rugby Amateur

FIRA (the Federation Internationale de Rugby Amateur) was formed in 1934. Its foundation owes much to the decision to ban France from the Five Nations Championship in 1931. Anxious to maintain international standards, France sought fixtures with neighbouring European countries. In 1934 FIRA was launched at a meeting in Hannover, West Germany, with representatives from France, Italy, Spain, Catalonia, Holland, Belgium, Portugal and Romania.

FIRA now enjoys a standing second only to the RFU. It also shows just how remarkable a contribution that France, who oversee FIRA from their Paris offices, has made to international rugby, not always appreciated by those who frown on inventiveness.

The applications to join FIRA flood in. Argentina joined from 1987, while Canada and the USA have expressed interest. FIRA could soon contain a solid phalanx of countries just below International Board recognition. And in this section of teams involved in the FIRA competetion there is a focus on the Soviet Union, a possible rugby force for the next World Cup?

Spain is another European country searching for an improved international fixture list to complement the growing interest in the game. Here they are seen playing England Under-23 at Twickenham in 1986.

FIRA Championship 1954–87

	1954	1966	1967	1968	1969	1970	1971	1972	1973	1974	1975	1976	1977	1978	1979	1980	1981	1982	1983	1984	1985	1986/7
France	1	1	1	1	2	1	1	1	1	1	2	1	2	1	1	1	2	1	4	1	1	1
Italy	2	3	2			3	4				3	2	3	5	4	3	4	2	2	3	3	4
Spain	3										5	4	3	6								
Romania		2	3	2	1	2	2	2	2	2	1	3	1	2	2	2	1	3	1	2	4	3
Czechoslovakia		4		3	3	4		4			5			6								
Belgium				4																		
Poland					4					4		4	5	4	5	5	5			6		
Morocco							3	3	4	5			6			6			5	5		
Spain								3	3	4							6				5	
W. Germany													6					4	6			
USSR															3	4	3	5	3	4	2	2
Tunisia																					6	5
Portugal																						6

FIRA MEMBERSHIP 1987

	Foundation	No of clubs	Players		Foundation	No of clubs	Players
East Germany	1948	21	1200	Morocco†	1956	14	1780
West Germany†	1900	68	4265	Mexico	1972	14	380
Belgium†	1931	44	3031	Mauritius	1976	3	55
Bulgaria	1967	12	1200	Poland†	1956	22	2100
Denmark	1950	24	2120	Portugal†	1957	40	4000
Spain*	1923	180	12 120	Romania*	1914	198	16 880
Finland	1981	4	250	Sweden†	1931	58	2300
France*	1920	1785	191 600	Switzerland	1971	20	1000
Holland†	1932	101	6000	Senegal	1977	8	620
Israel	1971	7	350	Czechoslovakia†	1926	32	2950
Italy*	1928	314	25 772	Tunisia*	1970	38	1000
Ivory Coast	1973	11	1000	USSR*	1966	260	21 000
Luxembourg	1973	4	160	Yugoslavia	1954	23	2800
Malagassy	1964	66	1970				

* Group A in 1987–8   †Group B in 1987–8

Chile, Paraguay, Barbados, Hong Kong, Solomon Islands, Taiwan and Western Samoa became members in July 1987.

Holland, constantly frustrated in their aim to secure a more permanent role among Europe's elite, entertain Queensland in 1986. The tourists – with several full internationals – won 54–4.

SOVIET UNION – RUGBY GIANTS OF TOMORROW?

Number of clubs 260
Number of players 21 000
Colours Red and white
Foundation 1966
Headquarters
  Luzhnetskaya Nab 8
  119270 Moscow

Whatever happened in the World Cup, the Soviet Union should have been there on merit. Two victories against France 'A' in France within four years (the French including at least eight internationals), plus wins against Italy and Romania, have established their credibility beyond doubt.

Rugby reached the Soviet Union via university contacts in France and Romania, and the Gallic roots are ingrained. In the first game Dynamo Moscow beat Institute of PE Moscow 6–0 in 1933, and the first inter-city game the same year saw Moscow defeat Minsk 6–0. Moscow Dynamo won the first championship of six teams in 1934, but the war years destroyed records, and progression. In 1957 at the Moscow Youth Games, France, Romania, Czechoslovakia and Llanelli sent teams. Rugby was included in most of the Communist Spartakiads of the era. The Rugby Federation of the Soviet Union was founded in 1966, its first president was none other than Mr Ilyushin, chairman of the aircraft company that bears the family name. An experimental league was organized in 1967 for three years, with Baumann University winning in 1968. From 1969 the championship has been run on a national basis, with the main strongholds in Central Russia, the Ukraine, Uzbekhistan, Belorussia and Georgia, who have recently produced Stroiteli Kutasi, a team capable of matching the best in the country.

The Soviets entered FIRA in 1974, and were members of the élite group in 1978. They have now beaten every team in the competition at least once. Only top-class experience is lacking.

CURRENT STRUCTURE

A first division operates with ten clubs plus two regional second divisions each with eight clubs. After each has played each other once, the top six teams in the first division play each other again to find national champions on a league basis. The bottom four clubs join the leading two from each of the second divisions, and play each other, while the tailenders also play in a league. In that manner a series of rankings exists from 1–8, 9–16, and 17–28. The aim presumably is to cut travel costs and widen the fixture list.

THREE SOVIET STARS

Igor Mironov
Born in 1959, Mironov plays for the VVA Gagarin club, and is captain of club and country. An Air Force officer, he scored 11 points in the 15–9 defeat of France and all 16 in the 16–14 win over Italy in the 1986-7 FIRA championship. He is the team's kicker, a drop goal expert, and leading try scorer. A left wing, he has been clocked at 10.8 seconds for 100 metres.

Alexandr Tikhonov
Born in 1961 and another from the VVA Gagarin club. Like Mironov, works for the Air Force and is a tall lock forward who is a fine athlete despite his bulk. Gained international respect by comprehensively outplaying Jean Condom, the experienced French international, and Constantin, the top Romanian, in significant Soviet victories.

Sergei Goniani
Born 1956, he has been in the national team since 1979. A modern full-back, capable of devastating counter-attack, but sometimes poorly positioned in defence. Has benefited from the Soviet policy of keeping the same squad together for several years. Plays for the Fili Moscow club, though is trying to organize a transfer. Ran 10.9 seconds for 100 metres in his younger days.

INTERNATIONALS – USSR v WORLD CUP COUNTRIES SINCE 1982

1982-3
W v France, 12–6 (Merignac)
L v Italy, 12–10 (Catania)
L v Romania, 15–10 (Kiev)

1983-4
L v France, 32–3 (Moscow)
W v Italy, 16–7 (Kiev)
L v Romania, 19–3 (Bucharest)

1984-5
L v France, 36–21 (Tulle)
L v Italy, 13–12 (L'Aquila)
W v Romania, 14–6 (Kiev)

1985–6
L v France, 7–14 (Leningrad)
W v Italy, 15–13 (Moscow)
L v Romania, 13–16 (Bucharest)

1986-7
W v France, 15–9 (Begles)
W v Italy, 16–14 (Genoa)
L v Romania, 12–13 (Moscow)
France normally field an 'A' XV containing at least eight internationals.

WESTERN SAMOA

Number of clubs 10
Number of players 350
Foundation 1927 (affiliated to NZRFU)
Headquarters Apia

Western Samoa's first international was in 1924 against Fiji in Apia. The Fijians had to play the match at 7 a.m. so that the locals could get to work. Fiji won 6–0 as well as having to negotiate a large tree in the centre of the field.

So much have the Samoans learnt from playing Fiji and Tonga that, in recent seasons, they have embarrassed those more powerful sides by winning the three-cornered Pacific championship. New Zealand have encouraged tours, and many Samoans have found work in the country. Bryan Williams, New Zealand's legendary threequarter, is one of several Kiwis of Samoan descent.

Wales visited Western Samoa in 1986 for a full international:

WESTERN SAMOA	14	T: Tafua, Palamo PG: Ailupo (2)
WALES	32	T: Titley (2), R. Moriarty, Bowen C: Dacey (2) PG : Dacey (3) DG: J. Davies

OTHER CHAMPIONSHIPS

Competitions, Cups and tournaments have mushroomed throughout the world – from the powerful Pacific championship with World Cup nations Fiji and Tonga playing Western Samoa, against whom some countries award caps. Here is a selection of lesser rugby powers.

CONFEDERATION OF AFRICAN RUGBY AMATEUR (founded 1985)

The following countries are already members of FIRA and have automatic membership to CARA: Tunisia, Morocco, Senegal, Ivory Coast, Malagassy (Madagascar), Mauritius. FIRA propose to elect the remaining countries into their affiliation:

	Foundation	No of clubs	Players
Comoro Islands	1986	2	75
Kenya	1921	11	600
Liberia	1985	3	100
Sierra Leone	1967	7	225
Tanzania	1953	1	25
Uganda	1953	1	25
Zambia	1900	13	475
Zimbabwe (see World Cup Junior Nations)			

CARIBBEAN NATIONS

	Foundation	No of clubs	Players
Bahamas	1962	4	125
Barbados	1964	1	75
Bermuda	1964	5	425
Cayman Islands	1972	4	80
Guadeloupe	1976	6	270
Guyana	N/A	1	50
Jamaica	1959	8	250
Martinique	1976	10	415
St Lucia		1	40
Trinidad & Tobago	1927	10	375
Virgin Islands (USA)	N/A	1	40
Virgin Islands (GB)	N/A	1	40

PACIFIC NATIONS
(Excluding Fiji and Tonga)

	Foundation	No of clubs	Players
Western Samoa	1927	12	475
Cook Islands	N/A	3	200
New Caledonia	N/A	9	500
Solomon Islands	N/A	3	150
Tahiti	1960	11	600
Wallis & Futuna	N/A	2	90

Note: Hawaii (9 clubs – 1200 players) belongs to the USA.

ASIAN COUNTRIES
(Excluding Japan)

	Foundation	No of clubs	Players
Brunei	1975	8	500
Hong Kong	1952	8	375
India	1980	150*	7500*
Indonesia	1971	5	115
Korea (South)	N/A	27	1650
Malaysia	N/A	10	350
Papua New Guinea	N/A	7	280
Sabah	1966	8	350
Sarawak	N/A	7	200
Singapore	N/A	16	800
Sri Lanka	1878	15	450
Taiwan	N/A	12	450
Thailand	1937	40	1750

Unconfirmed   N/A – Details not available.

Martin Tamu (Papua New Guinea), shepherded by two team-mates, scores a spectacular try against the United States at the Hong Kong Sevens.

Rugby in China – action from Teintsin's 12 points to 3 victory over Shanghai in 1912.

Dusty Hare

Nottingham, Leicester and England

Dusty Hare, christened William Henry, and born on 29 November 1952, is the record points scorer in rugby union history. Safely past 6000 points, one may ask when will it end? Then again, how long is a piece of string?

Educated at Magnus GS, Dusty was raised on the family farm at South Clifton, on the Notts-Lincs border, where he now farms nearly 3000 sheep. He used to practise goalkicking out in the fields. He joined the local Newark club, and progressed to the nearest first-class club, Nottingham.

In his early days a cricket career beckoned. He made ten appearances for Nottinghamshire between 1971 and 1977 alongside Sir Garfield Sobers. Yet such illustrious company did not prevent him concentrating eventually on the winter game. Dusty moved from Nottingham to Leicester and was part of their outstanding John Player Cup winning team in the three years from 1979. He added the odd try and drop goal to the repertoire, the points clicked by and Sam Doble's old record of 3651 was obliterated.

Unlike his rival J. P. R. Williams, Hare is the less flamboyant type of full-back. Quiet, unobtrusive and a deadly kicker, his game is founded on consistency. He hardly misses a game.

He made his international debut against Wales in 1974 in a rare England win. He became England's most capped full-back with 25 appearances in the white shirt. Yet between 1974 and 1982 he won just 12 caps, was dropped five times while England employed six full-backs. Despite this he still managed a new English record of 240 points.

Of all the kicks he has taken,

the two at the death against Wales in 1980 and again the following year live in the memory. The first was a last-minute kick to clinch the game 9–8 en route to the Grand Slam; the second, same time, same spot, different stadium, was blown past the Cardiff posts by a relieved Welsh nation.

In 1984 Dusty Hare retired from international rugby despite pleas to change his mind. A few years earlier England hadn't really wanted him. He continues to play for Leicester, and all the time the points keep mounting up.

Dusty Hare (in white, second from left) turns away as his injury-time penalty gives England a 9–8 victory against Wales at Twickenham during England's Grand Slam year of 1980.

The World Points record

Nottingham	1800
England	240 (record)
British Lions	88
Representative	639*
Leicester	3452*

*still accruing

ACKNOWLEDGEMENTS AND BIBLIOGRAPHY

The author is grateful for factual and statistical verification from books, annuals and periodicals from all over the world. Many thanks are due to the legions of rugby writers, officials and historians for their patience, help and guidance. I am also indebted to Graham Edge and Ian Morrison for their aid in the collation of the book, and to John English for his editorial work.

The following publications have been essential works of reference:
South African Rugby Writers Annual : Quintus van Rooyen; *Men in Black*: R. H. Chester and N. C. McMillan (MOA Publications); *Encyclopedia of New Zealand Rugby*: R. H. Chester and N. C. McMillan (MOA Publications); *Rugby Almanacks 1980–86*: R. H. Chester and N. C. McMillan (MOA Publications); *Playfair Rugby Annuals 1946–73*; *Rothmans Yearbooks 1971–87*: Vivian Jenkins and Stephen Jones (Queen Anne Press); *Guinness Book of Rugby Facts and Feats* (1st and 2nd Editions); *The International Championship 1883–1983*: Terry Godwin (Collins Willow); *History of Welsh International Rugby*: John Billot (Ron Jones Publications); *The History of Scottish Rugby*: Sandy Thorburn (Johnston and Bacon); *One Hundred Years of Irish Rugby*: Edmund Van Esbeck (G and M); *Fabuleuse Historie du Rugby*: Henri Garcia (O.D.I.L.); *History of Australian Rugby*: Jack Pollard; plus information from Leo McKern (Argentina); E. D. Hagarty (Canada and USA); Jean-Louis Barthes (FIRA); Luciano Ravaguani (Italy), and Jonty Winch (Rhodesia/Zimbabwe).

All photographs courtesy Coloursport, except the following: *Illustrated London News* 14, 32, 62, 64, 75, 113, 120 (top), 123 (centre, bottom), 127, 131 (left)
Peter Bush/Coloursport 41
Doug Sturrock/Canadian Rugby Union 120 (bottom), 128

INDEX

In references to specific matches, *Away teams* are indicated in *italics*. Page numbers in **bold** indicate the inclusion of illustrations.

Index compiled by David Wilson